JUL

COMING FULL CIRCLE

NEW DIRECTIONS IN NATIVE AMERICAN STUDIES

Colin G. Calloway and K. Tsianina Lomawaima, General Editors

COMING FULL CIRCLE

THE SENECA NATION OF INDIANS
1848–1934

Laurence M. Hauptman

UNIVERSITY OF OKLAHOMA PRESS : NORMAN

Library of Congress Cataloging-in-Publication Data

Names: Hauptman, Laurence M., author.
Title: Coming full circle : the Seneca Nation of Indians, 1848–1934 / Laurence M.
    Hauptman.
Other titles: New directions in Native American studies ; v. 17.
Description: Norman : University of Oklahoma Press, [2019] | Series: New directions
    in Native American studies series ; volume 17 | Includes bibliographical references
    and index.
Identifiers: LCCN 2018031332 | ISBN 978-0-8061-6269-0 (hardcover : alk. paper)
Subjects: LCSH: Seneca Nation of Indians—History—19th century. | Seneca Nation of
    Indians—History—20th century.
Classification: LCC E99.S3 H345 2019 | DDC 974.7004/975546—dc23
LC record available at https://lccn.loc.gov/2018031332

Coming Full Circle: The Seneca Nation of Indians, 1848–1934 is Volume 17 in the New
Directions in Native American Studies series.

To Ruth, my partner for half a century,
who has made everything good in my life possible

•◄►•

CONTENTS

•◄►•

ILLUSTRATIONS

Figures

Tables

Maps

•◀▶•

PREFACE

The present study is a prequel to my book *In the Shadow of Kinzua: The Seneca Nation of Indians since World War II* (2014). It treats the history of the Seneca Nation of Indians starting with its political revolution in 1848, the concluding date of my book *Conspiracy of Interests: Iroquois Dispossession and the Rise of New York State* (1999). The book ends in 1934, when Congress passed the Wheeler-Howard bill known as the Indian Reorganization Act (IRA), legislation I wrote about previously in *The Iroquois and the New Deal* (1981).[1] The title of this book, *Coming Full Circle: The Seneca Nation of Indians, 1848–1934*, is meant to be a double entendre. First, the referendum on the IRA was an attempt to introduce an elective system to the Senecas, even though they had adopted this form of government as early as 1848.[2] Second, I have now "come full circle" in my writings on the Senecas since I first began my academic career in the early 1970s, writing about the 1930s.

As with all my previous writings, this book is based on a combination of archival research, fieldwork, and interviews I have conducted with Onöndawa'ga:' (Senecas) and other Hodinöhsö:ni' (People of the Extended Lodge/Longhouse), and with non-Indian policy makers, since 1972.[3] It is an outgrowth of a massive, 933-page report commissioned by the Seneca Nation of Indians in April 2013. At that time the Seneca Nation president and council contracted with me to write a political history of its government, focusing on its leadership since 1848. I have pared down and edited this report considerably, while updating and adding new materials.[4]

Today, the Seneca Nation of Indians, a federally recognized American Indian nation, is composed of three territories—the Allegany (Ohi:yo'), Cattaraugus, (Ga'dägësgeo:nö'), and Oil Spring (Ga:no's) Reservations—all of which are located in southwestern New York State. It also has Indian trust lands in Buffalo and Niagara Falls, where it operates two of its three casinos/hotel resorts. The nation has a system of elected government that replaced its ruling council of chiefs in a revolution in 1848.[5] The Seneca Nation is separate from the Tonawanda Band of Senecas, another federally recognized America Indian nation in western New York, which retains a traditional Hodinöhsö:ni' government, ruled by a council of chiefs and clan mothers. The Senecas were one of the founding members of the Five Nations (later Six Nations), although Tonawanda sachems today are the sole Seneca voice represented in deliberations of the Iroquois Grand Council at Onondaga. For enrollment requirements then and now, the Seneca Nation follows the traditional rules of Iroquoian matrilineage.

From the Treaty of Big Tree in 1797 onward to the early 1960s, the Allegany Reservation, located in Cattaraugus County, was composed of 30,469 acres and was approximately thirty-five miles long on both sides of the Allegheny River, at a width of one to two and a half miles. Between 1960 and 1966, approximately ten thousand acres of this Seneca community was condemned and flooded in the construction of the U.S. Army Corps of Engineers' Kinzua Dam project. The Cattaraugus Indian Reservation, located in Cattaraugus, Chautauqua, and Erie Counties, is composed of 21,618 acres. It winds its way along nine and a half miles on both sides of Cattaraugus Creek. The Oil Spring Reservation, located on the border of Allegany and Cattaraugus Counties, is one mile square and, unlike the two previously mentioned reservations, is a nonresidential territory of the Seneca Nation. The Seneca Nation's Cornplanter Grant (Jonöhsade:gëh), a 660-acre residential community in Warren County, Pennsylvania, was two miles long and a half mile wide. However, the Kinzua Dam project flooded this territory between 1960 and 1966.[6]

Each of these Seneca Nation communities has had a distinct history. Much of the population of the Allegany Reservation is descended from families that migrated there from the 1760s onward. By the middle of the nineteenth century, 712 Senecas lived at Allegany while another 1,203 lived at Cattaraugus. Between 1784 and 1807, numerous Cayugas made their way to Cattaraugus. Eventually the Cayugas numbered more than 10 percent of the reservation's population, and the children of Cayuga fathers and Seneca mothers even rose to hold major elected Seneca Nation offices.[7]

The two other Seneca territories had far different histories. Oil Spring Reservation had been reserved for Handsome Lake (Sga:nyodai:yoh), the Seneca prophet, by the Holland Land Company in 1801, after it was mistakenly left out of the text of the 1797 federal treaty. Between 1791 and 1796, the governor and legislature of Pennsylvania recognized the personal domain of Chief Cornplanter on lands just below its border with New York State. The residents of this Cornplanter Grant, less than one hundred in number in the second half of the nineteenth century, included Senecas but also Cayugas, Onondagas, and non-Indian heirs of Chief Cornplanter. By the 1870s, the Onöndawa'ga:' on this territory, even though they had accepted allotment of their lands, were considered citizens of the Seneca Nation, shared in treaty annuities, and voted with their kin on the Allegany Reservation.[8]

Divisions within the Seneca Nation were quite noticeable by the second half of the nineteenth century. Several Protestant sects—Presbyterian, Baptist Methodist, and Quaker (and later Episcopal)—competed with one another for influence and souls. Meanwhile Longhouse followers at Newtown at Cattaraugus and at Coldspring at Allegany, facing attacks and being labeled pagans by whites as well as by some Senecas, attempted to isolate themselves as best they could in an effort to retain their rituals and separate way of life. Although Senecas were historically separated by residency as well as by lineage, a noticeable class system developed in the second half of the nineteenth century, dramatically affected by the influx of non-Indians and the leasing of Indian lands. On one hand, this diversity at times contributed to political chaos. On the other, as this book suggests, it forced the Senecas, in a highly sophisticated way, to find pragmatic solutions to the myriad of problems facing their nation. Remarkably, three years after the 1848 revolution that overthrew the council of chiefs, Seneca White, a former chief, was elected to the presidency of the Seneca Nation. Other former chiefs were elected president as early as the 1850s and 1860s.[9]

In the past as well as in more contemporary times, powerful politicians effectively dealt with separatist movements within the Seneca polity and prevented a permanent breakup. Despite intense and at times even mean-spirited political campaigns, the Senecas have been masters of broker politics, keeping their two very distinctive residential communities—the more populous Cattaraugus Reservation and the geographically larger Allegany Reservation—together through carefully worked-out compromises. They developed an electoral system by which these two major residential communities, separated in distance by thirty miles, alternated the offices of Seneca Nation president, treasurer, and clerk. At times this practical arrangement produced compromises that kept the nation from splitting apart as it had in the years 1838 to 1848. Because of frequent threats of land loss and state and federal intrusion on Onöndawa'ga:' sovereignty, bitter rivals were often forced to broker deals and work together. At times they joined with non-Indian allies, petitioning, bringing litigation, or testifying before state and federal committees. Their leadership cooperated by bringing lawsuits challenging state efforts to tax Indian lands, by protesting federal and state efforts to allot the Allegany and Cattaraugus Reservations, and by coming together to resist continuing efforts by New York officials to intervene in and assume jurisdictional control over Seneca internal affairs.

Although always highly critical of their structure of elected government, most members of the Seneca Nation accept it.[10] Indeed, the nation's political system has outlived nations carved out after World War I, such as Yugoslavia and Czechoslovakia. This staying power confirms the previous conclusions made by anthropologists Anthony F. C. Wallace and William N. Fenton and the eminent writer Edmund Wilson—namely that the Senecas were and remain quite savvy people who have had the great ability to adjust to and manage change, which allows them to maintain their separate existence as a federally recognized American Indian nation.[11]

Coming Full Circle begins with the events that led up to the Seneca revolution in 1848. This upheaval came after a decade of turmoil. On January 15, 1838, President Martin Van Buren's administration concluded a federal–Six Nations treaty at Buffalo Creek. Under this fraudulent treaty, consummated as a result of bribery, forgery, and alcohol, the Seneca ceded all their remaining New York lands, except the one-mile-square Oil Spring Reservation, to the Ogden Land Company, and the Six Nations as a whole relinquished their rights to Menominee lands in Wisconsin purchased for them by the United States. In return, the Indians accepted a 1,824,000-acre Kansas reservation set aside by the federal government for all six Iroquois nations as well as the Stockbridge-Munsee. The Indian nations had to occupy the Kansas lands

within five years or forfeit this reservation. For a total of 102,069 acres in
New York, the Indians were to receive $202,000—$100,000 of which was
to be invested in safe stocks by the president of the United States; the income
earned was to be returned to the Indians. The United States was to also
provide a modest sum to facilitate removal, establish schools, and purchase
farm equipment and livestock for the Indians' use.[12]

The treaty had far-reaching results. Some of the Indians on the Iroquois
version of the "Trail of Tears" died en route to or in Indian Territory of
cholera, exposure, or starvation. Some of the survivors returned to western
New York. In addition, the bitter in-fighting in tribal politics after the
treaty's consummation eventually led in 1848 to the creation of a new
political entity, the Seneca Nation of Indians; the overthrow of the council
of chiefs; and establishment of an elective system of government. Moreover,
the treaty led to a campaign to restore the Indian land base in New York,
resulting in the U.S. Senate's ratification of the United States–Seneca Treaty
of May 20, 1842. The Seneca regained the Allegany and Cattaraugus but
not the Buffalo Creek and Tonawanda Reservations. Only later was the
Tonawanda Band of Senecas, having permanently separated from the Seneca
Nation by retaining its chiefs' council, "allowed" to purchase a small part
of its reservation back from the Ogden Land Company. American Indian
claims under the Treaty of 1838 were not settled until the first decade of
the twentieth century in a major United States Court of Claims award.[13]

On December 4 and 5, 1848, on the Cattaraugus Reservation, seventy-
two Senecas, all men, overthrew their council of chiefs–directed government and adopted a written constitution, establishing elections. For the
first time, they had an elected president, treasurer, and clerk. Their new
constitution, drafted at the convention, required the nation to alternate
each of these offices at every tribal election. An equal number of elected
tribal councilors—eight today from both the Allegany and Cattaraugus
Indian Reservations—would make up the sixteen-member tribal council,
the legislative branch of government. A third branch of government, the
judiciary, would be composed of elected Seneca peacemakers from each
community, to mediate tribal legal disputes in the traditional way; surrogate
judges at both Allegany and Cattaraugus to handle probate matters; and
a court of appeals, composed today of six judges who hear appeals from
both the peacemakers and surrogate courts. The constitution has been
modified several times since its first revision in 1862. For example, in 1898

the amended Seneca constitution expanded the presidential term from one to two years. In 1964 Seneca women, who had operated effectively behind the scenes, were first allowed to vote, and in 1966 they were allowed to hold tribal offices for the first time.[14]

Coming Full Circle emphasizes Seneca agency. Chapter 1 questions the widely held view that the Seneca Nation's elected system was simply imposed upon it by outsiders—namely by Hicksite Quakers such as Philip Evan Thomas, Presbyterian missionary Asher Wright, and/or the Cayuga chief Dr. Peter Wilson. Instead, two issues came to the fore to cause the political upheaval—first, blaming the chiefs for the substantial land loss between 1797 and 1842; and second, criticism of these same chiefs for their corruption and for their inequitable distribution of treaty annuities. Chapter 2 focuses on attempts by the ex-chiefs to restore their council-led government in a counterrevolution and their ultimate decision to run for office in the new elective system of government. While fighting internal political battles, the new government nevertheless continued to meet challenges, including its determination to bring a legal action before the United States Supreme Court to fight off state and county efforts at taxation. It also had to contend with threats to its ownership of the Oil Spring Reservation, the building of railroads through Seneca territories, and the coming of the Civil War.

The narrative then shifts to Seneca efforts to maintain their way of life as Hodinöhsö:ni´ in the face of outside pressures and changes. Chapter 3 describes how the Seneca Nation's leadership attempted to rouse its people and win favor for its fragile electoral government structure by demanding justice and bringing two cases in federal court—a failed attempt to secure certain Cattaraugus lands taken in an unratified federal treaty in 1826; and a successful effort to win monetary compensation, however small, in its Kansas claims case. Importantly, chapter 4 clearly shows how cultural, religious, and social changes were incorporated into the Seneca world, thereby allowing for continuity of a separate Onöndowa´ga:´ identity.

Over the years, Hodinöhsö:ni´ have not only been focused on the immediate concerns of survival but have been taught that the Creator has mandated that they are responsible "for seven generations to come." The Senecas were especially concerned about the welfare of their children and their future. In this regard, chapter 5 focuses on health care, especially at the Thomas Asylum for Orphan and Destitute Indian Children, renamed the Thomas Indian School in 1905. Founded as a refuge for children, the school had a controversial history until it closed in 1957. However, its health records reveal much about the conditions at the school as well as in Seneca communities as a whole. From 1880 into the 1920s, the Seneca Council worked with Dr. Albert Lake, an extraordinary physician at the Thomas Asylum/School, to promote public health measures, eliminating smallpox as well as reducing the devastating impact of trachoma and tuberculosis and other contagions devastating the school and the Cattaraugus community at large.

The Senecas faced an immense struggle, since the Thomas Indian School, as well as all Indian schools, home and away, had an assimilationist focus and were designed to transform children away from traditional ways. Chapter 6 explores the roles and impact of New York State district schools that were first established among the Senecas in 1846. It also treats the education provided at the nearby Quaker School at Tunesassa, established in 1852. When the district schools were seen as ineffective and/or too much focused on assimilationist goals, Seneca parents, especially in the Longhouse neighborhoods, resisted by boycotting the schools or, as attendance statistics clearly reveal, allowing their children to be truants. Some Senecas, however, saw that the best alternative for their children was to send them away for their schooling. Unlike Indians in the trans-Mississippi West, no federal Indian agent forced these parents to send their children to far-off boarding schools. Hundreds went to the United States Indian Industrial School at Carlisle, Pennsylvania, between 1879 and 1918. Less known and described in chapter 7 were the seventy-nine Seneca children who attended Hampton Normal and Agricultural Institute in Virginia. This private school was academically better than the federally supported Carlisle, taught a marketable trade, was a viable alternative to the poor instruction of the district schools, and provided three meals a day and a safe haven for children.

The next three chapters deal with other Seneca efforts to retain their lands and control over their ways of life. The coming of the New York and Erie Railroad into their territory beginning in 1850 led to increased non-Indian settlement within Allegany Indian Reservation lands. By the mid-1870s, the number of non-Indians on the reservation was more than two thousand; thirty years later it reached eight thousand.[15] This development resulted in more than three thousand lease agreements with these outsiders. Consequently, the Seneca Nation faced pressure to allot its lands, a movement largely led by a small group of powerful southwestern New Yorkers historically opposed to Indian interests. As shown in chapters 8 and 9, the Senecas used a brilliant strategy and recruited powerful allies in the non-Indian world to ward off allotment, although they were forced into accepting long-term leasing on a significant chunk of Allegany territory. After two decades of bitter fighting, rivals William C. Hoag and Andrew John Jr., both powerful, multiterm presidents of the Seneca Nation, put away some of their contempt for each other and jointly resisted allotment bills in the early twentieth century. Long after these bills were defeated in Congress, state legislators and their allies on Capitol Hill pushed their agenda for state control over Indian affairs; denied Indian land claims; rejected Seneca jurisdiction over their rights to fish and hunt without a state license; and, despite Seneca objections, successfully created a major state park on the border of the Allegany Indian Reservation.

Coming Full Circle ends with the New Deal. By that time, the Seneca Nation of Indians' electoral system of government had been held together for more than eighty years. Consequently, the Senecas did not want to turn back the clock and fight the internal battles of the 1840s, 1850s, and 1860s all over again. They had established order out of chaos and feared that the IRA would bring into their world not only outside control but also increased political instability. It was no wonder that unlike many American Indian nations, they voted the IRA down, and not by a small margin.

In the post–World War II period, the Senecas faced problems similar to those they had encountered prior to and in the eight decades after their 1848 revolution. In 1948 and 1950, they once again challenged state efforts to transfer criminal and civil jurisdiction, but without success. However, the Seneca Nation did succeed in avoiding termination and, with it, the federal buyout of U.S. treaty obligations. The Senecas also resisted state efforts to impose taxes, this time on Indian-owned enterprises on their reservation treaty lands. Much like their response in the Kansas claims actions described in chapter 3, the Seneca Nation filed a series of court cases for monetary compensation before the Indian Claims Commission. Employing the same arguments used in attempts to secure lands back in the 1880s and 1890, attorneys for the Seneca Nation filed land claims suits, from 1985 onward, that resulted in the winning back of fifty-one acres of the Oil Spring Reservation in 2005.

By far the Senecas' greatest challenge in the postwar era came with the Army Corps of Engineers project to construct the Kinzua Dam, which resulted in the loss of nearly ten thousand acres. The Senecas had seen this type of highhandedness by outsiders before. The removal of hundreds of

Senecas from their homes on the Cornplanter Grant and on the Allegany Indian Reservation in the Kinzua Dam project must have reminded them of stories told by their elders about removal from the Buffalo Creek Reservation, their largest residential community, after the disastrous Treaty of 1838. If they were able to survive past times of trouble, including the forced removal from Buffalo Creek Reservation; rebuild their nation; and establish a new government that had functioned for more than one hundred years, Seneca Nation leaders undoubtedly believed they could do the same again.[16] Hence, in a very real way, Seneca history from the revolution of 1848 to the New Deal was prologue, years of preparation during which the leadership of the Seneca Nation learned valuable lessons to meet the many challenges they would face in the future.

Several other points need to be mentioned. First, some materials found in three of the chapters of this book appeared in quite different form in *Prologue: The Journal of the National Archives* (1977), the *Buffalo Law Review* (1998), and *New York History* (2014), as well as in my expert witness testimony before two houses of Congress on the Seneca Nation Settlement Act of 1990. Second, there are variations in spelling the place-name Allegany/Allegheny. The river, the valley, the state forest, the national forest, and the upper and lower reservoir created in the Kinzua Dam project are all spelled "Allegheny"; while Seneca territory and the nearby New York State Park are spelled "Allegany." Third, for consistency and the preferred spelling of Seneca names and places, I have relied on Phyllis Bardeau's *Definitive Seneca: It's in the Word*, edited by Jaré Cardinal and published by the Seneca–Iroquois National Museum in 2011.

New Paltz, New York
May 18, 2018

•◀▶•

ACKNOWLEDGMENTS

Numerous Onöndawa'ga:´—too many to individually thank—have contributed to my research over these many years. The former Seneca Nation of Indians president Todd Gates must be acknowledged for allowing me to bring part of my earlier report for the Seneca Nation of Indians to a wider audience. I should especially like to thank Martin Seneca Jr., former acting commissioner of Indian affairs and present senior attorney for the Seneca Nation, for suggesting this project to me in February 2013. Both Seneca and two former Seneca Nation presidents, Barry E. Snyder Sr. and Maurice "Moe" John Sr., encouraged my research at different stages of the project. Sean Crane, who has served as a key adviser to both the president and treasurer of the Seneca Nation, reported my findings to the Seneca leadership and helped me secure permission to reproduce materials presented in my report. Several other Senecas aided me immensely in my research. They include Rebecca Bowen, director of the Seneca Nation Archives; Dr. Randy John, professor emeritus of sociology at Saint Bonaventure University; Bruce Abrams, head of the Seneca Nation Maps and Boundaries Department; and David George-Shongo Jr., Seneca Nation museum director at the new Onöhsägweide´ Cultural Center.

I have also depended on the expertise of Andrew Arpy, James Folts, and William Gorman at the New York State Archives; and Nancy Horan, Paul Mercer, and Vicki Weiss, manuscript librarians at the New York State Library, who over the years have opened new doors for me in my examination of Seneca history. Airy Dixon, a western New Yorker by birth, helped me understand how the Senecas fit into the history of that region. Michael L. Oberg, SUNY Distinguished Professor of History at Geneseo, and Carl Benn, chair of the Department of History at Ryerson College in Toronto, provided advice about ways to improve an earlier version of this manuscript.

For the past thirty-five years, David Jaman of The Villages, Florida, has provided me with excellent technical assistance and overall advice on the formatting of this book. Most important, without my wife, Ruth, and her tolerance of my lifelong obsession for research and writing about Native Americans, I could not have completed my journey through Hodinöhsö:ni´ history. I dedicate this last of my books to her, the love of my life.

◆◀▶◆

MAPS

MAP 1. Eastern Iroquoia Today. Shown are the settlements of the Hodinöhsö:ni´
in eastern North America today. *Map by Joe Stoll.*

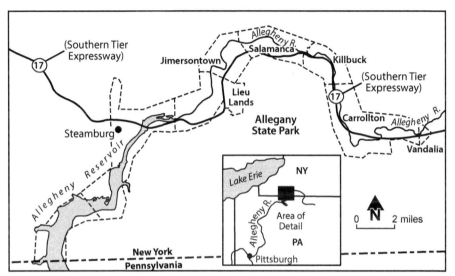

MAP 2. Allegany Indian Territory (Ohi:yo´) Today. *Map by Joe Stoll.*

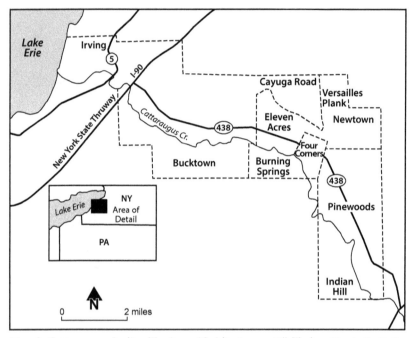

MAP 3. Cattaraugus Indian Territory (Ga´dägësgeo:nö´) Today. *Map by Joe Stoll.*

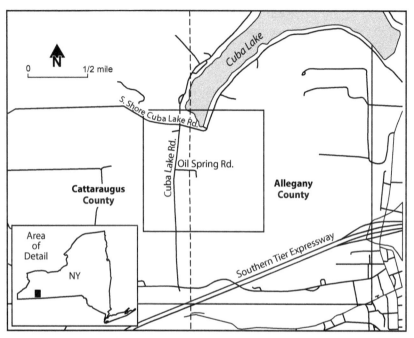

MAP 4. Oil Spring Indian (Ga:no's) Territory Today. *Map by Joe Stoll.*

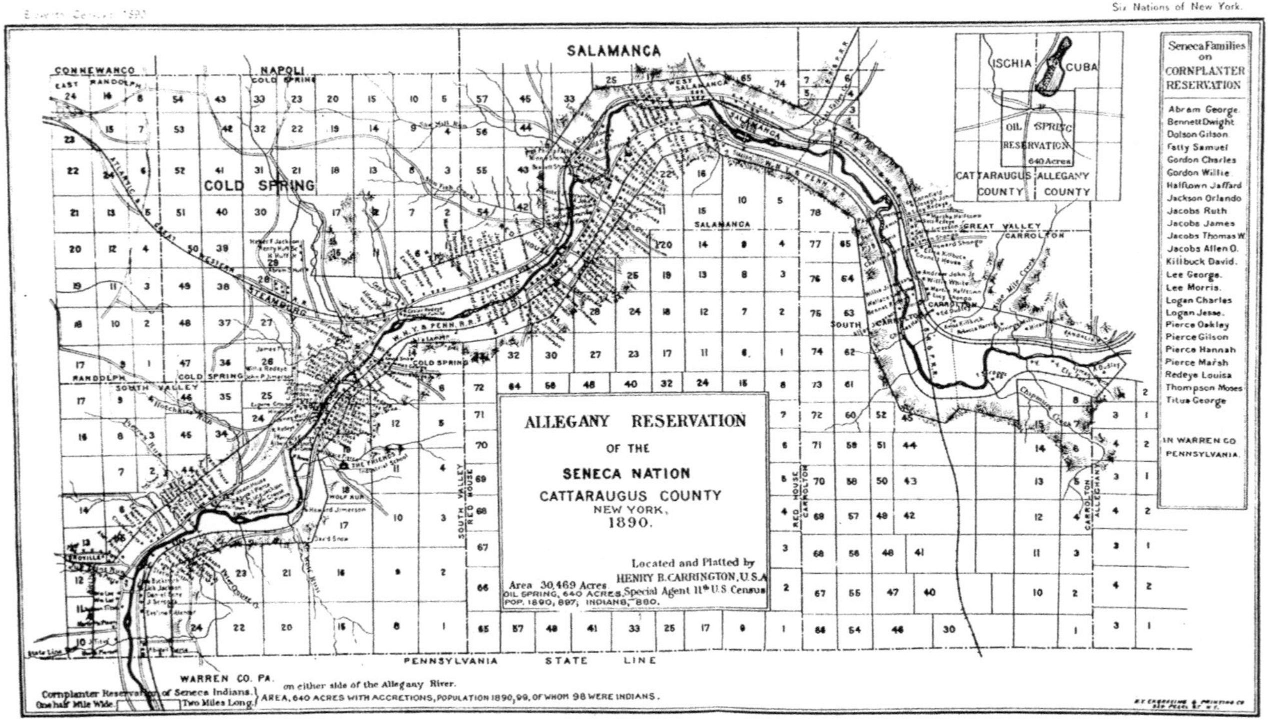

Map 5. Allegany Indian Territory and Environs, 1890. Besides showing family residences, schools, and houses of worship, this U.S. Census map reveals the existence of several rail lines that crossed the reservation and played an important role in Seneca history from 1850 onward. *Reprinted with assistance of the Seneca Nation Office of Maps and Boundaries from Thomas Donaldson, comp., The Six Nations of New York (Washington, D.C.: U.S. Census Printing Office, 1892).*

COMING FULL CIRCLE

•◄ 1 ►•

THE POLITICS OF BLAME

The Seneca Revolution of 1848

The revolution that produced a Seneca Nation elective system of government is largely misunderstood by contemporary Native Americans as well as by scholars today.[1] Although non-Senecas, both Indian and non-Indian, are usually credited or blamed for this historic event, the Seneca revolutionaries were not automatons merely following orders. In part, the misconceptions are a result of overreliance on Quaker publications, especially the correspondence of Hicksite Friend Philip Evan Thomas.[2] Both Seneca men and women were the principal actors and were most responsible themselves for the fateful decision to overturn their council of chiefs in 1848.

Although many immediate factors contributed to the change to an elected system, the major reason for this upheaval was clearly land loss. Seneca chiefs, fairly and unfairly, took most of the blame for dispossession and tribal decline. From the American Revolution until May 1842, the Seneca Nation was to be dispossessed of all its lands—fourteen counties of today's western New York State except for a one-square-mile uninhabitable territory, Oil Spring near Cuba, New York. In effect, by 1842 the Senecas were homeless people who were close to being fully removed to Indian Territory.[3]

One can hardly comprehend the level of stress on the Senecas in the period from 1797 to 1848. The pressures came from all directions—land speculators such as the powerful Ogden Land Company; canal and railroad interests tied to Albany politicos; presidents of the United States, especially

TABLE 1   Seneca Land Losses, 1797–1848

1797, September 15	Treaty—The Senecas cede most of their lands except for eleven territories. They reserve the right to hunt and fish in the ceded areas. One Seneca territory, Oil Spring, is inadvertently omitted from the original agreement, but it is later retained in a separate document and map given to Sga:nyodai:yoh (Handsome Lake) and preserved by Governor Blacksnake. *American State Papers*, 1:232.
1802, June 30	Treaty—The Senecas cede Canandaway territory and majority of lands along Lake Erie on the Cattaraugus Reservation. 7 Stat., 70.
1802, June 30	Treaty—The Senecas cede Little Beard's Town territory in the Genesee Valley to the United States. 7 Stat., 72.
1802, August 20	Treaty—The Senecas cede a one-mile strip along the Niagara River, from Buffalo Creek to Black Rock to the Stedman farm, but Senecas reserve fishing and camping rights. *American State Papers*, 1:664–65.
1815, September 12	Treaty—New York State "acquires" Grand Island and other islands in the Niagara River from the Senecas by state treaty. There is no federal commissioner present, nor is there ratification by the U.S. Senate. *Whipple Report*, 1:211–13.
1817–25	The Erie Canal is constructed, opening central and western New York for white settlement and increasing pressure on the Hodinöhsö:ni´. Buffalo and Rochester will become the ninth- and tenth-largest cities in the United States by the Civil War.
1822	The United States and Great Britain establish the international boundary along the Niagara River.
1823, September 3	Treaty—At the Treaty of Moscow, New York, land speculators John Greig and Henry Gibson of Canandaigua purchase most of the White Woman's Reservation (Gardeau) from the Senecas. The U.S. Senate never ratifies this "treaty."
1826, August 26	Treaty—In the Buffalo Creek Treaty of 1826, the Ogden Land Company "purchases" the remaining Seneca lands in the Genesee Valley, as well as parts of the Buffalo Creek, Tonawanda, and Cattaraugus territories. The U.S. Senate never ratifies this "treaty." *Whipple Report*, 1:23–24.

TABLE 1   (*continued*)

1832–51	The Erie Railroad is constructed through Seneca Country. Salamanca, in Allegany territory, soon becomes a major railroad hub. Leasing problems begin at Salamanca and environs and continue until the 1990s.
1838, January 15	Treaty—Despite blatant frauds committed by agents of the Ogden Land Company, the federal subagent, treaty negotiators, and some chiefs, the Senecas "cede" Allegany, Buffalo Creek, Cattaraugus, and Tonawanda territories. The treaty is never ratified by the required two-thirds of the U.S. Senate, although it is promulgated by President Van Buren. The Senecas and other Hodinöhsö:ni´ are to remove to Kansas, then the eastern part of Indian Territory. 7 Stat., 550.
1842, May 20	Treaty—Senecas agree to a "compromise treaty" that returns only the Allegany and Cattaraugus territories to them. The Tonawanda Senecas, none of whom signed the 1838 and 1842 treaties, refuse to leave their homeland. The Tonawandas refer to this treaty as the "compromised treaty." The result is a permanent political split and two federally recognized Seneca governments in New York by 1857. 7 Stat., 586.
1848, December 4–5	Senecas at Allegany and Cattaraugus abandon governance by chiefs, form an elective system, and found the Seneca Nation of Indians.

Andrew Jackson and Martin Van Buren, who were intent on full removal of the Six Nations from New York; Whig politicians intent on allowing the Senecas to remain in New York, but only as taxpaying citizens under New York State laws; and Quakers from Philadelphia and Baltimore who assumed they knew what was best for the Senecas and too often meddled in tribal affairs. Internally, the Senecas faced a chaotic political situation, in part caused by the great diversity within their population and by ten sets of chiefs who were forced from their eleven separate reservations onto four residential territories between 1797 and 1826. Often split about what course to pursue, these chiefs, some honest and others not, chose different strategies to meet the overwhelming challenges caused by the rise of the Empire State. Unfortunately for the Senecas, powerful New Yorkers lusted after these Indians' pivotal location—namely, the access routes to the Great Lakes and the Ohio Country, the gateways to the heart of the North American continent. In 1790, approximately 1,000 non-Indians lived west of Seneca Lake; sixty years later, more than 660,000 non-Indians lived in western New York. As a result of the opening of the Erie Canal in 1825 and the construction of railroads from the 1830s onward, Rochester grew from nothing in 1814 to a thriving city of more than 36,000 people by 1850. Buffalo, a city incorporated in 1831, grew to 81,129 people by 1860, making it the ninth largest city in the United States by the Civil War.[4]

To be fair, the chiefs who were overthrown in the Seneca Revolution of 1848 were not all incompetent or corrupt, but too often they were powerless to resist forces set in motion by a rising American nation. They were increasingly split in part because they were a diverse body representing local reservation interests. Their enemies, nevertheless, accused all of them of favoring emigration, land sales, and cooperating with the likes of the corrupt federal subagent James Stryker.[5] Even when they expressed the need for reform, they could not extricate themselves from the web of shame surrounding the hated treaty of 1838.

On the other hand, some of the opponents of the chiefs' council in the 1840s also had baggage. They were hard-boiled Seneca politicians who skillfully used an approach that characterizes tribal elections right down to the present time: the politics of blame. After a final crisis in 1864–65, the majority of members of both sides agreed to fight future battles largely through the electoral process.

One of the problems faced in researching the creation of the Seneca Republic in 1848 is the dearth of materials about the revolutionaries and their opponents on the council of chiefs. The exceptions are the extensive writings of two very different chiefs who were bitter rivals: Dartmouth-educated Maris Pierce and Yale-educated Nathaniel T. Strong. The most important of the revolutionaries, Solomon W. McLane (also known as Solomon W. Lane), a schoolteacher and the first popularly elected president of the Seneca Nation, elected in May 1849, died shortly after he left office; only a few of his letters and petitions survive in the Quaker records and in the U.S. National Archives. McLane was born into the Turtle Clan on the Buffalo Creek Reservation, was five feet nine and stockily built, and was raised by the prominent chief Young King, a major Seneca opponent of Red Jacket.

By the 1840s, McLane was an advocate of temperance among the Senecas and was residing at Allegany with his wife, Sara Two Guns, and six children, four of whom died at an early age. After he left the presidency, McLane served as a peacemaker judge. In 1850, he and his wife joined Asher Wright's United Mission Church. He died soon after.[6]

No more than a bare majority of the Seneca people in 1848 were revolutionaries. As in most revolutions, a small number of people were actual plotters. Most of the revolutionaries as well as their opponents made their marks on petitions. Unlike McLane, most of the early leaders of the Seneca Republic could not read and write English and left no writings except petitions sent to Washington and Albany. According to anthropologist Thomas Abler, approximately 38 percent of the core group of chiefs and only 9 percent of the new governmental leadership could sign their names.[7]

The revolutionaries were a diverse coalition loosely held together by one unifying reality: their opposition to the chiefs and their rule. In his excellent account, Abler claims that Indians who had been forcibly removed from the Buffalo Creek Reservation and who largely resettled at Cattaraugus were not in the ranks of the revolutionaries. Nevertheless, he appears to overlook that the population at Cattaraugus also included angry Senecas from other territories that had been lost between 1797 and 1842, and that a significant number of disgruntled Cayuga and Onondaga refugees from Buffalo had also resettled at Cattaraugus. Their presence was a constant reminder of the failings of chiefly rule.[8]

Abler correctly has insisted that the U.S. government's distribution of annuity payments to Seneca heads of families rather than the chiefs contributed directly to the coming of the Seneca Revolution.[9] The annuity question did significantly affect the events of 1848, but opponents of the chiefs and their rule had a great amount of ammunition to use to incite a revolution without this issue. Abler and others have also suggested that the chiefs' political decisions to lease reservation lands for sawmills also led to criticisms of their rule. However, this and other leasing issues appear to be far less important, only becoming significant after 1850.[10]

While it is clear that a large number of Senecas appeared to be loyal to the chiefs even well after the revolution occurred, the Seneca Council of Chiefs and its actions had clearly alienated a significant number of the residents of Cattaraugus and Allegany. By the mid 1840s, the Seneca chiefs could not justify their questionable actions by employing appeals to the past glory of the Iroquois League. The ancient custom of consensus politics had long before disappeared and now internecine conflict was tearing apart the chiefs' council as well as the nation as a whole. After 1845, there was no way to turn back the clock. Early that year, the Seneca Council of Chiefs began to discuss what reforms they needed to undertake to redeem themselves in the eyes of reservation residents.

The first problem the chiefs had to face was how to distance themselves from the popularly held view that they were not protective enough of the Seneca estate. Despite the federal government's return of Allegany and Cattaraugus in 1842, the residents of these two communities had little confidence in federal and state officials' insistence that the treaty marked a new day, since the Buffalo Creek and Tonawanda Reservations were not returned in the same treaty. After all, federal and state officials had constantly ignored treaty guarantees since 1794. Washington's promises of protection were seen as worthless, since its "commitments" changed upon each new administration entering office. If some of the chiefs could be tricked and/or corrupted to sell all their residential territories, including Buffalo Creek, the largest Seneca reservation and the ritual center of the Iroquois Confederacy after the American Revolution, would Allegany and Cattaraugus be next?

The politics of blame was increasingly noticeable in the Seneca polity in the years approaching the revolution of 1848. The presence of six deposed Seneca leaders who supported emigration—Chiefs George Jemison, Thompson S. Harris, Billy Shanks, White Seneca, William Tall Chief and Sachem Little Johnson—continued to remind the people of the scandals of 1838. In May 1846, these deposed chiefs, along with 56 Senecas and 157 other members of the Six Nations, left for Indian Territory. Both White Seneca and Little Johnson perished in the miserable trek, while Jemison, a direct descendant of the white captive and adoptee Mary Jemison, was to slowly redeem himself with some within the Seneca polity and take part in the revolution of 1848.[11]

In January 1845, fifty Seneca chiefs met in council at Cattaraugus and began debating a series of reforms. Most in attendance apparently did not realize that what they would decide on would have far-ranging consequences and would lead to the undoing of their leadership three years later. Chief John Seneca, who had signed both the 1838 and 1842 treaties, presided and called the council to order. His family was one of the most prominent in Seneca history. The chief had been one of the ten original members of the

Seneca Mission Church at Buffalo Creek in the early 1820s. At that time, the chief and his entire family first came under the influence of missionary Thompson Harris (not the chief of the same name). John Seneca's father was White Chief, who along with his wife had converted to Christianity. John's two brothers were White Seneca and Seneca White, both chiefs and early Christian converts at Buffalo Creek. The family had become divided in the 1830s. Chief White Seneca became a leader of the Emigration Party while Chief Seneca White was a major opponent of removal to the West.[12]

Unlike the combative Israel Jemison, who was the most visible and activist chief in resisting the change of government in 1848 and after, Chief John Seneca was more of a behind-the-scenes mediator. He apparently had the respect of most of the chiefs and at least some of the later revolutionaries of 1848. In the last decade of his life, the chief clearly worked to bring back some level of harmony to his Seneca people. Although he never served as a delegate or signed the constitution of 1848 that overthrew the chiefs, Seneca was to be voted in as peacemaker and assessor in the first popular election for president under the new government. Importantly, just before he died in 1857, the now former chief was to be elected president of the Seneca Nation.

At the January 1845 meeting, Chief John Seneca described the urgency that brought the chiefs together in council. Remarkably honest in his admission of the past failures of the chiefs, Seneca insisted that a new generation of more educated tribal members had come to realize "that the ancient form of government was not adapted to the necessities of the nation in its present improved form." To save the nation from spies within and "unslumbering" and "rapacious enemies" without (presumably the Ogden Land Company), the chief urged reforming the Senecas' political institutions and divesting the chiefs "of the arbitrary and irresponsible power they had assumed."[13]

At this council, the proceedings were no longer based upon consensus, which was traditionally a part of the protocol before 1797. Only one major resolution was passed, although five chiefs in attendance refused to agree to it. The resolution stated:[14]

> Resolved: determine, ordain, publish, and declare that our political usages, customs, organizations and constitution be, and the same are hereby altered and amended, so that no sale or disposition of the whole or any part of our Lands hereafter to be made, shall be valid, or of any effect, unless the same be made in full and open Council of Chiefs and

Warriors of the Nation, and by the express assent of two-thirds of all
the Chiefs, and two-thirds of the whole residue of the male population
of the Nation of the age of twenty-one years, and upwards, whether
attending such Council or not; such assent to be given in writing, under
the hands and seals of the parties, in full and open Council of the
Chiefs and Warriors of the Nation, assembled together in one Council.

The wording of the resolution left out references to the roles of clan mothers, the "keepers of the kettle," who traditionally were viewed as protectors
of the land. The constitution of 1848 later made up for this omission by
adding the requirement that three-fourths of the "mothers of the nation" had
to approve future land sales before the Seneca Nation could legally alienate
its lands. Perhaps motivated by being bypassed, some women, later in 1848
and in 1849, sent petitions advocating a change away from chiefly rule to
an elected system of government. They favored a change in the distribution
of annuities from the chiefs directly to Senecas, including to the women,
and urged that these annuities be parceled out in one payment to the head
of a household in the spring rather than at two separate times of the year.
They pointed out that these changes would help Seneca families finance the
expense of planting crops.[15] In a disclaimer undoubtedly inserted to win some
tribal council support, the resolution stated that "nothing herein contained
shall, in any manner, alter, change, or effect lessen or diminish the rights,
powers, duties, privileges or authority of the Chiefs in any matter or respect
whatever." It further added that the resolution would be forwarded to the
president of the United States, Congress, and the governors and legislatures
of New York and Massachusetts.[16]

On May 8, 1845, prompted by Hicksite Quakers and Whigs, the New
York State Legislature passed "An Act for the Protection and Improvement of
the Seneca Indians Residing in the Cattaraugus Reservations in this State."
Once again, as in the past, the state gave promises of protection against
trespassers and whiskey sellers, but the act, nevertheless, clearly intruded
on Seneca sovereignty and on the powers of the existing chiefs' council.
Albany recognized the existence of the "Seneca Nation of Indians" as the
government on the Allegany, Cattaraugus, and Oil Spring Reservations and
"awarded" it the right to "prosecute and maintain in all courts of law and
equity in this state, any action, suit or proceeding which may be necessary
or proper to protect the rights and interests of said Indians and of the said

nation, in and to the said reservations." The act also "allowed" actions for damages suffered by the Indians "in common, or as a nation" in state courts.[17] It also "awarded" the chiefs the following rights:[18]

> laying out of lands for separate cultivation, improvement or occupancy, by and Indian and his family, and the quantity of each; and make by-laws for laying roads and highways, and among the same; for regulating fences and protecting and improving their common lands, for regulating fences and preventing trespassers by cattle or otherwise; and to provide a penalty, not exceeding five dollars, for violating or disobeying any such regulation or by-laws. . . . The said chiefs at any such meeting may admit any Indian or tribe to become an inhabitant of their reservation and to enjoy the same privileges with them.

Importantly, the act of 1845 established annual Seneca elections each May for the positions of tribal clerk, treasurer, two marshals, and peacemaker judges/mediators. One provision even allowed New York's governor to nominate, with consent of the state senate, a person "who shall have been a counselor in the supreme court of this state for three years or more, to be an attorney of the Seneca Nation of Indians." This person "shall from time to time advise the said Indians respecting controversies between themselves, and between them or any of them, and any other person." Other sections of the legislation "granted" the Seneca peacemaker justices or a majority of them the right to call meetings of the chiefs. To satisfy the Quakers, Longhouse followers of Handsome Lake (Sga:nyodai:yoh), and other prohibitionists, the act made it a crime punishable by law to sell or give any Seneca "spirituous liquor or any intoxicating drink." The new state legislation also outlined Seneca voting qualifications and terms of office; described the specific duties and legal responsibilities of the peacemaker courts, treasurer, and clerk of the Seneca Nation; allowed for legal appeal to a jury of six chiefs; made it a state crime to offer false testimony in a tribal court; gave the chiefs the final say in assigning lands for cultivation; and provided individual Indians the right to sell timber on lands assigned to them but limited their rights elsewhere and set penalties. Other legislation in this period dealt with the establishment of state schools for the Seneca, providing for the education of Indian youths at state normal schools, and recognized Indian common law marriages and the right of Seneca peacemaker courts to marry Indians "with the like force and effect as if by a justice of the peace."[19]

For much of 1845 through 1847, the chiefs' attention was directed away from dealing with internal threats to their hold on government. While their opponents were gaining momentum, the chiefs had to contend with numerous concerns, including repercussions caused by the frauds committed by James Stryker, the federal subagent just prior to, during, and after the Treaty of 1838; the wooing of Senecas to join the migration out of New York to Indian Territory; calls to take back some of the survivors of the disastrous trek west; the onset of a major typhus epidemic; new more intrusive state legislation; and federal changes in disbursing annuities. In councils at Cattaraugus in August, October, and December 1845, the chiefs expressed fear of removal, although the Quakers in attendance tried to calm those fears. In August at the council house, Chief Israel Jemison expressed his apprehension: "We are settled in our minds not to go beyond the Mississippi. We are settled and building houses and making improvements. It is my desire now that no separation may take place among our people, but that all may settle and live in permanent peace."[20] At the same meeting, John Mitten revealed the suspicions held by the council—namely that the crisis of removal had not yet ended. He insisted that if the white men had "once murdered the Son of God, they would be more easily induced to destroy the Indian."[21]

The chiefs further splintered when a council composed of twenty-five members assembled in October 1845 and agreed to abide by the state law of May 8 that had established Seneca elections as well as the responsibilities and terms of office. Chief Pierce and others viewed the legislation as intrusive, one that struck a blow to "our old customs and usages."[22] Subsequently, a greater schism in the council resulted when Chiefs John Kennedy and Nathaniel Strong decided to participate in this first tribal election that involved officers other than president; the two Cattaraugus chiefs were voted into office the following year—Kennedy as clerk and the highly controversial Strong as peacemaker.[23] By December 1845, in an attempt to "unite together," the chiefs directed their attention by drafting an appeal to Washington, asking Congress to redress wrongs by providing the Senecas with "the money we have been cheated of."[24]

To stem criticism of their support of the state act of 1845 and to discuss the recent emigration of some Senecas to the West, the Hicksite Quakers held a meeting at Cattaraugus in June 1846 to try to heal the breach. Twenty-five Indians, including Chiefs Blacksnake, Israel Jemison, John

Kennedy, and Henry Two Guns, attended the meeting. Importantly, about half of the attendees were women. The Hicksites insisted that their support of the 1845 act was only intended to help the Indians out of dangers and that they were attempting to bring them relief. Not seeing the act as a threat to tribal sovereignty, these paternalistic Quakers claimed the act was passed out of benevolence by state legislators in Albany. Two Senecas in attendance, John Cook and Young Chief, endorsed Hicksite efforts. Cook, later one of the revolutionaries of 1848, pointed out that the Quakers had always been our constant unswerving friends."[25] Perhaps to win the women's support for their legislative and educational efforts and apparently aware of the important customary role of women in Seneca society, Philip Evan Thomas, the spokesman for the Hicksites in attendance, then announced plans for the establishment of a "Female Manual Training School at Cattaraugus."[26]

From 1784 to 1842, federal and state treaties had dispossessed the Onöndowa'ga:' of 99 percent of their lands as a result of the unsavory actions and influence of Oliver Phelps, Nathaniel Gorham, Robert Morris, Joseph Ellicott, Peter Porter, David A. and Thomas Ludlow Ogden, and Joseph Fellows. State legislators and postrevolutionary governors of New York collaborated with these interests, in hopes of building a transportation network and populating the central and western regions of the state. The ties between Albany and Washington became blurred especially in the Jacksonian Indian removal era when Governor Martin Van Buren became vice president and later president of the United States. Consequently, Seneca political leaders were well aware of how class and power realities operated in America. Perhaps with this in mind, some Senecas believed that they would be better off having their own advocate representing them in the highest circles of American government.

From 1838 to just before his death in 1861, Philip Evan Thomas, former commissioner of the Chesapeake and Ohio Canal, founder and director of the Baltimore and Ohio Railroad, and president of the Merchants' Bank of Baltimore, became the most prominent member of the Hicksite branch of the Society of Friends involved in Onöndowa'ga:' political affairs.[27] As a most accomplished businessman and philanthropist, who better was there to represent the Senecas as an envoy on Capitol Hill in the fight against continuing talk of removal? The Senecas realized that Thomas's connections could be useful in lobbying for their needs. Because of his lobbying efforts against Seneca removal to Indian Territory and his success in securing the return of both the Allegany and Cattaraugus Indian Reservations in the federal treaty of 1842, the Senecas adopted Thomas in 1845 and appointed him as their envoy to Washington. He served as the Seneca ambassador to Washington in several different Seneca Nation administrations into the late 1850s.[28] After they officially made him Seneca envoy to Washington for the second time, in December 1848, the Senecas bestowed him with a new name—Hai-wa-noh´—meaning "impressive voice, or one who is listened to."[29] Moreover, as a philanthropist interested in promoting education, he won support from some among the Senecas. Importantly, Thomas also encouraged and financially supported Presbyterian missionary Asher Wright's efforts to establish the Thomas Asylum for Orphan and Destitute Indian Children, later renamed the Thomas Indian School, which was founded in 1855.[30]

Thomas's writings were often slanted in favor of overthrowing the chiefs' council. On August 28, 1846, he wrote the commissioner of Indian affairs about the chaotic situation in the Seneca Nation. He recommended the 1845 New York State law establishing elections and not recognizing the special rights of the chiefs as the first step in bringing a semblance of order. In his correspondence, Thomas also discounted petitions of chiefs protesting the proposed change in distributing annuity payments. He condemned some of the chiefs and used his Washington connections to have Chief Maris Pierce removed as the U.S. interpreter, replacing him with his personal candidate, Dr. Peter Wilson, a Cayuga chief and a graduate of Geneva Medical College.[31]

Wilson devoted more of his time to securing political and land rights for the Cayugas within the Seneca Nation than he did practicing medicine.[32] On numerous occasions, Senecas criticized him for his alleged public intoxication and womanizing. As an outsider, a Cayuga living at Cattaraugus, he was resented for his meddling in internal Seneca Nation tribal politics. He was also resented by many Senecas for encouraging emigration to the West and later for bringing the survivors back to Cattaraugus. The Hicksites, especially Thomas, and prominent Seneca leaders such as John Luke, a leading revolutionary in 1848, nevertheless continued to support Wilson, perhaps since the Cayuga chief spoke out against continuation of the Seneca chiefs' council. Wilson stoked popular fears by suggesting that the Ogden Land Company would return to plague the Indians and that the council of chiefs would once again be corrupted and would repeat its "mistakes" of 1838.[33]

Wilson became the spokesman for numerous Cayugas residing on Seneca reservations who had no land rights. He had also helped the Cayugas, who had left for Indian Territory in 1846 and had suffered greatly in the trek, by coming to the aid of the few survivors who returned to Seneca Country. Some Senecas supported Wilson as well. His was an impressive lineage since he was a grandson of the Seneca chief Farmers Brother, a hero of the War of 1812. He was also to receive support from some Senecas married to Cayugas. While not the Indian agency physician, Wilson appears to have won some Seneca support, working alongside agency physician and missionary Asher Wright during a major typhus epidemic that killed seventy residents of Cattaraugus in 1847.[34]

Throughout the period leading up to the Seneca revolution, Wilson corresponded with his benefactor Thomas, reporting to him about the turmoil occurring within the Seneca Nation.[35] On March 10, 1848, Thomas wrote a letter to Commissioner William Medill, not only revealing his own views about the existing government of chiefs but also predicting the coming revolution:[36] "People are beginning to be restive under the irresponsible government of their chiefs and are even looking to the establishment of a Representative Republic. Their first resolution movement was to deprive the chiefs of power to sell their lands, the next was to take from the appointment of their municipal officers, and now it is manifest a position of them are disposed to take from their chiefs any control over the nation's funds."

After receiving information from Wilson about a public meeting scheduled to be held at Cattaraugus, Thomas wrote to Medill once again, indicating that a political upheaval was about to take place. On September 9, 1848, Thomas indicated to the commissioner that an explosion was imminent: "There is reason to believe they [Cattaraugus Senecas] are approaching towards serious convulsion, and perhaps a radical change in their form of government." He continued by pointing out that a "large majority of Warriors appear to have lost all confidence in the chiefs. . . ." Wilson had told him that the participants had voted with "great unanimity" to abolish the council of chiefs by the end of the year.[37]

Later, after the revolution of 1848, some Senecas accused Wilson, Thomas, and to a much lesser degree Wright of plotting the upheaval. Wilson's enemies could easily see his hand since the constitution drafted that December provided that all Indian residents of Allegany and Cattaraugus, whether Seneca or not, could vote in Seneca Nation elections. This provision, modified in 1862, allowed only male Senecas twenty-one years or older to vote in Seneca Nation elections. Although Wright clearly favored changes in the Seneca government, he denied attending secret meetings where the revolution was plotted even though he had served as the translator at the constitutional convention. Wright later acknowledged that he had suggested the clause requiring the approval of three-quarters of the "mothers of the nation" in any future alienation of Seneca Nation lands.[38]

Although greatly influenced by the ideas of Thomas, Wilson, and Wright, the Senecas who made the revolution did not receive their orders from Thomas, Wilson, or Wright, since a general feeling of discontent about the chiefs and their leadership existed within Seneca communities. To create more distrust for chiefly rule, the issue of annuity payments came to the fore in the three years before the revolution. The traditional way was for federal and state officials to distribute annuities to the chiefs at separate times throughout the year. The chiefs would then parcel out the moneys in any way they chose fit. Although state legislators attempted to reduce the power of the chiefs in a law in 1845, they later reversed this decision and voted instead to allow the council of chiefs to appoint a committee to receive and distribute the state–Indian treaty annuities. In 1847 Congress passed legislation allowing federal agents to distribute annuities per capita. The council of chiefs reacted immediately, insisting that a distribution by the Indian subagent to households should not proceed since the chiefs' custom was being violated.[39]

In the same year, two community groups arose to challenge the chiefs— one group composed of some warriors and a second group representing some Seneca women. From January through October 1848, the warriors sent three petitions to the War Department, then in charge of administering Indian policy. On October 11, a petition signed by the warriors urged the commissioner of Indian affairs to ignore the protest of the chiefs "until you receive an expression of our people who are in favor of the proposed change in the distribution of annuities." The petitioners in opposition to the chiefs' position included some of the revolutionaries who drafted the Seneca constitution of December 1848.[40] On October 13, six Seneca women—Gaa-nah-hoh, Julia Dennis, Polly Johnson, Martha Phillips, Jane Scott, and Betsy Snow—proclaimed that the women of the Seneca Nation had "equal rights" to the annuities "with the men and with the chiefs." They added that the chiefs, warriors, men, and children were "all on the same footing."[41]

A month later, Robert Shankland , the new federal subagent, attempted to distribute annuities to Seneca heads of families at the council house on the Cattaraugus Reservation. After he began distributing moneys to individuals and not chiefs, a scuffle ensued; tribal marshals removed the combatants, including two of the chiefs. Shankland later reported that he admired the chiefs' determination to challenge on the annuity issue but that he "disliked their system of tactics and regretted their obstinancy."[42] He then journeyed to Allegany to carry out his work there. The venerable Governor Blacksnake, well over ninety years of age, and other chiefs there had previously sent their own protest that favored the chiefs' position on the annuity question. In a passing comment about his efforts to distribute these moneys at Allegany, Shankland noted that he had been surprised by the number of individual Senecas who had refused to take their annuities and expressed support for the chiefs.[43]

The continued backing of the chiefs in some quarters at Allegany and Cattaraugus should not be surprising even after what had transpired since 1797. Their ranks included distinguished Senecas, including Governor Blacksnake, John Seneca, and Seneca White. Nevertheless, the chiefs' political opponents grouped the chiefs together and held them collectively responsible for the sins of the past. By 1848, a sizable number of Senecas had come to believe that the chiefs were incapable of protecting the remaining Seneca land base. This was frequently expressed, even as the Senecas debated the annuity issue.

The Seneca revolutionaries were pragmatic folks who clearly saw the need for change. Without question, they took the advantage presented to them. This was their chance to overthrow a system that had increasingly been viewed by many Senecas as ineffective in preventing land loss and unfair and even corrupt in the distribution of annuities. The revolutionaries were capable of successfully using the politics of blame to castigate their opponents. The successful repeated election of John Luke to the presidency in the 1850s and early 1860s also proves the revolutionaries' significant political acumen, one not found again in Seneca Nation politics until the presidential administrations of William C. Hoag, from the 1890s into the 1920s.

At the December 4, 1848, convention, seventy delegates joined with McLane and William Jimerson to sign the constitution overthrowing the council of chiefs and their rule. Under the constitution, whose official language was drafted by Cattaraugus County attorney Chester Howe, the Seneca revolutionaries created a new elected system of government. Elections were set annually in May, and the Seneca Nation Tribal Council would hold its meeting once a year, on the first day of June, but extra sessions could be convened by the president in case of crises.[44] Later, in 1898, the constitution was amended to provide for elections every two years, beginning in 1900. It is interesting to note that in the first decades, pay scales were infinitesimal. By the mid-1850s, the president and clerk of the Seneca Nation received $50 and the treasurer $46 a year. Although there were exceptions, annual tribal councilor salaries were in the $10 to $20 range. The "poormaster" had a salary of $20 a year, while the "Marshall Deputy" received $40 annually.[45]

Who were the revolutionaries who overthrew the chiefs in 1848? Much is still a mystery, especially the role that John Luke played in the revolution. A "John Luke" appears as a chief on Tonawanda Seneca petitions against the Buffalo Creek Treaty of 1838; however, there is no reference in the records to him being that same revolutionary. The proponents of the new election system included one emigration leader, George Jemison. In addition, as Abler has pointed out, the revolutionaries were much younger than the chiefs. Perhaps surprising to contemporary Onöndowa'ga:', more Christian-acculturated Senecas were represented in the ranks of the chiefs than in those of the revolutionaries. Indeed, not one of the delegates to the constitutional convention was a member of Wright's United Mission Church (now the Wright Memorial Church). Opponents of the revolution of 1848 were represented as congregants, including Chief Seneca White, Henry Two Guns, and John Jacket, Red Jacket's grandson. Despite their opposition to the government installed in 1848, all three men later ran for and were elected presidents of the Seneca Nation. Seneca White broke with missionary Wright and resigned his membership immediately after the revolution.[46]

Some of the notables who made their mark on the new Seneca constitution included Luke and John Cook, who had offered high praise for the Quakers in 1846. At least thirteen of the delegates had previously placed their names on petitions as headmen or warriors of the Seneca Nation—Cook, Big Chief, John General, John Greenblanket, Thomas Halfwhite, John Jimeson, Alexander Tallchief, Little Joe, Peter and Thomas Snow, John Wilson, Young Joe, and Solomon O'Bail, the latter a descendant of Cornplanter. Four had signed the Buffalo Creek Treaty of 1838—John Bark, John Bennett, George Jemison, and John Tallchief. Two of these men—Bennett and Jemison—had been implicated in the corruption scandals surrounding the treaty. Four of the delegates had put their names on the compromise treaty of 1842—Bark, Jemison, George Deer, and John Pierce.[47]

Several of the provisions in the constitution of 1848, especially sections 14 and 16, were controversial from the time of their adoption. In a clear restriction of tribal sovereignty, section 14 gave the council "the power to make any laws not inconsistent with the Constitution of the United States or of the State of New York." Section 16, repealed in 1868, stated: "The rights of any member of the ancient Confederacy of the Iroquois to the occupancy of our lands and other privileges shall be respected as heretofore."[48]

After the constitutional convention ended, the chiefs sent a protest, notarized by Reverend Wright, which they forwarded via their chairman, Thomas Jimeson, to President James Polk. They urged the lame duck president not to be swayed by "a certain portion of the warriors" who acted to abolish "our ancient legislature of government." The chiefs asked Polk to suspend judgment and not recognize the new government. There were familiar names on the memorial, among them Israel Jemison, Seneca White, Maris Pierce, and Nathaniel T. Strong. On this and later protests against the revolutionaries would appear the names of three future popularly elected presidents of the Seneca Nation: Henry Two Guns, Zachariah Jimeson, and John Jacket.[49]

Six weeks later, the chiefs made their most impassioned plea to President Polk: "Very soon a chief will be no body; but when the chiefs are no bodies, what will the people be? Where the interference of the chiefs is destroyed, the people will be without law—when our councils are without power, our people are arrested—we are Indians, not white men."[50]

From December 1848 through February 1849, supporters and opponents of the new government flooded Washington and Albany with petitions and sent delegates to lobby, attempting to convince legislators either to accept or reject recognition of the new government. On January 29, 1849, fifty-one of the headmen and warriors, including Harrison Halftown, who later served in the elected government as Seneca Nation clerk for more than two decades, petitioned President Polk. They insisted that the chiefs had been misrepresented by their enemies. They opposed the new government, which they claimed was composed of discredited chiefs who had been deposed for violating custom, even accusing them of being drunkards.[51]

The Polk administration, nevertheless, recognized the new government on February 2, 1849.[52] Yet the chiefs continued to push, hoping for a reversal of the decision since a new president, Zachary Taylor, was to take office the following month. The chiefs sent two former rivals, Maris Pierce and Nathaniel Strong, to Washington in an attempt to head off federal recognition of the new governmental structure. Now ex-chiefs, these two men argued that the Senecas, still wards, were not yet prepared for this new system of democratic government.[53]

McLane, who had been drafted into the position of provisional president of the Seneca Nation at the December 4 constitutional convention, countered the chiefs' moves. He wrote to Washington officials, repeating the litany of complaints against the council of chiefs. McLane insisted that the chiefs had to be held accountable to the people "for their acts however offensive they might be." While praising Thomas and the other Quakers, he insisted that they had not interfered in the final Seneca tribal decision to establish a new form of government.[54] In April, twenty women who supported the new government countered the chiefs' moves by sending a petition to the new president, Zachary Taylor, trying to discredit Pierce and his mission by bringing up the chiefs' past ineffective rule. They also claimed that the ex-chiefs were attempting to "thwart the public will."[55] While the Seneca proponents of the election system were lobbying, Thomas and the Hicksites used their political connections to counter the chiefs' petitions.[56]

Unable to get anywhere with Washington officials, the ex-chiefs then directed their attention to Albany. Hoping to stop state recognition, the chiefs directly appealed to the New York State Legislature. Pierce's new strategy was to try to play the state against the federal government. On March 13, Pierce wrote President Taylor, repeating some of his earlier condemnations of the new government. Once again, he pointed out that the creation of the new government was merely the act of a minority within the Seneca Nation. Pierce insisted that the change from chiefs' rule would interfere with existing or potential legal suits, that federal recognition would interfere with laws passed by the New York State Legislature, and that the Indian Office's recognition of the new government in February was illegal since, in his strange logic, New York State had to recognize the new Seneca government first! Pierce's convoluted logic convinced no one in Albany.[57]

On April 11, 1849, the New York State Legislature passed a law recognizing the Seneca Republic and its new government. The same day, the legislature passed an "Act to Benefit the Indians." The act recognized Indian common law marriages and the right of Seneca peacemaker courts to marry Indians "with the same force and effect as if by a justice of the peace." In a move clearly intended not to benefit the Indians, section 7 of the law "allowed" the Indian governments to divide their land and allot it to Indian individuals or families in "severalty and in fee simple, according to the laws of this state." However, it prevented the alienation of these lands "to any person other than the occupant, or his or her family." Section 11 "allowed" the New York State commissioners of the land office to accept "such sums of money as such Indians may wish to put in trust with the state of New York," where it would be "vested in good and safe securities by the comptroller, or in stocks of this state bearing interest at the rate of six per cent."[58]

On May 1, 1849, the Seneca Nation held its first popular election for president under its new constitution. McLane's National Ticket received 187 of the 307 votes cast. At least some of the supporters of the now ex-chiefs boycotted the election in protest. McLane was elected president, William Jemerson was elected clerk and one of the peacemakers, and Andrew John Sr. was elected treasurer. Two future elected Seneca presidents—Luke from Cattaraugus and Peter Jimeson from Allegany—were elected councilors. Luke also was elected superintendent of schools. Most of the councilors who were elected had been delegates at the December 1848 constitutional convention. Among the councilors elected from Cattaraugus was George Jemison, the controversial former pro-emigration chief. In this election, some of the chiefs participated, but not for the presidency of the Seneca Nation. In the election of May 1, John Seneca, the consensus builder and well-respected reformer of 1845, won two positions: peacemaker and assessor. Other chiefs who participated met defeat at the polls. Chiefs Seneca White and Maris Pierce were defeated for the position of peacemaker, Chief Thomas Jimeson for treasurer, and Chief Owen Blacksnake for marshal. Pierce was also was defeated for the position of Seneca Nation clerk.[59]

On the day after the election, President Taylor wrote his "children and friends" in the Seneca Nation. He insisted that the Indian Office's February decision to recognize the new tribal governmental structure had been done by a proper department of the U.S. government. Attempting to deflect criticism to the previous administration, Taylor added that the decision had been made (a month before) before he had assumed the presidency.[60]

The chiefs refused to accept Taylor's decision as being the final word. For the next decade and a half, the majority of these ex-chiefs, now referred to as the Old Chiefs Party, attempted to reassert their powers both through appeals and protests to Washington. They also added a new tactic: they would enter the new electoral process and attempt to win the presidency of the Seneca Nation. Although they were to frequently win this office, their counterrevolutionary efforts to resurrect the chiefs were to ultimately fail.

•◄ 2 ►•

SURVIVING THE
COUNTERREVOLUTION,
1849–1868

After the nation's first popular election for president in May 1849, the Senecas faced new pressures from within and from without. Although opponents of the 1848 constitution entered the electoral process and ran a full slate of candidates in 1851, the political battles between the supporters and opponents of the new system of elected government led to a stalemate, with both sides alternating electoral victories. Despite the political impasse, the nation did achieve two notable, but temporary, legal victories—one related to New York State efforts to tax Indian lands from 1840 to 1867; the other an ejectment case involving the Oil Spring Reservation that was decided in the Senecas' favor by the New York State Court of Appeals in 1861. Most importantly, the Seneca Nation survived these crises that seriously threatened the continued existence of its fragile new elective system of governance.

In the backdrop of sectional conflict that led to the American Civil War, the revolutionaries and the ex-chiefs and their supporters waged what appeared to a never-ending campaign to thwart the other's political ambitions. Abler has rightly pointed out that this process led to the evolution of political parties within the Seneca Nation.[1] By May 1851, the supporters of the former National Ticket had become the Warriors Party, and those who favored the return of the council overthrown in 1848 became known as the Old Chiefs Party. Yet the bitter rivalry persisted and continued to result in efforts to reinstall the chiefs. It also led to continuing political paralysis and resulted in ineffective efforts to deal with increasing pressures caused by timber stripping and leasing for much of the early 1850s. By 1852, Stephen Osborne, the federal Indian agent, reported to Commissioner of Indian Affairs Luke Lea about the chaotic situation: "I am persuaded that fierce quarrels among the Indians themselves about their own government and laws have been great, if not the principal cause of their sad situation. There has been a continued strife upon these reservations ever since the so-called revolution brought about the new government."[2]

The great divide within the Seneca polity had not closed from the time of federal recognition of the new government in 1849. On November 7, in response to repeated chiefs' efforts to overturn federal and state recognition of the new government, President McLane and Clerk Zachariah Jimeson wrote Secretary of the Interior Thomas Ewing. They once again tried to justify the revolution by maintaining that the old form of government was weak and corrupt, thereby allowing land speculators to take advantage of the Senecas. McLane and Jimeson noted that the new method of annuity distribution by the federal agent to individual Senecas would stop the chiefs from defrauding the people. They insisted that the council of chiefs had left the Senecas in poverty and with "no security to their prosperity and their homes" and that the new "Representative Republic was based upon free and democratic principles and that it was now in successful operation." The two officials emphasized that the chiefs should have no reason to complain, since all tribal members now had the same protection and guarantees of their property and person. They sarcastically pointed out that the chiefs had the same powers they had previously, "except the power to enrich themselves by venally selling the houses and homes of their kindred from under them, making them homeless and turning them out to perish."[3]

On November 29, 1849, Maris Pierce, now identifying himself as "chief warrior," wrote a lengthy letter to his mentor, Joseph Elkinton, the Orthodox Friend, teacher, and longtime Quaker School principal at Allegany. Pierce reflected on the tumultuous events of 1848 and 1849. He claimed that the new elected leaders of the Seneca Nation had little outside support beyond the Hicksites and Peter Wilson, the U.S. interpreter. Once again, he condemned Wilson, stating that the Cayuga had no right to voice his opinions in council. He insisted that his Seneca people were totally unprepared for "governing by a democratic government," were not "instructed sufficiently

[in] the art of self government," and had "not attained that degree of republican stability to exercise the right of suffrage." Pierce expressed his fears that the change in government would be a first step in a process whereby the Senecas would be reduced to the same fate as other tribes "bordering the Atlantic Ocean" had experienced. He predicted that the "chiefs and old men and the best of the nation will resist, until one or both fall into the hands of the enemy, and thus we may yet see the Senecas moving to the westward or scattering thro[ugh] the country homeless."[4]

In February 1850, Pierce again wrote to Elkinton, explaining that because of the ex-chiefs' resistance to the new government, the work of the Seneca Nation government was at a standstill and that the ex-chiefs refused to put forth candidates in the annual election.[5] In May 1850, Zachariah Jimeson won the presidency, and the ex-chiefs and their supporters boycotted the election. Nevertheless, ex-chief John Seneca once again was elected peacemaker.[6] Chief Pierce and other members of the overthrown chiefs' council continued to blame Thomas and the Hicksites. Refusing to admit that the chiefs had brought these sweeping changes on themselves, he wrote: "If the Hicksite would let us alone, we can get along better, but now they are using their influence to break us down, both at Washington City and in this state."[7]

Early in 1851, the majority of ex-chiefs made a fateful decision. While still committed to lobbying for and initiating the return of the chiefs' council, they decided to run a slate of candidates, with what they dubbed the Old Chiefs Party, for all the governmental offices, including president of the Seneca Nation. On May 6, 1851, ex-chief Seneca White was elected president, Maris Pierce clerk, and Israel Jemison treasurer of the Seneca Nation. The ex-chiefs and their supporters won election as councilors as well. These included three future presidents—Jacob Blacksnake, Henry Two Guns, and John Jacket. John Seneca was elected peacemaker.[6] Immediately after the election, Pierce wrote Elkinton that the Old Chiefs Party had won nearly twice the number of votes than the opposition. He gleefully added that Philip Thomas would finally see that the chiefs were the majority "in black and white."[8]

The ex-chiefs were once again determined to push for the end of the electoral system and a return to a government of chiefs. In March 1852, Jacob Blacksnake, Seneca White, Maris Pierce, Israel Jemison, John Jacket (Red Jacket's grandson), and other Seneca councilors of the Old Chiefs Party sent petitions to both the president of the United States and the New York State Legislature. In them they blamed Peter Wilson and the Cayugas as well as "false hearted Senecas" and the Quakers, "who have good hearts, and mean kindly, but who believe without seeing and are easily imposed upon by people who can flatter and lie." These Senecas insisted that it was wrong for the Great Father at Washington recognize the new government. The Old Chiefs Party pointed to their victory at the polls in 1851 as evidence that they "possess the confidence of their people." They indicated that they had participated in the last election "with the vowed intention of getting rid of it." Calling the constitution of 1848 "odious," they described it as being a "mysterious" instrument, a "paper constitution for a people who could not read until this year, exercised by elected officers who could not write."[9]

The Senecas elected the ex-chiefs to office in May 1852, with Jacob Blacksnake winning the presidency, Israel Jemison reelected treasurer, and Nathaniel T. Strong elected clerk. Strong had cooperated with disgraced federal subagent James Stryker in pushing an emigration agenda in 1838, but now he was rehabilitated in the eyes of a majority of Senecas. Upon this second straight electoral victory, the ex-chiefs were once again determined to push for the end of the election system and a return to a government of chiefs. On July 8, 1852, they petitioned President Millard Fillmore, requesting him to send a commissioner to Seneca Country to determine the truth about the split within the nation. They insisted that the new government created under the constitution of 1848 "was not in force, but was a paper document." The ex-chiefs pointed out the spreading of lies about how they were ready to once again sell Seneca lands and that Wilson and Shankland, had been too hasty pushing for federal recognition of the new government. They insisted that the change had occurred without the chiefs being fully heard. The ex-chiefs concluded: "We believe it is your duty to correct the error of your predecessor if you don't who will."[10]

Eight days later, Fillmore responded by writing to the commissioner of Indian affairs, recommending that attorney Chester Howe and the new federal agent, Stephen Osborne, hold a plebiscite on the matter. Nevertheless, the president noted that he had great doubts about whether the Senecas had the "sufficient intelligence to maintain a republican form of government." He added that once the issue was settled in a plebiscite, all efforts to reverse the decision would end for "a reasonable length of time—say ten years" before there could be protest and application for another change of government.[11]

In September 1852, the ex-chiefs, now the Old Chiefs Party, sponsored a convention chaired by Owen Blacksnake, attempting to abolish the constitution of 1848. They wrote, "Resolved: The convention recommends the abrogation of the constitution of December 4, 1848 and for the restoration of the government by Chiefs as amended by the Ordinance of 1845, by in every respect as existed before."[12] John Luke and John Hudson, two representatives of the Warriors Party in attendance, protested this action. Luke, Hudson, and Peter Snow—later Seneca president, in the early 1870s—then sent a memorial to Fillmore on September 29, condemning the ex-chiefs' action. They insisted that under a provision of the 1848 constitution, the tribal government structure could not be amended for five years after October 2, 1850. They urged Fillmore not to take action until May 1853, when a new election was scheduled to be held.[13]

The Old Chiefs Party continued to push for a new constitution and the return to chiefly rule. In January 1855, at a quickly called Seneca convention, their delegates drafted a new constitution in an attempt to void the 1848 document. These efforts proved fruitless because the proposal failed to receive a constitutional majority—namely, two-thirds of the votes of all members present, a requirement set forth in the 1848 constitution. The chiefs' opponents, led by John Luke, petitioned the Office of Indian Affairs, referring to the ex-chiefs' actions as "unconstitutional" since the ex-chiefs had held the convention without proper notice.[14] Luke and his allies did not stop there. They claimed that the supporters of the Old Chiefs Party were merely a small vocal minority and urged that Commissioner George Manypenny not listen to them. The supporters of the revolution defended the electoral changes of 1848 and once again pointed out the past corruption of members of the chiefs' council. Luke and his followers then warned the commissioner of the continued "corruption and the rapacious actions of land speculators who promote dissensions and troubles among our peoples." They specifically targeted ex-chief Strong, since he had been "very active in obtaining the fraudulent treaty" (1838). They also accused him of still being "under the pay of the land speculators."[15] Despite its successes at the ballot box in 1851, 1852, and 1854, the Old Chiefs Party continued to fail in its efforts to have the president of the United States, Congress, or the Indian Office reverse its decision of 1849 and support a change back to chiefly rule.[16]

During this period of political instability, the Senecas continued to face challenges from beyond their borders. On June 28, 1850, the Seneca government leased a 145-acre right-of-way—11.66 miles of track through the Allegany Reservation—to the New York and Erie Railroad for $3,000.

The easement agreement did not have the required approval by the federal government but was "confirmed" by an act of the New York State Legislature. On May 14, 1851, the railroad line from the New York City metropolitan area to Buffalo was officially completed in a golden spike ceremony at Cuba, New York. During the Civil War, this railroad leased an additional 23.85 acres for $2,385 for the construction, occupancy, and maintenance of its rail activities. This second easement laid the foundation for the founding of the city of Salamanca, a major railroad nexus on the Allegany Indian Reservation. James McHenry, an English iron magnate, and his friend and business associate the marquess of Salamanca, a Spanish royalist who made a fortune investing and building rail lines throughout Europe, soon after extended the Atlantic and Great Western Railroad 369 miles from today's Allegany Reservation to Dayton. By 1866 this second railroad had constructed a spur line south to Oil City, Pennsylvania, to take advantage of the newly discovered petroleum fields. The Seneca Nation also leased a right-of-way to the Buffalo and Pittsburgh Railroad.[17]

Importantly, the railroads had opened up the southwestern corridor of New York State, leading to increased white settlement and exploitation of the region's natural resources. By 1865 these rail lines had established train stations as well as depots and machine shops on Seneca lands. New communities—Carrollton, Great Valley, Red House, Vandalia, Salamanca, and Shongo (West Salamanca)—sprang up within the borders of the Allegany Reservation. At a time when there was political turmoil and internal bickering after the revolution of 1848, outsiders seeking homesteads, farms, and/or employment with the railroads made leasing agreements with individual Senecas or just began to settle on Allegany without formal permission. It should be noted that more than a few Seneca entrepreneurs, going against the regulations of their nation, took advantage of the weakness of their own tribal government as well as the inability of federal Indian agents to stop or supervise some of these individual leasing agreements.[18]

Even before completion of the New York and Erie Railroad, lumber mills were slowly transforming the Upper Allegheny Valley region. The burning of the plentiful oak, elm, maple, beech, and birch trees, which were subsequently doused with dripping water, produced black salts, or potash, used by farmers to fertilize their fields. One acre of land could produce four hundred pounds of potash, which sold for $10. Commercial water-powered mills soon followed, cutting pine, hemlock, and large hardwoods. The abundance of hemlock, with the high concentration of tannin in its bark, was especially essential for leather processing. By the Civil War, Buffalo and Rochester, among the ten largest cities in population in the United States and within one hundred miles of the Allegany Reservation, needed more and more lumber for the construction of homes and commercial buildings. By the 1880s, band saws had come into use. They made it possible to construct and employ larger mills. With easy access to rail transportation, furniture manufacturing became a major part of the southwestern New York economy. By the end of the century, the wood chemical industry began operating on and around the Allegany Reservation, producing acetate of lime, acetic acid, charcoal, wood alcohol, and other products, such as railroad ties made from lumber treated with creosote.[19]

As early as 1852, Seneca leaders had pointed out that their communities had become poorer and more wretched, since tribal lands were being denuded of timber and "everywhere invaded and trespassed on by whites."[20] Little was accomplished until 1861, when a "timber agent" was appointed to remove and prosecute intruders.[21] In January 1857, Nathaniel Strong wrote the commissioner of Indian affairs, indicating that "portions of the reservation [Cattaraugus] are now coveted with swarms of white men cutting saw logs for the Buffalo and Erie Railroad otherwise called 'Lake Shore Road.' The forests are full of shanties and wood cutting machines are erected." Taking a swipe at the elected government installed in 1848, ex-chief Strong bemoaned that there were no longer outspoken chiefs to condemn the practice.[22] In the same year, federal Indian agent Marcus Johnson noted in his official report to the commissioner of Indian affairs that the quick and easy money from timber stripping would only provide temporary relief, since the hardwoods were fast disappearing. The federal agent saw this as a good thing, since it might lead Senecas to take up farming, the desired plan of the Quakers.[23]

In 1866 the Society of Friends' Philadelphia Yearly Meeting described what had resulted in the decade and a half since the New York and Erie lease of 1850 and sounded an alarm, fearing that the Senecas could ultimately lose control of their lands. The Quaker report warned that the increasing white population around the Senecas was "of low moral character and expose them to corrupting examples and associations and present temptations which they [the Senecas] have not firmness to resist." It added: "The Rail Roads and stations on the Allegheny [sic] Reservation greatly increase the evils which proceed from this cause; and it must continue to operate so long as the Indians are located around or near the villages.[24]

At the same time, the successful drilling of a well in western Pennsylvania by Colonel Samuel Drake in 1859 led to an oil rush in southwestern New York, and whites began to seek leases for drilling from the Seneca Nation Council. In 1865 Job Moses sank the region's first oil well near the now defunct village of Limestone, which bordered the Allegany Reservation.[25] Questionable oil leases on the Allegany Reservation soon became a major issue in Seneca politics and even led to the impeachment of Job King, the nation's president in the late 1870s.[26] By the mid-1880s, the Bradford Oil Field, which encompassed 85,000 acres in McKean County, Pennsylvania, and south-central Cattaraugus County, New York, was one of the most prolific oil fields in the world.[27]

In the face of these challenges, two concerns brought the opposing Seneca parties together during the two decades after the Seneca Revolution. The first involved the Oil Spring Reservation. From the 1830s onward, non-Indians had come onto this territory, known to them as the first place oil was "discovered" in North America, and some had established a mill there. Many Senecas viewed the territory with its petroleum/medicinal spring as a holy place, associated with the life of their prophet Handsome Lake, who had saved the reservation after the Treaty of Big Tree. In the 1850s, non-Indians attempted to wrest ownership of the territory from the Senecas. This crisis led the Seneca Nation's rival parties to put aside their internal political differences.

From 1855 to 1861, both parties, led by presidents John Seneca, John Luke, and Isaac Halftown, fought to save the reservation from being overrun by squatters. They began a major ejectment case, *Seneca Nation v. Philonus Pattison*, which ended up in the New York State Court of Appeals. A second action was directed by the Seneca against Seymour, Gallagher, Chamberlain, and Clark for the northeast quarter of the Oil Spring tract. The Seymour was Horatio Seymour, a major canal promoter and later a governor of New York State and a Democratic candidate for president of the United States in the 1860s. The case turned on evidence produced in testimony by Governor Blacksnake, a nephew of Handsome Lake and a prominent Allegany Seneca ex-chief. At trial, the aged chief, possibly 107 years of age, produced an original map made by Joseph Ellicott of the Holland Land Company, indicating that the Oil Spring territory was Seneca property. The case was subsequently appealed to the New York Court of Appeals, and a decision was rendered for the Senecas.[28]

Despite this legal victory, the Senecas faced more travail with construction of the Genesee Valley Canal from 1858 to 1863 and its Oil Spring Reservoir (Cuba Lake), a dam on Oil Creek. In 1863 and then again in 1868, the New York State Legislature authorized the raising of the water level of Oil Creek Reservoir. Seneca lands were appropriated for the reservoir, but some tribal lands that were not taken for the project were damaged and flooded.[29] The repercussions of the state's appropriation of these lands and the subsequent leasing of cottages along the lake reverberated for the next century and a half. Only in 2005 was a land claim settlement reached, with the return of fifty-one acres to the Seneca Nation.[30]

Besides the coming of railroads and the threat to lands on Oil Spring Reservation, the already-beleaguered government of the Seneca Nation faced another crisis, one even greater, emanating from the outside. It involved retaining ownership of the Allegany and Cattaraugus Reservations. The two rival parties once again came together to petition the Office of Indian Affairs in Washington and the governor and state legislature in Albany. They also filed actions in state and federal courts. The issue was directly tied to taxation of reservation lands.

The effort to tax Seneca lands had begun in 1840 and 1841, when the state legislature passed two bills giving Allegany, Cattaraugus, and Erie Counties the right to tax tribal members for the maintenance of roads and bridges.[31] The Senecas refused to pay these taxes. In 1853, in response to a request by the Cattaraugus County Board of Supervisors, the New York State comptroller issued orders of foreclosure. From January to June 1856, 13,300 acres of Seneca lands, including 8,000 at Coldspring at Allegany and 3,600 at Cattaraugus, were foreclosed and put up for sale for nonpayment of taxes. One non-Indian, Harvey Baldwin, alone purchased 7,200 acres of these foreclosed lands.[32]

This new threat evoked a vociferous response from both the Senecas and the Quakers.[33] The Senecas temporarily put away their bitter rivalries and joined together to fight the taxes. President Luke and six tribal councilors, including his former political rival ex-chief Seneca White and two other future presidents of the Seneca Nation, sent memorials to Governor Myron Clark and the New York State Legislature, as well as to the commissioner of Indian affairs in Washington. In a quite deferential manner, the Senecas petitioned for help because of the nation's weakness in dealing with the "more mature intellect and consummate artifice of the Anglo-Saxon race" and fear that "there is a strong reason to believe the [Indian] race will be exterminated."[34] On the other hand, in their petitions the Senecas demanded justice and in a sophisticated way drew ammunition from the American past. They equated their resistance to that of colonists before the American Revolution. The petitioners then asked that the state legislature grant relief by making provisions "for the redemption of said lands, or for such further, or other relief as in your wisdom may be equitable and shall efficiently protect the rights of your petitioners."[35]

Philip Thomas led the Quaker effort to stop the imposition of the taxes, which he interpreted as a new way to force the removal of the Senecas from the state. During this struggle, he continued to serve the Senecas as an envoy every time the revolutionaries, now known as the New Government Party, defeated the Old Chiefs Party in the 1850s, since he was totally committed to supporting the electoral structure of Seneca government.[36] He never regained favor from most of the ex-chiefs, but he did redeem himself in some quarters when he helped fund the establishment of the Thomas Asylum for Orphan and Destitute Indian Children at Cattaraugus in 1855. In the same period, other members of the Society of Friends redeemed themselves in the eyes of some Senecas by establishing the Quaker School at Tunesassa, just off the Allegany Reservation.[37]

In the mid-1850s, Thomas repeated his case against Indian removal policies, frequently condemning the rapacious land sharks that seemed to always be around the Senecas, attempting to get at their lands. Thomas vehemently opposed reopening treaty negotiations with federal officials for fear that this type of action might lead once again to talk of removal of Indians to the West. Instead, Thomas continued to urge the Tonawandas to join their kin and relocate to the Cattaraugus Reservation, just as the majority of Buffalo Creek Senecas had done in the mid-1840s. His position did not change over time, which put him in direct conflict with the Tonawanda Senecas' Council of Chiefs, which continued to blame him and the Hicksites for not doing enough to get their lands back.[38]

In response to Seneca and Quaker protests, Commissioner Manypenny recommended that the New York State comptroller cancel the deeds and remit payment to the purchasers of Indian lands.[39] Subsequently, in 1857 the New York State Senate's judiciary committee issued a report stating that the Senecas' title to Allegany and Cattaraugus territories was "original, absolute, and exclusive" and not held by either New York State or the United States, and that Albany "had no right to tax them." The report added that the Senecas "are rather to be regarded as a distinct and independent nation, having a constitution and representative government of their own."[40]

In 1857 the state senate passed an "Act to Relieve the Seneca Nation of Indians From Certain Taxes on the Allegany and Cattaraugus Reservations," which returned seventy-two hundred acres to the Seneca Nation. It also stated: "No tax shall hereafter be assessed or imposed on either of said reservations, or any part thereof, for any purpose whatsoever so long as said reservations remain the property of the Seneca Nation." The purchasers of Indian lands at foreclosure sales were to be fully paid, with 7 percent interest per annum added in their reimbursement.[41] At a time when the country was in a major depression, the interest rate appears to be another Albany boondoggle.

In 1865 the New York State Court of Appeals, the highest court in the Empire State, reversed the legislature's act of 1857 and recognized Albany's right to tax Indian lands. The Seneca Nation then appealed the troublesome decision to the United States Supreme Court. In another twist of fate, Justice Samuel Nelson of Cooperstown was to render the majority opinion in the case *The New York Indians*, decided in 1867. Nelson had written the favorable majority opinion for the Tonawanda Senecas in the *Fellows v. Blacksmith* case of 1857. That case had recognized the Tonawandas as a political entity apart from the Seneca Nation, thereby allowing them to make a separate federal treaty to repurchase part of their lands from the Ogden Land Company.[42] The much-maligned Nelson, who had made the malodorous decision in the *Dred Scott v. Sandford* case, apparently viewed Native Americans differently from blacks, based on his interpretation of their treaties. Justice Nelson argued that the Cattaraugus County Board of Supervisors could not levy taxes before the Indians were scheduled to be removed to the West under the Buffalo Creek Treaty of 1838 and that state laws authorizing county officials to do so were unconstitutional. Citing his earlier decision in *Fellows v. Blacksmith*, Nelson insisted that the Senecas were entitled to "undisturbed enjoyment" in their ancient possessions from generation to generation until they sold their lands, they were formally removed from them, or their tribe ceased to exist. In a firm rebuke to Albany legislators, he added that "the rights of the Indians do not depend on this or any statutes of the states, but upon treaties, which are the supreme law of the land; it is to these treaties we must look to ascertain the nature of these rights, and the extent of them." Nelson concluded: "The time for the surrender of possession [1845, five years after the president's proclamation of the Buffalo Creek Treaty of 1838] according to their consent given in the treaty, had not expired when these taxes were levied." Hence the "taxation of the lands was premature."[43] Yet county officials as early as 1871 refused to consider the matter dead.[44] Despite the United States Supreme Court ruling in *New York Indians,* the issue of taxing Seneca lands was hardly resolved and has continued right down to the present day.[45]

In the midst of internal battles over their form of government, land issues related to Oil Spring, and the imposition of taxation by outsiders, the Senecas, as all Americans, were affected dramatically by the coming of the Civil War. More than one hundred Senecas fought as Union foot soldiers in the war. Although New York State refused to allow Indians to enlist in the first year of the war, other states allowed them entry from the first. In November 1861, the controversial ex-chief Nathaniel Strong, whose son later enlisted in the war effort, wrote Commissioner of Indian Affairs William Dole, objecting to the New York State's racial restrictions about enlistment. He questioned why Dutch, Irish, French, German, and English soldiers were allowed into the Union army but Indians were excluded. He indicated that his people were eager to serve as "Indian warriors and soldiers."[46]

The next month, to get around this restriction, some Allegany Senecas went to Harrisburg and joined up with Company K of the Fifty-Seventh Pennsylvania Volunteer Infantry Regiment. They saw action in the Peninsula Campaign. The first casualty in the unit was Cornelius Plummer, killed at Fair Oaks in June 1862. Of the twelve Seneca soldiers in Company K, two were killed in action, one died of tuberculosis, four were discharged for injuries incurred in service, and at least two were listed as deserters.[47]

Eventually, after the restriction in New York State was lifted in March 1862, more than one hundred Indians from Allegany and Cattaraugus territories joined the Union army.[48] Several Senecas joined Company D of the 132nd New York State Volunteer Infantry, the most famous Iroquois fighting unit, and received commendations at Batchelors Creek and Kinston, North Carolina. Nineteen-year-old Cattaraugus Seneca William Kennedy of the 132nd was captured and died at Andersonville Prison in 1864; Foster Hudson, a twenty-three-year-old from Cattaraugus, was shot and killed at

Jackson's Mill, North Carolina, one month before General Lee's surrender at Appomattox Courthouse.[49] Other Senecas served in the Fourteenth New York Heavy Artillery, the Twenty-Fourth New York Cavalry, and the Thirteenth New York Volunteer Infantry. Two members of the Seneca Nation—Jacob Halftown and Oliver Silverheels—earned citations for bravery at the Battle of Spotsylvania Courthouse in the late spring of 1864. After Confederates killed one of his regimental comrades, Silverheels camouflaged his body from head to foot with the foliage of pine boughs. With a rifle in hand, he "sneaked" up behind a Confederate sharpshooter who had perched in a tree before the Union lines, and he captured the rebel soldier.[50]

Tribal officials frequently complained to the War Department about the recruitment of underage Seneca boys, enticed by military bounties and by the excitement of replicating the warrior skills of the past. Eventually the War Department discharged some of these youngsters, but only after the Senecas sent petitions to Washington and after a Six Nations official delegation conferred with President Lincoln.[51] With numerous males away in military service, those left behind—primarily the women, children, and aged—had difficulty making ends meet. To survive, individual Senecas made more and more leasing arrangements without seeking out tribal or federal Indian agent approval. To make things even worse, a major smallpox epidemic struck the Seneca territories during the war.[52]

While many of their men were away at war, the Old Chiefs Party attempted a counterrevolution, challenging the presidency of Henry Silverheels. In October 1864, the Senecas amended their 1848 constitution. By a vote of thirty-four to eleven at a constitutional convention, Old Chiefs Party delegates passed a resolution calling for restoration of the council of chiefs, to be chosen according to the rules and customs of the Iroquois Confederacy. This action produced an immediate crisis. A month later, the Iroquois Confederacy's Grand Council intervened in the political crisis to support the move and attempted to add Seneca Nation sachems to it proceedings.[53] A reconstituted chiefs' council then tried to abolish the 1848 constitution and attempted to remove President Silverheels, ironically an ex-chief, and the councilors allied to him. This action of removing the duly elected officers was then certified by A. Sim Logan, the previously elected clerk of the Seneca Nation. Silverheels and the councilors who were removed then appealed to Commissioner Dole, who refused to sanction any of the actions of the counterrevolutionaries.[54] Silverheels and his allied councilors, reinstated by the Office of Indian Affairs, then forced Logan and his supporters to resign. Significantly, the next year, the Senecas reelected Silverheels president, indicating that by that time the return to chiefly rule was not supported by a majority of the nation.[55] While there were later challenges to the Seneca Nations' election system, none was as formidable as this crisis during the latter part of the Civil War.[56]

Although this 1864–65 effort to change the government failed, the battle had a major impact for the next forty years. Seneca leadership demonstrated its elasticity by making a 180-degree shift. Attempting to generate unity in their severely divided communities, which were increasingly affected by the growing presence of non-Indians seeking leases, Seneca Presidents Isaac Halftown, Peter Sundown, William Crouse, and William Nephew and their councils reversed Silverheels's course. While Seneca leadership from the 1850s through the mid-1860s had been reluctant to openly challenge the legality of past treaties for fear that these actions might revive federal interest in removing the Senecas to the Indian Territory, the four presidents and their successors now sought to join with other Hodinöhsö:ni´ communities to push back. After the formal end of federal Indian treaty-making in 1871, they lobbied Congress for compensation, bringing two major court actions. In the process, they strengthened Seneca nationalism and repaired some broken ties with the Iroquois Grand Council by jointly seeking federal compensation in the Kansas claims case. In the process, they created more support for the governmental structure created in 1848, providing it with a strong enough foundation to survive well into the future.

•◄ 3 ►•

ASSERTING SOVEREIGNTY

Two Cases

E ven while facing bitter internal political struggles, outside threats of taxation and land loss, and the horrors caused by participating in the Civil War, the Seneca Nation leadership lobbied to gain recognition for its grievances under two federal treaties. In two separate cases from 1858 to 1906, the Senecas sought compensation for the fraudulent "takes" of their land and for promoting Indian removal to the West.[1] These two lengthy litigations were to have very different results. The first of these efforts—the Kansas Claims case—first arose in tribal council discussions in the late 1850s. This successful court case led to a small monetary award to individual Senecas in 1905 and spurred later legal actions against the United States on other issues before the Indian Claims Commission from 1946 to 1977.[2] The second case—*Seneca Nation v. Harrison B. Christy*—which was started in the early 1880s, involved a land take set forth in provisions of the federal treaty of 1826 involving the Cattaraugus Indian Reservation. This important case originated the argument that state violation of the federal Trade and Intercourse Acts (1790–1834) was sufficient evidence to allow American Indians in the thirteen original states to bring their cases into federal court. This argument was later used by attorneys for the Seneca Nation and for other Hodinöhsö:ni´ in land claims cases decided from 1974 to 2006.[3]

Both the Kansas claims case and the *Christy* case involved treaties negoti-ated at the Buffalo Creek Reservation and federal inabilities to carry out fiduciary responsibilities to protect Seneca interests. Under the provisions of the Buffalo Creek Treaty of 1838, the U.S. government had ceded to the Senecas 1,824,000 acres "directly west of the State of Missouri" to entice them to leave New York. Article 3 of this treaty required that "such of the tribes of the New York Indians as do not accept and agree to remove to the country set apart for their new homes within five years, or such other time as the president may, from time to time appoint, shall forfeit all interest in the lands so set apart, to the United States."[4] Approximately two hundred Hodinöhsö:ni´ emigrated to the Kansas in 1846. Some of them died of disease, and most had returned to New York by 1847. Eventually, only thirty-two so-called New York Indians remained in the West; they later received patents or certificates of allotment in Kansas.[5] In a federal treaty concluded on November 5, 1857, the Tonawanda Senecas relinquished all their rights and title to these Kansas lands. They used the money from the sale of their interest to buy back 7,500 acres of their reservation lands from the Ogden Land Company.[6]

By 1857 the "New York Indian Reservation" in eastern Kansas had been overrun by trespassers in the aftermath of the Kansas-Nebraska Act of 1854. In the sectional conflict that led to "Bleeding Kansas," the Indians were the real losers, with squatters using excuses of promoting slavery or free soil to lay claim to the lands.[7] That fall, while the Tonawanda Senecas negotiated a new treaty with the federal government, Commissioner of Indian Affairs James W. Denver reported on the lands assigned to the "New York Indians" in Kansas and proposed a solution. He recommended the allotment of these lands to the few Six Nations people living there and the selling off of the rest, presumably to satisfy those non-Indians rushing into the territory. Denver maintained that those who had been already removed to lands in the West "should be assigned the three hundred and twenty acres promised to them, and the remainder of the lands be brought into the market for the benefit of our citizens who are rapidly filling up the territory."[8]

News of this chaotic situation in Kansas spread eastward. On June 2, 1858, the Seneca Nation elected governing body passed a resolution in support of the Senecas' Tonawanda kin and the ratification of the federal treaty that had been worked out the year before. However, Seneca Nation councilors were wary of bringing up the issue of Kansas lands, since the Ogden Land Company still had the preemptive claim to both the Allegany and Cattaraugus Reservations. Fear of removal still ran deep in the minds and hearts of the Senecas. Consequently, the councilors refused to pursue the issue of claims under the Treaty of 1838. The council's resolution maintained that "the question of the West land called Kansas Territory be rejected as we Senecas had nothing to do or right of said lands as long as we don't go there." The resolution further stated that that those circulating petitions among the Senecas on the Allegany and Cattaraugus Reservations "with the view for a re-opening of negotiations" and promoting emigration to the West would be viewed "as enemies to the well-being of our nation."[9]

Two months later, President Edward Pierce reiterated these concerns. He quickly dismissed those pushing for a new federal Seneca Nation treaty involving Kansas claims. He maintained that its pursuit by "these defrauded class of Seneca people," through the holding of meetings, councils, and conventions and sending delegations to Washington, was a precious waste of time and money, and he warned that its proponents were delusional with a "false expectation of a rich harvest."[10] Some Senecas were also suspicious about the claim, since it was being pushed by the controversial Peter Wilson and Nathaniel T. Strong.[11] Once Pierce left office and was succeeded by John Luke in 1859 and Isaac Halftown in 1860, Seneca support for this claims effort slowly gained momentum.

On March 21, 1859, following the commissioner's recommendation, the secretary of the interior ordered the appropriation of the lands in eastern Kansas as well as an official census of the "New York Indians" there to determine compensation.[12] The following year, President James Buchanan issued an executive order making these lands part of the national domain and allowing a survey. Commissioner of Indian Affairs Alfred Greenwood then ordered the allotment and sale of these parcels. The thirty-two New York Indians still there were to receive allotments of 320 acres each, and the remaining lands were to be thrown open and sold off to non-Indians, many of whom were already occupying Indian lands as squatter and trespassers. The land was eventually sold off at $1.34 per acre. Since the cost of surveying was a mere twelve cents per acre, the federal government made $1.22 per acre. The only other expense that Washington incurred was $9,464.08 in the removal of approximately two hundred Indians to the West in 1846.[13] Hence the United States made a significant profit doing a "land office business" at the expense of the Indians.

Although there were delays in considering the claim because of the outbreak of the Civil War and the massive number of refugees fleeing Confederate-held Indian Territory into Kansas, the Office of Indian Affairs nevertheless was determined to proceed on the matter, since its agents received complaints about conditions there.[14] In the fall of 1862, Commissioner of Indian Affairs William Dole wrote that with the exception of the Tonawanda Senecas and the Wisconsin Oneidas, who had agreed to swap their Kansas claim to remain on their 65,400-acre reservation in the environs of Green Bay, "these Indians have very unadjusted claims against the United States, arising under the provisions and stipulations of the Buffalo Creek Treaty of January 15, 1838." After considering the issue, Dole recommended congressional action to deal with both the Six Nations Indians who resided in New York and the handful who had emigrated and were still in Kansas.[15] Subsequently, he met with a Six Nations delegation in Washington.

In late January 1864, one of those delegates, Maris Pierce, who had long given up in his attempt to restore chiefly rule, was now teaching school at Cattaraugus. The highly educated Pierce, a man with great communication skills in both English and Seneca, was included as part of a Six Nations delegation to Washington, even though ex-chiefs were no longer represented on the Iroquois Grand Council. He met with Commissioner Dole and urged him to support a new treaty and/or legislation to resolve claims under the Treaty of 1838. Later, over tea with President and Mrs. Lincoln at the White House, Pierce brought the Kansas claim to the president's attention. He also urged Lincoln to order the discharge of underage Hodinöhsö:ni´ who had been enticed into military service. Lincoln made an impression on the ex-chief. Pierce commented that the president was a "good man" and that he was hopeful about justice for the Indians.[16]

From February through April 1864, representatives of the Grand Council continued to lobby in Washington for a resolution of the Six Nations' claim. Besides Pierce, other delegates included Nathaniel Strong, Israel Jemison, Peter Wilson, Daniel Two Guns, Joshua Turkey, and Tuscarora chief John Mountpleasant. On March 28, 1864, putting away their personal vendetta, Pierce and Strong then joined with Jemison in sending a petition to President Lincoln. They asked for the president's support in resolving the Kansas claims.[17] A month later, the same Six Nations delegates wrote Commissioner Dole, asking him to nominate General John H. Martindale, "a true friend of the Indians of New York," as a federal treaty commissioner to settle the issue.[18] Pierce indicated to his wife that the federal government officials appeared "willing to make a treaty with us, either to give us 320 acres of land a head or pay us in some money, although they do not like to do that."[19]

In the spring of 1864, Commissioner Dole sent his assistant, Charles Mix, to a Grand Council meeting at Cattaraugus to discuss the Six Nations Kansas claims. He showed up just when counterrevolutionaries were once again attempting to seize control of the Seneca Nation's government. President Silverheels and his supporters feared that opening up new discussions about the Treaty of 1838 might once again revive calls for Seneca removal from New York to Indian Territory. Using this as an excuse, his political opponents temporarily replaced him and his allied councilors and installed a new council of chiefs sanctioned by the Grand Council.[20]

Immediately after his arrival at the council, presided over by Onondaga sachem Samuel George, Mix became embroiled in a dispute with Jemison and Wilson. At the beginning of the council, Mix demanded to see the credentials of the delegates present to determine if they were official representatives of their tribes. Mix's action was seen as a break with long-standing council protocol. Jemison responded by insisting that Mix submit his own credentials first, and Wilson snapped in by stating that his people were on "an equal footing" in council with the federal government. Mix refused to hand over his official papers and "submit to the dictation" of the Indians and left the meeting in a huff. Federal Indian agent John Manley wrote in his report that the new government officers showed "disrespect and indignity" to the commissioner's representative at the council. He made it clear that President Silverheels had nothing to do with "this insult" and that what most Senecas wanted was to extinguish their title to their Kansas lands and receive "a just and fair compensation" from it. He labeled the disturbance an attempt to overthrow the constitution and republican form of government and "to foist upon them [Senecas] their old barbarism and irresponsible mode of government by chiefs."[21] Subsequently, Nathaniel Strong and John Kennedy Jr., deploring the treatment of Mix, apologized for it.[22]

President Silverheels later said that his opponents' behavior and use of the issue of the Kansas claims was actually a concerted effort to destroy the Seneca Nation's "recent republican constitution and government." He insisted that they "doubtless hoped to effect such a settlement" and present themselves as being "instrumental in inducing the [United States] government to take steps to liquidate our claim for compensation for the Kansas lands."[23] Thus it was no accident that the Indian Office in Washington favored the reinstallation of Silverheels and his supporters on the council, which subsequently occurred.

The issue of the Kansas claims did not disappear however, and the lob-bying for a new treaty gradually won acceptance. In the fall of 1865, the Senecas asked for a commissioner to be sent again to negotiate and adjust their claims in Kansas.[24] Both Seneca presidents Isaac Halftown and Peter Snow in the late 1860s pushed hard in this direction. Indeed, from 1867 though William C. Hoag's presidency in 1905, the Kansas claims case was one of the major concerns of Seneca tribal councils. It was as well a major focus of the Grand Council at Onondaga, which since 1848 had remained at odds with the Seneca Nation. At times throughout the late nineteenth century, the chiefs there disagreed with the Seneca elected tribal council about the leadership and strategies to use in pursuing the claim.

In 1867 Pierce detailed the progress relative to the claim. Although by this time there was significant community support for these efforts, the Senecas nevertheless were divided about strategies. Strong pushed for one set of claims agents to represent the nation, and Wilson for another. A third group representing four councilors from Cattaraugus insisted that the nation did not have to hire any at all. Pierce apparently was with the third group, complaining to a Quaker friend that the claims agents would allegedly get twenty-five cents of every dollar if hired.[25]

On December 4, 1868, at the Cattaraugus Council House, federal officials in the Indian Office reached an acceptable agreement on a new treaty with the Six Nations chiefs and the tribal council of the Seneca Nation. Among its provisions, the United States agreed to pay off the claim to the Indians, including members of the Seneca Nation, out of moneys the United States had obtained by selling the remaining "New York Indian Reservation" lands. However, the treaty never went beyond the Senate Committee on Indian Affairs. The push for a new treaty failed. The committee maintained that the Indians had forfeited their rights under the Treaty of 1838, since they had not complied with the requirement about removal en masse from New York within five years of the treaty's formal presidential proclamation, which had occurred in 1840.[26] Other efforts to push for a new treaty dealing with this claim failed in Congress when the U.S. government formally stopped making treaties with Indian nations in 1871.[27]

For the next three decades, the issue took a convoluted course in Congress and the courts. Congress held hearings on bills to deal with resolving the matter, but each time the effort went down to defeat. In 1874 Senator Reuben Fenton of New York introduced Bill S. 640, which called for the settlement of the claim and for the appointment of a special agent to make a full and complete registry of Six Nations Indians entitled to compensation. Once again, the bill never became law.[28] A major stumbling block frequently arose. Throughout the 1880s and into the early 1890s, congressmen as well as commissioners of Indian affairs once again continued to question whether the Senecas and other Hodinöhsö:ni´ had forfeited their title to Kansas lands.[29]

The Senecas continued to make their case. In late January and early February 1883, two Seneca delegates—Andrew John Jr. and Clerk Harrison Halftown—went to Washington to lobby for a settlement. They insisted that moneys from a claims settlement could be used to create a new industrial school on one of the Seneca reservations.[30] This was not the last time John lobbied on Capitol Hill. John, an Allegany Seneca, was elected president four times—in 1886, 1887, 1888, and 1890. He became a familiar face in Washington as a lobbyist and later as a tour guide for visiting Indian delegations to the Office of Indian Affairs and at the Smithsonian Institution.[31]

Finally, after a quarter of a century of lobbying, on January 28, 1893, Congress authorized the United States Court of Claims to hear, determine, and enter a judgment on the claims of certain Indians who were parties to the Buffalo Creek Treaty of 1838.[32] In 1895 the court of claims decided that the "New York Indians" had abandoned their claim and thereby dismissed the case. On appeal, the decision was overturned and remanded back to the court of claims. On November 14, 1898, the court of claims reversed its earlier decision and awarded $1,967,056 to the Hodinöhsö:ni´. The U.S. government then appealed the decision. On March 20, 1899, the United States Supreme Court affirmed the court of claims award. The court held that the "New York Indians" had legal title to "1,824,000 acres in the present state of Kansas," "that there was no uncertainty as to the land granted or to the identity of the grantees," and that "the Indians had neither forfeited nor abandoned" their claim (except for the Tonawandas and Wisconsin Oneidas) and consequently were "entitled to judgment."[33] On February 9, 1900, Congress appropriated $1,998,744.46 to pay the judgment and accrued interest on the claim.[34] In 1904, out of the 4,803 "New York Indians," 1,657 Senecas at Allegany and Cattaraugus were deemed eligible, and each individual Seneca was entitled to a 2,234th of the total fund.[35]

To facilitate the process of distribution, on August 22, 1901, the commissioner of Indian affairs instructed federal Indian agent B. B. Weber to send the most up-to-date Seneca census, one that had been collected earlier by agent A. W. Ferrin. The list, containing the names of all Senecas alive on November 30, 1901, would then be approved and signed by the president of the Seneca Nation, who would forward it to the commissioner for certification purposes. Weber subsequently sent a list of 2,245 names—984 at Allegany and 1,261 at Cattaraugus.[36]

From 1903 to 1905, Special Agent Guion Miller was assigned to do research, scrutinize names, and prepare lists of residents of both Allegany and Cattaraugus who were entitled to "Kansas money." He also prepared lists of those not eligible. All Indians who sought moneys had to provide documentation that they were tribal members or "descendants of such persons or that they were affiliated or associated with one of said tribes" on January 15, 1838, and "further establish that since said date of 1838 they have not affiliated with any tribe of Indians other than one of the tribe of New York Indians parties to said treaty."[37]

Applicants were denied based upon a number of factors. They included those with no evidence of bloodlines back to 1838, honorary adoptees into the Senecas, members of other tribes who had already accepted allotments, and descendants of fathers or grandfathers who had taken white brides. The Tonawanda Senecas were ineligible because they had sold their Kansas claim in the federal treaty of 1857 to buy back part of their New York reservation lost in 1842, while the Senecas living at Grand River Reserve in Canada were also denied, since these Indians had left New York well before the Treaty of 1838. In the largest category of denials—sixty-eight separate cases that included about 130 individuals—Guion and the Indian Office followed the ruling of the secretary of the interior that the children of white mothers and Seneca fathers were not entitled to share in the fund.[38] Some descendants challenged Guion's findings. Most notable was Hattie R. Calhoun of Cattaraugus, whose case and appeal dragged on for several years. Guion maintained in his report that the "applicant's mother was a white woman, and neither his mother nor applicant was ever recognized by the tribe, and neither has ever drawn annuities with the tribe."[39]

In the lengthy process of evaluating the applicants, Seneca tribal officials William C. Hoag and Chester C. Lay had to give sworn testimony about the merits of individual applicants. In Case 2352, Hoag indicated that the applicant was a Canadian. In another case he stated that the female applicant had applied for adoption as a Seneca but that it was not granted. In another instance, Lay indicated that he had never heard of a man claiming Seneca descent.[40]

The Seneca Nation faced an electoral crisis that interfered with the distribution of "Kansas money." On November 1, 1904, in a disputed election between candidates of the Senecas' People's Party and their Republican Party, electoral inspectors at Cattaraugus failed to properly carry out their duties, allegedly because of "carelessness, inefficiency, or willful intent." They also failed to certify the votes at Allegany. The vote would have favored Hoag and his People's Party candidates. The party's candidates then tried unsuccessfully to take the oath of office and assume their positions on the tribal council. This effort was resisted by the Seneca Republican Party, and the result was that the People's Party then brought suit in state court, attempting to compel the canvassers to reconvene and declare it the winner of the vote at Cattaraugus. The crisis continued into 1905, just when there was a final resolution of the forty-five-year-old Kansas claims.[41]

After the crisis was finally resolved in Hoag's favor, the Seneca Nation government filed a brief indicating that some of the Indians not on the list to receive payment in the Kansas claims settlement were entitled to be included in the award. On May 18, 1905, the court of claims nevertheless finalized approval of the Kansas claims award and rejected appeals by applicants who had been denied.[42] On July 22, Senecas at Coldspring received a partial payment of $100. Two days later the partial distribution took place at Cattaraugus. On orders from Washington, federal Indian agent Weber was strictly authorized to distribute "Kansas money" regardless of "sex, age, or family relations, and . . . minors' warrants could be delivered only to duly qualified guardians."[43] It is important to note that until the awards of the Indian Claims Commission in the late 1960s and 1970s, the allocation of "Kansas money" in 1905 and 1906 was the only compensation the Senecas and other Hodinöhsö:ni´ ever received for the "surrender" of more than 150 square miles of what is today's western New York State. These lands included the loss of six Seneca reservations and the reduction in size of two others as a result of the fraudulent treaties of 1826 and 1838.

The second case brought by the Seneca Nation involved specific lands at Cattaraugus lost in the Buffalo Creek Treaty of August 31, 1826.[44] In this test case, *Seneca Nation v. Harrison B. Christy*, the Senecas sought legal redress for the fraudulent "take" of 5,129 acres of tribal lands at Cattaraugus.[45] In the 1826 treaty, the Senecas had ceded all of their remaining

Genesee Valley lands, including the Big Tree, Canawaugus, and Squawkie Hill Reservations in Livingston County; the remaining two square miles at the Gardeau Reservation in Wyoming County; and the sixteen-square-mile Caneadea Reservation in Allegany County. In addition, under this "treaty," the size of the Buffalo Creek, Tonawanda, and Cattaraugus Reservations were substantially reduced—Buffalo Creek by 36,638 acres, Tonawanda by 33,409 acres, and Cattaraugus by 5,120 acres. Overall the treaty reduced the total Seneca land base by 86,887 acres.[46]

The Senecas questioned the legal validity of the "treaty" of 1826 from the start because it had been consummated through bribery and was never ratified by the U.S. Senate. Nevertheless, on February 16, 1827, Commissioner of Indian Affairs Thomas McKenney questioned whether Senate approval was even necessary on the treaty, since a federal commissioner had been present at its signing, and, after all, "the President was the true guardian of Seneca interest." Despite McKenney's statement, President John Quincy Adams submitted the treaty to the Senate "for their advice and consent" on February 24, 1827.[47] On February 29, 1828, the Senate, by a vote of twenty to twenty, failed to ratify it"[48] Until April 4, 1828, the Senate also placed an "injunction of secrecy" over treaty deliberations. On that day, the Senate passed the following ambiguous resolution: "That by the refusal of the Senate to ratify the treaty with the Seneca Indians, it is not intended to express any disapprobation of the terms of the contract entered into by individuals who are parties to that contract, but merely to disclaim the necessity of an interference by the Senate with the subject matter."[49] On May 28, because of growing Indian and Quaker protests, President Adams appointed Richard Montgomery Livingston to investigate the events surrounding the treaty. Livingston's report confirms the fraud perpetrated at the treaty council. Livingston maintained that until August 1826, the Seneca chiefs had "disputed about religion, but clung to the common object of retaining their lands." At no time since the founding of the Ogden Land Company in 1810 until ten days after the council of 1826 had been in session "were any of the chiefs, willing to convey any of their lands." The investigator then explained what had transpired to get Seneca "approval."[50]

Livingston indicated that immediately after the War of 1812, the Ogdens gave $5,000 each to the government agent and interpreter and one other interpreter to "influence" certain Senecas. "The Agents [probably Jasper Parrish and Horatio Jones] thus retained were empowered to enlist in the

service, by liberal . . . stipends for life, such as the chiefs as might be won."
Until 1826 these efforts failed. The appointment of Oliver Forward, the
federal treaty commissioner, to push a land transaction was done "without
the solicitation or privity of the tribe." Forward then convened a council
on August 11, 1826, employing arguments "addressed to the hopes and
fears of the nation," implying that removal to the West was the only other
option. "The terrors of a removal enchained their minds in duress," leading
them to submit "to sell a part to preserve the residue." Livingston claimed
that Ogden Land Company proprietors and Forward had had a secret
rendezvous at Rochester prior to the council, at which they perfected their
strategy. He added that Dr. Jacob Jemison, a physician and one of several
interpreters employed at the treaty grounds, was in the pay of the Ogden
Land Company. Livingston also pointed a finger at many of the chiefs,
especially the Christian faction who resided around the Seneca mission at
Buffalo Creek, who had become dependent on federal annuities and other
"rewards." In late December 1828, Livingston sent his final report to Peter
B. Porter, the secretary of war.[51] Undoubtedly because of its negative findings
and Secretary Porter's connection to the Ogden Land Company, the report
went nowhere. The treaty was never resubmitted to the U.S. Senate for its
advice and consent.

The Senecas never forgot this injustice and frequently brought the issue
up to federal and state officials, some of whom agreed with their cause.
Even the state assembly's anti-Indian Special Committee to Investigate the
Indian Problem of the State of New York, commonly known as the Whipple
Committee, acknowledged in its final report in 1889: "This treaty [of 1826]
was never ratified by the Senate of the United States, or proclaimed by
the president, and the Indians have for a long time past claimed that the
treaty was invalid for this reason."[52] Writing in 1950, Henry S. Manley,
the former assistant attorney general of New York State, insisted that treaty
commissioner Forward had "received money from an Ogden Land Company
trustee, as did Jemison and other interpreters, and some of the Seneca chiefs
themselves."[53]

Although the Senecas had a half century of grievances built up after the
1826 treaty, the pursuit of this land claim came immediately after internal
political crises caused by two disputed elections in the 1870s. In one of the
elections, three separate individuals claimed to be the rightfully elected
president of the Seneca Nation. In 1879 the Seneca Nation Tribal Council

impeached Job King.[54] Perhaps as a way to heal wounds and unite the divided populace, the Seneca leadership—President John Jacket, Clerk Andrew John Jr., and Treasurer Cyrus Crouse—filed a petition with the Office of Indian Affairs on January 5, 1881. The Seneca Nation Tribal Council memorial to Washington indicated that they were "praying that they may be put into possession of certain lands in the State of New York, accompanying which is copy [*sic*] of a treaty entered into in 1826, between said Indians and Robert Troup, Thomas L. Ogden, and Benjamin W. Rogers [Ogden Land Company]." They appealed for federal intervention in the case on the grounds that this agreement was illegal:[55]

> 1st. No person or persons executing or signing the same was in any manner authorized to act for or bind the Seneca Nation or the people of the Seneca tribe of Indians.
>
> 2nd. The sale was not made by or under the authority of the United States and has not been ratified or confirmed or published by the President or Congress.
>
> 3rd. The sale was in violation of the laws and constitution of the State of New York, and of the Statutes of the United States.
>
> 4th. That the persons claiming title under the said pretended treaty procured the signatures of those pretending to act for your petitioners by paying them large bribes for their individual benefit, and by promising and paying the more influential, life annuities. . . .
>
> 5th. That the sum of $48,216 agreed to be paid to your petitioners by said pretended treaty has never been paid to them. That a large part thereof was about that time deposited by the said Robert Troup, Thomas L. Ogden, and Benjamin W. Rogers, in the Ontario County Bank, subject to their own control, where it remained until about the year 1853, when it was removed without the knowledge or consent of the Seneca tribe or Nation; and is now in the U.S. Treasury.

This Senecas' appeal was largely ignored. In the same year, Benjamin Casler, the federal Indian agent, commented that "the Senecas claim that they have been defrauded out of this land [at Cattaraugus] and did not receive its full value." He indicated that "they are anxious that the general government shall see they have justice." Casler noted that the Seneca Nation had "on one or two occasions sent delegations to Washington to induce the department to take some action in the matter, but this without effect."[56] In the meantime, the Seneca Nation of Indians filed suit, a legal action in the Supreme Court of New York State in Erie County, on October 13, 1885, to recover lands in the town of Brant known as the mile strip. It had been part of the Cattaraugus Indian Reservation from the Treaty of Big Tree in 1797 until the federal–Seneca treaty of 1826. This action of ejectment and for damages was brought against Harrison B. Christy of Brant, who had secured one hundred acres of these lands more than fifty years previous from the Ogden Land Company. The land, situated in Erie County, had an estimated value of $50 per acre by the 1880s. The Seneca Nation brought the case under a New York State law of 1845 that gave it the right to prosecute and maintain any action, suit, or proceeding in all courts of law and equity.[57]

In 1885 the Seneca Council was increasingly under fire. The nation was financially bankrupt, and the councilors were coming under fire for profiting by their own personal leasing arrangements. The federal Indian agent maintained that funds received from land leases had been squandered by the councilors in useless legislation and had largely led to bribery and other forms of corruption.[58]

The Seneca Nation action of ejectment against Harrison Christy reached the Erie County Circuit Court in April 1887. James Clark Strong and his brother John of Buffalo served as the Senecas' attorneys in the case. A passionate advocate for the rights of American Indians, Strong also represented the Canadian Cayuga Indians in their claim against New York State and wrote books about his earlier frontier and Civil War experiences. In his briefs he argued that the federal Trade and Intercourse Act of 1802 required the presence of a federal treaty commissioner to properly supervise any sale, lease, or conveyance from a federally recognized tribe to protect American Indian interests and that the ratification of the 1826 treaty by the U.S. Senate had never occurred.[59]

In 1887 an Erie County court rendered a verdict for Christy. The Senecas then appealed to the New York State Supreme Court, where the previous decision was affirmed. The New York State Supreme Court gave judgment to Christy, insisting first that the federal–Seneca treaty of 1826 was a valid transaction under the Trade and Intercourse Act of 1802, since a federal commissioner had been present to supervise the negotiations, and second that the Senecas' action was barred by the statute of limitations.[60] The

Senecas then appealed the unfavorable decision all the way up to the New York State Court of Appeals.

In April 1891, the court of appeals rendered a unanimous decision in an opinion written by Charles Andrews, chief judge of the court in 1881 and 1882 and again from 1893 to 1897 and one of the longest-serving jurists on the state's highest court. The judge, it is clear, had no intention of casting aspersions on the major state political leaders of the past who had facilitated the "take" of Indian lands. In 1891, at a time when Americans were reflecting on the so-called closing of the frontier and seeing the Indians as a vanishing race, Andrews was not inclined to set a revolutionary precedent by finding for the Senecas. He would hardly agree to add lands to a reservation, Cattaraugus, an Indian land base that was being considered for allotment by Albany and Washington officials at precisely that time.[61]

Much of what Andrews wrote in his decision reflected the majority opinion held by whites in central New York at the time. His contact with the Hodinöhsö:ni´ had been with the Onondagas, whose sixty-one-hundred-acre reservation lay at the southern boundary of the city of Syracuse. Much like the Senecas, the Onondagas were facing increasing pressures for allotment. The Whipple Committee's report in 1889 had presented racist testimony by Dr. C. M. Sims, chancellor of Syracuse University, who seven years earlier had conducted his own report for the state legislature that had recommended land in severalty for the Onondagas.[62] Even many reformers of the age believed that Native Americans had to accept private property to be saved and brought into the American polity as quickly as possible and that the best legal protection was to bestow U.S. citizenship on them. Behind these attitudes was the seldom-challenged assumption that it was possible to "kill the Indian" but "save the man."[63]

Andrews insisted that the Seneca claim challenged not only the title of every purchaser and holder of lands within the boundaries of the Treaty of 1826 but also all title to many millions of acres in the state.[64] He readily admitted improprieties involving the treaty but then tried to justify why so many eminent New Yorkers in the past had violated federal Indian laws.[65] Despite his obvious qualms, Justice Andrews nevertheless insisted that the Ogdens' purchase of Seneca lands in 1826 was valid, since it was done in the presence of and with the approval of commissioners both of Massachusetts and New York pursuant to requirements set forth in the Hartford Convention, a 1786 New York–Massachusetts compact dealing with state jurisdiction over and preemption to Hodinöhsö:ni´ lands in central and western New York. To Andrews, the deed executed in 1826 was made valid also "by the voluntary surrender and abandonment by the Indian occupants of the land," making the ratification of the federal treaty between the United States and the Senecas unnecessary. He added that the clause in the U.S. Constitution prohibiting states from entering into treaties did "not preclude a state having the pre-emption right to Indian lands, from dealing with the Indian tribes directly, for the extinguishment of the Indian title." To Andrews, the "true spirit and intent" of the 1802 federal Trade and Intercourse Act was to allow a state or its agents to enter into treaties or other agreements with Indian tribes within its borders, "provided it was entered into in the presence of and with the approval of a commissioner of the United States appointed to attend the same, and that such a treaty is within the true meaning of the proviso, a treaty held under the authority of the United States, and requires no ratification or proclamation by the federal authorities." Besides, the judge concluded, the Senecas' sale of the land was subsequently confirmed retroactively and made good by an act of Congress in 1846, which authorized the president of the United States to receive from the Ontario Bank money and securities representing the purchase price of the lands. These moneys were deposited in the Treasury of the United States in 1855. Despite its retroactive nature, Andrews claimed that the act of receiving these moneys under federal statute and their administration as a trust fund for the benefit of the Senecas "furnishes the most emphatic evidence of a ratification."[66]

This was no minor decision. It was seen as vital to the state, with implications far and wide. On April 24, 1891, the *New York Times* hailed the court of appeals decision as "one of local, state, and national importance alike."[67] Two weeks later, the *Cattaraugus Republican* went even further in its support for the decision: "If the claim of the plaintiffs had been substantiated, it would have not only challenged the title of every purchaser and holder of lands included in the Ogden Land Company's purchase of August 31, 1826, but also the title to millions of acres of lands in the state under similar treaties with the Indians."[68] Hence, four months after the Wounded Knee massacre, chapters in American history had to be rewritten. Courts tried to excuse the actions of great statesmen who had contributed so much to the rise of the Empire State and the nation as a whole. One year after Andrews's opinion, a ninety-nine-year lease to Salamanca went into effect, with the Senecas receiving a pittance. The implications were clear: a vanishing, "antiquated" race had to give way to "American Progress" symbolized by the railroad yards in the white city arising on the Allegany Reservation.

Five years later, the Christy case, on a writ of error, reached the United States Supreme Court. In a brief opinion of the case decided seven to zero on April 18, 1896, Chief Justice Melville Fuller dismissed the writ of error, insisting that the federal courts were "without jurisdiction" in the matter since the New York Court of Appeals decision was decided "upon a distinct and independent ground, not involving a Federal question." In effect, the United States Supreme Court in 1896 did not see a constitutional issue and did not see violations of the Trade and Intercourse Acts as allowing the Indians standing in federal courts.[69]

The court's defense of the Ogden Land Company's acquisition of lands of the Seneca Nation at the Cattaraugus Indian Reservation in 1826 can easily be seen as an egregious decision when judged in the context of Seneca history from 1797 to 1828. Yet it took another eight decades for the federal courts to question the decision in *Christy*. In January 1974, the U.S. Supreme Court, with eight justices participating, overturned 143 years of U.S. jurisprudence with the case *Oneida Indian Nation of New York State, et al. v. County of Oneida, New York, et al.* The decision allowed this Indian nation, as well as the Seneca Nation later in its numerous filings, access to federal courts in the pursuit of land claims litigation. Importantly, the Oneidas used the exact same argument that the Senecas and their attorneys had tried to use without success in the *Christy* case. The U.S. Supreme Court held that the federal Trade and Intercourse Acts were applicable to the original thirteen states, including New York, thus opening up the federal courts to the Oneidas as well as to other Indian nations seeking to get back land in the original thirteen states of the Union.[70] Thus the Senecas and their attorneys, the Strong brothers, were the precursors of the modern eastern Indian land claims movement, setting the legal agenda for eastern Native American nations until 2006, when the Supreme Court closed the door on such actions for the immediate future.[71]

Besides fighting for justice in the alien environment of the white man's courts, the Seneca Nation found itself in a rapidly changing world in the second half of the nineteenth century. To cope and to maintain their separate Onöndowa'ga:' identity, the Senecas had to selectively adapt. While holding onto some of their long-held traditions, they had to adjust to the new realities and pressures brought by non-Indians, finding ways of resistance to avoid being submerged within the dominant white world. While they had been exposed to the realities of the market economy and Christianity for two centuries, they found themselves no longer isolated by geography and were now surrounded by economic, cultural, and religious forces that thoroughly permeated their communities.

CONTINUITY AND CHANGE
IN THE SENECA NATION

The U.S. census of 1890 reveals some of the changes within Seneca Nation communities since the revolution of 1848. However, it also indicates Seneca adaptation and resistance to change. Of the 1,882 Cattaraugus Senecas, 505 could not speak English. Of the 897 Senecas at Allegany, 275 could converse only in Seneca. At the Cornplanter Grant, thirty-five out of ninety-two could not speak English. Although employment statistics were incomplete, out of the 492 respondents at Cattaraugus, 186 listed themselves as farmers, 244 as laborers, 19 as carpenters, 24 as housekeepers, 7 as musicians, 4 as mechanics, and 2 as "show people." At Allegany, out of the 291 who complied with the survey, 120 were listed as farmers, 149 as laborers, 4 as mechanics, 2 as domestics, 2 as laundresses, 1 as a carpenter, 1 as a trapper, and 1 as a housekeeper. On the Cornplanter Grant, the census report indicated sixteen laborers, twelve farmers, three "housewives," and one each of the following: ferryman, lumberman, and musician.[1]

In the same census, 301 Senecas were listed as members of four churches—the Presbyterian church at Allegany and the Presbyterian, Baptist, and Methodist churches at Cattaraugus.[2] A few years after this census, an Episcopal church was established at Cattaraugus. Each of these Protestant denominations, along with teachers at the Quaker School at Tunesassa, inculcated Senecas with their values and beliefs. Traditional Hodinöhsö:ni´ religion was not static and had also experienced change. Where there had been four longhouses spreading the ancient traditional message of the Gayaneshä´go:wa:h, the Hodinöhsö:ni´ Great (Binding) Law of Peace, by the last decades of the nineteenth century, only two—the Coldspring Longhouse at Allegany and at the Newtown Longhouse at Cattaraugus— were preaching the Gaiwi:yo:h (Good Message), which was based upon the visions of Handsome Lake.[3] By the second decade of the twentieth century, the numbers of Longhouse followers had dwindled precipitously, although the influence the Gaiwi:yo:h remained a powerful force in Seneca society.[4] The annual ritual cycle, from the midwinter ceremony to the Thanksgiving address in fall, remained a touchstone of Seneca identity and separated all Senecas, Longhouse and Christian, whether they participated or not, from the non-Indian world. At Newtown, lacrosse, the Senecas' national sport, was centered around the longhouse, and preachers of the Longhouse religion, such as Delos Kettle and Edward Cornplanter, promoted the "Creator's Game" among all Senecas. It is no coincidence that even today, the box lacrosse fields are located next to the Newtown and Coldspring Longhouses.

Handsome Lake, the Seneca prophet, had urged his followers not to abandon the four sacred rituals/ceremonies, namely the Feather Dance, Thanksgiving Dance, personal chant, and bowl game. He had condemned the drinking of whiskey, playing the fiddle, and gambling in dice games, all introduced by whites. Much like Protestant clerics of the time, he urged his followers to confess their sins, stop abortions, and put an end to the witchcraft they had practiced in the past. Handsome Lake had encouraged the transformation of women's roles in his visions and teachings and preached that men could now enter the formerly exclusive province of Seneca women: tending to the fields with the planting and harvesting of maize, beans, and squash, known to Hodinöhsö:ni´ as the Three Sisters. By recommending this change, he was promoting the acceptance of a new economy, one that allowed men to farm with a plow for the first time, although not all men heeded the prophet's message and women continued their old ways of horticulture. Handsome Lake, while maintaining calendrical rituals, taught that the traditional religion "was basically compatible with practical social and technological reforms dictated by the new reservation-bound existence."[5]

Thus, while the Good Message of Handsome Lake provided a mechanism for accommodationist change within Hodinöhsö:ni´ society, it also reaffirmed the previous teachings of the Gayaneshä´go:wa:h, the ancient Great Law of the Iroquois. Handsome Lake was not totally breaking with traditional beliefs and gender roles, since the Gaiwi:yo:h importantly reinforced both clans and the matrilineality. Although clan matrons no longer chose the chiefs after 1848, Seneca women never completely abandoned their important role in horticulture, and Seneca matrilineage defines identity and continues to the present day. Anthropologist Elisabeth Tooker perceptively observed that "the reforms introduced by Handsome Lake merely adapted Iroquois religion to changed conditions. They did not change the basic structure of the Iroquois ritual and belief systems." She noted that Iroquois religion was quite different from the Judeo-Christian tradition, although the "reforms of Handsome Lake did make Iroquois religion more like Christianity in certain superficial ways, and so in a sense permitted the old Iroquois view of the world to persist beneath the guise of a religion apparently more influenced by Christianity."[6]

From the time of Handsome Lake's death in 1815 to the middle of the nineteenth century, Tonawanda chiefs John Sky and later Jemmy Johnson and John Blacksmith helped spread the Gaiwi:yo:h. However, they did not set the prophet's teachings in stone. Although some anthropologists, such as Wallace and Merle Deardorff, credit ex-chief Owen Blacksnake for establishing the Gaiwi:yo:h at Allegany, others, such as Tooker, argue more persuasively that the religion continued to evolve and take different forms on different reservations even in the second half of the nineteenth century.[7] According to Arthur C. Parker, around 1876 preachers of the Gaiwi:yo:h met at Coldspring, the old home of Handsome Lake, to compare versions that each saw as correct. Seneca president and former chief John Jacket, Red Jacket's grandson, was chosen to settle forever the words of the Gaiwi:yo:h and write it down using Asher Wright's orthography of the Seneca language. The preachers then went off to Cattaraugus, where they memorized "the parts in which they were faulty and soon after the original written text was somehow destroyed."[8]

Although there is some question about the accuracy of this story, Seneca preachers of the Gaiwi:yo:h from both Allegany and Cattaraugus were nevertheless quite important in spreading the religion, somewhat like Christian missionaries. In the process, they found ways to restore Seneca Nation connections to the chiefs at Tonawanda and to the sachems on the Grand Council at Onondaga that had been severed in the revolution in 1848 and its aftermath. To accomplish this, Seneca Longhouse preachers used their knowledge of the Gaiwi:yo:h and taught it at longhouses in other

Hodinöhsö:ni´ communities.[9] Another way was to promote lacrosse, known to the Hodinöhsö:ni´ as the Creator's game.

The role of Edward Cornplanter, a member of the Wolf Clan and the principal preacher of the Gaiwi:yo:h at the Newtown Longhouse, illustrates this point. Edward's reputation went far beyond the walls of the Newtown Longhouse at Cattaraugus.[10] His famous son, Jesse, described his father's vital role: "Dad was the sole authority. He knew every bit of songs and ceremonies, not only one group or kind. His versions were of the old Cattaraugus Village variety and not imported [from] elsewhere." According to his son, he knew "all the histories of every song or groups of them. . . . Then he was the best in Feather Dance Songs."[11] Edward was also the coach/director of the Newtown Lacrosse Club, which played throughout the Northeast, against all comers, Indian and non-Indian, in the first two decades of the twentieth century. In 1909 Edward Cornplanter preached on the teachings of Handsome Lake at the annual fall address at Onondaga.[12] Thus, sixty years after the overthrow of the council of chiefs and the expulsion of the Seneca Nation from the Iroquois Confederacy, Seneca Longhouse preachers continued to play a vital role in educating *all* Hodinöhsö:ni´ about the prophet's message, the meaning of specific rituals, and how ceremonies needed to be performed.

Historians writing about Onöndowa´ga:´ society after the revolution of 1848 have emphasized that Seneca women's political influence sharply declined throughout the nineteenth and well into the twentieth century.[13] It should be noted that women suffrage became a reality within the Seneca Nation only in 1964. Two years later, women finally achieved the right to hold tribally elected offices. Indeed, not one woman has held the office of president of the Seneca Nation of Indians since the founding of its form of elective government in 1848.[14] The evidence of women's political decline is clearly there, but there are exceptions. First, during a disputed election in the late 1870s, at a time when some Allegany Senecas attempted to push secession from their Indian nation, thirty-three women intervened, this time attempting to bring in Quaker mediation efforts to settle the dispute.[15] Second, in the 1930s, Alice Lee Jemison served as the Seneca Nation's "eyes and ears" on Capitol Hill while lobbying against the Indian Reorganization Act.[16] Moreover, in the economic, educational, and social realms, Seneca women's leadership roles have remained vital for Seneca cultural survival. Besides the maintenance of the matrilineage since 1848, Seneca women have actually expanded some of their roles, especially in the areas of health-care delivery and education.

The Gayaneshä´go:wa:h had clearly set forth women's traditional economic, political, and social roles in Hodinöhsö:ni´ society.[17] The "woman chief," or clan matron, was the trustee, owning the titles of all chiefs. Clan matrons had the power to nominate as well as initiate the removal of errant chiefs, to participate in village and tribal decision making, and to determine the fate of war captives. They acted as trustees for all tribal property and had to be consulted especially on matters relating to Hodinöhsö:ni´ lands. A senior matron designated areas surrounding the village where firewood was collected and where work parties of women planted, cultivated, and harvested the Three Sisters—beans, maize, and squash. Even with the vast political changes taking place after the revolution of 1848, Seneca women continued to manage their garden plots, and they provided much of the crops and crafts sold at agricultural fairs on and off the reservations in the second half of the nineteenth century. They also continued to be in charge of adoption and naming ceremonies, and their roles in child rearing expanded, since children's uncles had shared this role with them in the past.[18]

By the second half of the eighteenth century, large longhouse residences in palisaded villages gave way to smaller "creolized" longhouses in villages without stockades. According to archaeologist Kurt Jordan, log cabins became common residences and resulted in nuclear family households after the American Revolution:[19] "Families became patrilineal with respect to name and inheritance, the Indian men taking an English name, or an English translation of an Indian name, as a surname and transmitting, along with inheritance rights to real estate [plowshare rights; not fee simple title] in the white style."[20] Yet, as late as the Treaty of 1794 at Canandaigua, Seneca matrons appointed Red Jacket as their spokesman and were successful in checking Cornplanter's threats of joining with the Indians in the Ohio Valley and waging war against the United States. In 1797 clan matrons removed Red Jacket as their spokesman and directly made land cessions at the Treaty of Big Tree.[21]

This treaty was a clear turning point in Seneca women's political influences. Their voices in the political realm were muted and their concerns were often bypassed in decisions relating to tribal lands until just before the events that led to the Seneca Revolution. Although the Seneca constitution of 1848 included a provision, section 6, maintaining that no lands could be sold without the consent of "three-quarters of the mothers of the nation," their status was further reduced by the political upheaval, since clan matrons had no longer the power to raise or remove chiefs in the ancient manner.[22] Anthropologist Diane Rothenberg has pointed out that this "radical change in political structure" was the "culmination of the loss of female power."[23]

As in religious expression, change in the roles of Seneca women occurred over time but also reflected cultural continuity. For much of the nineteenth century and well into the twentieth century, Seneca women's roles were still mostly centered in the clearing. Moreover, each Christian denomination represented in Seneca Nation territories attempted to wean women away from tending their gardens, an effort that did not completely succeed.[24] Despite missionary teachings, the matrilineage that defined Onöndowa'ga:' identity continued. Seneca women did not totally abandon their horticultural work in their fields and were still heavily involved in gathering herbs. They also developed small-scale cash-producing activities. These included specializing in craft production by selling their beadwork, baskets, and pots, and marketing sassafras.[25] They did this at the Erie County Fair or at agricultural fairs at Allegany and Cattaraugus that became quite popular after the Civil War. With the coming of the Erie Railroad in 1850 and the rapid growth of the non-Indian population, new markets for women's crafts in and around the Seneca reservations further developed. In addition, the Senecas' proximity to the important tourist industry at Niagara Falls gave women a major market for their crafts.[26]

In the social setting of everyday reservation existence, women's involvement in community organizations, such as those that promoted temperance and philanthropy, was especially important. One of the many moral teachings espoused by Handsome Lake, as well as missionaries entering Seneca territories, was abstinence from alcohol. Anthony Wallace states that "Handsome Lake was not content merely to condemn drinking as a sin; he went to some pains to just explain what were the social evils attendant upon drinking: family quarrels, mistreatment of children, lowered economic productivity, and mayhem and murder at drinking parties."[27] The message of the prophet, an individual whose own life had been negatively affected by drink, rang true to many Senecas, Longhouse and Christian, in the nineteenth century. Indeed, the message actually brought some unity to severely divided Seneca communities. Both the emerging Longhouse religion, which came about in the first half of the nineteenth century throughout Iroquoia, and Christian congregations founded on reservations during the same era warned about similar dangers. In both instances, imbibing was seen as violating the Creator's teachings. Although men were the officeholders in the temperance movement and played in bands promoting abstinence, women were a major force, since their families' survival and their communities' tranquility often depended on their involvement. Newspaper reports were filled with stories of alcohol abuse leading to family tragedies—accidental deaths, violence, and incarceration.[28]

In March 1832 an Iroquois temperance society was established at the Cattaraugus Indian Reservation. It soon joined with one founded earlier at the Tuscarora Indian Reservation.[29] From the 1830s onward, women, especially in the growing Christian congregations on Seneca reservations, were mainstays of this organization. They held meetings to promote abstinence as well as hard work, education, and moral reform. Clergy and members of churches, especially Asher and Laura Wright's United Mission Church at Cattaraugus, were leaders in the movement. After the deaths of these two missionaries, M. F. Trippe, a Presbyterian missionary, took over the crusade against "demon rum." By mid-century, at church gatherings and temperance meetings, Senecas sang hymns, read passages from the Scriptures, and signed abstinence pledges. In schools, students were encouraged "to draw up a pledge to give up tobacco and fire water, which was signed by all the older pupils."[30]

With the coming of the railroad in 1850 and the pouring of outsiders onto the Allegany Reservation over the next five decades, the city of Salamanca arose, and with it, fifty saloons in Seneca territory. The census report of 1890 went so far as to describe the nearby village of Carrollton as a "drunkard-manufacturing center."[31] Despite federal and state legislation forbidding the sale of alcohol to Indians and Seneca Nation protests against whiskey sellers, whites and Indians had easy access to alcohol in this hardscrabble railroad town, and laws regulating sales were loosely enforced.[32] Hence it is not surprising that by 1890, 10 percent of the all women and men at Allegany and Cattaraugus were members of temperance organizations.[33]

An important feature of the temperance movement was the rise of Seneca-directed brass bands. The popularity of band music among the Hodinöhsö:ni´ was heavily influenced by three factors in the second half of the nineteenth century: the proximity of master brass instrument makers in Buffalo, the rise of marching bands and their music during and after the Civil War, and the prominence of martial band music in the curriculum of Indian boarding schools such as Carlisle in their efforts to promote "Americanization."[34] To promote abstinence, temperance, and other ideals, cornet bands, most prominently those directed by the Lay family, especially

Chester C. and Sylvester Jr., both members of the United Mission Church at Cattaraugus, played at church gatherings and at reservation and county fairs. Other prominent musicians included A. Sim Logan, Orlando Doxtater, Alfred Logan, Charles Wilson, and T. Francis Jemison.[35] In 1878 the federal Indian agent described a large temperance meeting held in June 1877 at Cattaraugus, one attended by twelve hundred people, including neighboring whites. Two cornet bands played excellent music while Seneca women prepared and sold well-cooked meats, chickens, bread, cakes, and pastry of "great variety and good quality." The Senecas in attendance refrained from profanity and "not one intoxicated person" was present.[36]

Besides promoting temperance, the bands at agricultural fairs aimed to encourage Seneca men to become farmers. Influenced by the success of the Erie County Fair, which began in 1820, and the New York State Fair, which began two decades later, Senecas and other Hodinöhsö:ni´ formed the Iroquois Agricultural Society in the antebellum era. This organization promoted fairs at both Allegany and Cattaraugus and encouraged competition for prize money for agricultural products. Featured booths marketed Indian crafts and athletic events, including footraces, lacrosse, and horse racing. Although churches sponsored these fairs, their timing corresponded to the traditional harvest festivals held by Longhouse Senecas at Newtown and Coldspring.

In October 1877, cornet bands performed inside and outside the United Mission Church and at the Cattaraugus Agricultural Fair. The crowds were quite large and included Oneida Indians from as far away as Green Bay, Wisconsin.[37] It was probably no coincidence that Seneca politicians used these fairs to win votes. Musician Chester C. Lay of Cattaraugus was elected president of the Seneca Nation, as was William C. Hoag, a member of the Six Nations Temperance Society and the most prosperous farmer at Allegany. In 1876 the different reservation branches of the Iroquois temperance organizations took the name Six Nations Temperance Society of the United States and Canada.[38]

Two years earlier Frances Willard had founded the Women's Christian Temperance Union in Cleveland. This national association favored an assimilationist program, supporting missionary work, efforts at allotting Indian lands, and making Native Americans U.S. citizens. Nevertheless, in 1884 a WCTU chapter was established on the Cattaraugus Reservation. It was headed by Lydia Pierce, an Onondaga, who continued to promote abstinence right into the 1920s.[39] Just before World War II, the numerous temperance societies throughout Iroquoia morphed into the Peter Doctor Memorial Indian Scholarship Foundation, administered largely by Seneca and Tuscarora women.[40]

Besides their advocacy of temperance, women were especially active in philanthropic pursuits. In May 1880, they organized the Seneca Female Benevolent Society at Allegany. The officers of the organization, which was better known as a sewing society, were President Jane Jimeson, Vice President Effie Jimeson, Treasurer Jane Shongo, and Secretary B. A. Blinkey. The money collected in fund-raisers went to purchase calico, lining, stuffing, thread, and needles for quilting items for the less fortunate.[41] In the mid-1880s and onward, many Seneca women went off to school at Hampton and Carlisle. Most were trained to manage their own households, serve as seamstresses, or work as domestics, although some became teachers in district schools, or school matrons and nurses in federal Indian boarding schools throughout Indian Country.[42]

With the passage of the Nineteenth Amendment of the United States Constitution in August 1920, the right of American women to vote was now guaranteed. The same year, approximately twenty-four enrolled Onöndowa'ga:' women and men put their names on a petition calling for the right of Seneca women to vote. However, there is no record of this petition being presented to the Seneca Nation Council in its minutes.[43] During the next four decades, other suffrage efforts failed in council. Finally, largely because of women's essential work as volunteers during the Kinzua crisis, the Seneca Nation voted in favor of allowing women the right to vote and hold elected office in the mid-1960s.[44]

While Seneca women's roles were still largely centered in the clearing—namely, on reservation life—men remained much more mobile. Although some turned to farming and others continued to hunt, trap, and fish on and just off their reservations, Seneca men also enlisted in America's far-off wars; preached in Longhouse ceremonies on other reservations; labored in new cash-producing enterprises such as lumbering and rafting, bringing logs down the Allegany River; were employed at tanning mills, in railroad work, or in road construction; served as longshoreman or ship hands on steamers on the Great Lakes; and even performed as entertainers and musicians, as "Plains Indians" in Wild West shows, and as acrobats in circuses. By 1900 the city of Buffalo had a population of 352,387, substantial industry with major rail connections, the leading grain storage port in the country, and

access to the Erie Canal. The following year, it hosted a world's fair, the
Pan-American Exposition, which drew eight million visitors to the city. At
the turn of the twentieth century, with the establishment of steel mills at
Lackawanna, just south of Buffalo, Senecas were hired as factory workers at a
massive plant that became Bethlehem Steel in the early 1920s. By that time
ironwork, not solely the province of Mohawks, had attracted residents of
Cattaraugus and Allegany, who migrated with their families to urban settings
in western New York. In the process of relocating for job opportunities, they
established a major Seneca community around Cottage Street in Buffalo.[45]
The possibility of greater employment opportunities attracted more and more
Senecas to the city. By the 1920s, only 993 out of more than 21,000 acres
were being used for agriculture at Cattaraugus; at Allegany, 5,209 of more
than 30,000 acres were under cultivation, although on each reservation,
women maintained their small gardens.[46]

The importance of athletics in Seneca society throws added light on
men's roles and how they dealt with change from 1848 to 1934. Indeed,
examining the history of sport is no frivolous pursuit but rather a significant
way to study American social and cultural history. Although snowsnake
and other community games remained popular, and great Seneca athletes
such as Bemus and Hawley Pierce and Isaac Seneca starred on Carlisle's
legendary football teams and later in professional football, long-distance
running and lacrosse were most important in these years.[47] Seneca athletes
in these sports became hometown heroes, adapting their traditional roles by
competing in regional, national, and international events. Both competitive
sports generated a great feeling of Seneca pride and nationalism and diffused
tensions within residential communities. They also opened new economic
opportunities for those skilled enough to play for pay as professional athletes.

Long-distance running has been a vital part of Hodinöhsö:ni´ tradition.
Historically, Six Nations runners were not merely athletes intent on "going
for the gold." They summoned councils, conveyed intelligence from nation
to nation, and warned of impending danger. Significantly, runners conveyed
messages and carried stringed wampum to symbolize their official role, diplomatic protocol, and/or the truth of their words. For energy during their
demanding tasks, runners carried bearskin or deerskin pouches attached to
light belts on their breechclouts; the pouches contained pounded parched corn
intermixed with maple sugar. According to Lewis Henry Morgan in his classic
League of the Ho-de-no-sau-neé, or Iroquois (1851), "Swiftness of foot was an

acquirement, among the Iroquois, which brought the individual into high repute."[48] For example, during the War of 1812, Onondaga runner Samuel George carried official messages, traveling from the Buffalo Creek Reservation to the arsenal at Canandaigua and back, approximately 150 miles, in two days! It is no coincidence that George became a spokesman for the Iroquois Confederacy and became Wolf Clan sachem in the 1850s and that he met and negotiated with President Abraham Lincoln in the White House during the Civil War.[49] To this day, Six Nations sachems still designate "runners," using the term to describe a person who serves the confederacy as a conduit for the conduct of essential business and who is accorded respect as a community leader, worthy of other higher positions of authority and prestige.[50]

By the 1830s, Seneca runners were not simply carrying out their customary roles as messengers carrying important council decrees. They were now winning accolades for their competitive running in interracial contests at horse tracks, taking on all comers for prize money. Most of these competitive races also involved heavy betting at taverns and challenges made in local newspapers. The most famous Seneca runner was John Steeprock. By the 1850s and 1860s, Seneca runners, including Isaac Hill, Albert Smith, Strong Smoke, and one mentioned in newspaper accounts only as Sundown, were achieving distinction in long-distance competition.[51]

Lewis Bennett, popularly known as Deerfoot, was the first superstar athlete in Iroquoia, with exploits on two continents. He was the acknowledged king of competitive long-distance running in the early 1860s, setting world records for distances of ten to twelve miles. No Seneca before or since has matched his athletic achievements. He repeatedly won long-distance races at ten thousand meters or more. Deerfoot was a product of his Seneca culture, having trained and developed his running strategies first by playing lacrosse. He excelled at lacrosse because of his exceptional endurance more than his blinding sprint speed. Between 5 feet 10½ and 6 feet tall and weighing 162 pounds, he was a force to be reckoned with, both as a lacrosse player and later as a long-distance runner. From 1862 to 1897, Deerfoot's mark of eleven miles, 970 yards in the one-hour run stood as the world record. He was also the most influential long-distance runner before the reestablishment of the marathon race at the Olympic Games in 1896. Indeed, he reshaped the sport by introducing strategies that later legends of running—Emil Zátopek of Czechoslovakia and Paavo Nurmi of Finland—used at the Olympics in the twentieth century.[52]

According to an interview conducted by Harriet Maxwell Converse in 1894, Bennett was born in 1830 and given the name Hut-geh-so-do-neh, or "He Peeks through the Door." At the time of his birth, his family resided on the Buffalo Creek Reservation, the Senecas' largest and most populated reservation, lands that make up the present city of Buffalo and environs. The Bennetts were Presbyterians, members of Asher Wright's Seneca Mission Church. After the Treaty of Buffalo Creek in 1838, the Bennett family refused to go west to Kansas, then part of Indian Territory. Instead, they moved onto Cattaraugus Indian Reservation, where they lived the rest of their lives.[53] There, during the mid-1850s, Deerfoot was drawn to running, not just because of his skill as a lacrosse player or a hunter but because of the success of earlier Seneca competitive runners such as John Steeprock and because of the significant prize money to be made in the sport by the 1850s.

Deerfoot was the master of pedestrianism, a professional distance-running sport popular in the nineteenth century, especially in Great Britain. Official challenges were advertised in the press by event promoters, who were too often unsavory characters, and terms were negotiated at prominent taverns and inns that were often adjacent to cricket fields or horse tracks. Promoters served as managers as well as trainers and gave their runners colorful names, such as Crowcatcher, American Deer, and Young England, to sell the event to the public. Pedestrian races were quite popular, attracting thousands of paid admissions. A major part of the attraction was that spectators were encouraged to bet heavily on the races. Victors were rewarded with prize money, sometimes a share of the admission receipts, and a championship cup.

Deerfoot's prowess first came to the public's attention at Fredonia in 1856, when he defeated John Stetson, "the pride of New England," in a five-mile race, which he ran in twenty-five minutes flat. He followed up with a series of four- to twenty-mile races at locations between Buffalo and Boston. On June 21, 1861, he raced at National Racecourse, a horse-trotting venue in Corona, Queens, against several British pedestrians brought to the United States by promoter/trainer George Martin. Although Deerfoot lost the race, Martin was impressed by the Seneca's performance and with his potential. As a skilled race promoter, Martin was also taken aback by Bennett's swagger; his Seneca running attire, which included an eagle feather, a breechclout with wampum appliqué, and moccasins; and his physicality, since he ran bare-chested. Seeing the box office potential of an Indian, the entrepreneur invited Bennett to join his "stable" of runners in London.[54]

Deerfoot was hardly the first Seneca to journey to England. Other American Indians, including Senecas, had preceded Deerfoot. Too often they were gawked at and presented as relics of the ancient past that were fast disappearing from the planet, much like dinosaurs. Other times they were presented as noble or bloodthirsty "savages."[55] In the late summer of 1861, Deerfoot arrived in Great Britain and began a twenty-two-month whirlwind tour, with competitive running events and exhibitions though England, Scotland, and Ireland. In the following eighty-seven weeks, he ran 130 races, an average of one race every four and a half days, often at a distance of ten miles or more. In his whirlwind tour, he captivated crowds of thousands of onlookers by breaking every record for ten to twelve miles in existence.[56]

Deerfoot's appearance was quite dramatic, and he undoubtedly shocked many in Victorian England when he removed his wolf skin cape/blanket and revealed his tall lithe body with his chest fully exposed. From head to toe, he played the role of Indian, in a manner that suggested that at least some of his actions were choreographed by Martin. At his first race, on September 16, 1861, Deerfoot wore an eagle feather in his headband, which designated his Seneca heritage; a modified breechclout (actually more of a skirt) ornamented with porcupine quillwork, beads, wampum, and jingling bells; and beautifully crafted moccasins. At later races, officials made him wear long drawers and a knitted woolen shirt instead of running bare-chested and wearing a skirt/breechclout.[57]

The race on September 16, his first victory in Great Britain, was followed by his winning twenty-six of his next twenty-eight challenge races—at four, six, ten, and twelve miles. Crowds of up to fifteen thousand people witnessed the Deerfoot phenomenon. The size of the winner's purses also increased, and the Seneca soon became the rage of London. One of his fans was Prince Edward, known to the public as Bertie—the bon vivant son of Queen Victoria, who later ascended the throne as King Edward VII. A play based on Deerfoot's exploits opened at the Royal Olympic Theater, and a dance piece was written and performed in his honor.[58] On December 4, 1861, Deerfoot participated at Cambridge in a six-mile race at the university's Cricket Club. Upward of six thousand people, including Prince Edward, were in attendance. There the prince watched the Seneca outperform his British rivals. At the awards ceremony, he presented Deerfoot with two bank notes of £15 each and a trophy.[59] An article in an April 1862 issue of *Bell's Life*, Great Britain's leading sporting magazine, observed that the

Seneca "is now acknowledged the most extraordinary pedestrian that has ever appeared in England."[60]

Because of Deerfoot's overwhelming success, the payout in the betting line became infinitesimal, since he was viewed as a sure thing. When he infrequently finished second, the British and American press accused him and agent Martin of fixing the race.[61] Moreover, his entertainment as an "exotic Indian runner" in London and other major venues in Great Britain soon began to wear thin, and paid admission crowds subsequently became smaller. To meet the challenge of declining interest in pedestrian competition, Martin devised a race tour, more like a traveling circus, which included eighty stops and sixteen major races in fourteen weeks. Willing to do anything to attract publicity, Martin apparently even convinced Deerfoot to stage a mock scalping in a tavern. The tour started in Tonbridge on May 7 and ended at Manchester on September 1, 1862. Much of it was set for the English countryside and smaller cities, although the tour made stops at Bath, in Wales, and in Edinburgh and Glasgow in Scotland, as well as several venues in Ireland. Perhaps as many as 150,000 people attended over the course of the tour. When crowds dwindled and the tour ran out of money, Martin returned to London, where Deerfoot was to rekindle his magic as a long-distance runner.[62]

On October 27, 1862, in the Brompton area of London, in a one-hour race before four to five thousand spectators, the Seneca broke William "the American Deer" Jackson's world record. However, an ugly incident during a six-mile race at the Copenhagen Grounds at Wandsworth threatened to stain his reputation. There, Deerfoot raced into the stands after a spectator. Although no account of this incident suggests why he took this uncharacteristic action, one can only speculate that he was being taunted. On January 12, 1863, Deerfoot beat his own mark in a one-hour race by running eleven miles, 790 yards, setting a world record, at the Hackney Wick, a one-acre track behind a famous pub in East London. In another one-hour race in London on February 23, he won the £100 prize after his opponents fell by the wayside and couldn't complete the race. On Good Friday, April 3, 1863, once again competing at Brompton, Deerfoot faced William "the Crowcatcher" Lang, who was given a hundred-yard head start in this handicap race. The Seneca extended his one-hour record to eleven miles, 797 yards. However, the race was set for twelve miles, and Lang crossed the twelve-mile finish line ahead of the Seneca.[63]

In his last four races in Great Britain, in April 1863, the Seneca failed to finish. Realizing that he was no longer at the top of his game and disturbed by the catcalls of fair-weather English fans, Deerfoot returned to Cattaraugus. He continued to run professionally until 1870, when he reached the age of forty. He participated in events at a variety of venues, including county fairs and city parks in Boston, Cleveland, Chicago, Detroit, Saint Louis, and Syracuse, and on Hodinöhsö:ni´ reservations. Much like the great Jesse Owens after the 1936 Olympics, he even ran against racehorses in exhibitions.[64]

In retirement from racing, the famous Cattaraugus Seneca runner remained a celebrity for the rest of his life. He was an honored guest, along with other prominent Hodinöhsö:ni´, at the 1893 Columbian Exposition in Chicago. There he again made headlines—this time when a deranged woman stabbed him on the street. Surviving, he returned to Cattaraugus and spent his last years there. On January 18, 1896, Deerfoot died at his home at Cattaraugus.[65] Ironically, his death occurred the same year the modern Olympic Games were revived in Greece. The Athens Olympics brought new attention to long-distance running by making the marathon the crowning event on the last day.

Deerfoot was buried in an unmarked grave on the reservation. Because of his international fame, Harriet Maxwell Converse and Joseph Keppler Jr. (also known as Udo J. Keppler), a political cartoonist and editor of the highly influential *Puck* magazine, both white advocates for the Six Nations, arranged for his reburial in Buffalo's Forest Lawn Cemetery in the shadow of Red Jacket's monument and next to the graves of Ely Parker and Chiefs Young King, Little Billy, Captain Pollard, Destroy Town, and Tall Peter.[66]

Lewis Bennett should be remembered as one of the most extraordinary athletes of his time. Although his pedestrian races were far from home and involved prize money, he never left his roots, wearing his Seneca feather, depending not on sprint speed but on endurance gained from years of playing lacrosse, and residing all his life in Seneca territory, be it at Buffalo Creek or later Cattaraugus. His achievements came in a foreign environment just two decades after his Seneca people had faced removal to the trans-Mississippi frontier. In an age when Native American equality was not recognized, racial theories—even those held by eminent scholars of the age—reinforced outright bigotry and violence against minorities. It should also be pointed out that while Deerfoot was racing in Great Britain in the early 1860s, newspapers, even in London, Dublin, and Edinburgh, carried stories about the U.S. Army's frontier wars with the Navajos and Apaches in the Southwest and the Sioux in Minnesota. Although the times forced him to play a stereotyped role, Deerfoot nevertheless challenged the racial assumptions and theories of the era by besting the fastest white men in pedestrian races, much like what Jesse Owens later accomplished.

Other Senecas followed Deerfoot's path to fame. Most important were the brothers of Bemus and Hawley Pierce—Frank, Jerry, and Tom—Allegany Senecas who excelled in track and field at Carlisle and at Amateur Athletic Union meets. Frank Pierce, the most successful of the three runners, ran the marathon at the 1904 Olympic Games in Saint Louis, which coincided with the Louisiana Purchase Centennial Exposition. Racing in the sweltering heat and humidity in August, most of the runners, including Pierce, failed to finish the race, which was won by Englishman Thomas Hicks.[67]

Other sports brought pride and strengthened Seneca nationalism as well. Most important was lacrosse. Traditionally, lacrosse, or *dewa 'ë:ö '*, has served several major functions in Seneca society. These functions range from ritual and medicinal to diplomatic (by facilitating alliances and attempting conflict resolution between rival parties and nations) to sheer entertainment. The game is seen as a gift of the Creator and was used as a way to directly appeal to the Creator for help. Thus it is not surprising that even today many conservative Hodinöhsö:ni´ consider lacrosse paraphernalia, especially sticks (*dewa'ë:ö 'ga 'hnya '*), to be sacred objects.[68]

Evidence of the importance of lacrosse as a ritual is found throughout the scholarly literature. It has been used as a medicine game and has often been employed in an effort to heal. Individuals have the right to request that a game be held on behalf of someone suffering from an illness. In 1815 Handsome Lake was on his deathbed at Onondaga. According to Wallace, the Hodinöhsö:ni´organized a lacrosse game to attempt to restore his health and cheer him up: "The people tried to amuse him by playing a game of lacrosse in his honor. It was a beautiful day and they brought him out so that he might see the play. Soon he desired to be taken back into the house."[69]

Lacrosse was also a feature at the Iroquoian condolence ritual. Among the Senecas, one or more clans traditionally constituted a moiety (either of two groups into which a society is divided). According to William N. Fenton, distinct moieties acted "reciprocally to condole and bury each other's dead." They then played a game of lacrosse, "a game that anciently discharged social tensions—to cheer some depressed person."[70] Moreover, at the end of the solemn condolence ritual, which was transformed in the colonial era into an integral part of forest diplomacy, lacrosse and social dancing followed a feast to bind ties and establish alliances. Lacrosse was a vehicle to unite people and to encourage social interaction. When disharmony occurred within the Hodinöhsö:ni´ or between them and rival nations, lacrosse was a way to promote a settlement short of war. Fenton maintains that "village chiefs encouraged lacrosse matches with neighboring towns, both to keep warriors fit and to discourage intervillage feuds and warfare."[71]

The traditional Seneca game, no longer played exclusively by men, was a no-holds-barred athletic contest. Although today's box lacrosse on reservations, known as boxla and played with six competitors, is considered rough by many, it is quite mild compared to how the game was played by Senecas in the past. In traditional Seneca field lacrosse, the rough-and-tumble game included charging, ramming, slashing, tackling, tripping, wrestling, and even using one's stick to strike an opponent—all of which was considered legal and not penalized. There was little protective gear—no shoulder pads or elbow pads. Besides their moccasins, participants wore only the *ani:nodashä´*, or Hodinöhsö:ni´ breechcloth. To gather strength and luck for this violence, players kept amulets and talismans, including miniature *gagöhsa´* (medicine masks), with them. In preparation, they also bathed, stringently fasted, and used emetics, including decoctions of the bark of spotted alder and red willow. Indian herbalists dispensed a decoction of red osier bark for the players to drink and to rub on their legs. Since injuries were commonplace, Seneca traditional doctors used indigenous remedies and were often present to handle major wounds. Betting was a regular feature of the game.[72]

Seneca lacrosse sticks in the mid-nineteenth century were far different from contemporary ones. Unlike a modern stick, a dewa'ë:ö´ga ´hnya´ was whittled down from a five-foot piece of hickory to its proper size and shape, and its netted end was bent through a steaming process. In *League of the Ho-de-no-sau-nee, or Iroquois,* Lewis Henry Morgan stated that lacrosse sticks lacked guard strings, and thus sticks had no pockets to catch the ball. He indicated that the slightest jarring would result in a player losing the ball. Morgan said the game involved running in fits and starts and passing and that the Senecas had a difficult task of balancing the ball on the taut webbing. The traditional lacrosse ball—ë´hoshä´—was about two and one-quarter inches in circumference and differed from the contemporary rubber ball used today. The most common ball then in use contained an interior of cotton thread and was covered with one piece of buckskin, sewed like a baseball. Fields were five hundred yards long or more, and the number of players varied, with one account suggesting as many as one hundred on a team. Unlike the two-hour-or-so matches broadcast on ESPN2, a traditional game might start at midday, be suspended at dusk, and continue over the next day or two.[73]

Lacrosse was already changing by Morgan's time. In Canada it began to attract non-Indians. The first international rules of field lacrosse were established in 1867 in Montreal by William George Beers, a dentist. Unlike traditional dewa´ë:ö´, field lacrosse was soon transformed into a sport with many rules and with ten players (now twelve) on a side.[74] As historian Donald Fisher has pointed out, field lacrosse, which became popular at private colleges in the East at the turn of the twentieth century, was soon viewed by its white participants and fans as a "game of manliness" for gentleman.[75]

In the first decade of the twentieth century, Edward Cornplanter's Newtown Longhouse team would journey far from Seneca communities to play for pay. At the Pan-American Exhibition in Buffalo in 1901, the *New York Times* reported a match between the Tonawanda Seneca team and the "Pagan Indians of Cattaraugus."[76] Cornplanter's team also played in New York City, Hoboken, and Canada in the years before World War I. Often they met stiff competition from the Crescent Athletic Club and college teams, including those from Stevens Institute and Cornell.[77] The games were rough-and-tumble affairs, resulting in injuries, and were reported much like frontier conflicts between the U.S. Cavalry and Indians. After a hard-fought victory by the Cattaraugus team at Stevens Institute, a news story opened with the following sentence: "A war party of Seneca Indians armed with lacrosse sticks met a like number of men wearing the colors of Stevens Institute yesterday on the famous old field of St. George's Cricket Club at Hoboken, N.J."[78]

Between 1900 and 1912, the private Hobart College in Geneva, New York, frequently held contests with the Seneca team from Cattaraugus Reservation. Hobart's student newspaper characterized the contest as "strength and the speed of the forest against the brains of the white man."[79] Another reporter depicted the Senecas as "descendants of Hiawatha and Minnehaha." The story went on to describe the contest, declaring that a "tribe of Red Skins, armed with war whoops, lacrosse sticks, and an abundance of nerve and skill, sallied forth in full war paint to take by storm the camp of Mr.

Hobart's paleface warriors."[80] Despite the efforts of Cornplanter and others to dispel misconceptions, the college world of field lacrosse continued to stereotype Indian players for decades to come.

With the rise of professional non-Indian lacrosse leagues in Ontario and western New York in the 1920s and 1930s, some Senecas joined teams to make a living. Victor Twoguns turned back to lacrosse after his days as an amateur Golden Gloves boxer had ended. In an interview in the 1980s, he repeatedly described what had motivated him: "We made good money at lacrosse. We stayed right in Rochester. They paid our board and eighteen dollars a week besides. We played three times a week. On Friday nights we played at home. Sometimes we went to Geneva on Saturday night. Sunday nights we went to Syracuse to play. So we made pretty good money."[81] One major venue was Edgerton Park in Rochester, where Francis Kettle, later president of the Seneca Nation, played and coached. His two star players, both from the Six Nations Reserve, were Arleigh Hill, a Seneca, and Harold W. Smith, a Mohawk whose film name was Jay Silverheels, known in the *Lone Ranger* movies and television shows as Tonto.[82]

In the 1930s, Six Nations people began to play and watch box lacrosse, or boxla, a six-player game. Boxla began at Newtown on the Cattaraugus Reservation and at other reservations in Iroquoia after World War II. Yet Senecas continued to play professional lacrosse; William "Gumps" Abrams and Nelson Bally Huff became hall-of-famers in professional leagues in Ontario in the 1940s and 1950s. Seneca Oren Lyons, an Onondaga faithkeeper, was recognized twice as an all-American goalie on Syracuse University's legendary lacrosse teams in the mid-1950s. Importantly, all three of these men spent much of their lives teaching youngsters the fundamentals of the Creator's game, instilling in them its central role in Hodinöhsö:ni´ culture.[83]

While Senecas were adapting to change by drawing from the strength of their own cultural traditions, they faced incredible challenges. Perhaps the greatest one involved health matters. The census of 1890 reveals an extremely high infant mortality rate at Allegany, Cattaraugus, and Cornplanter. The death rate for the age group newborn to one year was 22 percent.[84] The Senecas' and their physicians' efforts to improve public health conditions, especially for children, was another form of resistance, a vital part of their history that has been skipped over by previous scholars.

FIGURE 1. Maris B. Pierce, a former Seneca chief, a teacher on the Cattaraugus Reservation, and one of three American Indian graduates of Dartmouth College before 1900. He was a key opponent of the Seneca revolutionaries of 1848. Part of a Six Nations delegation to meet with President Lincoln in the White House in 1864, he was instrumental in convincing Senecas to pursue their Kansas claims. *Courtesy Buffalo History Museum Library.*

FIGURE 2 (*opposite, top*). Governor Blacksnake (Tëwönyas), circa 1850. The former Allegany Seneca chief and a nephew of Handsome Lake, the Seneca prophet, helped save the Oil Spring territory (Ga:no's) with his testimony in court. *Reprinted from Thomas Donaldson, comp.,* The Six Nations of New York *(Washington, DC: U.S. Census Printing Office, 1892).*

FIGURE 3 (*opposite, bottom*). Edward Cornplanter (or Sosondó:wa, which means "Deep Night"). The Newtown Longhouse preacher-teacher spread the "Good Message" of Handsome Lake throughout Iroquoia. He was also a promoter of lacrosse, known among the Hodinöhsö:ni´ as the Creator's game. *Courtesy Seneca–Iroquois National Museum, Seneca Nation of Indians.*

FIGURE 4. Many Britons, Irish, and Scots saw this romanticized, early 1860s image of Lewis Bennett, popularly known as Deerfoot, perhaps the greatest long-distance runner of the nineteenth century. He is pictured wearing a headdress of one feather, symbolizing his Seneca Nation. Bare-chested, shocking to many in Victorian England, the Cattaraugus Seneca is also wearing a skirt rather than a breechclout, made of porcupine quill appliqué with attached feathers, bells, and wampum. Instead of highly crafted moccasins, he is pictured wearing leprechaun-style running shoes. On the table is the wolf robe he wore before races.

FIGURE 5. Lay's Band. Chester C. Lay and Sylvester C. Lay Jr. were accomplished musicians in the late nineteenth and first years of the twentieth century. The Lays' band, one of several among the Senecas, promoted temperance and played at Iroquois agricultural fairs, county fairs, and temperance conventions. Chester C. Lay was also a member of the board of managers of the Thomas Asylum/School and president of the Seneca Nation in 1889. *Courtesy Seneca–Iroquois National Museum, Seneca Nation of Indians.*

HEALTH MATTERS

In 1855, during the height of the attempts to overthrow the Seneca Nation's elected government and replace it with a council of chiefs, Presbyterian missionary Asher Wright, with the assistance of his wife, Laura, founded the Thomas Asylum for Orphan and Destitute Indian Children on the Cattaraugus Indian Reservation. The institution was named after Philip Thomas, who had personally bequeathed funds for its operation.[1] The asylum received and cared for destitute and orphaned children from all the reservations in New York State, as far away as the Shinnecock Reservation at Southampton, Long Island, but more than 80 percent of the children during its century of existence were from reservations in western New York.[2] The asylum was initially part of a reform movement of its day, serving, in the words of historian Marilyn Holt, as an enclave of "child rescue" for orphans and abandoned, abused, malnourished, and neglected youngsters, and it was specifically devoted to the improvement of care for these children.[3]

Seneca Nation tribal members, most notably President Andrew John Jr., donated lands for the asylum. Prominent Senecas served on its board of managers from the first. Of the initial ten board members, five were Senecas: Zachariah L. Jimeson, two-time president of the Seneca Nation; Sylvester Lay Sr., later president of the Seneca Nation; and Wallace King, Joshua Pierce, and Lewis Seneca. By the end of the century, that board of managers included other prominent tribal leaders such as Seneca presidents William Hoag and

Chester C. Lay and Treasurer Walter "Boots" Kennedy. It is important to note that the asylum also had Hodinöhsö:ni´ employees as early as the first decade of its operation and later employed Hodinöhsö:ni´ teachers.[4]

The records of the Thomas Asylum/School contain the best documentation we have about Seneca health conditions for an eighty-plus-year period. Its dispensary/infirmary/clinic/hospital facility, located at the center of the Cattaraugus Indian Reservation, was the major health facility for Senecas in the reservation's residential territories. From 1855 to 1922, the Thomas Asylum/School had two major health providers—missionary Wright and Dr. Albert D. Lake—and their reports and correspondence provide the best records of medical conditions within the Seneca Nation during this period. It should be noted, however, that these records have major limitations, such as cultural bias; their focus on pediatric and adolescent health matters and not on prenatal care, infant mortality, or adult medicine; and their silence on mental health and physical and sexual abuse.

In 1875, following the death of Asher Wright, the institution was on the verge of closing and had limited financial resources. That's when William P. Letchworth, a prominent businessman and reformer from western New York and a former vice chairman of the New York State Board of Charities, intervened to save the institution. By an act of the state legislature, management, supervision, and control of the asylum was transferred to the Board of Charities. It became a state institution, and the Board of Charities required administrators to furnish resident Indian children "such care, moral training and education, and such instruction in husbandry and the arts of civilization, as they shall prescribe in their rules and by-laws."[5] The next year, Daniel Sherman, the federal Indian agent, referred to the institution as "a model Indian school under the best of instruction and discipline."[6] Two decades later, the *Cattaraugus Republican,* referring to the students as "inmates," praised the asylum for teaching boys agriculture and trade skills such as carpentry in the making of window frames and cases, teaching girls sewing and cooking, and teaching both the "table manners of civilization."[7]

In 1898 the asylum offered regents examinations. Seven years later, the Board of Charities renamed the institution the Thomas Indian School. By that time, the institution offered eight grades of instruction. A ninth grade was added in 1930, a year after the Board of Charities changed its name to the Department of Social Welfare.[8] All students had to leave the institution when they reached the age of sixteen and seek to survive on their own. In 1931, while maintaining its medical facility and opening it up for Cattaraugus residents, the Thomas Indian School admitted day students from the Cattaraugus Indian Reservation for the first time. Since the day students could return to their homes at Cattaraugus after their classes each afternoon, their experiences at the school were far different than those orphaned, destitute, or neglected children placed in the institution by parents, legal guardians, or county welfare agencies. By then the extensive complex of 332 acres had nine redbrick buildings, an employees' residence, an infirmary/hospital, a schoolhouse, four dormitories, a dining room and kitchen, a gymnasium, a carpentry shop, a powerhouse, an icehouse/greenhouse, a chicken house, and stables.[9]

As at federal Indian boarding schools, the coeducational institution provided both academic and vocational coursework. Asylum and later school administrators assigned gender-specific training and duties—boys learned and did industrial and farmwork; girls did domestic tasks. Some children transferred to off-reservation boarding schools, such as Hampton. At the age of sixteen, students who had completed their training at Thomas were sent to live with and work for white people in their homes and businesses, allegedly to gain an appreciation of "civilized life." The asylum's and later the school's emphasis on transforming the children away from their tribal ways created an unsettling experience and trauma for many, but not all.[10] William Clement Bryant, who headed the Thomas Asylum's board of managers, set forth the institution's assimilationist objectives in his report in 1890. He stated that the institution was not merely a "temporary sanctuary for orphaned and outcast Indian children" but one that aimed "to develop and build character, to transform its inmates into thoughtful, thrifty, virtuous men and women, examples and incentives to their less favored brethren, who are struggling in that dreary interval which separates barbarism from civilization."[11]

The regimentation of student life was made clear in Superintendent Emily Lincoln's annual report for 1910: "No regular correspondence is kept up with guardians of children placed here, *but the school devotes one day each month to letter writing and each child has the privilege of writing a letter to parent, guardian, or friend*" (emphasis added). The superintendent added: "All letters in regard to the welfare of children are cheerfully answered and in case of serious illness of any child, their nearest kin is communicated with."[12] Yet not all Senecas were affected by the rigidity of the school and its assimilationist focus.

Opinions about the institution varied, depending on a student's particular treatment there. The school's leadership and policies implemented by school superintendents also varied widely over a one-hundred-year period. Some administrators, such as Superintendents George and Emily Lincoln from the mid-1890s through World War I, received high marks. Others, such as John C. Brennan from the 1920s into the 1940s, were criticized for their high-handedness, strict discipline, and cultural insensitivity. In addition, certain students were emotionally and psychologically stronger than others and were better at navigating the strict rules of the institution. And the views of orphans and destitute children who resided at the institution were generally less favorable than those of day students who returned home to their families each night. Finally, all children, whether able or not, had to leave the institution when they reached the age of sixteen and had to survive on their own or be placed with families, some of whom had little concern for the children's welfare and future.[13]

Besides learning to psychologically adjust to the regimentation they encountered at the institution, the children frequently faced repeated health crises that rapidly spread through the institution and Cattaraugus Reservation as a whole. These included epidemics of influenza, measles, smallpox, trachoma, and tuberculosis. Although the asylum received some state moneys from its inception. it was a private institution in its first two decades. During the Civil War, the underbudgeted asylum was especially hard hit with illnesses. In 1864 Wright indicated that the federal government provided $2,000; New York State $1,607.76; the Society of Friends $625; the American Board of Commissioners of Foreign Missions $100; children's treaty annuities $161.30; and other charitable donations $250.[14]

Indian health care was not based much on altruism or concern for the state's Indian communities. In 1889 the state assembly's *Whipple Report* primarily blamed non-Indian officials for the poor state of health care delivery on New York reservations. The report added: "The aid from the state and nation and from public charity is not enough to support the Indian in comfort and decency and health, but it is just enough to discourage and destroy effort on his part to assist himself. If the laws are set right the schools and missionaries will do the rest."[15] As late as 1930, another state legislative report admitted that Albany's focus was not on Indian health care as such but "was almost solely that of protecting the citizenry of the State from communicable disease arising on the reservation, particularly smallpox."[16]

The federal government was even more neglectful in serving the health needs of the Hodinöhsö:ni´. The Thomas Asylum/School never operated as a federal institution, although at times it received a small allocation from Washington based on its stated educational mission to bring "civilization" to the Indians. While federal Indian agents complained about health conditions, Washington's involvement nevertheless was minimal. In the 1870s and again in 1888, the federal government did hire doctors to vaccinate the Senecas against smallpox. By the later date, it also operated, off and on, a small infirmary at Cattaraugus.[17] It must be noted that the first comprehensive federal Indian health study was published in 1903 and that the Federal Indian Medical Service, later the Indian Health Service, was established only in 1908. IHS did not provide medical care to the Seneca Nation until 1976.[18]

Asher Wright served both spiritual and medical needs while residing first on the Senecas' Buffalo Creek Reservation and later on the Cattaraugus Reservation. During his missionary work with the Senecas, he practiced medicine at four widely scattered Seneca communities: Allegany, Buffalo Creek, Cattaraugus, and Tonawanda. From 1855 to his death in 1875, he also served as the physician at the Thomas Asylum. His medical training was limited to a one-year residence at Dartmouth Medical School. In July 1873, federal Indian agent Daniel Sherman described Wright as an "honest man" who resided in the center of Cattaraugus, "the most populous reservation in the agency," and who had practiced "medicine for over twenty-five years" (actually more than forty years) and treated "the sick at the Thomas Asylum for Orphan and Destitute Indians which he helped found." Although "not a graduate of any medical college . . . he is a scientific man, has a good knowledge both theoretical and practical of medicine of the human system of diseases, and has a very extensive experience in the treatment of disease among the Indians in the agency."[19] Nine days earlier Wright had told Sherman how he had come to medicine. While preparing for missionary work, he had made himself "acquainted with medical, surgical and obstetrical works such as were considered good authority at that time, but did not undertake to graduate at a medical college." He added that since then he had "endeavored to keep posted as far as possible in the progress of medical science."[20] In the eulogy at Wright's memorial service in 1875, Frederick Parker, nephew of Ely S. Parker, praised the heroic deeds of the missionary and his wife, Laura, during health crises: "Their hearts and hands were always open for the benefit of the Nation. When cholera and smallpox half ravaged our [Cattaraugus] Reservation, when no one would go near those who were sick, Mr. and Mrs. Wright went to their homes and ministered to them. They were angels of mercy."[21]

Wright's correspondence reveals much about health matters within Seneca communities from his mission at Buffalo Creek in the 1830s to his death at Cattaraugus in 1875. Except for medicine sent from Washington to help combat the cholera epidemic at Buffalo Creek in 1832, Wright was not helped by either the federal or state government until shortly before his death in 1875. In the fall and winter of 1847–48, he ministered to the needs of Senecas stricken with either typhoid or typhus, which killed between fifty and seventy adults. Just prior to this outbreak, twenty to thirty others, mostly children, perished in a measles epidemic; twenty others, old and young, died from dysentery.[22]

Wright spent approximately $100 a year out of his own pocket to buy medicines to treat his patients.[23] Only in 1874, when Commissioner of Indian Affairs Edward Smith visited Seneca Country, did the federal government promise Wright medical supplies, in lieu of paying him a salary. Because Wright died shortly after the supplies arrived, the federal government, despite Agent Sherman's efforts, insisted they be returned.[24] Hoping to prevent the loss of these supplies, Sherman wrote that Wright had been "a skillful physician as well as a faithful missionary." The federal Indian agent indicated that for years Wright had supplied medicines to the Indians in this agency at his own expense as auxiliary to his mission work.[25]

Once the Thomas Asylum was founded in the mid-1850s, Wright and his family were faced with providing for the care of orphans and malnourished children from all over Iroquoia. He and his family were frequent defenders of the reputation of the asylum and the medical care provided there. In 1863 two children died—one from meningitis. The other was a sickly child who had managed to survive for seven years at the asylum. Despite the Wrights' and the staffs' efforts to meet health challenges, they were overwhelmed at times by periodic epidemics that struck both the asylum and the Cattaraugus Reservation. During the Civil War, at a time of political turmoil during Henry Silverheels's presidency, epidemics of measles and smallpox struck. At the Thomas Asylum in 1864, thirty-five children out of fifty-eight contracted measles. Eight of these children died from the disease and/or from resulting complications, including dysentery. Fearing the loss of confidence in his management of the asylum, Wright and his son Arthur tried to rationalize the tragedy in a later report to the federal Indian agent. Arthur insisted that the institution had gone into substantial financial debt fighting the outbreak. The missionary later claimed that the number of deaths that year was the same as the total for the entire first decade of the asylum's operation. He also indicated that there was a higher mortality rate outside the asylum's walls on the Cattaraugus Reservation. He told the Indian agent that there was an obvious need for better provisions for the sick and recommended that improved facilities be constructed to guard against the spread of contagions. The recommendations were ignored.[26]

In one of Wright's letters to the federal Indian agent, he claimed that Hodinöhsö:ni´ traditional medicine was slowly fading away. However, he pointed out that the some "pagans" still journeyed to Grand River Reserve in Canada to visit an Indian practitioner. Wright readily admitted that elderly reservation women were his major competitors since they served in all cases as midwives. He observed that there were fewer old-time herbalists in Seneca Country but that "almost every old women knows of remedies which have been used successfully in one or more cases." The missionary implied that most Indians had little remaining prejudice about seeing a white doctor and in fact "seem, however, to prefer" to go to a white physician "in all serious cases if they can but obtain the money of paying him." He blamed whatever reluctance there was in seeking out white physicians on their fees, saying, "with many [Senecas] it is insurmountable."[27] Despite this assertion, two months after the missionary's death, a "Native doctor or medicine man" led a protest against a schoolteacher at Cattaraugus for allowing Dr. E. D. Meader to vaccinate the children at a school in "one of the Pagan districts."[28]

Wright also indicated that the major illnesses he saw in his patients were diseases of the chest and that "diseases of the respiratory organs take the first rank."[29] In 1888 there was a 10 percent annual mortality rate from tuberculosis among the Senecas.[30] By 1909 tuberculosis was the major scourge of Indians throughout the United States, resulting in 40 percent of all Indian deaths; the mortality rate was 60 percent higher than the non-Indian rate.[31] Wright also pointed out that he rarely saw patients with rheumatic fever, scarlet fever, and typhus; that the Senecas had the same rates as white communities for cancer, blindness, deafness, epilepsy, and various forms of paralysis; and that croup (whooping cough), diphtheria, and meningitis were less than in white communities.[32]

Just after Wright's death, in April 1875, the federal government hired seven physicians at a total cost of $480 to vaccinate Hodinöhsö:ni´ on the reservations in New York. To administer vaccinations on the Seneca reservations, the government hired local Angola doctor Watson Curtis as the physician at $.41 per day and Laura Wright, Asher Wright's widow, as assistant physician at $.685 per day. Curtis was later replaced by E. D. Meader. The seven physicians were able to vaccinate only 1,880 out of 3,856 Indians across New York State, since, according to the federal Indian agent, there was significant resistance in the "pagan districts."[33] Because of delays in paying the physicians, the agent then recommended that tribal federal annuity moneys be used to hire an agency physician. At a time when there were two disputed tribal elections, in 1876 and 1878, the issue of using federal annuities for the hiring of an agency physician split the residential communities of Allegany and Cattaraugus. In a Seneca Nation resolution of July 1877 offered by Hiram Dennis of Cattaraugus and Peter Shongo of Allegany, the tribal council appropriated $150 each to hire a physician and an assistant physician. The moneys were specifically to be taken out of federal annuities for payments to households in Cattaraugus territory, not from Allegany. Although Sherman finally received support from the Seneca Nation Tribal Council, his idea was overwhelmingly criticized by the Seneca populace at large, since there had been no popular referendum on the issue. His proposal was later rejected by the Office of Indian Affairs. Undoubtedly, some of the protesting Senecas equated the action of the council with the past arbitrary action of the chiefs regarding how annuities were dispensed. The issue inflamed passions and split the nation as it had from 1845 to 1848.[34]

Sherman tried to hire Watson Curtis as the first salaried Indian agency physician, at $150 per year, and to hire Laura Wright as his assistant physician, at $250 per year.[35] After Curtis protested his low salary and the difficulty of traveling on the bad local roads, the federal Indian agent searched for a replacement. While Sherman was attempting to secure the services of an agency physician, another epidemic struck the asylum. In 1876, one matron at the asylum died of pneumonia.[36] The next year, Sherman hired Albert D. Lake, a thirty-one-year-old from Perrysburg, New York, described by the federal Indian agent as a "reliable and competent physician."[37] Lake was assisted by Laura Wright. Although she was not completely accepted by some followers of the Longhouse religion in the Newtown neighborhood, she persevered and apparently brought comfort there to some desperately suffering from disease and malnutrition.[38] In 1877 both were hired by Sherman at a salary of $125 a year, later raised to $200 per annum, to serve the medical needs of widely scattered Hodinöhsö:ni´ reservations that stretched three hundred miles across New York State. [39] Wright served in her official role until 1880; she continued to serve the medical and spiritual needs of the Cattaraugus community until her death in 1886.[40]

In 1880, the New York State Board of Charities hired Lake as a part-time pediatric and adolescent physician at the Thomas Asylum.[41] He visited the institution once a week in the 1880s and then twice a week until 1922. A leading physician and public health advocate in western New York State, he was clearly not motivated to serve because of salary or any other financial compensation package. During the height of an influenza epidemic, he received merely $33.34 per month. In the last year of Lake's medical service at the school, the state was still paying him only $50 month, or approximately $6 a visit.[42] Later in the 1880s, Lake was hired in his second role, as the physician in charge of the Cattaraugus Reservation infirmary.[43] Although a non-Indian, Lake worked closely with the Seneca Nation leadership and was frequently critical of Albany and its failures to provide for the health needs of the Seneca Nation and the children at the Thomas Asylum. He also had to deal with superintendents, managers, and teachers of the Thomas Asylum/School whose abilities, honesty, cultural sensitivities, and even mental stability were sometimes called into question.[44] Although he favored allotment of tribal lands and with it the extension of U.S. citizenship to the Senecas, the records nevertheless indicate that he was an outspoken public health advocate for Native Americans at Cattaraugus and at other Hodinöhsö:ni´ communities. His measures to counter the scourges of tuberculosis, trachoma, and measles at the Thomas Indian School were far ahead of the pediatrics and adolescent medicine practiced at federal Indian boarding schools at the time.[45] On his death in 1923, after forty-three years of service, the Thomas Indian School board of managers reflected on his contributions during his long career and passed a resolution hailing his service. The board insisted that he was "a man of unquestionable integrity, of unflinching purpose, and one who never compromised with wrong. He was a man of strong personality, an orator, a diplomat, a patriot. He was a leader of his profession and a recognized authority on many medical questions. He was often sought as expert counsel." The resolution added that Lake "has always taken a special interest in the Indian and was one of the best informed on Indian problems. He solicitously guarded the health and interests of the School and has been a prime factor in the development of the Institution. His counsel and advice will long be missed."[46] Eighty years after his death, Doctor Lake's portrait was still displayed on the wall in the first-floor room of the old Thomas Indian School hospital/infirmary/clinic, which by then was being used by the Seneca Nation of Indians as their courthouse on the Cattaraugus Indian Reservation.[47]

Lake's background and training were impressive. The son of a physician, he was born on February 22, 1846, in North Collins, just off Cattaraugus territory. He attended Springville Academy and then the University of Michigan. In the years after the Civil War, he attended the Cleveland Medical College, now the prestigious Case Western Reserve School of Medicine. He wrote his required thesis on the importance of and improvements in anesthetizing patients. After graduation he married and set up a medical practice in New Albion in 1871. Subsequently he moved his practice to Perrysburg, where he was elected town supervisor. Later he transferred his medical office to Gowanda. On several occasions, Lake was elected president of the Cattaraugus County Medical Society; he also served on the society's hygiene committee. Later he was a delegate to the annual meetings of the New York State Medical Society and was on staff of Niagara University in Lewiston.[48]

Lake, as a determined public health advocate, made yearly recommendations in his physician's report to Albany; all of them were reprinted in Thomas Indian School's annual reports to the New York State Legislature. Some dealt with the health concerns of the school population, some with the health of Seneca and Cayuga residents of Cattaraugus, and still others with the health problems faced by Native Americans statewide. Almost every year, Lake recommended new dormitory construction.[49] Since the original buildings at the Thomas Asylum were wooden structures and heated by burning wood, he was especially worried that fires would break out and threaten the safety of the children. He also recommended the installation of steam heating in the buildings.[50] In 1908, although pointing out that there had been a decrease in tuberculosis cases at the school, Lake warned "that the over-crowding of our dormitories may soon be followed by more cases in the future." He noted that congested quarters bred disease and recommended that an upper floor of the school be converted into an isolation ward for contagious patients. Constantly concerned with the welfare of the children at the school, he urged in the same report that the state build a school gymnasium, arguing that this would not merely be for the enjoyment of students and staff but would improve overall physical fitness.[51] In 1910 he insisted that there was insufficient ventilation in the dormitories and that it "would not be difficult to devise some means whereby this condition could be improved."[52] Two years later, after a visit by two members of U.S. Public Health Service, including an oculist, Lake advised that better lighting be installed in the crowded carpentry shop to alleviate the danger of machines causing mishaps. Later, in 1921, he called for the construction of a new carpentry shop to relieve the dangerous conditions and the threat of injury there.[53] In 1915 Lake recommended the erection of a sewage disposal plant after a health emergency caused by the overflow of Cattaraugus Creek.[54]

Over time, Lake's frustrations in dealing with bureaucrats and politicians led him to become more vocal in his criticisms of Albany officials and state legislators. Perhaps because of his high standing within the medical community and his past political position as a town supervisor, he was protected from dismissal from state employment. His criticisms were most apparent in his report for 1911. The physician openly condemned the state for ignoring the health needs of Indians statewide and not promoting public health education on reservations. He insisted that the state legislature needed to empower the newly established state Department of Health to instruct Indians on the reservations, not just at the Thomas Indian School, on the best ways to prevent and manage infectious diseases. Lake realized that there was a direct connection between infectious diseases found at the school and those in the Hodinöhsö:ni´ communities at Cattaraugus and around the state, since Thomas employees, both Indian and non-Indian, traveled outside the immediate grounds of the school, as did students who journeyed back to visit their reservation communities. Lake noted that he had previously consulted with some Hodinöhsö:ni´, referring to them as "intelligent and very receptive to instruction," and concluded "that whenever they have learned of the modern methods employed to prevent infection, they have almost invariably followed such instruction."[55] Then Lake chastised the state's response to Indian health care, calling it lamentable that "the Indian population of the State of New York, amounting to more than 5,000, should be entirely ignored in the crusade which has shown such splendid results throughout the State. It is proper for me to say that without doubt all this would be changed if the Legislature would place in the hands of the State Commissioner of Health sufficient funds to allow him to do the necessary work."[56]

In the same report, after praising the construction of new dormitories and extensive walkways and approaches to the buildings, which in his medical opinion allowed "the children to remain more in the fresh air during the season when the ground is damp from frequent rain fall," the physician then went so far as to accuse Albany officials of violating state health laws. He argued: "The statute provides that each child be given 600 cubic feet of air space. With 185 pupils we afford to each 500 cubic feet or perhaps slightly less." He warned: "It seems to me that we cannot go beyond this point unless additional buildings are provided, without much danger of a marked increase in the number of cases of tuberculosis."[57] When thirty-three influenza cases broke out at the school in 1916, Lake repeated his charge that a state law—the one that required "600 feet of air space per individual in dormitories"—was being violated, pointing out that the conditions added "greatly to the danger of infection, if communicable disease should occur."[58]

The physician apparently was emboldened to take a more assertive position on Indian health care at the school and the state reservations by his growing reputation as an expert on Indian health matters. He lectured widely on the need to improve Indian medical care, speaking out critically about the lack of federal, state, and local efforts. In 1910 he attended the Lake Mohonk Conference of Friends of the Indian and Other Dependent Peoples and addressed the reformers, mostly paternalistic do-gooders, about his work as the singular health professional at the Thomas Indian School. He pointed out that there was confusion because on the one hand, the federal government administered the New York Indian agency, and on the other hand, state-hired physicians were employed on the same reservations. The result was that the "State Commissioner of Health and the health boards adjacent to the reservations are not at all clear as to their powers, and the consequence is that no vital statistics are obtained, and no restraint whatever, in most instances, is placed upon the extension of epidemic diseases."[59]

From 1880 until an accident in 1922 forced him into retirement, Lake made a weekly visit—later extended to two days per week—to treat the children at Thomas. Right from the beginning, he was praised for his expertise and his untiring efforts and recommended for renewal of his contract.[60] The physician's greatest achievements there were in fighting scourges of smallpox, polio, trachoma, and tuberculosis, both the more viral consumption and the less deadly scrofula. Indeed, his public health measures seem to have succeeded more than those at federal Indian boarding schools administered by the Office of Indian Affairs in same period.[61]

The last major outbreak of smallpox in Seneca Country occurred in 1888. At least eight residents of Cattaraugus and Allegany perished in the outbreak. Lake vaccinated five hundred Indians to stop the spread of the disease. This was no easy task, because many Senecas, especially Longhouse followers, were reluctant to be vaccinated. The disease appears to have all but disappeared as a major threat at the school and on the two residential territories by the second decade of the twentieth century in part because of Lake's efforts in winning acceptance of vaccination among Longhouse Senecas.[62]

In 1916 New York State faced the most serious epidemic of polio in its history. The disease struck mostly children, especially under the age of ten. More than thirteen thousand cases and far more than three thousand deaths were reported. Yet not one case occurred at the Thomas Indian School.[63] In 1912 alone there were more than thirty-nine thousand cases of trachoma among American Indians nationwide. Trachoma, a viral disease of the eye, was caused by unsanitary conditions and led to blindness throughout Indian Country well into the twentieth century. Although there were two reported cases of trachoma at the Thomas Indian School in 1917, the viral disease appears to have been virtually wiped out by the end of World War I among the Hodinöhsö:ni´ in New York.[64]

In 1882 the German bacteriologist Dr. Robert Koch isolated the immediate cause of tuberculosis. Yet Albany had no organized effort to stem the spread of the disease until 1906.[65] Lake, however, had already taken steps to limit the spread of tuberculosis. In 1888 he had described tuberculosis as the greatest of all health concerns at the school and on the Cattaraugus Reservation. The physician indicated that approximately one hundred of the eighteen hundred residents of the reservation, mostly those from infancy to age thirty-five, died each year from the disease and that one-third of all Seneca children died of the disease before age five.[66] It is important to note that the disease declined at the school more rapidly than at other Indian boarding schools, from sixteen cases of both forms of tuberculosis and two deaths in 1904 to four cases in 1921.[67]

Despite his efforts, the physician was less successful in other areas. Epidemics of measles struck the school in 1907, with half of the student body becoming ill. A more serious strain of this disease occurred in 1918, resulting in 111 cases and three deaths. In the same year, 25 percent were affected by impetigo, a highly contagious skin rash. An outbreak of German measles struck in 1914, with nearly 20 percent of the students contracting the disease. In 1911 thirty-seven students contracted whooping cough, and in 1915, 16 percent of the students enrolled came down with scarlet fever.[68]

Lake's greatest challenge was his attempts to contain the influenza that struck Cattaraugus every late fall and winter. By 1918, even with the building of more boys' and girls' dormitories, the Thomas Indian School was over capacity. More than 200 students were living in residence halls with a 140-student capacity. To make things worse, in the same year, the state's appropriation for food at the institution was cut by one-third.[69] But nothing Lake faced was like what struck the institution, New York State, the United States, and the planet in the fall of 1918.[70] A world pandemic of the H1V1 flu was to kill half a million Americans and fifty million people worldwide, much more than all the casualties of World War I. In New York State alone, 61,015 people died from influenza and its complications, namely pneumonia, during 1918. In Buffalo from September 1918 through March 1919, there were more than 3,075 deaths from the disease and the pneumonia that often followed from it.[71] More than 13 percent of the Hodinöhsö:ni'—eight hundred Indians—contracted the disease, and eighty—mostly adults in the prime of their lives—perished.[72]

From the fall of 1918 through the end of March 1919, 211 cases of what was dubbed the Spanish flu were recorded at the Thomas Indian School. Six children and four employees, including teacher Louise Courtney, died. Disaster first struck in October 1918, during the last days of President Frank Patterson's administration, when the first cases of influenza appeared at the school. On October 25, the superintendent noted in his diary that there were already 174 cases: 11 employees and 163 children. Two days later he noted that there were 190 cases. On October 27, the superintendent wrote: "More cases this morning so we have about two hundred. Everyone worked to care for the sick." On Halloween, three children—Archie Logan (Onondaga), Hamilton Jimerson (Allegany Seneca), and Elin Bennett (Cattaraugus Seneca)—died of pneumonia, a complication of the H1V1 virus. The epidemic swept through the institution, with the outbreak continuing into February, when Hazel Thompson, a Tuscarora, succumbed after a fever of 106 degrees.[73] Only one pupil in the entire school, Rubena Jacobs, escaped contracting the disease. She later described the outbreak: "Most of them [the girls] were down in bed. They were delirious. I remember one time I had to pass out soup to the beds. They lost some pupils and some teachers. It was a terrible flu epidemic."[74] The relatives of the sick children and employees paid visits to help out, or joined with the undertaker to make funeral arrangements for the deceased. Because of the outbreak, Sunday church services and Sunday school were called off, although Thanksgiving dinner was not suspended.[75]

The death rate among the Seneca Nation from the pandemic of 1918–19 would have been much greater if not for community's response during the new administration of President William Hoag, the work of Lake, and a fortunate happenstance: the timely visit of Nancy Seneca Phillips, the first Seneca to become a trained nurse, who heroically tended to those affected. A graduate of Carlisle and the nursing program at Philadelphia's Chirurgical Hospital (now the University of Pennsylvania), she had worked for two decades as a nurse in the Indian Service in South Dakota and Oklahoma.[76] The Thomas superintendent wrote: "During the influenza epidemic, I do not know what we would have done if the Indian People had not come to our assistance, for it was just impossible to get nurses or any help from places around us." He went onto to give his obligatory thanks to Henry Lechtreker, an inspector for the state Board of Charities, for helping in his brief residence during the outbreak. Quite significantly, however, the superintendent personally pointed to Seneca's efforts: "We were extremely fortunate in having on our reservation at the time Mrs. Benjamin Phillips, formerly Miss Nancy Seneca, a trained nurse of this reservation, but now of Garber, Oklahoma, and her husband, who came and rendered us valuable assistance during this epidemic."[77]

In his physician's report in 1919, Lake blamed the high rate of influenza at the school partly on a lack of isolation wards and "in not finding sufficient competent nurses [except for Phillips] to handle the epidemic."[78] Indeed, for the entire month of March 1919, there was no state-employed nurse on staff, although one was hired the next month.[79] To prevent a recurrence of the epidemic, as well as the spread of diphtheria and tuberculosis, the physician advised "having larger isolation wards so that these carriers and infectious cases may not convey the disease to others, and I earnestly recommend an isolation hospital containing wards not of large dimensions be provided for the institution."[80]

In 1920, with the hope that his report would bring additional funding from the Board of Charities and the state legislature, Lake pointed out that with the closing of the Carlisle Indian School, the Thomas Indian School was "the only place accessible for resident pupils of all the reservations of the state."[81] A year later, in 1921, he continued his advocacy by urging the construction of an industrial building for carpentry, since the conditions of the older building were dangerous and ripe for injury.[82] In 1922, Lake, now seventy-six years of age, was injured in an automobile accident and was forced to retire.[83]

In the early morning hours of March 13, 1923, Lake died of heart disease at the age of seventy-seven.[84] Until the early 1970s, when Seneca women in the Health Action Group and Lionel John took up the cause of improving Indian health care, no other person, Indian or non-Indian, had done more for improving Seneca medical services and improving public health awareness than the outspoken advocate Albert Lake. It was no coincidence that several improvements pushed by the physician came to fruition. Within three years of Lake's death, a shop building for carpentry and a gymnasium were opened, and the infirmary was slightly expanded. Six years after Lake's death, the New York Department of Social Welfare, formerly the Board of Charities, received state funding for the building of a "hospital" at the school, but it was more an infirmary or clinic.[85]

As a result of Lake's efforts and conditions exposed during the influenza epidemic, other changes were implemented over the next ten years. Until 1919, the state Department of Health, founded as the New York State Board of Health in 1891, had not been involved in monitoring health conditions on Seneca reservations. However, that year the state made its first major health study of the Hodinöhsö:ni´. Soon afterward, the Department of Health for the very first time assigned a nurse to the Allegany Reservation. In 1928 "travelling children's units" of public health nurses, funded by both the state and Erie County, made visits to Cattaraugus to examine children and vaccinate them against typhoid, diphtheria, and scarlet fever. In a major agency report to the legislature in 1930, the Health Department recommended a sizable increase in funding to provide more extensive services "than [are] given to rural citizens generally."[86] Nevertheless, much of the work done by Lake in cooperation with the Seneca Council soon faded into history.

The new three-story "hospital," a fireproof brick building with a bed capacity of thirty-two, opened at the Thomas Indian School in 1931. The state facility was severely underfunded from the beginning. Although it was open to all Indian residents of the Cattaraugus Reservation, New York State allocated a mere $869.51 for its medical supplies in 1936–37.[87] The hospital also had no easy access for the elderly and physically challenged at its entrance; narrow hallways made it difficult to maneuver for patients in wheelchairs; and there was no elevator![88] Despite Lake's efforts to fix the sewage disposal system at the Thomas Indian School, untreated waste from that institution and from the Gowanda State Hospital for the Insane and a nearby tannery and glue factory flowed into Cattaraugus Creek, right past the school, and contaminated wells and polluted swimming and fishing areas through the entire length of the Cattaraugus Indian Reservation.[89]

Seneca leaders, from Raymond Jimerson in the early 1930s to Calvin "Kelly" John in the late 1960s, had to face one crisis after another—the Great Depression, World War II, the Korean War, Kinzua, and termination—which took focus away from health care delivery for Seneca communities. The Thomas Indian School closed its doors forever in June 1957.[90] However, a part-time clinic in the school's "hospital" continued to operate. The clinic's location on the old school grounds limited its efficacy. Some Senecas avoided making needed visits to the clinic since they still had bad memories of being harshly disciplined, humiliated, or even abused at the school, especially in the years after Lake's death during the administration of Superintendent John C. Brennan.[91] As late as the 1960s and early 1970s, two part-time doctors worked alternate weeks at the clinic. Although there was a pediatric clinic to deal with the needs of children, it was open for only four hours on Thursday mornings. Moreover, at that time Albany's total funding for Seneca services—education, health, and social services at Cattaraugus—was merely $137,592, out of a paltry budget of $769,765 for all the reservation communities in the state.[92]

In the 1970s, Lionel John and a determined coterie of women—the Health Action Group—convinced the Seneca Nation Council to focus on improved health matters, resulting in establishment of the first IHS facilities in the Northeast.[93] Nevertheless, one can greatly appreciate the early efforts of Asher and Laura Wright and Albert Lake in working with Seneca Nation leadership to improve health conditions and fight the scourges that ravaged Indian communities. Although they were not successful in many areas and often faced intractable bureaucrats in Washington and Albany, they were an essential part of the greater Seneca struggle to survive in a hostile world.

In traditional thought, Hodinöhsö:ni´ refer to the importance of looking well into the future—namely to "the seven generations to come." Consequently, the welfare of their children was their constant and overwhelming concern. One of the greatest challenges the Senecas faced involved the education of their children, especially when the state, religious societies, and private school administrators and teachers, holding distinct opinions and values, were put in charge of this great responsibility. Unlike some Native Americans in the trans-Mississippi West, Seneca parents were not forced to send their children to far-off federal boarding schools. Nor did the state have a compulsory law to require Indian children's attendance until 1900, and even well after that legislation was passed, it was hardly enforced. Although Seneca parents had limited options, most of which were less than desirable, they were actors in making the following choices: (1) having their children remain close to home, being educated either at state district schools or the Quaker School at Tunesassa; (2) encouraging or allowing their children to be truants, avoiding attendance at these same schools; or (3) joining with other Native Americans and sending their children to Indian boarding schools.

•◄ 6 ►•

KEEPING THEIR CHILDREN NEARBY

Both Public and Private Schools

Throughout their history since 1848, one of the greatest challenges the Senecas faced involved the education of their children. Historically, the Senecas had good reason to distrust state, religious, and private school administrators and teachers intent on transforming their children away from Onöndowa'ga:' ways. Educational policies initiated by racist educators, parsimonious bureaucrats, and poorly trained and underpaid teachers too often denied the worth of Hodinöhsö:ni' culture.[1] Only in 1975 did the New York State Board of Regents, in a policy statement, finally recognize that Native Americans "prefer to retain their specific tribal cultural identities and life styles and that they wish to exercise the prerogatives of adopting only those components of the dominant culture that meet their needs. In American history, the State and Federal attempts to terminate tribes, to dissolve their reservation status, and to relocate their people into urban settings have been unsuccessful."[2]

Two years before the revolution of 1848, the New York State Legislature enacted a law authorizing its superintendent of common schools, the predecessor of both the state superintendent of public instruction and the state commissioner of education, to provide for school buildings and annual appropriations for the education of American Indians on four reservations: Allegany, Cattaraugus, Onondaga, and Saint Regis (Akwesasne). Later, state-administered district schools were established at Shinnecock (1848),

Tonawanda and Tuscarora (1856), Oneida (1857), and Poospatuck (1875). The two schools at Oneida were closed in 1889. As a result of the movement to centralize smaller rural districts into larger ones beginning in 1931, allegedly for better administrative and financial efficiency, and efforts from the mid-1950s onward to promote racial integration, the remaining Seneca district schools closed down.[3]

The movement for centralization of smaller districts occurred across the border on the Cornplanter Grant as well. In 1857, after receiving a small subsidy from the Pennsylvania State Legislature in Harrisburg, Marsh Pierce, the grandson of Chief Cornplanter, opened a small wooden schoolhouse to serve the educational needs of his small community. A newer brick one was erected in 1903 and financed by the state. This small school, which each year educated two or three dozen pupils, including some whites, was closed in 1953 and the students were transferred to public schools in nearby Warren, Pennsylvania.[4]

The last Seneca Nation district school in New York remained open at Allegany until 1965, when its land was taken for construction of the Kinzua Dam.[5] Today only one all-Indian reservation school remains in western New York—at Tuscarora. Now the majority of Seneca Nation children attend public schools in two nearby districts, Gowanda and Salamanca; a smaller number are registered in the Lake Shore School District. Seneca children living in Buffalo attend public schools within its city limits. In each district, Seneca children are a racial minority.

One of the first enactments of the state legislature relating to American Indian education passed in 1856. It was entitled "An Act to facilitate education and civilization among the Indians residing within the state."[6] This stated assimilationist direction in educational policies was in every superintendent of public instruction report from 1854 well into the twentieth century. In 1858 the superintendent of public instruction observed that two major problems existed in teaching the Senecas: first, Seneca residences were scattered along a forty-mile corridor of the Allegany Reservation; and second, many of the Indians on the Allegany and Cattaraugus Reservations only spoke Seneca. In addressing the second "problem," the local superintendent of Seneca district schools added: "One obstacle to a rapid improvement in their studies, is found in the pertinacity with which they adhere to their own language, rendering the English virtually a foreign tongue, and instruction therein almost as difficult and tedious as it would be for a teacher in one of the common schools of the state, to instruct his pupils in Latin or Greek by the use of those languages colloquially."[7] Thirty years later, Joseph Hazard, the local superintendent of the schools at Cattaraugus and Allegany, complained to the state superintendent of public instruction that families who spoke Seneca in their households, especially in what he labeled "pagan" districts, meaning those neighborhoods occupied by followers of the Longhouse religion, were "a hindrance to the work of the schools."[8]

By the end of the Civil War, seven state districts schools were in operation for two twelve-week sessions at Cattaraugus, and six were in operation at Allegany. By 1879 seventeen schools were in operation.[9] Most of the moneys—$2,117 of a total amount of $2,678.05—went to teacher salaries at the two reservations. Of that amount, Quakers from the Philadelphia Yearly Meeting had donated $300 to extend the school term another month at certain districts, while the Seneca Council itself appropriated $500 and local reservation residents provided the kindling wood as well as the necessary labor to maintain the schoolhouses. E. M. Petit, the local superintendent for the Indian schools and later a member of the board of managers at the Thomas Asylum, observed that progress was the result of the system of schools and Albany's "benevolent care and liberal policy," myopically commenting: "Now, a stranger passing through the Cattaraugus reservation would see but little in the costume of the people or the general appearance of the country to remind him that he was in an Indian settlement."[10]

In 1866 the Seneca Nation Council appropriated $500 to aid in the building of schoolhouses and continued to allocate some of its own moneys for the maintenance of these schools.[11] However, the local school superintendent frequently complained about who should undertake repairs of school buildings, who should clear the fields around schoolhouses, and who should supply the firewood for the one- and two-room district schools so that classrooms would be warm enough for students to learn.[12] The state eventually supplied moneys for firewood to heat the district schools, but the controversy seems to have continued, since the local school superintendent stated that he had to close the schools in frigid weather and insisted that the Senecas should not be required to supply wood for kindling to warm the classrooms.[13] It should be noted that many problems faced in educating the Senecas in these district schools were similar to problems faced by poor whites throughout rural New York State in the second half of the nineteenth century—namely, high teacher turnover, poor salaries, and inadequate facilities.[14]

Superintendents frequently complained about their inability to retain teachers, blaming it on the low pay scale and the alleged privations and hardships that teachers had to endure. Until a 1943 state law, teachers in Indian district schools were paid far less than their counterparts in non-Indian schools. For two twelve-week sessions of instruction in 1866, the salaries of six teachers at Allegany totaled $793; the total for seven teachers at Cattaraugus was $1,324.[15] On September 30, 1868, Superintendent Petit reported that an additional three district schools had opened and that the instruction would be for two sessions of sixteen weeks each. He listed teachers' salaries, which now ranged from $96 to $240 a year.[16] In 1888 the Whipple Committee reported that teachers' salaries in district schools had fallen much lower, to $7.10 per week. The cost savings appear to result from gender discrimination, since almost all the teachers were women by then.[17] As late as 1923, the problem of teacher retention in the Indian district schools continued, since according to the inspector of special schools, after they gained experience, teachers went off to seek more lucrative positions.[18]

On December 13, 1871, the local superintendent of reservation schools suggested that because Indian teachers could speak the language, they had succeeded better than white teachers. He also indicated that there was a cost savings if he hired Indians as teachers, since they received lower salaries.[19] Teachers of Hodinöhsö:ni´ ancestry were hired from the 1850s onward, including ex-chief Maris Pierce (and his non-Indian wife, Mary), Abbie Parker, Hattie and Daniel Two Guns and Hattie Pierce. Both Parker and Pierce were graduates of Fredonia Normal School, now SUNY Fredonia.[20] In 1874 John Archer, superintendent of the Seneca district schools at Cattaraugus and Allegany, commented that the six Indian teachers "do not do as well as our own people." However, the following year he admitted that at least three were "succeeding admirably."[21] A decade later, despite the success of two female Indian teachers at Cattaraugus, the local school superintendent, continued to push for a whites-only hiring policy.[22]

Archer was to find himself in hot water three times during his tenure as superintendent for the district schools at Allegany and Cattaraugus. First he faced an open rebellion in Newtown, the Longhouse district of Cattaraugus, caused by a teacher's attempt to require vaccinations against smallpox.[23] The second crisis was more widespread and directed at Archer himself and his authoritarian approach to hiring, retaining, and firing teachers. Seneca-appointed Indian school trustees had locked the schoolhouse doors and refused admittance to the teachers in a protest against the superintendent's arbitrary power, haughtiness, and disdain for the Senecas in general. Archer blamed it on Seneca "trustees" who often thought they had the same power as trustees of white schools. To Archer, the label "trustee" was "a misnomer and should be at once dropped, and the name marshal, or some other name equally applicable should be given to them."[24] The school superintendent continued to be controversial, and his authority was once more challenged in 1879.[25] Not surprisingly, he was replaced the following year.

From the time the state legislature established district schools in 1846 to well into the twentieth century, school administrators expressed frustrations about getting Seneca parents to send their children to these schools. The authoritarian tendencies of some superintendents of Seneca schools, such as John Archer, did not help attract pupils. Less than 50 percent of registered students, youngsters under the age of twelve, showed up for school, leading officials to lobby the state legislature for the passage of a compulsory education bill by the turn of the twentieth century. In part, this was an indication of dissatisfaction on the part of some Seneca parents and their children with the curriculum, the quality and lack of cultural sensitivity of the teachers, the assimilationist focus of the schools, and the poor state of the school facilities. Weather conditions in the winter in western New York; unheated, dilapidated schoolhouses located too far from certain residences; and periodic epidemics also drove down daily attendance. However, a major reason for the lack of attendance by Senecas was their need to go to work to supplement their meager family incomes.[26]

Residents of Allegany and Cattaraugus clearly resented school administrators meddling in Seneca religious and political affairs, pushing an agenda to solve what they labeled the "Indian problem." Indeed, Albany's master plan went well beyond educational policies. W. H. Campbell, the superintendent of the Seneca schools, saw the enemy as the Longhouse people, who he claimed retarded progress. He insisted that it was remarkable that a people with churches in their midst, "where Christians weekly assemble to worship the only true and living God, should remain sunk in the depths of superstition." The superintendent blamed the highly influential ex-chief Owen Blacksnake, the senior preacher at the Coldspring Longhouse, and his son for making pledges never to attend church or be buried in church cemeteries. Campbell advocated citizenship as "a way to make a man of the Indian." After all, he insisted, thousands of immigrants "whose qualifications for citizenship are not to be compared with those of many of the Indians" are made citizens. Although the Senecas had "given up their tomahawk, war paint, feathers, and moccasins and have material items such as a silver watch," they were no better off. He maintained that the "people are still backward and to quite an extent ignorant and indolent, and their advancement is still slow but sure." His solution to the "Indian problem" was clear: "Give us railroads, telegraphs and public schools, and the children of the forest will in principle soon be white men, and we will extend them the hand of citizenship."[27]

In 1888 and 1889, a New York State Assembly committee, headed by James Whipple of Salamanca, investigated the "Indian problem." The final report issued by the committee demeaned Hodinöhsö:ni´ beliefs, customs, and leadership and advocated the breakup of all tribally held lands. A significant part of that investigation dealt with Indian schools. The committee reported that 700 students were registered for school at Cattaraugus and Allegany but that only 237 appeared daily. Committee members never questioned why the truancy rate was so high, what was being taught in the schools, or the teachers' qualifications.[28] The report added: "Many of the Indians are indifferent to the schools and some people oppose their establishment." It further indicated that teachers' salaries were quite low—$7 per week for two sixteen-week sessions—and that "suitable teachers" were needed but difficult to hire at that rate.[29] The report concluded: "These Indian people have been kept as 'wards' or children long enough. They should now be educated to be men, not Indians, and it is the earnest belief of the committee that when the suggestions made, or at least the more important of them are accomplished facts and the Indians of the State are absorbed into the great mass of the American people, then, and not before, will the Indian 'problem' be solved."[30]

Most of the annual reports of the superintendent of public instruction and later those of the state Department of Education well into the 1920s are pro forma and deal merely with physical improvements to school buildings or are statistical in nature. However, some are quite revealing. As early as 1891, Joseph Hazard, longtime superintendent of the Seneca schools, advocated closing the Indian district schools and combining their student populations with those of neighboring white schools. Although never admitting that his rationale was influenced by cost-cutting, he noted that in most of the existing Indian district schools, some non-Indian children were already in attendance and that, as a result, some of the Indian "parents appreciate the benefit derived from the association of the white and Indian children."[31] The next year, G. W. Boyce, the new local superintendent, noted that he faced several problems. First, because the schools were widely scattered over a three-county area, he had not yet visited every schoolhouse, resulting in "the difficulty and expense of supervision." In his report, he stressed that he tried to hire the best teachers he could, "but the best will not go into these Schools for the pay that is allowed."[32]

For more than fifty years after the filing of the *Whipple Report*, administrators continued to complain about the high degree of Indian student absences/truancy. In 1897 the local school superintendent indicated that only 42 percent of the children showed up daily at the district's schools—more at Cattaraugus than Allegany. Consequently, he recommended that a compulsory attendance law be enacted by the state legislature.[33] Two years later he reiterated the call for compulsory attendance, blaming the truancy on Indian migratory habits and the fact that students forced to return from boarding schools had no desire to continue their education by attending reservation district schools. Nowhere was there an admission that the district schools were of poor quality and that the returned students were no longer willing to take another form of regimentation so typical of Indian boarding schools of the era.[34] As late as 1914, the annual report of the commissioner of education went so far as to slander reservation communities, blaming the Indians for their "lack of initiative, ambition, perseverance, judgment, standards of morality, and, above all, leadership." The report continued by insisting that "the ultimate end" of the "educational work on the reservations is the dissolution of tribal relations, the allotment of land in severalty and the assimilation of the people with the white race."[35]

From the mid-1880s to his death in 1913, Andrew S. Draper, the most highly influential educator in New York State at the time, pushed this agenda. His ideas were at the forefront of Indian educational policies in New York State when he served as superintendent for public instruction from 1886 to 1892 and as commissioner of education from 1902 to 1913. In his annual report in 1888, Draper insisted: "The lands should be divided among the Indians and conveyed to them, to be inalienable for a period of twenty five years. They should be made citizens and given the privileges and charged with the obligations and responsibilities which go with citizenship." He added: "The only ambition which is discernible among them is one to perpetuate their national or tribal identity, and they reason that schools and churches are destroying them."[36] Later he fully endorsed the *Whipple Report*'s recommendations and promoted allotment policies, buying out the Ogden claim, and "rewarding" the Senecas with U.S. citizenship.[37] He frequently received press attention as an "expert" on Indian matters. He traveled around the state and to reformers' meetings at Lake Mohonk, pushing his ideas.[38] According to one scholar, Draper specifically urged schooling of children to "instill Anglo-American sociocultural values," which would "facilitate their assimilation into society."[39]

In his annual report for 1888, Draper first described that the school year had been extended to thirty-two weeks in the Indian schools and that the state legislature had put more of taxpayers' money into repairing thirteen district schoolhouses at Allegany and Cattaraugus. He implied, however, that the state was throwing money at the "Indian problem" and that the policy was "not very promising" and did little to "prepare Indian children for citizenship." He then blamed the victim. Draper indicated that the real reason for the "Indian problem" were Indian parents. Incredibly, he suggested that the orphans at the Thomas Asylum were better off than pupils in the state district schools, since they were more controlled and had little contact with outside corrupting family influences.[40]

Superintendent Draper went on to advocate the "breaking up of the reservation system" and the absorption of these "wards into the citizenship of the State." He endorsed the principles of the Dawes Act and its extension to the Hodinöhsö:ni´, who had been excluded from its provisions a year earlier. He justified the idea by referring to the reservations in New York as "nests of uncontrolled vice," where "superstition reigns supreme," where "impure ceremonies are practiced by pagans," where no law operates to protect or punish, where "chronic barbarism" exists, and where too few Indians speak English. Bemoaning this state of affairs, he questioned why it continued to exist "in the heart of our orderly and Christian Nation." Although recognizing state treaty obligations to the Hodinöhsö:ni´ that needed to be fulfilled "in equivalents if not in kind," Draper insisted that "when treaties perpetuate barbarism and protect vice, they should be broken." After all, he maintained, the Hodinöhsö:ni´ "are not to be considered equals; they are unfortunates; they are the children of the State."[41]

The superintendent also pushed the transfer of Indian students from the reservation to Indian boarding schools. By recommending this policy,

Draper was actually proposing cost savings. If the Senecas and other Indians from New York were dispersed to off-reservation federal Indian industrial schools such as Carlisle or private schools subsidized by the federal government such as Hampton, the state would save money and these institutions would be better equipped to put Draper's assimilationist program into effect. It appears to be no coincidence that Hodinöhsö:ni´ enrollment at these two off-reservation boarding schools shot up dramatically after 1888.[42] Meanwhile, from 1878 to 1903, the overall attendance of Indian students at district schools shrank, from 673 to 309.[43] Thus, while Albany officials continued to advocate state jurisdiction over the Indians, the state actually shifted much of its financial responsibilities for educating the Hodinöhsö:ni´ to the federal government.

In an attempt to stop Indian truancy, in 1900 the New York State Legislature enacted a bill introduced by Albert T. Fancher, Salamanca resident and the Republican boss of Cattaraugus County. It called for the compulsory education of Indian children on the Allegany and Cattaraugus Reservations. Parents who failed to comply were to be charged with a misdemeanor and fined $5 a day or jailed for not more than ten days. If they repeated the offense, they could be imprisoned for up to thirty days. Yet Seneca Nation officials failed to enforce this state law in their territories. Student nonattendance at district schools continued to be a vexing problem to local and Albany school administrators for the next several decades.[44]

By the 1920s, the Indian districts, now under the administration of the New York State Department of Education, were classified as "special schools" and headed by Dr. A. C. Hill, who administered Indian education together with schools for delinquents and institutions for neglected, deaf, and blind children. By that time, seventeen Indian district schools were still in operation at Allegany and Cattaraugus, with an approximate enrollment of three hundred students. Hill was also a member of the Everett Commission, a state legislative committee investigating Indian Affairs from 1920 to 1922. Perhaps with the exception of Andrew Draper, Hill put his personal stamp on Indian education policy more than any single state administrator until the board of regents policy statement of 1975.[45]

Much of Hill's report focused on teachers within Indian district schools. By this time, the majority of teachers were underpaid women. He praised Adele Waterman, a Hodinöhsö:ni´ teacher at Cattaraugus, who had resigned due to an illness that subsequently proved fatal. Waterman had promoted the highest welfare of her people, had acted more as a social worker than a teacher, and had not limited her school day to classroom instruction. Hill then discussed the major problem of retaining competent teachers. He maintained that "as soon as a teacher has gained a knowledge of the art and becomes in the truest sense useful, she naturedly seeks a more lucrative position." The Indian schools "therefore become in a sense training schools for teachers."[46]

Hill, as was true of other administrators since the 1880s, advocated that Congress transfer its authority over New York Indians to the state, which he deemed necessary for progress. In the annual report of the New York State Education Department for 1923, he readily admitted the past failures of the district schools but blamed much of the problems on Indian parents for "the retardation of their children" and their failures to cooperate with the compulsory school law of the state. He insisted that past Albany policies—the state's maintaining of schools, paying their road taxes, and providing free health care—had retarded Indian progress by creating dependency and that Indians' failure to prosper was "their own fault." He also blamed the poor level of instruction found at the schools on what he referred to as the lawlessness on the reservations, which he partially attributed to the "propaganda of unrest." In Darwinist fashion, he observed: "*It seems to me the duty of the white race to direct the course of primitive and dependent people during the period of transition to from savagery to civilization*" (emphasis added). Hill added: "The Iroquois are nearer the goal than any other American Indians but still need direction until they are firmly on their feet as self-reliant communities in a cosmopolitan nation."[47]

In his report, Hill also proposed a new policy direction, one that was to be put in place from the 1930s onward in New York State. Hill advocated the closing of all Indian district schools. To him, "the future of Indian education was not in retaining the separate existence of Indian schools forever, but encouraging the mingling with the white race in off-reservation public schools." Citing Richard Henry Pratt, the former superintendent at Carlisle as his authority, he stressed an assimilationist goal—namely, that the future of the Indians was not in retaining the separate tribal existence on reservations forever but the scattering of their populations, which would lead to their mingling with the white race.[48]

In December 1930, New York State commissioner of education Frank P. Graves, in a report to the state legislature, suggested the closing of the six district schools at Allegany and consolidating them into one. Because of the improved roads at Cattaraugus, Graves indicated, it was becoming more feasible to close all the district schools there and "transport the children to a consolidated school," presumably off the reservation. Despite claiming improvements in Indian education in state schools, Graves indicated that only 25 of 936 Indian high school students statewide had earned regents diplomas.[49]

In 1931 the state began to shut down the Indian district schools, a process that continued within the Seneca Nation for several decades. That year, the Thomas Indian School began to accept day students.[50] Teachers in the Indian district schools began leaving for neighboring school districts.[51] By 1953 there were only two schools operating within the Seneca Nation—the Allegany School and the Thomas Indian School. In his report, the commissioner insisted that he was committed "to mak[ing] Cattaraugus Reservation part of the Gowanda district and Allegany part of the Salamanca district."[52] Subsequently, in 1954, the New York State Legislature passed a bill allocating $201,060.86 as "special aid [to school districts] for integration of Indian pupils.[53]

The movement to close the separate Indian district schools also reflected the educational direction of the times, which classified all nonwhites as racial minorities having the same interests and problems. This thinking was later reflected in the historic 1954 Supreme Court decision *Brown v. Board of Education*, which ruled against the principle of separate but equal and challenged the policies of separating children into racially segregated schools. Although the case involved African Americans in Topeka, Kansas, its far-reaching impact was on the racially separate Indian schools across the country. Thus by 1960 only three Indian public schools were operating on reservations in New York, and only one was in Seneca Nation territory.

Seneca educator Alberta Austin's interviews with Seneca elders who attended state district schools from the late 1890s into the 1920s provide us with community insights. In these interviews, there are frequent references to how difficult it was to get to these schools, since no transportation was provided to the children; they walked significant distances in all kinds of weather to attend. From these accounts, it is clear that both the quality of instruction and the discipline at these schools varied considerably.

Some Senecas, such as Caroline Hewitt at Cattaraugus, who attended district school before going off to Hampton Institute in 1905, maintained that she was allowed to speak Seneca. Florence Parker was not disciplined for speaking her native language in a classroom of fifteen students in the same time period in district school 10 school at Allegany. But Seneca Bernice Crouse insisted that before she was transferred to Tunesassa, she was not allowed to speak her native tongue at the school at Steamburg. Around the time of World War I, at district school 7 at Newtown, Elsie Johnson indicated she could talk Seneca only at recess, while Rachel White, at the same school, was spanked and forced to stand in the corner if she spoke Seneca.[54] Esther Sundown, who attended district schools in the 1920s, was more critical. She asserted that besides being physically punished by a teacher, who hit her hands with a board for speaking Seneca, "they [the white teachers] try to change our way of thinking and then they blame us for being savages. It's not true. It's when our people went to the white schools that we learned to be savages."[55] It appears from these interviews, as well as from the author's fieldwork, that when the teachers were Hodinöhsö:ni´ themselves, such as Pauline Seneca, the Cayuga wife of Seneca Nation president Cornelius Seneca, and Flora Heron, Lottie Lay, and Nora Patterson, children appeared to be more geared to learning their lessons in arithmetic, geography, and reading and writing English.[56]

Students in District 7—the Longhouse neighborhood at Newtown—had the most difficulty with the schools.[57] Elsie Jimerson noted that the "Indian people who believed in the Indian way didn't send their children to school." In her class in District 7, she had no history books but concentrated on reading, spelling, arithmetic, and geography.[58] Rachel White reported to Alberta Austin that she was "not taught anything about Indians" in the District 7 school. Although she was punished by her parents for skipping school, she was glad she did so, since she became educated in the ways of the Longhouse. Instead of attending school, she went to the Newtown Longhouse if there were ceremonies in progress.[59]

In 1852, on a much more limited scale than at the numerous state district schools, the Philadelphia Yearly Meeting of Friends, long active in Seneca Country, established a school just outside the boundaries of the Allegany territory near the Pennsylvania border. This Quaker boarding school at Tunesassa, which accepted some day students, continued in operation until 1938. At its height of operation, fifty boys and girls attended the school yearly. The school educated more than twelve hundred girls and boys, including future presidents of the Seneca Nation, during its eighty-six-year history.[60]

In 1798 three Quakers from Philadelphia—Halliday Jackson, Henry Simmons, and Joel Swayne—made their way to Allegany Seneca Country, intent on spreading the Gospel.[61] They were not the first proselytizers of Christianity to enter the world of the Senecas. In the 1650s the Jesuits had made their appearance in what is now western New York; a century later, Presbyterian missionary Samuel Kirkland attempted to establish a mission. Both efforts were to fail. In the early nineteenth century, numerous missionaries, both Presbyterian and Baptist, followed the Quakers' lead and begin to establish missions at Buffalo Creek.

The timing of the 1798 arrival of three Quakers in the Upper Allegany Valley proved to be opportune. In the wake of the "whirlwind," the Seneca term for the American Revolution, Cornplanter had sought help from the outside. In 1797 the Treaty of Big Tree had resulted in major tribal land losses and initiated the reservation period for the Senecas. Fears of land jobbers such as Robert and Thomas Morris, agents of the Holland Land Company and New York State officials, drove the Senecas to look for allies. As the late Anthony F. C. Wallace has elegantly written, the Senecas not only faced the loss of their military strength and prime position at the gateway to the Ohio Country, but were also beset with internal political and social pressures that were to soon give rise to the emergence of their prophet, Handsome Lake.[62]

In the next 140 years, the Quakers were to effect a revolutionary change in Seneca life. Initially their focus was to make converts; establishing schools was "often a means to an end."[63] In the process of proselytizing, they taught arithmetic to encourage entrepreneurial skills and literacy to prevent the Indians from being defrauded of their lands by outsiders. After a decade of contact, the Seneca leadership, including Cornplanter, Handsome Lake and Captain Strong, requested that the Quakers establish a school. After initial setbacks from 1811 to 1813, in 1816 the Quakers sent twenty-one-year-old Joseph Elkinton to establish a school at Tunesassa. The next year the school was shifted, with the help of Thomas Halftown, to Coldspring.[64]

Although the Quakers are often presented as less intrusive than other religious groups in their dealings with the Senecas, this was not really the case, as we have already seen in discussions about the Hicksites and Philip Thomas in the period 1838 to 1848. Historian Jill Kinney, in her carefully presented and balanced account of Quaker education among the Senecas from 1798 to 1852, convincingly writes that the Senecas saw advantages to Friends "helping them negotiate the American legal system when necessary and to write for them when correspondence with whites were desired."[65] Kinney observes that the Quakers at times "did not always understand the implications of their words and actions." However, she maintains that their impact on Seneca culture was nevertheless unmistakable:[66]

> In addition to altering gender roles, promoting private property, teaching and emphasizing the English language, introducing new commodities and ways of thinking, condemning serial monogamy and easy divorce, advocating the keeping of domestic livestock and otherwise altering the food consumed by Senecas, and engaging in many other teachings and activities which had an influence on the Senecas, Quakers most assuredly did seek to alter the religion of the Seneca people in subtle and sometimes not so subtle ways. In the Seneca world, culture and religion were so closely connected that it was difficult to differentiate between them. Their everyday lives involved many things that were done in connection with their belief system, from growing crops to practicing the healing arts. Quakers often promoted ideas directly opposed to Seneca beliefs because of profound cultural misunderstandings between the two groups.

Despite being threatened with death for meddling in Seneca internal political affairs and for advocating changes in Seneca land tenure to fee simple title, Elkinton had slowly gained some acceptance by the 1830s.[67] The Quaker did this in part by mentoring promising Senecas such as Maris and his brother Joseph Pierce. He then hired them as teachers in his school and later encouraged Maris to go further in his education at Dartmouth College, where he was graduated in 1840.[68] Moreover, as a result of land losses, the rapid growth of non-Indian settlement in western New York that encroached on Seneca territory, and the nefarious treaties at Buffalo Creek in 1826 and 1838, more and more Senecas began to seek out ways to fight back, thus giving impetus to the need to master English through Western schooling. Elkinton clearly used this argument to promote his work. Nor was he alone in making this argument; rival Presbyterian missionaries William Hall and Asher Wright were also making this pitch.[69] While competing with the Presbyterians, Elkinton had to deal with a major schism in the Society of Friends that had arisen in the late 1820s. By 1840, the Orthodox Friend Elkinton soon had to contend with the more assertive presence of Philip Evan Thomas and the growing Hicksite Quaker influence at Cattaraugus.[70]

As a result of the lobbying efforts by Elkinton, Robert Scotton, and Josiah Tatum, the Philadelphia Yearly Meeting of Friends established the Tunesassa School in South Valley Township, Cattaraugus County, on lands adjacent to the Allegany Indian Reservation. The school opened on January 2, 1852. What preceded its founding were Quaker discussions with Owen Blacksnake, David and Harrison Halftown, Jacob Shongo, and Robert and Sky Pierce. The representatives of the Philadelphia Yearly Meeting offered the Senecas a free education for their children that was to emphasize literature and promote the mechanical arts. Subsequently, the Philadelphia Yearly Meeting of Friends initially purchased title to 692 acres to establish the boarding school but later sold off 225 acres to local farmers. It cleared 75 of the remaining 467 acres around the school.[71]

The Quaker School was free to all Hodinöhsö:ni´. However, families of students were responsible for their children's clothing and also were responsible for providing firewood for the school.[72] The initial class in 1852 included six girls—Elizabeth, Hannah, and Emma Curry and Laura Bowen, Lucinda Pierce, and Lucy Snow. The school, which first admitted day students who lived nearby, was largely transformed into a coeducational boarding school by the late 1860s. Its enrollment had shot up to thirty students by 1877.[73] Students there performed gender-specific roles, as was true at the Thomas Asylum/School. Male students at Tunesassa were to spend part of the day outside of class doing farmwork to raise crops, which were then sold to support the upkeep of the school. In 1871, during Abner Woolman's administration of the school, twenty-five girls were in attendance and were taught "the proper performance of household duties customary to civilized life, as well as in all branches of school instruction."[74] They were instructed in the "domestic arts" and expected to do the required housework, sewing, and work in the kitchen and laundry room, although some were trained as potential teachers.

In an interview conducted by Charles E. Congdon, a Salamanca attorney and local historian, Alice White, a prominent member of the Wolf Clan from Coldspring who attended the school in the 1870s, recalled that one of the older students there at the time was William C. Hoag, who was in charge of running the gristmill. Hoag would later manage his own farm, become the most prominent farmer (of more than one thousand acres) at Allegany, found the Six Nations Agricultural Society, and help establish the Indian Village at the New York State Fair. He would also become the most powerful individual in Seneca politics from 1890 to his death in 1927.[75] White went on to describe what students faced at the school. Abbie Mott, a stern-looking women, served as the school's principal. White blamed Mott for the horrendous conditions at the school and claimed that the children were "always hungry and dirty" and full of lice. Mott was always cross, and Alice's mother temporarily removed Alice from the school. She noted that when Aaron Dewees and his son took over as principals, conditions improved dramatically and her mother allowed her to return to the school.[76]

Aaron Dewees Jr., who had served two years previously as assistant superintendent, took over the administration of Tunesassa from his father in the mid-1880s, continuing in that capacity until 1894. In February 1886, the boarding school burned to the ground. It was rebuilt with funds provided by the Philadelphia Yearly Meeting and other benefactors. The school was rebuilt with improved facilities, including better dormitories, two classrooms, a dining hall, a kitchen, a pantry, a family parlor, a nursery, sewing rooms, a washroom with indoor plumbing, and lavatories. With new and more attractive facilities, the number of applicants to the school rapidly increased. The school had reached its capacity of fifty-two by 1909.[77]

At a Whipple Committee hearing at held at the school in 1888, Superintendent Dewees described the rebuilt institution. It had a two-story building with a basement and a furnace heating system, two classrooms and a meeting room on the first floor, and sleeping rooms on the second floor, plus farm barns. At the hearing, Dewees also provided a brief history of Quaker educational efforts among the Senecas. Questioned by Judge Oliver Vreeland, the committee's counsel, Dewees then stated that the institution had five other employees: "Two ladies, a matron, assistant and governess." He continued by informing the committee that Quaker educational efforts were initially opposed by many Indians, since the Senecas were afraid of being "led into a trap." However, "some of the chiefs favored the schools."[78] Dewees then answered questions from committee members about the boarding school's rules, curriculum, and teaching methods:[79]

Q. Do you use the English language in the school?

A. . . . We do not allow them to use the English language while here, and each child is required to report each day any infringement of this rule; we have several children who have not broken this rule this term, except when their parents or friends visit them. . . .

Q. Are the children taught anything except book learning?

A. Yes, sir: the girls are instructed in house-work and sewing, and the boys in farming.

Q. Do you teach them trades?

A. No, sir.

Q. How many days in the week do you have school?

A. Every day but Sunday; we have three half-holidays in the week; we have school about five and a half hours each weekday.

Q. Do you have any services on Sunday?

A. On Sundays we have Scripture lessons.

Q. What branches do you teach in the day school?

A. Usually the common branches only, but we have now one studying algebra, who has taken geometry and philosophy.

Q. You teach them Scripture lessons, you say?

A. Yes, sir: we make no effort to teach religious faith except to give moral lessons and lessons from the Scripture, and to lead them to profit by our example, and we make no difference between pagan [a pejorative term for Longhouse] and Christian children.

Q. Are they always able to speak English when they come?

A. No sir: some of them speak no English. . . .

Q. Do some of the children remain only a term or so?

A. A few remain only a term or two, but many of them much longer; I think they would average 16 years old when they leave; those who remain until they are 16 usually remain two or four years longer.

From later interviews conducted and transcribed by Alberta Austin, we have intimate portraits of life at the school, especially in the last three decades before the school's closing in 1938. Perry Jemison from Cattaraugus, who was sent as a young boy to Tunesassa, recalled being homesick, having been separated from his mother for the very first time.[80] Nettie Watt resented that she and other Hodinöhsö:ni´ students were not allowed to speak Seneca at the school. On the other hand, Dema Stoffer acknowledged that, unlike other students there, she was not punished for speaking her native tongue.[81]

Stoffer mentioned that she learned algebra, biology, and Latin there but no knowledge of "Indian culture."[82]

Unlike the state's Indian district schools and the Thomas Indian School, Tunesassa did not inflict corporal punishment on its wayward pupils, a point of criticism against it made by the *Whipple Report*.[83] Florence Lay, who also complained about not being able to speak Seneca at Tunesassa, indicated that there was "a lot of Bible reading" at the school. "We learned a lot of Bible verses, especially when we were punished." According to Lay, the students accused of breaking school rules were locked up in the school's attic and required to memorize passages of the Bible. "Sometime, it took three to four days, but they did feed us. That was their biggest punishment."[84]

Bernice Crouse, who entered the school at nine years of age after transferring from a state-run Indian district school, indicated that her initial coursework, taught by all-white instructors, included reading, writing, and arithmetic and later, in the eighth grade, algebra, biology, and Latin. She was also "taught the proper way of doing things." Crouse was assigned gender-specific chores; she was required to make boys' beds, mend and iron clothes, wait on tables in the dining room, help out in the kitchen, and work two days a week in the bakery to prepare her for housekeeper work in Bradford. Although all students were required to attend church services, Crouse recalled downtime playing "longball" and listening to music on the phonograph.[85] Iva Calendine repeated Crouse's reference to girls' duties at the school and was less positive about her experience at Tunesassa. She objected to having to get up at 5:00 A.M. to make bread and to the staff's strict discipline and regimentation, including required student attendance for one hour of prayer and contemplation at Quaker meetings. Her reaction was to fall asleep during the prayer meetings and run away from the school.[86]

Hazel Pierce Black was the most adamant about her dislike of the school. She had been transferred against her will to Tunesassa from a state district school at Cattaraugus, where she was lucky to have had Pauline Seneca as her teacher. She stated that the level of education at the boarding school was rudimentary compared to what she was taught at the district school. Black, who hoped to become a nurse, reacted against the school's low standards and the gender stereotyping: "Their curriculum was very basic. The training was more to prepare girls for homemaking and the boys for farm work." Later, Black became a student at the Thomas Indian School, where she was forced to catch up because it had higher academic standards than Tunesassa.[87]

By the time of the Great Depression, the school was financially insolvent. To deal with this emergency, the Philadelphia Yearly Meeting decided to rent out the school and its facilities for the summer months as a "resort" for Allegany State Park visitors. Other major problems with the school were revealed in a report commissioned by the Philadelphia Yearly Meeting in 1931. In it, Edith Newlin, the superintendent of the Quaker schools, questioned the outdatedness and relevancy of the institution's curriculum, which emphasized agriculture and neglected changes happening in the new industrial America. She also criticized the austere, highly regimented manner in which the school was administered, which she claimed interfered with learning. Newlin recommended encouraging more friendly interaction between the children and staff, including celebrating birthdays, which hadn't been a part of school life.[88]

In the 1930s, Quaker School administrators faced other criticisms as well. Unlike the Thomas Indian School, there was no physician specifically assigned to handle medical emergencies right through the time the school closed in 1938. The school was cited for violations: the boys' dormitory was below the standards set in New York State's fire code and the institution had no on-site medical facility. These criticisms and the school's bleak financial picture led to Tunesassa's closing. Most of the few remaining Seneca students were transferred to the few remaining Indian district schools, to off-reservation public schools, or to the Thomas Indian School.[89]

The Quaker School nevertheless had left its mark on Seneca life and leadership. Among the students who attended the school were five presidents of the Seneca Nation of Indians: Wilford Crouse, William C. Hoag, Calvin "Kelly" John, Francis Kettle, and Frank Patterson. Other prominent Seneca pupils included Cordelia Abrams, DeForest Billy, Gladys John, Wini Kettle, Dema Stoffer, and Nettie and Harry Watt, all of whom played major roles in fighting federal termination policies, fighting the Army Corps of Engineers' construction of the Kinzua Dam, and/or helping rebuild the Seneca Nation in the quarter century after this massive project was completed in 1966.[90]

In a certain way, keeping their children close to home was a Seneca attempt to hold Onöndawa'ga:' families together, even though parents were quite aware that state district schools and the Quaker School had severe limitations, including inadequate, assimilationist, and even racist instruction. Other Senecas, as described in chapter 7, saw that sending their children to far-off boarding schools would provide them with three meals a day and skills that parents believed were necessary for survival in America's new industrial order. In both instances, families had to make uncomfortable compromises, ones that were to shape the Seneca world for generations.

•◀ 7 ▶•

SENDING THEIR CHILDREN AWAY

Seneca Students at Hampton Institute, 1884–1923

From the mid-1880s onward, numerous Seneca families sent their children away to Indian boarding schools in Pennsylvania and Virginia and as far west as Haskell Indian School in Kansas. Although all schools at that time had an assimilationist focus and Native students often faced harsh discipline and regimentation at these schools, many Hodinöhsö:ni´ parents viewed boarding school education as the only way for their children to escape poverty and the poor instruction provided in the numerous state district schools, as well as the virulent racism surrounding their communities. Schools on or near the reservations were unequipped to meet the needs of Hodinöhsö:ni´ students. While the Thomas Asylum/School provided training in agriculture and carpentry, the institution had a limited capacity of two hundred students and its policies allowed children to attend only to the age of sixteen. The nearby Quaker-run school at Tunesassa, which emphasized Euro-American methods of agriculture, was even smaller, with a capacity of fifty. Consequently, many Seneca and other Hodinöhsö:ni´ parents reluctantly made the difficult decision to send their children away for schooling.

Seneca parents looked around and saw their world rapidly changing. Their concern about their children's future was further prompted by witnessing the unsettled political situations within the Seneca Nation, a situation intensified by the arrival of thousands of non-Indians pouring in after completion of

114

the New York and Erie Railroad in 1850 and the leasing of lands on the Allegany Indian Reservation. Moreover, Senecas on the Cattaraugus Indian Reservation frequently faced outright racism when they traveled to, passed through, or attempted to shop at the nearby town of Gowanda. For generations, Senecas were unwelcome visitors in what John Mohawk, a resident of Cattaraugus, would label an "anti-Indian border town."[1] Thus sending children away from western New York was seen as a viable alternative, a way to insulate them from the harsh realities faced by Senecas at home.

The most famous Indian schools was the United States Indian Industrial School at Carlisle, Pennsylvania, founded in 1879. Most of the approximately ten thousand to twelve thousand Indians who attended spent only a few years there. Despite its fame, one largely based on its legendary football team, the school had minimal academic standards. Until it closed its doors in 1918, a total of 629 Senecas, the third largest contingent of Indian children, attended the school. They included not only enrolled members of the Seneca Nation but children from the separate Tonawanda Band from New York and Senecas from Oklahoma.[2]

Seneca attendance at Carlisle was no accident. Captain Richard Henry Pratt, the institution's founder and superintendent, had been born in Rushford, New York, close to three Seneca Nation territories: Allegany, Cattaraugus, and Oil Spring. Moreover, Glenn "Pop" Warner, the school's legendary football coach, was born in nearby Springville. Among the most famous students to attend the school were four Senecas: Isaac and Hawley Seneca, Nancy Seneca (Phillips), and Bemus Pierce. Both Isaac Seneca and Bemus Pierce were all-American football stars who later played professional football. Pierce was also Pop Warner's assistant coach from 1900 to 1912 and served as head coach when Warner was on leave in 1906. Nancy Seneca became one of the first Indian trained nurses in the United States. Hodinöhsö:ni´ were attracted to the school not just for its athletics but also for its internationally acclaimed music program, especially its marching band. Carlisle closed in 1918.[3]

An analysis of the numerous Senecas at Carlisle is a book in itself. A much more feasible way to study the impact of boarding schools is to focus on the seventy-nine Senecas from Allegany, Cattaraugus, and Cornplanter who attended Hampton Normal and Agricultural Institute, a private secondary school, from 1884 to 1923. The history of Seneca attendance there is an important but neglected story, one that especially influenced educational, political, religious, and social life on the Cattaraugus Indian Reservation.[4] Senecas even established a branch of the Hampton alumni association on this reservation.[5] Importantly, it must be emphasized that Hampton, despite being a private boarding school, founded in 1868, directly influenced the establishment of and the curriculum at the federal Indian boarding school system.

Contemporary Senecas know more about Native Americans at the more famous United States Indian Industrial School at Carlisle, Pennsylvania, than about the numerous Senecas who attended Hampton. Hampton is also a mystery since the school is remembered today as an educational institution for African Americans. Indeed, many Senecas can't comprehend why some of their ancestors were sent away to a segregated "black school" and not to federal Indian boarding schools such as Carlisle. Hampton's importance was first brought home to the author in interviews in the 1970s at Cattaraugus with the Reverend W. David Owl, a well-respected Cherokee missionary among the Senecas who graduated from Hampton in 1915, and by meeting Caroline Glennora Cleopatra (Cleo) Hewitt, a beloved Seneca elder and longtime music teacher on the reservation. She was a child protégé, an accomplished violinist and pianist who devoted her entire life to her Seneca people.[6]

Despite Hampton being a private school for African Americans, the academic/vocational model of its Indian program was later adopted by federal Indian boarding schools throughout the country.[7] Samuel Chapman Armstrong, Hampton's founder, attempted to combine "cultural uplift with moral and manual training." He believed in educating the "head, heart and the hand."[8] Armstrong was a former colonel who had commanded black troops during the Civil War. The son of missionaries who had served the American Board of Commissioners for Foreign Missions in Hawaii, Armstrong became heavily involved after the war with the efforts of the American Missionary Association and the Freedmen's Bureau. In 1868, during Reconstruction, Armstrong established the school to provide industrial education and agricultural instruction for ex-slaves. Although Hampton continued to serve the black community after Reconstruction, Armstrong initiated his Indian program in 1877. Approached by Captain Pratt, Armstrong admitted sixty-two Indians to his Virginia school the following year.[9]

Between 1878 and 1923, 1,451 Native American students—518 girls and 933 boys representing sixty-five tribes—attended Hampton. One hundred fifty-six of these students graduated from the school. One hundred and fifteen Senecas, including Tonawandas, attended the Hampton program. Seventy-nine of the Senecas—forty-two males and thirty-seven females—were from Allegany, Cattaraugus, and Cornplanter. Twelve of these seventy-nine Senecas—seven girls and five boys—were to graduate, a graduation rate second only to that of the Sioux. The first Seneca Nation student to arrive at the school was seven-year-old Annie Scott from Cattaraugus. She had been sent to Hampton in the fall of 1884. Two weeks after her arrival and before her official attendance, she died of measles, allegedly contracted before she reached the school. Perhaps because of this death, it took another eight years for the next Senecas to attend the school.[10]

The Seneca experience at Hampton challenges the often-held assumption that all Native American students who attended far-off boarding schools in the late nineteenth and early twentieth century became lost souls caught between two worlds. The Senecas interacted with students from far different tribes, African Americans, and even some youngsters from overseas. Compared to the numerous Plains and southwestern Indians in attendance, the Senecas and other Hodinöhsö:ni´ were far more savvy about the white world and white educational institutions. Their ancestors had had hundreds of years of experience with the non-Indian world and its efforts to "civilize" them thorough conversion and education. Although some Seneca children, especially the boys, had difficulty adjusting to the school's rules and regulations and the separation from their families back home, their experiences previous to attending Hampton were far different than pupils from Indian nations in the trans-Mississippi West. They were clearly better prepared to deal with change. Unlike the numerous Plains Indians, who had little or no knowledge of English, all the Seneca students were transfers from state district schools, the Thomas Asylum, or the Quaker School and had years of previous education. Before going off to Virginia, a few Senecas had even attended Lincoln Institute in Philadelphia, a school established for blacks during Reconstruction.[11] Although they were encouraged by their ministers, parents, or guardians to attend the Virginia school, they were not forced by a federal Indian agent, although several apparently did not want to leave Seneca Country. Their ancestors had served the Union in the War of 1812 and the Civil War, unlike the sons and daughters of Apache, Cheyenne, Comanche, Kiowa, Navajo, and Lakota warriors who had fought the American frontier army in the 1860s, 1870s, and 1880s.

TABLE 2 **Allegany and Cattaraugus Girls at Hampton Institute**

	Territory	Years	Occupation	Other Information
Alice Armstrong	Cattaraugus	1893–94		Married Isaac Parker
Tillie Bluesky	Cattaraugus	1906–9	Housekeeper; church worker	
Emily Brooks	Cattaraugus	1893–98	Domestic servant; homemaker	Married Hampton attendee Walter Kennedy
Ellen Crouse	Allegany	1892–95	Homemaker; Woman's Christian Temperance Union	Married Joel Scanandore; two daughters attended Hampton
Elsie Doxtator	Cattaraugus	1918–22	Domestic servant	Married Hampton attendee Lewis B. Williams; completed high school in Massachusetts
Lucinda Doxtator	Cattaraugus	1918–22	Homemaker	Married Hampton attendee Thomas Reed
Helen George	Cattaraugus	1893–98; graduate	Teacher	
Francis Halftown	Allegany	1910	Domestic servant; housekeeper	Left due to poor eyesight
Harriet Halftown	Cattaraugus	1908–10	Housekeeper	Married Frank Williams
Irene Halftown	Allegany	1914–16	Housekeeper	Married Bert Harris; died 1921
Caroline Glennora Cleopatra Hewitt	Cattaraugus	1905–12; graduate	Music teacher at Cattaraugus for forty years	Did postgraduate work at Carlisle and Dana Musical Institute; niece of J. N. B. Hewitt, Chester C. Lay, and Theodore F. Jamerson Sr.
Alice (Edita) Jemison	Allegany	1908–12	Teacher	Married Hampton attendee Edison Crouse; left school when government funding ran out in her senior year
Floria Jamison	Allegany	1908–10	Domestic servant; housekeeper	Married Raymond Gordon
Norah Jamison (Redeye)	Cattaraugus	1914–19; graduate	Teacher	
Irene Jemison	Cattaraugus	1892–95; graduate	Teacher; clerk: boys' school matron; farm laborer	

TABLE 2   (*continued*)

	Territory	Years	Occupation	Other Information
Delora John	Cattaraugus	1908–10	Government employee; housekeeper	Married Hampton attendee Eli Beardsley
Jennie Mohawk	Cattaraugus	1906–7	Domestic servant; housekeeper	Married Elgin Golden
Gertrude Pierce	Cattaraugus	1911–12	Domestic servant; cook; homemaker	Married David Mabie
Irene Pierce	Cattaraugus	1913–15	Domestic servant; telegraph operator; homemaker	Married Hampton attendee Henry Webster
Marian Pierce	Cattaraugus	1906–7	Beautician; domestic servant	Married Elias Scanandore; returned home at parents' request
Rose Poodre (Gatwatah)	Cattaraugus	1900–1; Carlisle graduate	Homemaker; farmer	Married Louis LeRoy and later Eli S. Parker
Elsie Scanandore (Cutting Flowers)	Allegany	1921–23		Last Seneca Nation student at Hampton's Indian program; daughter of Ellen Crouse and sister of Lydia Scanandore; completed high school in Pennsylvania
Lydia Scanandore	Allegany	1915–17	Domestic servant; housekeeper	Married Theodore Jackson; sister of Elsie Scanandore
Clara Schingler (Schindlee)	Cattaraugus	1906–7	Domestic servant; housekeeper	Married Hampton attendee Carl Parker
Annie Scott	Cattaraugus	1884; died of measles within two weeks of arrival		
Lettie Scott	Cattaraugus	1892–94; Carlisle graduate	Teacher; Red Cross worker	Teacher in state district schools; expert basket maker

TABLE 2   **Allegany and Cattaraugus Girls at Hampton Institute** (*continued*)

	Territory	Years	Occupation	Other Information
Bernedena Seneca	Cattaraugus	1903–7; graduate	Laborer; domestic servant	Sister of Hampton attendee Elnora Seneca and Cornelius Seneca
Elnora Seneca	Cattaraugus	1897–1900	Laundress; seamstress	Described in school records as a "fine woman"; mother of Alice Lee Jemison; sister of Cornelius Seneca and Hampton attendee Bernedena Seneca; married Hampton attendee Alonzo Lee
Gladys Seneca	Cattaraugus	1916–19	Homemaker; church volunteer	Married Walter Nephew
Florence Silverheels	Cattaraugus	1898–1907; graduate	School matron; domestic servant; homemaker	Married Arthur Wahkolee
Miami Smith	Cattaraugus	1893–94	Laundress	Married Elyn Pierce
Evelyn Snow	Cattaraugus	1910–11	Domestic servant	
Julia Snow	Cattaraugus	1910–13	Teacher	Married S. Renville; died 1919
Mildred Snow	Cattaraugus	1906–7; a transfer from Carlisle	Sunday school teacher; domestic servant	Described in school records as "very religious"; married Philip Garlow
Jennie Tall Chief	Cattaraugus	1906–8	Housekeeper	Married Hampton attendee George Skye; later married George Button
Julia Tall Chief	Cattaraugus	1906–7	Housekeeper	Married Arthur Doxtator
Evelyn Twoguns	Cattaraugus	1905–9; graduate	Teacher; school and hospital matron; clerk	Postgraduate education in business and matron administration at Hampton

Sources: Hampton student files, Hampton University Archives; Brudvig, "Bridging the Cultural Divide"; Brudvig, "Hampton Normal & Agricultural Institute"; Owl, "Hampton Indians at Cattaraugus"; and interviews. Because of privacy concerns, the charts do not include disciplinary actions, such as suspensions or dismissals, brought against specific Senecas.

TABLE 3   Allegany, Cattaraugus, and Cornplanter Boys at Hampton Institute

	Territory	Years	Occupation	Other Information
Lucius Bishop	Cattaraugus	1893–98; graduate	Farmer; machinist; musician	Performer in New York City
Charles Conklin	Cattaraugus	1906		Ran away after twelve days at Hampton
Lawrence Cooper	Allegany	1912; 1914–16	Laborer	
Chester Crouse	Allegany	1892–94	Farmer	Died 1907
Edison Crouse	Allegany	1910–12	Telegraph operator; poultry farmer	Married Hampton attendee Alice Jamison
George Crouse (Jarnoh)	Allegany	1892–97	Farmer; machinist	"Hard worker" according to school records
George W. Crouse	Allegany	1914–15		Ran away after seven months
Samuel George	Cattaraugus	1892–98; machinist certificate; graduate	Machinist	Interview about his Hampton years available online
Wallace George	Cattaraugus	1897–1902; graduate	Machinist	Married Hampton attendee Julia Lee
Bennett Gordon	Allegany	1903–5		
Victor Gordon	Cornplanter	1911		Left after three and a half weeks; wanted to be civil engineer
James Greene	Cattaraugus	1903–7; machinist certificate; graduate	BIA clerk	
Laverne Leonard Jemison	Cattaraugus	1911–12	Laborer in steel mills at Lackawanna	Left because government funding ran out
Harry Jimerson	Cattaraugus	1907–8		Died 1913
Leroy Jimerson	Cattaraugus	1907–10; carpenter's certificate	Carpenter; farmer; foreman of WPA Seneca Arts Project	President of the Iroquois Temperance League; brother of Ray Jimerson

TABLE 3   **Allegany, Cattaraugus, and Cornplanter Boys at Hampton Institute**
(*continued*)

	Territory	Years	Occupation	Other Information
Peter Jimerson	Allegany	1903–5		Later attended Montana State University
Ray Jimerson	Cattaraugus	1911–16; certificate of agriculture	Farmer; supplier of pulp wood and firewood	Twice president and treasurer of the Seneca Nation
Theodore Jimerson	Cattaraugus	1914–18; graduate	Farmer; laborer in machine shop; inventor	Married Hampton attendee Ethel Charles
Wilbur Jimerson	Cattaraugus	1907–8	Farmer; machinist	
Harry John	Allegany	1911–12	Farmer; school employee; laborer on railroad	
Mitchell Johnnyjohn	Cattaraugus	1907–8		
Harvey Johnson	Cattaraugus	1915–16	Postal worker; factory worker	Left because homesick
Francis Kennedy	Cattaraugus	1893–99	Laborer and owner of auto repair shop in New York City	Interview about his Hampton experience available online
Walter Kennedy	Cattaraugus	1893–97	Farmer; general laborer	Married Hampton attendee Emily Banks
Carl (Karl) Lay	Cattaraugus	1908–12	Farmer; disciplinarian at Thomas Indian School; machinist; farmer	Seneca Nation director of adult education and recreation; cousin of Caroline Hewitt
Percival Lay	Cattaraugus	1908–10	Machinist; farmer	Served as engineer in boiler room at Thomas Indian School
William Lay	Cattaraugus	1904–9; graduate of Haskell, 1911	Forest Service employee	Described in school records as a "leader"; marine veteran of World War I
Asher Wright Parker	Cornplanter	1898–99; ran away and joined navy	Bookkeeper; construction worker	

TABLE 3 *(continued)*

	Territory	Years	Occupation	Other Information
Carl Maxwell	Cattaraugus	1910–12	Machinist	Married Hampton attendee Clara Schingler
Nicholson Henry Parker	Cattaraugus	1910–12	Machinist; farmer; carpenter	
James Patterson	Cattaraugus	1892–95	Farmer; laborer	Married Hampton attendee Mattie Sundown
Clarence Plummer	Allegany	1897–1907	Handyman; railroad employee; farmer	
Solomon Scott	Cattaraugus	1906–8	Laborer; farmer	Left due to father's illness
Ulysses Scott	Cattaraugus	1907–9	Farmer	
Wilbur Seneca	Cattaraugus	1911–12	Machinist	
Leroy Snow	Allegany	1909–12	Machinist; farmer	Seneca Nation tribal councilor
Archie Tall Chief	Cattaraugus	1912–13	Laborer; farmer	Left due to needs of family
DeForest Turkey	Cattaraugus	1893–97	Steamboat engineer; musician; farmer; laborer	
Herbert Washburn (Two Clouds)	Cattaraugus	1898–99		
Cephas Watt (Breaks)	Allegany	1911–12	Farmer; railroad employee; lumber mill employee; tribal councilor	Left because government funding ran out
James White	Cattaraugus	1892–93	Farmer; laborer	

Sources: Hampton student files, Hampton University Archives; Brudvig, "Bridging the Cultural Divide"; Brudvig, "Hampton Normal & Agricultural Institute"; Owl, "Hampton Indians at Cattaraugus"; and interviews. Because of privacy concerns, the charts do not include disciplinary actions, such as suspensions or dismissals, brought against specific Senecas.

The first major recruitment of Onöndowa'ga:' started just two years after the massacre of Lakotas at Wounded Knee in 1890. By then, Hampton had a much more rigorous curriculum than federal Indian boarding schools and attracted more highly motivated, more academically accomplished Indian students. The school must also be looked at as a self-contained institution, a safe haven for Native Americans and African Americans to learn both academic and vocational skills to help themselves and their families earn a living and survive in a hostile world. The Senecas' arrival at the school occurred when more blacks were being lynched than at any time in American history. Thus, to both races, Hampton was not merely another boarding school intent on indoctrinating the values of the more powerful white world.

Impoverished Seneca parents knew that Hampton would provide their children with three meals a day, improved medical care, and a more advanced trade school education than was offered at the Thomas Asylum or the Quaker School at Tunesassa. Hampton also had a full-time physician (Martha Waldron) and hospital and was seen as an alternative—a way for parents to protect their children. Deaths of students at Hampton from any cause were rare after 1890. Tuberculosis was ravaging Indian Country and depopulating reservations, but not one of the Seneca children died of this disease at Hampton.[12] Although the Virginia school was not completely free of the race hate found in the larger society, the students were more isolated from the virulent prejudices that existed at the time in western New York.

While the Hampton founder believed that racial minorities should accept mainstream American values, Armstrong's motivation was "not simply to promote a form of social control."[13] He stressed the need to inculcate his charges, whether black or Indian, with the gospel of work and the dignity of labor, combined with Christian teachings. Through discipline and hard work, he and his successor/protégé, Hollis Burke Frissell, would instill the Protestant work ethic and produce self-reliant individuals—farmers, mechanics, tradesmen, domestics, nurses, teachers, and school matrons—since the past enslavement of blacks and the so-called "savagery" (Armstrong's word) of the Indians had to be overcome. They had to be led to "civilization" through a Hampton-styled education, one that combined "cultural uplift" with moral and manual training.[14]

Armstrong and Frissell were also practical administrators and not entirely utopian dreamers. They saw that by adding the Indian program to Hampton, they would also be able to secure moneys from the federal government for each Native American student in attendance, which would bolster the institution's financial health. It should be pointed out that, unlike Indian students from the trans-Mississippi West, whose attendance at the school was subsidized by the federal Office of Indian Affairs, Hodinöhsö:ni´ children did not get tuition and subsidies for room and board until 1893 and initially depended upon the philanthropy of private donors.[15] Thus it is not surprising that Seneca enrollment at the school sped up after that date and declined after 1912, when the federal government slashed the subsidy for Hampton's Indian program. At its height, congressional appropriation for the education of Native Americans at the school was more than $200,000.[16]

Native Americans were enrolled in several separate divisions of Hampton and taught in very different ways, since they entered with different levels of education and English language abilities. Some, mostly western Indians with little or no knowledge of English, were admitted to a basic course of literacy and introduced to "obedience, courtesy and other qualities." A second level, preparatory to admission to the normal school, included study of arithmetic, drawing, economics, geography, history, physiology, singing, reading English texts, public speaking, and learning to write grammatically. The normal school, or third level, actually equivalent to high school, included course work in "practical" knowledge in arithmetic and science that could be applied to various occupations and trades. There was also an emphasis on civics and economics to prepare Indians for U.S. citizenship in the future. The more successful students at the senior level, both male and female, were also trained in the basics of teaching methods and entered a special program at the Whittier elementary school, formerly the Butler School, at Hampton.[17]

While academic course work in English, geography, history, mathematics, and science was coeducational, agricultural and industrial training was exclusively for the boys, starting from the lowest division of education at Hampton onward. To gain an appreciation of "the habits of regular industry" and leave Hampton "with a knowledge of some honorable occupation" by means of which they could "earn a living in a civilized community," the boys worked part of each day as apprentices, learning practical knowledge of blacksmithing, carpentry, farming, harness making, livestock management, printing, and shoemaking.[18] During the summer months, some of the boys were sent off to gain practical agricultural experiences on the farm at the Hampton's annex in Massachusetts.[19] To be sure, Hampton's administrators viewed labor on this working farm or on "outings" as a way advance acculturation of the Indians into the dominant white capitalist world of the late nineteenth century.[20] Armstrong's "Technical Round, introduced first in 1886," provided the Indians general training in various trades such as carpentry and blacksmithing.

Although the girls studied the same academic subjects as the boys, their instruction at boarding schools such as Hampton had a quite different focus and was hardly equal to that of the males.[21] Principal Frissell's report for 1894 indicated that Indian girls were instructed in "domestic science and etiquette." They were taught housework, seamstress skills including dressmaking and mending clothes, and cooking and baking.[22] Thus, although a few of the Seneca girls became teachers, it was no coincidence that most of them ended up working as domestics and seamstresses after they left the school.[23]

To illustrate a Hampton Indian boy's curriculum, we can examine the course work that W. David Owl undertook in the last four years before his graduation in 1915. To satisfactorily complete his first year, he had to pass general science, literature, blacksmithing, and trade school mathematics. The second year he took botany and soils, literature, blacksmithing II, physical geography, physics, and mechanical drawing; the third year literature, chemistry, American history, geometry, animal husbandry, and mechanical drawing; and finally, in the fourth year, algebra, psychology, economics, wheelwrighting, and shoemaking.[24]

Armstrong and Frissell set out to train the Indians for American citizenship and suffrage, and to value private ownership of property, the goal espoused by the majority of reformers of Indian policy in the post–Civil War era. Much like federal Indian boarding schools, Hampton required military-style discipline for every male student, who were dressed in uniforms and performed precision drills on the parade grounds.[25] Both male and female students, black and Indian, were included in the school's celebrations of Columbus Day and the "discovery" of America and Thanksgiving, where they were told how "noble" Indians such as Squanto, Samoset, and Massasoit had helped the Pilgrim "fathers" found America. Hampton Indian students, both girls and boys, were featured performers commemorating the four hundredth anniversary of the "discovery" of America at Chicago's Columbian Exposition. They also were required participants in the Columbia Roll Call pageant on Indian Citizenship Day, February 8, which celebrated congressional passage of the Dawes General Allotment Act of 1887, legislation that contributed to the significant alienation of tribal lands in the trans-Mississippi West but that provided Native Americans a route to U.S. citizenship.[26] Because of her expertise on the violin, Cleo Hewitt was a featured musician at several Dawes Act commemorations.[27]

Although Hampton was not church affiliated, it did receive funding from missionary societies, and its program had more of a religious underpinning than Carlisle's, since Pratt had a disdain for missionaries. Historian Jon Brudvig, who has written the best study of Hampton's Indian program, observes that unlike Pratt's uncompromising belief in the need to rapidly transform the Indians, Armstrong believed in gradualism. At Hampton students took course work on the Bible, were encouraged to say their prayers before dining and bedtime, and were required to attend chapel as well as Sunday services. Christianity permeated student life and the school promoted proseltyzing.[28] Importantly, unlike Captain Pratt's focus at Carlisle, students at Hampton were encouraged to recognize their responsibilities as Christians to serve the group and society as a whole, not just to further individual pursuits. These same values were quite compatible with old Indian beliefs. Religious affiliation also appears to have affected the selection process for admission to the school. It was no coincidence that almost all the Seneca attendees were members of churches on the Allegany, Cattaraugus, or Cornplanter territories, with the largest number being associated with the United Mission, the Presbyterian church at Cattaraugus. In addition, M. F. Trippe, the Presbyterian missionary at Allegany, aided in the recruitment of Seneca children.[29]

Two non-Indian Hampton employees, initially Clara M. Snow and later Caroline Andrus, undertook recruitment trips to Seneca Country. In 1892 Snow brought twenty-five Native American youngsters from New York, including eight Seneca Nation children—Lettie Scott, Chester and George Crouse, Samuel George, Irene Jemison, James Patterson, and James White from Cattaraugus and Ellen Crouse from Allegany—to Hampton.[30] Snow was a teacher of arithmetic and Bible studies, while Andrus was the director of the school's Indian program.[31] In several articles for the *Southern Workman*, Hampton's magazine, Snow described her recruiting trips. From her writings, it is clear that she was aided in her efforts by the Foreign Missionary Board of the Presbyterian Church and by the Philadelphia Yearly Meeting of Friends, the two Protestant sects most historically tied to the Senecas.[32]

In her first journey to recruit Senecas in northwestern Pennsylvania and southwestern New York, Snow wrote that she was "surprised by the eagerness of the Indians for education." She claimed that on "every reservation parents begged me to take their children." The Hampton recruiter insisted that these same parents recognized the need to send their children away from what she saw as corrupting influences and the need to provide both the girls and boys "with restraint and wise management."[33] Besides having much more expansive course work than federal Indian boarding schools at the time, Hampton was also more selective in admitting students. On her recruitment trips to Cornplanter and Tunesassa, Snow indicated that her intent was to give those students selected the advantage of Hampton's first-class trade school education. Unlike Captain Pratt, who envisioned that the educated Indians at Carlisle would not "return to the blanket," she referred to those admitted to Hampton as future tribal leaders. To comfort those not chosen, Snow suggested that those Senecas who had not met Hampton standards would still have the opportunity to go to the Carlisle or Lincoln Institute.[34] To uphold Hampton's academic standards emphasized by the recruiters, the school administrators instituted an admissions test in 1898.[35]

Some Seneca parents definitely viewed Hampton admission as an opportunity and as a place of refuge for their youngsters. Their children's education in the state district schools was inferior, and the Quaker School at Tunesassa was often too full to admit more students. For the most part, until the early 1930s, the Thomas Asylum/School, which had better instruction, was open only to the most financially desperate or orphans and had to release its students to the world at age sixteen. According to a reading of Seneca applications to Hampton, both the Quaker School and Thomas were feeder schools for Hampton.[36]

With both a sense of apprehension and adventure, Cleo Hewitt and the other Seneca children made their journey to Dixie. Youngsters went off and struggled together in their strange new surroundings. Some of these children were retracing their fathers' and grandfathers' steps, since many Senecas had fought for the Union army in Virginia during the Civil War three decades earlier. Hampton student Evelyn Twoguns's father, Noah, had served in the Union army before he had served as a Seneca councilor.[37] Just as the Civil War had shaped their ancestors' lives, the Hampton experience was to permanently affect Seneca youngsters, for good and also for bad. Undoubtedly, some of the pain of separation from home was lessened by the large numbers of Hodinöhsö:ni´ in attendance at the school, especially Oneidas, who numbered 193 students. To help them adjust to their new surroundings, Charles Doxon, an Onondaga student, had established a Hodinöhsö:ni´ club there in the 1880s.[38]

Cleo Hewitt was among the thirty-seven Seneca girls at Hampton. Half of them attended during the first decade of the twentieth century. Seven from Cattaraugus—Hewitt, Helen George, Norah Jamison, Irene Jemison, Bernedena Seneca, Florence Silverheels, and Evelyn Twoguns—received academic degrees. Twoguns returned to take postgraduate work at Hampton. It should be pointed out that the loss of federal government funding and family emergencies at home prevented several others from completing their education at Hampton; two were graduated from Carlisle, and several others later completed schooling elsewhere. One girl was forced to leave because of failing eyesight. Three were punished or expelled: one suspended for leaving her outing without permission, one disciplined for interracial flirting with a white chauffeur, and one dismissed for being ill and for her "unsatisfactory conduct."[39]

As in many Indian boarding schools at the time, both girls and boys were sent to work in the outside world, to learn white society's ways, in a determined effort by school administrators to "civilize" the Indian students. These outings varied, resulting in everything from lasting friendships to outright exploitation.[40] W. David Owl was sent to work at Mohonk Mountain House to learn about the mores and manners of America's elite. At this leading resort, where the annual Lake Mohonk Conference of Friends of the Indian and Other Dependent Peoples was held, Owl established the first recreational program and a lifetime connection with the family of the owners of the resort.[41]

Other outings were not so smooth or were hardly "appreciated" by the Seneca students. One Seneca girl decided to absent herself from her outing and was disciplined.[42] Moreover, there was a clear exploitative element to the program. Several Seneca girls were sent to "Millionaires' Row," the mansions of the superrich along Rhode Island Avenue in Newport, Rhode Island, to serve as domestics. Elnora Seneca was paid $1.50 per week for three and a half months of servant duties in an effort to "civilize" her.[43] Evelyn Twoguns worked there for two summers and was paid $2.50 per week for four months to sweep and dust the mansion and help the laundress. In the required performance report on Evelyn's outing, Mrs. W. J. Easton, her hostess, described her as having "excellent spirit, conduct, [and] neatness" and commented that she was "quick and quiet." Although Twoguns "had the *privilege* of going wherever she wished to" (emphasis added), she did not, since she spent the time caring for a sick employee. Perhaps in an effort to justify the poor wage scale, Easton added that she gave Evelyn "shoes, a ring, and some extra money when we had company." She concluded that she was very pleased with Evelyn.[44] Thus Twoguns, who later worked as a teacher and school matron in Indian schools and as a matron in Indian hospitals in Nebraska, New Mexico, and Oklahoma, was trained, like so many other black and Native women who attended Hampton, to be a domestic servant for America's elite.

Cleo Hewitt's outings reveal much about her independent spirit. In her first outing, she tolerated the experience and even praised her sponsors. She was accepting of her low status and low pay. In 1908 and 1909, her responsibilities were to do general housework—namely to iron, sew, and wash bottles at homes at Great Barrington and Monterey, Massachusetts, and in Plainville, Connecticut. Her pay was between $9 and $10 a month for approximately three months.[45] However, in 1910 she was assigned to the home of Grace B. Lawton, on Millionaires' Row in Newport. Hewitt appears to have resisted her employer at every turn, even though she was given a slight raise, to $12 a month. Lawton's evaluation was scathing: "If you have any jurisdiction over the future of Carolyn—do not suggest housework of any kind. She has no interest in it and is unobserving"; nor "is she strong enough for housework of any kind." It may be suggested that Hewitt, an accomplished musician, an orphan who had survived the academic rigor of Hampton, and now a young woman of twenty, was clearly fed up with being an exploited servant.[46]

In October 1905 Hewitt had entered Hampton, where six other Senecas were in attendance. She was from an impressive lineage and was well versed in the Seneca language and in herbalism. Born at Cattaraugus in 1890, she was the daughter of Hattie Lee and Aaron Hewitt. Her mother, a Cattaraugus Seneca, was a teacher, and her father, a Tuscarora, was a musician. One of her uncles was Chester C. Lay, the famous Indian bandleader who had been elected president of the Seneca Nation in 1889. She was taught the violin by another relative, Sylvester C. Lay Jr., who had been on the council of the Seneca Nation. J. N. B. Hewitt, the famous anthropologist of Tuscarora ancestry at of the Bureau of American Ethnology at the

Smithsonian Institution, was her paternal uncle, whom she visited from time to time in Washington, D.C.[47]

In 1893, when Hewitt was three, her mother died; her father died in 1901. Consequently, she went to live with her aunt, Martha Jamerson, the wife of Theodore F. Jamerson Sr., another musician, who had been elected president of the Seneca Nation in 1897. Martha became her legal guardian. For seven years, beginning in 1897, she attended a state district school at Cattaraugus and volunteered as a teacher's helper at the Thomas Asylum/ School, where her family members served on the board of managers. Prior to her attendance at Hampton, for a brief time she also attended an intermediate school in Angola, New York. On Hewitt's Hampton application form, she indicated that she wanted to become a kindergarten teacher because she liked helping out at Thomas.[48]

After her graduation from Hampton, she spent a year at Carlisle taking business courses. One teacher there encouraged her to go to a conservatory to do postgraduate training on the violin. However, she had no financial resources to pursue her dream. Instead she sought employment as a matron and a teacher and gave private violin and piano lessons.

Hewitt's first teaching position was at the district school on the Tonawanda Reservation in 1913. The following year she served as a matron at the Thomas Indian School and later that year secured a teaching position in an off-reservation school at Indian Falls, New York, just off the Tonawanda Reservation. From 1915 through 1919, she taught on the Cattaraugus Indian Reservation in district schools 4 and 2 and supplemented her meager salary by giving violin lessons to children in the community. For four years in the 1920s, she was a resident at the prestigious Dana Musical Institute in Warren, Ohio, where she did advanced training on the violin. Hewitt continued to give private music lessons to support her postgraduate education there. She returned to Cattaraugus in 1926, securing a permanent position as the music teacher at the Thomas Indian School. For the next three decades, she—along with her dearest friend, Pauline Seneca—taught at the school. She also gave private piano and violin lessons for many years in the Cattaraugus territory.[49] When I knew her in the 1970s, she was hard of hearing and could no longer enjoy listening to music.

Along with Evelyn Twoguns and Florence Silverheels, Hewitt was the most accomplished Seneca girl at Hampton. Her grades improved every year, with one exception. She repeatedly had problems passing mathematics, but on the whole, her teachers evaluated her highly. Teacher Edith Dobie indicated that she had ability, was succeeding in her studies, and had "excellent moral character." This was not surprising since she was a devout Presbyterian, a member of the United Mission Church at Cattaraugus, and a regular churchgoer.[50]

Forty-two Seneca boys—twenty-nine from Cattaraugus, eleven from Allegany, and two from Cornplanter—attended Hampton and had quite different experiences there and afterward. One five graduated, although several received agricultural and machinist certificates. One other later graduated from Haskell. Seven married women who had attended Hampton. Like their female counterparts, most male Senecas who attended Hampton eventually had more than one occupation in their lifetime. The school's records list ten as becoming machinists, plus seven laborers, eight farmers, three railroad employees, two musicians, two carpenters, one ironworker, one disciplinarian at the Thomas Indian School (Carl Lay, Cleo Hewitt's cousin from Cattaraugus), one clerk in the Bureau of Indian Affairs, one steamboat engineer, one Forest Service employee, one telegraph operator, and one owner of an automobile repair shop in New York City (Francis Kennedy).[51]

Apparently, Seneca boys had a more difficult time adjusting than the girls.[52] Victor Gordon from Cornplanter found the academic program lacking at Hampton, since he wanted to study engineering, and he left after a month at the school.[53] Both Archie Tallchief and Solon Scott left because of the needs of their families back home at Cattaraugus.[54] Asher Wright Parker from Cornplanter ran away from the school and joined the navy in 1898.[55] One Cattaraugus Seneca left Hampton because of "the want of interest," while another left because he was suffering from homesickness. Seven Senecas—16 percent—were dismissed for poor academic performance or for school infractions. One student from Allegany was told not to return to Hampton Institute unless he could "show better spirit in class," while another from the same territory was expelled for "unsatisfactory conduct." One Cattaraugus student was expelled for drinking alcohol, while another from the same territory was dismissed for "using vulgar language at the dinner table." Still another was dismissed because he had impregnated a Hampton coed.[56]

Prominent Senecas who attended included Ray Jimerson, twice elected president and treasurer of the Seneca Nation in the 1920s and 1930s.

Jimerson had arrived with his chums Laverne Leonard Jemison, Wilbur Seneca, and Cephas Watt in 1911.[57] His older brother LeRoy had earned a certificate in carpentry from the school in 1910. In 1916 Ray received a certificate in agriculture, but he was forced to leave the school before graduation because of his father's illness.[58] Later, in the late 1920s and early 1930s, Jimerson led the fight for Seneca hunting and fishing rights that had been restricted by state and federal courts and in legislative rulings.[59]

In Armstrong's and later Frissell's thinking, black students at Hampton would help lead the Indians to "civilization." To further these efforts, Armstrong felt, the more accomplished black students would serve as models of behavior, tutor English, teach certain skills, emphasize neatness, and enforce discipline. Advanced-level blacks would lead workshops, lead classes, and even command the required military drills for the separate Indian companies at the school. The "experiment" enforced separate seating at dining hall tables and in chapel. American Indian male students resided in a dormitory named the Wigwam, while black males were housed in separate residence halls. In contrast, at times Native American women were assigned black roommates.[60] Owl, a proud graduate of the school in 1915, claimed that while "the races were in a measure separate, the more basic school activities united into one big student body." He maintained that "the general assemblies, social gatherings, religious meetings . . . were all open to Indian students." Owl added: "A few of our Indian girls [one Seneca Nation student out of thirty-seven] married colored men and some of them developed congenially integrated families of culture. I know of no Indian male students who married a Negro girl."[61]

As the school records show, not all Senecas felt comfortable attending a school whose primary mission was to educate African Americans.[62] Fights broke out between black and Native students, but historian Donal Lindsey claims that despite racial tensions, there was for the most part an apparent lack of conflict between the two groups on campus: "Whenever the Hampton system pushed a black or Indian further than he could accommodate himself, some official of the institute could usually heal the fissure by pointing to the miseries of the other race."[63]

Some of the more academically accomplished blacks served as resident advisers in the separate Indian dormitories. They included Hampton's most famous graduate, Booker T. Washington. The famous educator at first opposed the admission of Indians to Hampton, fearing it would limit educational opportunities for blacks at the school. Thirty-five years later, when the Indian program was threatened with the loss of its federal subsidies, Washington, then principal of Tuskegee Institute, testified in favor of Hampton's commitment to educating Native Americans.[64] According to my interview in the 1970s with W. David Owl, Washington would periodically return to Hampton and come into the all-Indian dormitories, tell stories with moral lessons, and recite prayers with the children before they fell asleep.[65]

Hampton's importance to the Senecas is clearly documented. One Hampton alumna-alumnus couple—Ellen Crouse (Allegany Seneca) and Joel Scanandore (New York Oneida)—sent their two daughters, Elsie and Lydia, to the school. Bernedena Seneca followed in her sister Elnora's footsteps, as did their cousin Jacob Seneca, a Cayuga, in attending Hampton. Hodinöhsö:ni´ classmates such as Evelyn Twoguns, Cleo Hewitt, and Rogene Pierce (Cayuga) wrote to teachers and administrators, attended class reunions, and even made financial contributions to Hampton.[66] Twoguns sent her condolences when Booker T. Washington died and wrote to prospective students, endorsing the school and telling them that the teachers at Hampton would care more for them than those at the Indian schools of the day. In 1937 Twoguns indicated that she couldn't attend the reunion that year but that she had not "forgotten dear old Hampton."[67] Not surprisingly, about 30 percent the girls who attended the Virginia school married former Hampton students.[68]

Cleo Hewitt frequently wrote to the Hampton staff. In one letter, she indicated that she hoped more Indians would be encouraged to take up teaching as a career, since students on reservations would respond to them better than to non-Indian teachers. In another, she claimed that she was a faithful reader of the *Southern Workman* and that she had hung a picture of Hampton on her classroom wall in her school at Cattaraugus. The staff's admiration for Hewitt was mutual. To this day, Hampton University has a photograph of Hewitt and her students at Cattaraugus in 1918 hanging in its museum.[69]

In the 1912 budget for the year 1913, Congress, which had appropriated $167 per Indian student, reduced its funding to Hampton by more than 90 percent. Federal funding was reduced to $1,690.85 for Hampton's Indian program, and Indian student enrollment dropped 46 percent during the 1913–14 academic year. Only eight Seneca girls and four Seneca boys continued to attend after the 1912–13 academic year ended.[70] Hampton faced increased competition for students, staff, and funding from Indian boarding schools as well as with other black schools around the nation. Fewer and fewer Native American students coming to the Virginia school meant fewer intertribal friendships on Hampton's campus; Native students became more isolated. Indian boarding schools, especially Haskell, benefited by becoming more attractive to numerous Hodinöhsö:ni´.[71]

The decline of Hampton's Indian program was caused by other factors as well. Racism clearly entered the picture, especially during Woodrow Wilson's presidency. By 1915 the Ku Klux Klan had reappeared. According to historian David Wallace Adams, even though there was a limited association between the races, critics "saw in Hampton's biracial experiment a serious breach of the 'color line'" and a waste of American taxpayer money. Even though Booker T. Washington and Indian alumni came to the program's defense, the times of the paternalistic white reformers of Reconstruction had changed.[72] Moreover, Frissell, a strong advocate of the Indian program, died in 1917. Some involved in promoting the Indian program moved on to other positions outside Hampton, while others retired. With the loss of federal funding, some administrators at Hampton clearly lost interest in educating Native Americans, which was always a secondary objective to the school's original mission.[73]

During the last year, 1922–23, when all federal funding ended, two Senecas—Lucinda Doxtator of Cattaraugus and Elsie Scanandore ("Cutting Flowers") of Allegany, the daughter of Seneca alumna Ellen Crouse—were among the remaining eleven pupils in the program. Both girls finished their education in a high school in Massachusetts.[74] With the resignation of Caroline Andrus, the head of the Indian program, and the dismissal of two longtime faculty members, this experiment in Indian education came to an end in 1923.[75]

Hampton's Indian program had a great impact. Its founding in response to Richard Henry Pratt's urging directly led to congressional funding for the education of American Indians, however limited and assimilationist it was. Armstrong's willingness to initiate his "experiment" also led Pratt to establish Carlisle the next year. Other off-reservation federal Indian boarding schools—including Chilocco, Flandreau, Haskell, Pipestone, Phoenix, and Sherman—soon followed. According to Brudvig, these boarding schools "copied Hampton's blend of academic and vocational training." He concluded: "Hampton's greatest legacy was its American Indian alumni."[76] This was especially true at Cattaraugus. Importantly, the trials, tribulations, and successes of Senecas and other Hodinöhsö:ni´, both as students and alums, are preserved in one of the great archival collections on Native Americans, housed today at Hampton University.

Despite exposure to the white world's education at state district schools, the Quaker School, or faraway boarding schools such as Hampton, nothing could prepare these students for the immediate challenges that faced them, their families, and the Seneca Nation as a whole. They now had to face federal, state, and local efforts to confirm and extend long-term leasing at Allegany, to allot Seneca lands on both reservations to facilitate sales to non-Indians, and to acquire tribal resources. These concerns became the overwhelming focus of their attention well into the twentieth century.

FIGURE 6. Asher Wright. As the Presbyterian missionary to the Senecas, first on the Buffalo Creek Reservation and later at Cattaraugus, Wright, a noted linguist and scholar, was a major force in Seneca life from 1831 to his death in 1875. Besides promoting Christianity, he served as adviser, educator, notary, physician, and scribe. He and his wife, Laura, founded the Thomas Asylum for Orphan and Destitute Indian Children in 1855, and he served as its superintendent for two decades. *Courtesy Buffalo History Museum Library.*

FIGURE 7. Laura Wright. Serving with her husband on the Buffalo Creek and Cattaraugus Reservations, Wright was especially influential among Seneca women. She served as an adviser and educator at the Thomas Asylum and worked as the Indian agency's assistant physician at Cattaraugus after her husband's death. *Reprinted from Harriet S. Caswell,* Our Life among the Iroquois Indians *(Boston: Congregational Sunday School and Publishing Society, 1892).*

FIGURE 8. Dr. Albert D. Lake (1846–1923). Lake was the physician at the Thomas Asylum/School and the major health-care advocate for the Senecas and other Hodinöhsö:ni´ from 1880 until 1922. *New York State Archives.*

FIGURE 9. Girls' dormitory complex, Thomas Asylum, Cattaraugus Reservation, 1890s. Albert Lake saw these wooden-framed dormitories as firetraps and successfully lobbied for brick replacements. *New York State Archives.*

FIGURE 10. The Thomas Indian School complex showing Stewart Hall and other buildings, circa 1910. By this time, many of the buildings were of brick construction because Albert Lake had advocated it as a safety precaution against fires. *New York State Archives.*

FIGURE 11. Monument honoring Captain Richard Henry Pratt on the grounds of the former United States Indian Industrial School at Carlisle, Pennsylvania. Pratt, a former Union officer in the Civil War and an officer in frontier wars, founded the federal Indian boarding school in 1879. As superintendent there until 1904, he had a major influence on its students, curriculum, and military-styled discipline. More than six hundred Senecas from New York and Oklahoma attended the school before it closed in 1918. *Photograph by Donald Quigley.*

FIGURE 12. Nancy Seneca (Phillips). A graduate of the United States Indian Industrial School at Carlisle, Pennsylvania, in 1897, Seneca went on to attend the nursing program at Philadelphia's Chirurgical Hospital (now part of the University of Pennsylvania). For several decades she worked as a nurse and matron for the Indian Service. She later returned to help her Cattaraugus Senecas cope with the influenza pandemic of 1918–19. *Courtesy Cumberland County Historical Society, Carlisle, Pennsylvania.*

FIGURE 13 (*opposite, left*). Bemus Pierce in his football uniform. Pierce and his brother Hawley were legendary all-American football players at the United States Indian Industrial School at Carlisle, Pennsylvania. He later played professional football and coached, including at Carlisle in 1906 when Glenn "Pop" Warner was on leave. His brother Frank was a successful long-distance runner. As a member of the U.S. track and field team, Frank participated at the 1904 Olympics in Saint Louis. *Courtesy Cumberland County Historical Society, Carlisle, Pennsylvania.*

FIGURE 14 (*opposite, right*). Samuel Chapman Armstrong, founder and principal of Hampton Normal and Agricultural Institute. Armstrong established this private boarding school to educate freed African American slaves in 1868. From 1878 to 1923, the school also admitted American Indians, including seventy-nine Senecas from Allegany, Cattaraugus, and Cornplanter. Reprinted from Edith Armstrong Talbot, *Samuel Chapman Armstrong: A Biographical Study* (New York: Doubleday, Page, 1904).

144

FIGURE 17. Caroline Glennora Cleopatra Hewitt wearing a sweetgrass basket hat on a visit to see her uncle J. N. B. Hewitt, a renowned anthropologist of Tuscarora ancestry at the Smithsonian's Bureau of Ethnology, 1913. Taught the violin by her uncle Sylvester C. Lay Jr., Hewitt was a child musical prodigy. After graduating Hampton Institute, she taught for many years at the Thomas Indian School and also gave private lessons at Cattaraugus Indian Reservation. *Smithsonian Institution National Anthropological Archives, image NAA GN00985A.*

FIGURE 15 (*opposite, top*). Hampton Institute campus seen from Hampton Inlet, leading from Chesapeake Bay to the James River. *Photograph by Frances Benjamin Johnston, circa 1899–1900. Library of Congress, image LC-DIG-ppm sca-17491.*

FIGURE 16 (*opposite, bottom*). Native American male students had their own separate residence hall at Hampton Institute, called the Wigwam. *Courtesy Wisconsin Historical Society, image 26477.*

•◄ 8 ►•

PICK YOUR POISON

Unlike many millions of acres in Indian Country in the trans-Mississippi West, the lands of the Seneca Nation of Indians were never subdivided under the Dawes Act of 1887 or under subsequent congressional legislation. Individual Senecas have plowshare rights, known in law today as restricted fee title, on lands they occupy on the Allegany and Cattaraugus Indian Reservations. Onöndawa'ga:' cannot sell these lands to non-Senecas since ultimate title rests with their nation.[1] In the years between the Civil War and World War I, the Senecas escaped being included in provisions of federal allotment legislation. The Senecas understood that if Congress ever formally approved allotment and awarded unrestricted feet patents separate from their Indian nation's control, their lands could be subject to state and local taxation and foreclosure for nonpayment. And, like any non-Indian-owned property, the lands could be sold off.

The Senecas avoided this fate largely because of the existence of the Ogden preemptive claim to Seneca Nation lands, *the* reason the Allegany and Cattaraugus Reservations were exempted from the Dawes Act.[2] If these lands were allotted and subsequently sold off, all land sales had to be to the heirs of the Ogden Land Company, since the company retained the first right of purchase. By 1887, the heirs of the "Ogden proprietors" were numerous and scattered all over the world. Because of the Congress's reluctance to spend millions of dollars searching for the company's rightful heirs and then buy out their claims, the movement to allot the two reservations failed.[3]

From the Civil War until World War I, both Washington and Albany officials, pressured by white lessees on Allegany and their political representatives, grappled with the issue of buying out the company's preemptive right. Congressional and state legislators repeatedly introduced bills to extinguish the claim. Despite the federal and state governments' recognition of the legality of the claim, the Senecas and their supporters obfuscated the issue. Because they considered the federal treaties of 1826 and 1838 to be fraudulent, they questioned whether the Ogdens had any existing rights to their land.[4] Meanwhile, the agents representing some of the Ogden heirs made it difficult for a settlement, demanding more moneys from Washington than a conservative Congress wanted to spend. Thus the impasse helped the Senecas resist every effort to allot their lands.

Leasing pressures were directly related to the push for allotment.[5] Early in 1865, the New York State Legislature passed bills confirming illegal leasing arrangements made between non-Indians and Senecas.[6] When efforts at confirming all leases at the state level failed, the lessees and their representatives began to seek a solution at the federal level, which was opposed by the Senecas. On February 7, 1868, Israel Jemison, Saul Logan, and Peter Johnson sent a petition to the New York State Legislature complaining about the tribal council's failure to prevent trespassing by whites on Seneca territories and to regulate leasing by some of these outsiders. They specifically focused on the situation at Salamanca on the Allegany Reservation, which they indicated was "fraught with evils, for which there can be no compensating advantage." The three Cattaraugus Senecas insisted that "no whites should reside on any of the reservations of the state, except such as will be useful to us, as artisans and teachers." They added that the policy of leasing lands, except for "the purpose of public highways, as in the case of railroads," was "detrimental to the best interests of our Indian population."[7] Three days later, the Seneca Nation Council passed a resolution protesting "the confirming of such leases by the state legislature."[8]

In 1870 the white settlers at Salamanca received a setback in their efforts to confirm the legality of their lease arrangements with individual Senecas when Judge George Baker of the New York State Supreme Court declared all the leases null and void because they violated the federal Trade and

Intercourse Act of 1834, which gave the United States exclusive jurisdiction over Indian affairs, including the approval of leasing contracts.[9] In January 1871, both houses of the New York State Legislature passed a concurrent resolution asking Congress to grant legal title to the lessees on the Allegany Reservation.[10]

The Seneca Nation then began ejectment proceedings against some of the lessees. In response, Hudson Ansley, the town supervisor of Salamanca and later the state-appointed attorney for the Seneca Nation, sent a letter of protest to the commissioner of Indian affairs. He contended that Baker's decision was a "great injustice" and claimed that the whites had been "invited and encouraged to settle" upon the reservation. Ansley and the board of supervisors of Cattaraugus County further elaborated on their grievances and requested that the secretary of the interior appoint a commissioner to examine the matter with a view to legislation "to prevent further misunderstanding." Contending that the Senecas had sufficient land—"300 acres to each man, woman, and child"—Ansley sent a clear message: the federal government must allow and facilitate allotment of the Allegany Reservation.[11] A year later, Thomas Heller, a New York State assemblyman, toured the Allegany Reservation to determine what actions could be taken to bring "relief" to the leaseholders.[12]

The movement to get Congress to confirm the leases retroactively or to allot reservation lands gained impetus in 1873 when a local judge in Cattaraugus County, William Daniels, upheld the Seneca contention that the New York State Legislature had no legal authority to make laws regulating the use of Seneca lands. As long as the United States recognized the existence of the Seneca Nation and because of existing federal Indian treaties, Daniels argued, the state had no jurisdiction. The implications of this decision were significant because the railroad rights-of-way as well as the other leases had no federal authorization.[13]

With millions of dollars invested in and around the city of Salamanca by the early 1870s, the two thousand non-Indians there clamored for relief, by Congress either confirming the questionable leases or passing legislation facilitating the transfer of title from the Senecas to them. Congress was besieged by these lessees and their representatives, and it soon responded to this lobbying effort. On July 10, 1873, Ansley, now chairman of the local citizens committee, wrote in support of congressional legislation that had been introduced to "quiet title to the lands of the Seneca Nation of Indians" and to protect "white settlers on the Reservation from wrong and or injury which might be attempted by reason of the insufficiency of their title."[14]

While some individual Senecas were bypassing tribal approval and making leases with non-Indians, the Seneca leadership continued to voice opposition to confirming these same leases. On February 3, 1873, President Peter Snow and the Seneca Council sent a protest to Washington when a bill was introduced in Congress "to authorize the Cattaraugus and Allegany Indians in the State of New York to lease lands, confirm leases, quiet titles to their lands." The bill also provided for the buying out of the Ogden preemptive claim with moneys from the U.S. Treasury. On July 17 of that year, James Johnson, the tribal attorney, wrote to the Indian Office in Washington, questioning whether there was any federal law or treaty allowing leases to railroads.[15] The need to legitimize these same railroad leases, which had never been previously confirmed, was clearly the motivating factor behind passage of the first congressional leasing act affecting the Allegany territory, in February 1875.

Federal Indian agents were hardly objective in appraising the situation. After the Civil War, agent H. S. Cunningham wrote to the commissioner of Indian affairs, urging him to push for sale of the Allegany Indian Reservation.[16] Despite having an apparent conflict of interest because he served as federal Indian agent and counsel to the Seneca Nation at the same time, agent Daniel Sherman, who succeeded Cunningham, first pushed for confirmation of the numerous illegal leases made at Allegany and then urged the federal government to buy out the Ogden preemptive claim and allot the Allegany and Cattaraugus Reservations. He frequently praised New York State's "beneficial care" of the Indians and insisted that Albany had primary responsibility for and jurisdiction over the Senecas. By 1874 he urged the Indian Office in Washington to aid the leaseholders, "who are entitled to some relief." The federal Indian agent described the numerous ways the white lessees had improved Salamanca, including by bringing in more than a million dollars of financial investment to the city.[17]

In January 1874, Congressman Walter Sessions, an attorney from nearby Harmony, New York, introduced a bill into the House of Representatives. The bill was aimed at confirming existing leases, extinguishing the claims of the Ogden Land Company by a federal buyout, "allowing" the Senecas to allot their lands in severalty, and, if the majority of Indians agreed, giving them the "right" to sell their lands.[18] In response, on January 31, 1874,

President Peter Sundown and the Seneca Nation Council sent another petition to Washington, expressing their deepening concerns about the rapidly changing world at Allegany and what they referred to as the unlawful leasing that went against "the authority, laws, and customs of the Seneca Nation of Indians," as well as the laws of the United States.[19]

On June 3, 1874, now feeling the imminent threat of allotment, the Seneca Nation Council, meeting at Cattaraugus, passed a resolution condemning congressional efforts to confirm the leases retroactively. It sent this protest off to Washington. Newly elected president William Nephew, fifteen councilors, and the tribal clerk signed the petition. Two future presidents of the nation—Casler Redeye and Andrew John Jr.—were signatories, the latter official soon becoming the major voice opposing allotment in the years that followed. The petition argued against passage of the Sessions bill and maintained that confirmation of illegal lease violated federal treaties, the Trade and Intercourse Act of 1834, and New York State laws of 1813, 1821, and 1843 that involved trespass and timber stripping on Indian lands.[20]

Despite the Seneca protests, the lobbying effort had received backing from the Office of Indian Affairs. In the fall of 1874, Commissioner Edward Smith recommended a congressional appropriation of approximately $100,000, which would then be tendered to the Ogden Land Company "for a total relinquishment of their pre-emption right." He added that the agreement would thus end the existing Seneca claims against the United States for lands west of Missouri (their "Kansas claims") under provisions of the Buffalo Creek Treaty of 1838 and the subsequent Treaty of 1842.[21] Despite this recommendation, the commissioner's push for a buyout failed.

In January and early February 1875, Congress debated the Sessions bill. In the era of the Crédit Mobilier and other corruption scandals, Senators Morgan Hamilton of Texas, Thomas McCreery of Kentucky, John P. Stockton of New Jersey, and Thomas F. Bayard of Delaware opposed the bill, viewing it as a blatant attempt to get at Seneca Indian lands. Bayard, who later was appointed secretary of state, saw unwarranted outside intrusion, noting that the Senecas' views had to be respected, since they had their own tribal organization "with tribunals of justice and equity, according to their own rights." Thus the Seneca Nation's adoption of a republican form of government appears to have shaped the senator's opinion. Predictably, however, congressional supporters of railroad legislation pushed the Sessions bill. On the other hand, Senator Lewis Bogy from Missouri, who had served as commissioner of Indian affairs immediately after the Civil War, claimed that the Senecas actually favored the bill, an untruth. He added that because of their "inferior condition," they would benefit by living on less land and that by contact with white townspeople, they "would advance in a higher civilization." While admitting the illegality of the leases, Senator Reuben Fenton from southwestern New York (later governor of the state) defended the congressional right to confirm these leases.[22]

On February 19, 1875, President Ulysses Grant signed "An Act to Authorize the Seneca Nation of New York to Lease Lands Within the Cattaraugus and Allegany Reservations, and to Confirm Existing Leases" after the Senate passed the bill on the same day by a two-to-one margin. Because of strong opposition in Congress, the Sessions bill's provision about allotment in severalty was removed, along with mention of extinguishing the Ogden Land Company's preemptive claim. In the first section of the act, apparently not coincidental, Congress confirmed the existing railroad leases with the Senecas. The law also created a commission of three members to survey, locate, and establish proper boundaries and limits of the villages of Vandalia, Carrollton, Great Valley, Salamanca, West Salamanca, and Red House within the Allegany Reservation. These so-called congressional villages were subject to state jurisdiction and not to the customs or laws of the Seneca Nation. All existing individual leases with individual Indians or the Seneca Nation were now made confirmed and binding for a five-year period, after which they could be renewed for twelve more years. All future leases had to be made and approved by the Seneca Council. Importantly, all the money for the leases would be collected by the treasurer of the Seneca Nation. Interestingly, in an effort to win some Seneca support, one provision of the act stated that the Indians could not be taxed on their lands. Five years later, Congress was to extend this lease act for twelve more years, to expire on February 19, 1892.[23]

One day after passage of the 1875 congressional leasing act, the Seneca Nation Council sent a formal protest, indicating that the legislation that had just passed Congress occurred while the Seneca officials were still meeting to discuss the merits of the bill. The council then sent an official delegation to Washington—composed of President Nephew, Treasurer Andrew John Jr., and Clerk Harrison Halftown—to express their displeasure to officials of the Grant administration. They were especially concerned about the establishment of the congressional villages outside of Seneca jurisdiction as well as the makeup of the commission authorized to undertake the survey.[24] The three commissioners appointed by the Indian Office were Joseph Scattergood, a noted Philadelphia Quaker do-gooder; Henry Shanklin of Kansas; and John Manley, a former federal Indian agent.[25] Manley had made enemies when he had taken sides in the Seneca political crisis of 1864. Later he was accused of bribing President Job King, which led to a major Seneca political crisis in 1878 and 1879.[26]

The Seneca Council reluctantly agreed to the boundary survey after a new president—Casler Redeye—and a new council were elected in May 1875. Redeye realized that the Senecas were powerless to resist and could face a worst fate—allotment—if they took an unbending stand against the commission's survey. By the end of 1875, the three commissioners had laid out the congressional villages, totaling west to east 5,465 acres: Red House, 15 acres; West Salamanca, 750 acres; Salamanca, 2,000 acres; Great Valley, 260 acres; Carrollton, 2,200 acres; and Vandalia, 240 acres.[27]

In the mid-1870s, the Office of Indian Affairs as well as the local federal Indian agent began pushing the idea of a buyout of the Ogden preemption. In the fall of 1875, after his visit to Seneca Country, Commissioner Edward Smith reflected on the Senecas in his annual report. He praised New York officials for their benevolence in their treatment of these Hodinöhsö:ni´. He wrote that the Senecas were fortunate that New York State hadn't forced them west "as paupers and vagrants," "allowing them to remain on fertile portions of their original land," protecting "them in their property rights, and better than all, [maintaining] public schools according to the pro rata share of the state educational fund." Smith added that the Senecas were "fully prepared for citizenship, which they hesitate to accept, partly from fear of taxation and legal responsibilities for debts and partly for fear that the abandonment of their tribal government will result in their loss of their lands."[28]

Throughout the decade, federal Indian agent Sherman continued to push allotment in his reports to Washington. Annually, he recommended that the Ogden Land Company preemptive claim be extinguished, suggesting the Seneca annuity fund as a payoff to these land jobbers. He and later federal agents in the 1880s also gave the false impression that a large number of Senecas were in favor of fee simple title. In these reports, attempting to convince the commissioner of Indian affairs to support congressional legislation to allot the Allegany and Cattaraugus Reservations, Sherman noted that the small number of Senecas at Cornplanter had recently agreed to allotment and had made significant improvements since it had been implemented.[29]

The Senecas were handicapped by intense political feuds that spilled over into electoral crises just when the movement for allotment of Indian lands was gaining momentum. In May 1876, Myron Silverheels's Seneca Union Party and Harrison Halftown's Seneca Republican Party claimed victory and accused each other of buying votes. A special election had to be called. There, Andrew Fox of the Union Party was elected president.[30] Two years later, the bribery case against Job King became so intense that Laura Wright indicated that all business within the nation came to a halt. She added: "Their political affairs keep them in a continuous foment. . . . There are now two Presidents and two councils doing business, one at Allegany and one here [at Cattaraugus]."[31] On January 8, 1879, King was placed on trial. Despite his plea of not guilty and the flimsy evidence to support the charge, King was impeached as president by a vote of eight to four. Former president William Nephew was appointed in his place.[32] Some Allegany Senecas even attempted to push secession as a separate political governmental entity. Seeing that these series of political crises was threatening the viability of the Seneca Nation, thirty-three women, much as in the past, intervened, this time attempting to bring in Quaker mediation efforts to settle the dispute.[33]

Leasing furthered opportunities to use political office for financial gain during the Gilded Age, when corruption was prevalent nationwide. While the Seneca Nation faced financial bankruptcy, some of its leaders were lining their pockets, and growing class divisions became more noticeable within the Indian nation.[34] Temptation was always there, since as late as 1891, salaries for tribal officials were miniscule—the Seneca president, clerk, and treasurer each received $80 a year and councilors no more than $37 annually.[35] From 1881 to 1892, the Seneca Nation, exclusive of oil and mineral leasing, made approximately $120,000; $11,000 to $13,000 a year came from lease rentals.[36]

By the 1880s, two powerful Senecas—Andrew John Jr. and William C. Hoag—began to dominate the politics of the Seneca Nation. John was born at Vandalia and grew up at Red House on the Allegany territory. Later he resided at Cattaraugus. He was the son of one of the supporters of John Luke and the revolutionaries of 1848. His father, Andrew John Sr., had been treasurer of the Seneca Nation but had been accused of corruption in 1854 for allegedly misappropriating tribal funds.[37] Andrew John Jr., a physically imposing figure, was first elected as a tribal councilor in 1875 and as clerk of the Seneca Nation in 1880, right after the disputed elections of 1876 and 1878. He was reelected clerk in 1881. In 1886, as the Dawes allotment bill was being debated in Congress, John was elected president for the first time. He was reelected to the presidency in 1887, 1888, and 1890. He has been described as an "expert in applying the white man's methods of improving the opportunities of office" and a "steadfast upholder of his nation while never making unnecessary sacrifice of his personal interest for anybody."[38]

John frequently accused Albany and southwestern New York politicians and transportation, land, and mineral interests of conspiring to get at the Seneca land base. He was correct in his assessment, but it should be pointed out that there were also prominent Senecas with diverse backgrounds in favor of allotment, and not all of them could be classified as "sellouts." Some apparently were fed up with Seneca politics and politicians who had allowed leasing to get out of hand and/or had personally profited from some of these questionable dealings.[39]

Criticisms of John were quite biting and often led to character assassination by his political rivals. His Seneca opponents frequently criticized him for his numerous trips to Washington, which he claimed were necessitated by his opposition to both the extension of the leases and allotment.[40] On one occasion, Hoag falsely accused President John of coming to the defense of James Crawford, an alleged rum seller, while the president was lobbying in Albany.[41] On another, he was accused by Hoag of conspiring against the Seneca Nation Council and by profiting by some of his dealings.[42] After he lost office in a highly contested election in 1891, John was hired at $5 a day by the Smithsonian Institution's Bureau of American Ethnology to chaperone all Indian delegations arriving in Washington. These delegations were housed in Bainbridge House, where John resided when he was in Washington. This allowed him to strike up an acquaintance with visiting chiefs, which allowed him to win their confidence and get them photographed and measured, allowing casts to be made of their heads.[43]

John's rival, Hoag, was elected treasurer of the Seneca Nation in 1882 and remained the major figure in tribal politics until his death in 1927. He was elected Seneca Nation president ten times, treasurer twelve times, and clerk three times during this forty-five-year period. In 1898 a revision to the Seneca constitution modified the length of elected officeholders terms, from one to two years. Thus, in effect, Hoag served as president for a total of nineteen years. Constantly accused of skimming off tribal funds for personal use and stealing elections by buying votes, he nonetheless was returned to office regularly, alternating between president and treasurer of the Seneca Nation. To counter this image and enhance his political standing among his people, Hoag was the head of the Seneca branch of the Six Nations Temperance League and received favorable attention through this position. His political power was based not so much on his charisma as on his personal wealth. Hoag managed the largest farm—more than one thousand acres—at Allegany and employed numerous Senecas as laborers, which made them dependent on him. Although he profited significantly from questionable leasing agreements, he was opposed to allotment, which threatened his large landholdings. If the heads of households received 160 acres, as proscribed under the Dawes Act formula, Hoag stood to lose future income.[44]

Through his "precinct captains"—Franklin Patterson, eight-time president of the Seneca Nation and Walter "Boots" Kennedy, both of Cattaraugus—Hoag operated much like a New York City Tammany Hall political boss in his pursuit of power. He frequently alternated the presidency and the office of treasurer with his right-hand man Patterson to ensure his continuing influence and power. Despite his advocacy of temperance, he and his men were constantly accused of using alcohol as well as bribery to win elections. Once in Albany, in an attempt to repeal a statute allowing an appeal to New York State courts from a decision of the Seneca Council, Hoag allegedly "fixed a deal with the city police to get an Indian from Cattaraugus arrested for being drunk so that he could not appear before a legislative committee the next day in opposition to repeal." According to Charles Congdon, local historian of the Upper Allegany Valley and former attorney for the Seneca Nation, "that was typical of Willie's methods."[45] Among the words used to describe Hoag's machine were "a regular ring," "reactionary," and "corrupt."[46]

Although they constantly battled for political control, both John and Hoag rejected the idea of extending the Dawes Act to include the Senecas. Hoag favored extending the leases but did not support allotment. After all, Hoag's large landholdings of more than a thousand acres at Allegany and his dominance over the Seneca Council allowed him to make profitable leasing arrangements for himself, his family, and his political allies. They also gave him total control over dispensing money from the Seneca Nation treasury. Later, in 1897, John described just how the situation worked to Hoag's and his political allies' advantage. John said that Hoag's council had "enjoyed too much liberty in the apportionment of money accruing from the lands which are leased and rented to white men." He added: "Many of the heads of families are complaining about not receiving part of the money. . . . As it is now, the President of the nation—together with three men from each of the reservations, forming the Council has the distribution of the funds, and this has led to extravagance."[47] John later called for a congressional investigation of Seneca finances under Hoag's control. It is little wonder that Hoag and his political machine frequently accused John of his own extravagance in his lobbying efforts in Albany and Washington, and of conspiring against the interests of the Seneca Nation.[48]

On February 2, 1887, President Benjamin Harrison signed the Dawes Act into law. It authorized the president to determine what Indian lands were to be to be allotted, and it designated a formula for awarding allotments to heads of families, individuals over eighteen, orphans under eighteen, and single persons under eighteen born prior to the passage of the act. These lands were to be held as trust patents, modified later by the Burke Act of 1906 and other congressional legislation, which meant the lands patented and could not be alienated out of Indian hands for twenty-five years. Because of the complicated status caused by the Ogden preemption claim, section 8 of the act specifically excluded the reservations of the "Seneca Nation of New York Indians in the State of New York."[49]

In response to the exclusion of the Seneca Nation from the Dawes Act, the New York State Legislature decided to conduct an on-site investigation of the "Indian problem" in August 1888. Since the act had specifically excluded the Six Nations in its provisions because of the ambiguous implications of the Ogden preemptive claim, Albany turned its attention to "rectifying" this omission. The next year, the New York State Legislature created an assembly committee headed by attorney James Whipple of Salamanca, later state commissioner of fish and wildlife, to investigate the "Indian problem" in New York.

This committee held its first hearing at Allegany in August 1888. President Andrew John Jr. was the major witness countering the push for allotment. John was cross-examined over several days at Allegany by local judge Oliver S. Vreeland. While the judge attempted to paint a negative picture of Seneca beliefs and reservation life, John countered every question. As a Longhouse Seneca versed in his people's customs and highly educated in the non-Indian world, having been educated at Mansfield Normal School, he stood his ground in answering the racism-strewn questions posed by Judge Vreeland. Having been in tribal government since the early 1870s, John indicated that he had opposed the congressional leasing act of 1875 and that a consortium of scheming whites, a "ring," had taken advantage of leasing. The Seneca president told the Whipple Committee that he would not recommend renewing any of the lease contracts beyond twelve more years (1904) and that would end most of the problems created by Congress's five-year lease act of 1875 and twelve-year lease act of 1880. While admitting that some Senecas married to whites, such as John Kennedy, were in favor of land in severalty, John opposed this direction as well as efforts to extinguish the Ogden claim and making the Senecas citizens of the United States. In wrapping up his testimony, the Seneca president concluded: "I wish to say just one word more about the Ogden Land Company's claim; we claim they are merely to buy the land from the Senecas when the Seneca Nation wants to sell it to them; then they could buy it." He indicated that this would occur only when and if the Seneca Nation became "extinct." The Seneca president emphasized to Whipple Committee members that "the whites want to buy the land; the Indians don't want to sell any foot of land; you go right through the whole reservation, there is a few you will find that wants a change."[50]

Other prominent Senecas testified before the Whipple Committee. William C. Hoag, John's rival, whose political career was on the ascent, spoke briefly. He rejected the idea of making the Hodinöhsö:ni´ U.S. citizens because he feared that it would lead to tax burdens, foreclosure, and land loss. He backed up his argument by pointing to what had happened to the Oneidas in central New York when a state law in the early 1840s had allotted their lands; within four decades, the Oneidas had lost almost all their remaining territory.[51]

Harrison Halftown, longtime clerk of the Seneca Nation, focused his testimony on the finances of the Seneca Nation and the collection of rent by the tribal treasurer. Avoiding the word *corruption*, Halftown, obviously fed up with the situation, recommended bypassing the Seneca treasurer's office. He recommended that rental moneys be paid into a fund administered by the office of the secretary of the interior and be paid as an annuity and distributed per capita directly to individual Senecas. Although he personally favored becoming a U.S. citizen, Halftown, an eight-term Seneca Nation clerk who had served from 1858 onward, admitted that other Senecas would reject the idea. Halftown disputed a memorial sent by John and his councilors claiming that the white settlers at Allegany were "undesirable neighbors and detrimental to the peace and welfare of the [Seneca] people." He urged efforts to promote education by establishing a high school on the reservation and efforts to promote temperance.[52]

Much to the delight of Whipple Committee members, former tribal councilor Myron Silverheels praised the efforts of the Quakers and missionaries in educating his people and advocated citizenship for any Senecas so desiring it. A prominent farmer at Allegany, Silverheels was elected to the tribal council in 1876 and soon after ran unsuccessfully for president of the Seneca Nation as head of the Union Party. However, he soon became embroiled in the electoral crisis of 1878, and it appears that he did not politically recover after that since he never held elected office again. At the Whipple Committee hearings at Allegany in August 1888, Silverheels was asked whether there was corruption by tribal officials. He replied: "Yes sir: quite often, I know myself: and I think the right way is to let the government appoint a commission to appraise the land" (presumably after allotment in fee and before individual Seneca sales of individual parcels of Seneca lands). Then Silverheels indicated his feelings about the preemptive claim: "Well in regard to the Ogden Land Company, I think it would be right and good if they [white people] have to buy and pay them for this claim; if there is any division of the lands to be made there is no trouble; we cannot do anything."[53]

This committee's report was filed in 1889. It condemned Hodinöhsö:ni´ family life, cultural mores, and traditional and religious practices in all their communities in New York and strongly recommended changes in land patterns and the end of tribal governments. The committee urged the state legislature to ask Congress to extinguish the preemptive claim of the Ogden Land Company and recommended that after this buyout, Seneca Nation lands should be allotted in severalty, but with suitable restrictions as to alienation to whites and protection from judgments and other debts. The committee further recommended that New York State assume full jurisdiction over the Senecas and their lands and that they be made U.S. citizens.[54] The *Whipple Report* concluded: "This allotment in severalty ought not to be limited to a division of the possession of the land, but should comprise a *radical uprooting of the whole tribal system*, giving to each individual absolute ownership of his share of the land in fee" (emphasis added).[55]

While Whipple and other state legislators were planning to hold their investigation, Seneca officials petitioned the Office of Indian Affairs for help "to stop the increasing numbers of squatters, trespassers, and alcohol dispensers unlawfully entering the Allegany Reservation."[56] In response to queries about the leasing problems at Allegany, federal Indian agent T. W. Jackson filed a fifteen-page report with the commissioner of Indian affairs. He indicated that the Senecas were receiving a mere $5,000 from lease payments and noted that the Senecas had "no records of a great many of the leases." Jackson recommended that "some person should be appointed by the commissioner of Indian affairs to take charge of this matter, attend to the leasing of these lands, and the collection of rents, and the proceeds should be paid over to them per capita, the same as their annuities are paid, taking it entirely out of the hands of the council." He concluded: "I think the law should be amended so as to secure to Indians in some manner, so that they could not be defrauded out of it, a proper rental value for these lands."[57]

On September 19, 1890, Congress extended the Seneca leases for ninety-nine years, beginning on February 19, 1892. President Benjamin Harrison signed the bill into law eight days later. All the leases were undervalued even for 1892, and none had accelerator clauses that would take into account inflation over this lengthy period of time.[58] A decade later, federal Indian agent B. B. Weber reported that the twenty-three hundred Senecas received a mere $12,110.77, approximately $4 per Seneca, from leasing. Besides $6,785.15 from leasing in the congressional villages, they received other annual rents: $200 from railroads, $55 from telegraph and telephone lines, $40 from Oil Spring farmlands, and $500 from oil and gas leases (other than the Seneca Oil/South Penn Oil lease, which totaled $4530.77).[59]

While increasingly faced with the problems created by leasing, the Senecas had to contend with a greater threat: the continuing local, state, and federal pressures pushing allotment. Despite section 8 of the Dawes Act of 1887, the movement for allotment of the Seneca Nation reservations was not dead. In his annual report for 1887, after passage of the act, Commissioner of Indian Affairs John D. C. Atkins stretched the truth, stating that the Seneca leadership had expressed a desire to use a portion of their annuity funds ($11,000 per annum) and a capital of some $230,000 "to extinguish such [Ogden] claim" that prevented allotment in severalty. Atkins then repeated the recommendation made by so many past federal Indian agents since 1868—namely, that Congress should take steps to enact the necessary legislation, carry through with allotment, and make the Senecas U.S. citizens. He added: "As soon as this is accomplished, the services of an agent in that state [New York] can be dispensed with."[60]

Commissioners of Indian affairs as well as non-Indian Salamancans, their political allies in Albany and Washington, and some misguided reformers of Indian policy continued to push allotment as a solution to the "Indian problem." The majority of Senecas continued to resist these efforts, although some supported allotment and U.S. citizenship. After the filing of the assembly committee's report in 1889, Whipple and his allies in the New York State Legislature proposed several bills in their attempt to extinguish the Ogden claim, force fee simple title on the Senecas, and open up tribal lands for sale to non-Indians.[61]

In July 1890, President Andrew John Jr and a delegation of Seneca councilors went to Washington to protest, filing a formal petition with Commissioner of Indian Affairs Thomas L. Morgan. In it they indicated that the state legislature had attempted to act before getting the consent of the Seneca Nation, had ignored the Indians' strong objections, and had violated federal treaty guarantees made by George Washington. They also presented a protest to Albany about the legislature's efforts to push for lands in severalty.[62] In March 1891, the Seneca Council unanimously adopted a resolution opposing Whipple's continuing efforts—Bills 544 and 3683, which among other provisions attempted to extend the laws of New York State to Indian reservations and to make these lands taxable. Faced with the dilemma of resolving the Ogden claim, unwilling to pay for its extinguishment, and hearing from a vocal minority opposed to the bills, New York State governor David Hill vetoed the legislation.[63]

Both the *Whipple Report* and Whipple's bills before the legislature infuriated Harriet Maxwell Converse, an extraordinarily energetic advocate for the Senecas.[64] Converse's family had had close ties to the Senecas since the 1790s. They had adopted her grandfather Guy Maxwell as well as her father, Thomas, a wealthy merchant, railroad executive, and former congressman.[65] In 1881 in New York City, Converse met Ely Parker, a Tonawanda Seneca sachem and the first Native American appointed commissioner of Indian Affairs. Their chance encounter changed the direction of her life.[66] As a journalist, poet, philanthropist, amateur folklorist, and collector of Iroquoian art for museums, she became *the* chief publicist for the Senecas and the major non-Indian opponent of Albany's efforts to break up and allot their reservations. Right to her death in 1903, she continued to expose the special interests behind this movement to allot Seneca lands.[67]

In an age when many Americans viewed Native people as a "vanishing race," Converse's articles, books, lectures, and poems described the lives, customs, and contemporary problems facing living *Hodinöhsö:ni'*, influencing readers and gaining support to help them in various quarters. Her New York City apartment, a virtual museum of Iroquoian art and a literary salon of note, became a center for disseminating cultural and political information as well as helping Indians who had relocated to the city.[68] Despite inaccuracies in her writings and her collection of ritual objects for major museums, Converse was accepted by the Hodinöhsö:ni' because in part she was viewed as their chief publicist and patron of their arts.[69] More importantly, she was their advocate, challenging racial and cultural slurs and defending their civil and treaty rights, their traditional Longhouse religious practices, their lands, and their governments.[70] It is little wonder that she was an honored guest and frequent visitor at Seneca communities, advising the Indians on strategies to pursue and emphasizing the need for a unified front.[71]

On three separate occasions, the Hodinöhsö:ni' formally honored Converse in ways that reveals much about them. The Hodinöhsö:ni' have always defined friendship in terms of reciprocal obligations, and Converse understood this from the first time she was honored. On June 15, 1885, on the Cattaraugus Reservation, the Senecas named and adopted Converse into the Snipe Clan in a ceremony recognizing her for her writings. They bestowed her with the Seneca name Ga-Ya-Nes-Ha-Oh (Law Bearer), the same as was given to Chief Cornplanter a century earlier. At the ceremony, she pledged her commitment to help the Senecas.[72] After news reports credited Converse with helping to kill Whipple's bill, the Senecas honored her again. In June 1891, they gave her a new, more appropriate name: Ya-ie-wa-noh (The Watcher).[73] On September 18, 1891, the Iroquois Confederacy sachems installed her as a chief in a Condolence Council ritual at the Tonawanda Indian Reservation.[74]

Condolence Council rituals, known by the Senecas as the Hai Hai, are essential for understanding the Iroquois as well as their relations with outsiders—Indian and non-Indian.[75] In the ancient past as well as the present, they are for mourning dead chiefs, lifting up the minds of bereaved relatives, and installing their successors. William N. Fenton has written that there was another, more subtle function of the ceremony. Through the seriousness and religiosity of the Condolence Council, the Iroquois attempted to manipulate the white world to their advantage. Fenton concluded: "Whoever came to the Iroquois came on their own terms."[76] In effect, this ceremony was not just to simply thank Converse for her past help but was carefully designed to strengthen the link between her and the Hodinöhsö:ni' in future crises.

What was not comprehended by non-Indian news reporters writing about this ceremony was that Converse's installation as a chief was actually tied to the historic role of women set forth in the *Gayaneshä'go:wa:h*, the Hodinöhsö:ni' Great Law. In it, the woman chief or clan matron was responsible for overseeing and protecting the land.[77] That was the exact role Converse played as the Senecas' advocate until her death in 1903.[78]

While Converse was championing Hodinöhsö:ni' causes, Seneca politics remained divided, with John and Hoag continuing their battling.[79] Yet John and Hoag continued their political battles. Hoag's large landholdings and dominance over of the Seneca Council allowed him to make profitable leasing arrangements for himself, his family, and his political allies, but it also permitted him total control over dispensing money from the Seneca Nation treasury. Later, in 1897, John described how the system worked to Hoag's and his political allies' advantage. He insisted that Hoag's council had "enjoyed too much liberty in the apportionment of money accruing from the lands which are leased and rented to white men." John added: "Many of the heads of families are complaining about not receiving part of the money. As it is now, the president of the nation—together with three men from each of the reservations, forming the Council has the distribution of the funds, and this has led to extravagance."[80] Hoag retaliated by frequently accusing John of conspiring against the interests of the Seneca Nation and complained about John's extravagant lobbying efforts in Albany and Washington. Hoag and his People's Party members even supported a congressional bill aimed at investigating their Seneca rival.[81]

Local whites in the congressional villages seeking title to their leased lands and their supporters in the New York State Legislature in Albany continued to clamor for the allotment of Seneca lands. In 1899 southwestern New Yorkers elected Edward Vreeland to Congress. Vreeland, who became the most prominent proponent of allotment, was a Salamanca banker and the brother of Oliver Vreeland, the lead attorney for the Whipple Committee in 1888 and 1889.[82] The congressman was part of a small group of prominent individuals in Salamanca and environs, led by Albert T. Fancher, who had established themselves as a formidable force, a virtual oligarchy. They were interconnected by their financial dealings as well as by marriage. Fancher was a trustee of Congressman Vreeland's bank, while Whipple's son had married Vreeland's daughter.[83] Fancher, known later as the "father of Allegany State Park," was the Republican boss of Cattaraugus County until his death in 1930. Although he founded the Fancher Furniture Company, a major enterprise that employed hundreds of local workers, much of his personal fortune came from his skillful investing in oil exploration in Oklahoma Territory, Indiana, and southwestern New York. Some of Fancher's oil fields were later sold off to John D. Rockefeller.[83] Opposed to Seneca interests and lusting after Indian lands and resources, the Fancher ring took care of their allies and pushed Vreeland's allotment bills in Congress.

Vreeland's efforts gained momentum in 1900 when Theodore Roosevelt, then governor of New York, appointed a blue-ribbon committee to investigate the "Indian problem." The committee was headed by Philip Garrett, a leading Philadelphia Quaker and an official of the Indian Rights Association. In its recommendations, the committee supported allotment and, with it, the "awarding" of U.S. citizenship to the Senecas.[84] Reacting to this committee's recommendations, Chauncey H. Abrams, the Snipe Clan Tonawanda sachem on the Iroquois Grand Council, wrote Converse that he feared that "Roosevelt will work against the Indians and make us become citizens so I hope you will do all you could to help let us to have the congress let us live as we are."[85]

Throughout the 1890s, congressmen had introduced allotment bills as well as ones designed to extinguish the Ogden claim. Now Vreeland figured out a way for the federal government to save money by extinguishing the Ogden claim. His plan was to pay off the Ogdens with part of the $1.9 million that the Senecas were to receive as part of their Kansas claims award based on a recent court decision. Thus the United States Treasury would not be out more money than it was already obligated to pay to the Senecas. In his scheme, after the Ogdens were satisfied, the Allegany and Cattaraugus Reservations were to be divided among individual Indians under the Dawes Act formula, which would facilitate land sales to non-Indians.

After Theodore Roosevelt assumed the presidency after the assassination of William McKinley in 1901, Vreeland, the head of the House Banking Committee and a loyal Republican, went about cultivating a relationship with federal policy makers as well as some of the reformers of federal Indian policies.[86] He attended and spoke at reform gatherings, including the Lake Mohonk Conference of Friends of the Indian and Other Dependent Peoples. Despite Vreeland's less-than-honorable motives, a sizable number of policy reformers were hoodwinked into supporting his efforts, believing that providing citizenship to the Hodinöhsö:ni´ was their best last hope to survive the onslaught of "civilization," even if it required Indians to abandon their customs and traditional landholdings. Later, at the Lake Mohonk Conference, Garrett endorsed Vreeland's plan, referring to reservations as "cancers in the midst of the body politic" and asserting that the only reason there was Indian opposition was because "they want barbarism and not civilization."[87]

With all of Vreeland's backing, how did the Seneca Nation, impoverished and reeling from leasing problems, finally stop this decades-old effort to get at their lands? The anti-allotment forces that opposed Vreeland's bills were a diverse group. Importantly, despite their never-ending political battles, both Hoag and John and their supporters in the end vigorously resisted Vreeland's efforts. The sachems of the Iroquois Grand Council also joined with the Seneca Nation leadership in filing a formal protest against the bills. With congressional hearings scheduled in 1902, the Iroquois Grand Council challenged Vreeland's bills, insisting that they were clear violations of the federal treaty at Fort Stanwix.[88]

Five prominent non-Indians came to the Senecas' defense: Converse; William D. Walker, the Episcopal bishop of western New York; John Van Voorhis, a former Republican congressman and Rochester attorney for the Senecas; Senator Matthew Quay of Pennsylvania, who led the early opposition in Congress; and Representative William Sulzer, later mayor of New York City. Throughout the battle to defeat the Vreeland bills, Converse and her protégé Joseph Keppler Jr., editor of influential magazine *Puck*, worked with the Seneca leadership and helped coordinate the lobbying.[89] As a lifelong Episcopalian and noted philanthropist, Converse convinced Bishop Walker to take a stand against the Vreeland bills and appear with her at a series of meetings at the Cattaraugus Reservation and in Buffalo, and she suggested that Keppler get the bishop to secure the services of a prominent Buffalo law firm to aid Van Voorhis's efforts.[90] Converse and Keppler also convinced Judge Charles Andrews to write an article for newspapers challenging the Ogden land claim and questioning the congressional effort to pay off its preemption.[91] Since Converse faced financial difficulties because of her overly generous philanthropic efforts, she asked Keppler to pay for rail transportation to allow Seneca delegates to attend hearings and testify on Capitol Hill.[92]

In March 1902, the House of Representatives held hearings on Vreeland's Bill H.R. 12270, "for the allotment of lands in severalty among the Seneca Nation of New York Indians, and for other purposes." Although there were five other Senecas who testified, Andrew John Jr. was the major witness opposing the bill. After denying the validity of the Ogden Land Company's preemptive claim to Seneca lands, the three-time president of the Seneca Nation insisted that Seneca "title to lands has been firmly, solemnly, unanimously and most decidedly declared to be valid by the highest courts of appeal created by the Constitution of the United States and by that of New York." John argued the unfairness of forcing Senecas (and Tuscaroras) to pay for this buyout to the Ogdens by moneys the Indians were entitled to receive based on U.S. failures under treaties.[93] John was followed by Chester C. Lay, a former Seneca Nation president from Cattaraugus. Lay repeated much of what John testified to, arguing that it was not right to compel the Senecas to pay. He beseeched congressional committee members to provide "fair consideration in justice to my people."[94] Lay was followed by Myron Silverheels, who testified in the Seneca language. He once again favored allotment, insisting that the Senecas would not be poorer for agreeing to it and that great progress would result five years after passage.[95]

On March 21, just after the congressional hearing, one of Converse's articles appeared in the *Washington Times*. She praised those Indians testifying in opposition to the Vreeland bills and for pleading against the measures "in an intelligent and logical way." She rejected the idea of using the Kansas claims moneys to buy out the Ogden preemption since the Indians were legally entitled to be reimbursed for violations of their federal treaties. She insisted: "Therefore the question of today is not so much the rights of the land company as enforcing of them upon the Indians. If this claim is just and legal, the Government should protect its wards [the Senecas] in its provisions."[96]

Throughout 1902, other non-Indian supporters of the Senecas hammered away at Vreeland's bills. Bishop Walker, who had been adopted by the Senecas, had previously served the Episcopal Church in North Dakota, where he had witnessed the failures of federal Indian policies. He questioned the morality of using Seneca moneys awarded as compensation for the Treaty of Buffalo Creek to pay off the nefarious Ogdens. Walker later urged the reformers at Mohonk to listen to the Senecas' own pleas against the bills and not "to take from Naboth his little vineyard."[97] Attorney Van Voorhis pointed out that the Seneca Nation Council had vehemently opposed using the Kansas claims award to pay off the Ogden heirs. The Rochester attorney carefully showed that numerous non-Indian leaseholders at Allegany, who he claimed were already taking advantage of the Senecas, were backers of the bills. In his defense of the Seneca Nation, Van Voorhis tied the Vreeland bills to John D. Rockefeller's Standard Oil Company, a popular target for muckraking journalists of the time. Praising the Senecas, including their Longhouse followers, he insisted that these Indians were already "civilized" and thus did not require subdivision of their lands to further this goal.[98]

The key opposition in Congress to the Vreeland bills was initially led by Senator Quay, the powerful Republican boss of Pennsylvania. A no-nonsense, tough-minded senator who had won the Congressional Medal of Honor at the Battle of Fredericksburg in 1862, Quay had long opposed oil leasing and had arranged for at least one Iroquois delegation to meet personally with President Roosevelt. Proud of what he claimed was his distant Indian ancestry, the senator had become concerned about the plight of the Delawares of Oklahoma Territory, and he clearly equated their misfortune with that of the Senecas. As the key member of the Senate Indian Affairs Committee, he questioned why so many undervalued leases existed in Salamanca. He insisted that neither the president of the United States nor a congressional committee should determine when and if allotment should occur, and that the question should be decided by the majority of Senecas themselves in a plebiscite.[99] The fiscally conservative Quay was aided in the House of Representatives by liberal congressman William Sulzer, an anti–Tammany Hall Democrat reformer and later mayor of New York City, who was vehemently opposed to Standard Oil and its monopolistic practices. Until Quay's death in 1904, the two repeatedly stymied Vreeland and his efforts to subdivide Seneca lands.[100]

On December 15, 1902, the very day that one of his allotment bills cleared the House of Representatives, Vreeland made his motivation quite clear: "I represent 8,000 people upon these reservations who hold ninety-nine year leases from these Indians, and who want to get a title to their lands."[101] Despite his effective public relations work, two of his bills—H.R. 12270 and H.R. 7262, both of which subsequently passed the House of

Representatives—failed in the Senate. Despite the defeat, Vreeland continued to pursue his goal of allotment of Seneca lands.[102]

Despite Silverheels's testimony and continued infighting in the Seneca Nation, its membership was overwhelmingly united in opposition to Vreeland and his bills. On January 15, 1903, 629 adult Senecas filed a protest against the congressman's proposed legislation.[103] Perhaps realizing that the crisis of the Seneca land base was now the most serious one since 1838, both Hoag and John stopped fighting and began to address themselves to the real threat. Both men pointed out that vested interests were behind Vreeland's bills. John actively defended the Senecas at the Lake Mohonk Conference of Friends of the Indian and Other Dependent Peoples and in Washington before congressional committees. At Lake Mohonk, John condemned the Vreeland bills and appealed to white guilt over past treatment of the Indians: "It is the very same story from the time of Columbus. Once we had the whole domain: where are the Indians today? We have to fight all the time to keep the reservations that we have left."[104] On Capitol Hill, instead of taking the opportunity to lambast his Seneca political rivals, John directed his attacks on the principle of land in severalty: "If allotting lands can produce virtue and chastity and justice, allotment might be applied in the city of Washington, and perhaps elsewhere in this broad land."[105]

While John tried to convince the reformers that Vreeland was a scoundrel and that the congressman's objective was to get at the Seneca land base for his white constituents, Hoag used another tactic: a direct attack on the reformers. Hoag portrayed them as uninformed meddlers. He condemned the actions of the Indian Rights Association, the Lake Mohonk conferees, and members of the U.S. Board of Indian Commissioners. Hoag insisted that he "never could see anything that these Mohonk Lake people ever did for any of us. They go down there and have their pow wows, but I don't think it does anything." He pointed out: "Is this not a case in which the Indians need protection from their 'friends.'"[106]

Three months after Converse's death in November 1903, Seneca officials Hoag and Patterson met with Van Voorhis. They once again hired the attorney, contracting him for $2,500 to continue his fine work on the Senecas' behalf. They praised him for his efforts in 1902 in stopping Congress from using Seneca Kansas claims money to buy out the Ogdens. They indicated that the fight against the Vreeland bills had cost a "great many thousands" and that the cause had fiscally bankrupted the nation.[107] That same year, the

Vreeland bills once again came close to becoming law. However, after the United States Court of Claims awarded the Senecas their "Kansas money" in 1905, Vreeland's scheme was torpedoed, since Congress was not willing to pay out other moneys from the U.S. Treasury to satisfy the Ogden preemptive claim. In March 1906, Commissioner of Indian Affairs Francis Leupp labeled the Vreeland bills "an injustice," even though he previously supported allotment policies."[108]Although talk of allotment of Seneca lands continued until 1914, the movement in New York had peaked.

To be sure, the Senecas—a small Indian nation of fewer than twenty-five hundred members—were not much of a concern to most New Yorkers or to Americans as a whole. The push for land in severalty was not helped by the Ogden Land Company's claim and its history of defrauding Indians. In addition, the smell of oil and the nefarious history of leasing at Allegany had hurt Vreeland's allotment push. Although allotment was often couched in moralistic terms—uplifting the poor Indians to "civilization"—no amount of reform and missionary rhetoric could deny who some of the lessees were and what they sought. Oil fever was out in the open, white lessees were paying a pittance, and non-Indian title to Indian lands was demanded. Moreover, in an era of rising concerns about monopolies, especially that of the oil trust, John D. Rockefeller's association with Salamanca leasing damaged the movement for fee simple title. In the end, credit must be given to the two controversial Seneca leaders of the age—John and Hoag—who temporarily focused their attention on the threat of harmful congressional legislation and not on their long-standing bitter rivalry, as well as to the actions of five non-Indians: Converse, Walker, Van Voorhis, Quay, and Sulzer.

MORE INTRUDERS

On February 2, 1890, an article entitled "New York's Indians" appeared in the *New York Herald*. Much of the article dealt with the Seneca Nation and its relations with Albany. It was a clear condemnation of Andrew Draper and James Whipple as well as those interests in southwestern New York scheming to get at Indian lands through allotment legislation. In this remarkable article that went against commonly held stereotypes, the anonymous reporter insisted that state officials had "shamefully slandered" the Indians "for selfish reasons." The article quoted Presbyterian missionary M. F. Trippe, who stated that the Senecas were "misunderstood and abused people." Trippe added that the Senecas were not lazy, did not use profanity since there were "no swear words in their native language," and had a "sincere respect for women—their own women as well as those of whites." The reporter recognized the existence of corruption by Seneca politicians, suggesting that they could give pointers to Tammany men. However, the reporter then took a swipe at Albany's elected officials, maintaining that the Seneca Nation Council was as "honest and decent" as the state legislators found in Albany. Importantly, the article accurately identified why the Hodinöhsö:ni´ viewed state policy makers with such disdain: "Anything, however, which the State of New York may attempt to do for them will be viewed with suspicion. To them, 'New York' is synonymous with 'thief.'"[1]

While New York State officials were increasingly interfering in the Onöndowa'ga:' world, the federal government was also meddling into Seneca affairs. Federal court decisions and congressional legislation restricted Seneca sovereignty over their rights to fish and hunt. America's entry into World War I and the passage of military conscription created another crisis. Seneca efforts to reclaim lands at Oil Spring and their riparian rights in the Niagara River were ignored or were sidetracked by laws passed in Congress. Instead, after the war federal officials promoted U. S. citizenship as their way to solve the "Indian problem" and held hearings on Capitol Hill about transferring criminal and civil jurisdiction over the Hodinöhsö:ni' to New York State. Since the state's founding after the American Revolution, Albany had long sought to control Indian affairs. From 1785 onward, state officials had made numerous "treaties" with the Hodinöhsö:ni'. Many of these "accords" were in violation of the federal Trade and Intercourse Acts, since negotiations occurred without the presence of a federal treaty commissioner and without U.S. Senate ratification. Despite at times readily admitting questionable land titles, Albany officials dismissed Seneca and other Hodinöhsö:ni' land claims and extended state jurisdiction over what the Onöndowa'ga:' considered their own territory.[2] Consequently, before, during, and after World War I, the Senecas both protested the state's encroachment onto their nation's lands at Oil Spring and sought riparian rights along the Niagara River. They brought these claims before congressional and state legislative committees well into the 1920s, but without success.[3]

The state's governors, legislators, and agency commissioners, and their allies in Congress, pushed the idea of transferring complete control over Indian affairs to Albany. In 1888, 1900, 1906, 1915, 1920–22, and 1930, commissions were established and hearings were held to consider the move. A state legislative report in 1906 claimed that "the fact the jurisdiction respectively of the national and State governments is not clearly defined and that for some purposes the jurisdiction of both seems to be concurrent has proved to be a great misfortune to the Indians and has undoubtedly been the main cause of governmental neglect and their failure to make greater progress." Discounting Native American sovereignty and not encouraging efforts at tribal self-rule, the report recommended that the time had come "when public policy requires that the responsibility for the future of the Indians should be fixed and determined and that some systematic policy toward them be pursued in order to avoid a national and State disgrace."[4]

In the summer of 1915, New York State held a convention designed to revise its laws and adopt a new constitution. There, James Whipple once again came to the fore, this time serving as New York State commissioner of forest, fish, and game. Although not a member of the convention's Indian Affairs Committee, Whipple was considered by the delegates assigned to that committee the state's "expert" on Indian policies.[5] Consequently, he played a major role in the convention's deliberations on revising state Indian policies. The Indian Affairs Committee was headed by James P. Lindsay of North Tonawanda, New York, and included two members from the Buffalo area, one from the Adirondack region, one from Syracuse, and one from New York City.[6] Its report opened by recommending that the Indians should "be treated as civilized persons, and not as barbarians" and that they should be awarded "full citizenship" and no longer be viewed as "dependents in a state of tutelage" as they had been seen over the years.[7]

Despite these words that suggested a change for the better, the committee went on to hail the *Whipple Report*, claiming that the document provided a full and accurate picture on the "lands, moral and social condition, government and needs of the Indians."[8] The committee then launched an attack on the Indian courts, claiming that these bodies had absolute power over marriage and divorce and that women and their children had no protection in their determinations of cases. It recommended that New York State assume legal jurisdiction over the civil and criminal affairs of the Indians. The report added that New York State's constitution should be amended to abolish "inefficient and corrupt" Indian courts that the committee claimed existed on several reservations. It also recommended guaranteeing protection for Indians in state courts.[9] After all, the report stated, there was nothing to prevent state legislation from accomplishing these objectives since the "Federal Government has never assumed by treaty, or laws, to govern the Indians within this State."[10] Whether the Indians wanted these changes or not, the delegates to the 1915 convention concluded that all state laws relating to American Indians, except the one restricting alcohol sale to Indians, should be repealed and that the state should assume jurisdiction over Indians in all matters not specifically set forth in federal statutes and treaties.[11]

By 1915 Whipple was the head of a state agency that had had one of the most contentious relations with the Senecas. In the preceding years, state game wardens and local law enforcement officers had failed to acknowledge Seneca treaty rights to fish and hunt without state licenses on their reservations and within their historic territory, namely in the fourteen counties of western New York. In 1880 the state had first appointed game wardens, later called "conservation protectors." By 1886 the state legislature had already added two restrictions and fines to the game laws that directly affected hunting and fishing on the Cattaraugus Indian Reservation: one that affected the taking of partridges, woodcocks, snipes, and plovers; and the other forbidding the setting and taking of fish with nets or seines in Cattaraugus Creek. Under these laws, offenders, both Indian and non-Indian, could be arrested, charged with misdemeanors by county district attorneys, jailed, and fined.[12] In 1895 New York established the Fisheries, Game, and Forest Commission to regulate fishing and hunting, set seasonal restrictions, and attempt to stop poaching. This commission, in conjunction with the New York State Attorney General's Office, then set out writing its first code of enforcement.[13]

George Decker had helped write some of the state's fishing and hunting regulations when he served as the assistant attorney general of New York. Later, when these same regulations were all-too-frequently used to harass and prosecute Indians, Decker resigned and became the major advocate for the Hodinöhsö:ni´ fighting these same regulations and filing land claims suits against the state.[14] Decker and his Seneca supporters used the argument made in *United States v. Winans*, a 1905 U.S. Supreme Court case—namely that the Indians retained "reserved rights" even if these same rights were not specifically mentioned in a treaty. In the *Winans* case, the court held that a treaty is "not a grant of rights to the Indians, but a grant of rights from them."[15]

In 1915 Decker and the Senecas lost a major federal case, one that awarded the New York State Conservation Department the authority to unilaterally regulate Indian hunting and fishing off Seneca territories. Several Senecas—Lafayette Kennedy, Warren Kennedy, and Willis White Jr.—had been arrested for spearfishing, a time-old Indian technique, along Eighteen Mile Creek in Erie County, which was outside the boundaries of their Cattaraugus Reservation. Decker argued that the fishing was done in historical Seneca Country, lands sold to Robert Morris by the Treaty of Big Tree of 1797, and thus the Senecas had reserved treaty rights of hunting and fishing even after the sale. Having caught fish in their possession, they were arrested under section 176 of the New York State conservation law. The state supreme court dismissed the action, agreeing with Decker's argument. The case was then appealed. The appellate division reversed the lower court's decision. The case was affirmed by the New York State Court of Appeals, the Empire State's highest legal tribunal.[16]

Because of the court's interpretation of federal treaty law, Decker and the Senecas then appealed to the United States Supreme Court. In an opinion agreed to by six justices and written by Chief Justice Edward White, the nation's high court held that the New York State conservation law's prohibition against the taking of fish applied to Indians off-reservation. While recognizing the Senecas' reserved right to fish and hunt on their existing reservations, White nevertheless portrayed himself as a conservationist. He insisted that things had changed from the time "when game was plentiful" and that "under modern conditions," New York State officials had the right to establish regulations to preserve wildlife off Indian territories, specifically lands that had passed out of Indian hands in the Big Tree Treaty in 1797.[17]

The state's tentacles soon reached further into Seneca existence. For the next two decades, the Senecas continued to be arrested as poachers even on their existing residential territories. Seneca protests were frequent. The most articulate espousal of Indian treaty rights to hunt and fish was made at the hearings of the Everett Commission at the Allegany and Cattaraugus Indian Reservations in 1920. Although these hearings are best known for their emphasis on Hodinöhsö:ni´ land claims, the representatives from the Senecas at the two hearings mostly focused on federal treaties that guaranteed their rights to fish and hunt and the state's failure to recognize these rights. Among those Senecas who testified against state intrusion were President Franklin Patterson, Treasurer William Hoag, Councilors Walter "Boots" Kennedy and George Jemison, and Emily Tallchief, Chief Cornplanter's granddaughter. Other Senecas who testified included Francis Jamierson, John Van Aernum, and the attorney John Snyder, a controversial Seneca who served as the mouthpiece for President Patterson. All criticized the effort to transfer complete jurisdiction to the state, although Hoag and several others recognized that the state had historical, moral, and legal obligations to the Senecas that needed to be clarified.[18]

Testifying in Seneca and translated by President Patterson, Tallchief told how her eminent family had handed down the view to her that treaties had given the Senecas the freedom "to hunt and fish and cut down trees among the whites when they sold the land to the whites and that nobody ever said a word at that time."[19] Van Aernum described the situation the

Senecas faced and compared it Jews enslaved in ancient Egypt. He added: "We can no longer hunt and fish as we used to, nor camp along our lands, lakes, and rivers and fish. Our streams are polluted from factories beyond our reservation thus destroying our means of livelihood, we can no longer fish."[20]

Although sympathetic to the Indians' critique of past state policies. Chairman Edward Everett was ignorant of the nature of the Seneca Nation government, referring to tribal officials, including Patterson and Kennedy, as "chiefs." In the two hearings, at Cattaraugus on August 23 and at Allegany on August 26, Kennedy was the most effective in his testimony. Kennedy, a loyal member of Hoag's political machine, clearly laid out the Seneca argument against jurisdictional transfer. Making reference to federal treaties, the Seneca politician began his testimony by posing questions to Chairman Everett:[21]

(1) Do you consider the solemn pledge of the United States of any significance?

(2) Do you consider the Constitution of the United States of any significance?

(3) Then these lands of the Six Nations are outside of the territorial limits of the United States according to international law?

(4) Now that the Indians pledged the United States they would never claim land outside their territories. Am I right?

(5) Now the United States acknowledged all the lands to be the property of the Seneca Nation and will not disturb them, etc. [According to the Treaty of 1794 at Canandaigua], it shall remain theirs until they chose to sell to the United States. What do you mean when you say that?"

Chairman Everett answered in the affirmative to the first four questions. On the fifth question, Everett answered, "Just what the language says as far as I am concerned." He added: "It is a solemn pledge of faith, but you can't ask me to carry it out alone; but I will do my best to adjust the matter."[22] Then Kennedy specifically focused on Seneca rights to fish and hunt as specified in the Treaty of Big Tree in 1797. He described how the Seneca Nation deeded land to Robert Morris in a treaty sanctioned by the federal government, one that allowed the Indians to reserve their right to continue to fish and hunt on the ceded property. Kennedy continued: "New

York turns around and against conditions of the deed interferes with that right which we reserved, is that right?" He indicated that the Indians had been illegally arrested and fined for violations of state laws even though the Seneca Nation issued its own fishing and hunting licenses. Containing his anger, Kennedy concluded that state and local officials and law enforcement officers treated the Indians as if they were aliens.[23]

The *Everett Report,* completed in March 1922, was never accepted by the state legislature and governor largely because the chairman had agreed with the Hodinöhsö:ni´ about clouded state title to their lands after the Treaty of Fort Stanwix in 1784 and because other members of the commission had opposed the chairman's conclusions. The committee's censored report nevertheless spurred the Hodinöhsö:ni´ land claims movement in the 1920s, one that was revived in the 1960s and 1970s.

The Everett Commission had followed several major political stirrings in Iroquoia. State officials were not seen as the only intruders. During World War I, a renewed sense of Six Nations nationalism sprung up on both sides of the international boundary.[24] Several hundred Senecas fought in the war and even went over the international boundary and enlisted in the Canadian Expeditionary Force, which fought in France prior to the U.S. declaration of war in April 1917.[25] Some Senecas were killed in action and buried in cemeteries in France. Others, such as Jesse Cornplanter, who had been born at Cattaraugus, returned with neurasthenia, having been gassed in trench warfare.[26] However, a vocal minority of Hodinöhsö:ni´ opposed participation after both Canada and the United States instituted conscription. Congress passed the Selective Service Act of 1917, requiring that all males between the age of twenty-one and thirty-one register for the draft. From this pool, men could be selected for military service. Although noncitizens and temporary residents were exempted, noncitizen Indians such as most Hodinöhsö:ni´ were nevertheless forced to register and be subjected to the draft.[27] In a letter to Arthur C. Parker, Walter "Boots" Kennedy described the reaction to the draft by the Indians, claiming that "quite a number of young men . . . have failed to comply with this [registration] order."[28] At Allegany, Senecas opposed to serving in the war held rallies, made speeches advising the Indians not to register, and labeled the actions of tribal members who promoted registration as "selling out to the Government."[29]

After the end of the war, Hodinöhsö:ni´ activism arose partly in reaction to a successful decision rendered in a federal court of appeals land claims case, one that returned thirty-two acres to the Oneidas in New York.[30] As transnational people, the Hodinöhsö:ni´ in New York were also affected by their kin across the international boundary. In Canada, Chief Levi General (known as Deskaheh), with the help of attorney George Decker, attempted to bring Native complaints against the government in Ottawa before the League of Nations in an attempt to get to the World Court in the Hague. Among other issues, Deskaheh insisted that the Canadian government had interfered in Hodinöhsö:ni´ traditional affairs in its efforts to foist an elected council on the people of the Six Nations Reserve and had violated Indian border-crossing rights guaranteed in the Jay Treaty.[31]

Two years after the conclusion of the work of the Everett Commission, Congress passed the Indian Citizenship Act, one opposed by both the Seneca Nation Council and the Iroquois Grand Council at Onondaga. The reasoning was based on Hodinöhsö:ni´ tradition. They proudly saw themselves as Hodinöhsö:ni´, as separate nations with inherent sovereignty given to them by the Creator, not Washington. At a time when Native Americans were still losing their lands under allotment policies in other areas of Indian Country, they questioned the logic of how American Indian nations with federal treaties could at the same time become U.S. citizens. After all, citizenship was also historically equated with taxation and fears of land loss through foreclosures.[32]

In 1927 Congress passed the so-called Seneca Conservation Act, which awarded the state concurrent jurisdiction with the Senecas over fishing and hunting on the Allegany, Cattaraugus, and Oil Spring Reservations.[33] Seneca Nation leaders, most vociferously Ray Jimerson, strongly objected. Jimerson served as Seneca president from 1928 to 1930 and again from 1932 to 1934, and as treasurer from 1930 to 1932 and from 1934 to 1936. He also led the fight against congressional confirmation of illegal leases made on tribal lands along Lake Erie. Jimerson and Councilor Warren Kennedy, one of the Senecas prosecuted in the earlier case, led the fight to repeal the 1927 act. They were aided by Cephas Watt, a tribal councilor and member of the Coldspring Longhouse at Allegany, and Seneca activist Alice Lee Jemison, the niece of Cornelius Seneca, who handled most of the president's correspondence as his "girl Friday."

At the Senate Committee on Indian Affairs hearings in January 1933, the Senecas universally condemned the act of 1927. Councilor Warren Kennedy reacted to what he saw as a threat to Seneca sovereignty and treaty rights. He insisted that the Senecas did not want "the white conservation department down there on the reservation." Kennedy also feared that opening up the waters of the reservation for non-Indians to fish could clean out the streams, leaving nothing for the Indians. President Jimerson favored the idea of Indians granting licenses to non-Indians, but he was especially concerned about enforcement. He compared the situation to past timber stripping of reservation forests by outsiders and the failure of the federal authorities to prevent these criminal actions. The Seneca president added that he was also concerned that the frequent arrest of tribal members for fishing and hunting without state licenses on Seneca lands was putting a heavy financial burden on his nation, since the Senecas felt an obligation to pay for the expenses of defending their tribal members. At the end of his testimony, he presented a joint resolution of his tribal membership at both Allegany and Cattaraugus territories, insisting that Congress respect Seneca sovereignty and treaty rights by overturning the 1927 act.[34]

The Senecas continued to press their case.[35] Alice Lee Jemison became the Seneca Nation Council's lobbyist in Washington, championing a change.[36] In the late spring of 1935, Congress passed a bill sponsored by Representative Alfred Beiter and Senator James Mead that called for the repeal of the 1927 act and the end to concurrent jurisdiction on Seneca lands. However, President Franklin D. Roosevelt, the former governor of New York State, vetoed the bill. Presenting himself as a conservationist, Roosevelt insisted that the state had an obligation to pass laws to "limit the seasons during which hunting and fishing may be indulged in and the numbers of game and fish that may be taken within fixed periods. . . . It is, therefore, strictly true to say that the Indians are no more vested with a property interest in this game than are the people of the rest of the state or country."[37]

Until 1974 Senecas were subject to arrest and fines if caught without a state license, even if they fished and hunted on their own tribal lands. In that year, a local county court, in the case *People v. Redeye*, made a fateful decision. Senecas James and Judith Redeye and John and Patricia McStraw—had been arrested and convicted of hunting on the Allegany Reservation without a state-issued license. The court overturned the conviction, insisting that, according to federal law, the Senecas had the right to hunt and fish on their tribal lands without state-issued licenses.[38] Subsequently, the legislature overturned its past insistence on concurrent jurisdiction on Indian reservations in the state and allowed all enrolled tribal members to hunt, fish, and trap upon their reservations, "subject only to the rules, regulations and fish and wildlife laws established by the governing body of such reservation."[39]

The state's intrusion into Seneca Country also included Albany's creation of Allegany State Park. In 1921, without any advanced consultation with the Seneca Nation, the state legislature established the state park, New York's largest, which borders Allegany Indian territory.[40] Today 1.5 million vacationers visit the park annually.[41] Significantly, the park's creation brought Robert Moses, chairman of the New York State Council of Parks in 1924, into Seneca Country for the first time. Moses later pushed park development that became tied to the Kinzua Dam project.[42]

Cattaraugus County, one of the poorest counties in the state, faced a major economic downturn and the end of World War I. Forest lands had been denuded of much of their best timber. Tanneries started to close down.[43] The local wood chemical industry and furniture makers found themselves with limited supplies of needed hardwoods. Moreover, because of the great abundance of cheap oil from new fields in Venezuela, Mexico, and the Arabian Peninsula and declining manufacturing because of a postwar depression, the price of refined oil fell from $6.10 per barrel in 1920 to $3.65 per barrel in 1927 to $2.02 per barrel in 1932.[44]

Boss Albert T. Fancher of Cattaraugus County came to realize that establishing Allegany State Park would immensely benefit the economy of the region. He and his political ally Robert Moses saw that parks that would lead to highway construction, which would be an engine to further economic expansion. The Cattaraugus County boss envisioned numerous vacationers seeking out the area for recreation—camping, fishing, hunting, and picnicking—reviving the economy of nearby Salamanca. It was no coincidence that Fancher became an active member of the New York State Association, a private civic lobbying organization that in 1922 drafted *A Park Plan for New York State with a Proposal for the New Park Bond Issue*. Moses was secretary of and a driving force within this association. In the publication, Fancher and his supporters laid out his plans for the development of Allegany State Park.[45]

Fancher came to the realization that the supply of hardwoods within the immediate surroundings was no longer sufficient for the needs of his family's furniture company, which employed hundreds of workers in southwestern New York. Consequently, Fancher allied himself with scientists at the New York State College of Forestry in Syracuse and civic-minded reformers in Buffalo who were already promoting state forests and parks in an effort to reforest the region, an area devastated by unregulated cutting for nearly a century. Well aware of congressional passage of the Weeks Act of 1911, which allowed the federal government to buy forest lands in eastern states, Fancher began to advocate for the development of a national forest. For about a decade before the establishment of Allegany State Park, Pennsylvania congressmen were pushing for the creation of a national forest just across the New York State line.[46] Unlike New York state parks, national forests allow logging as well as drilling for oil and gas. Boss Fancher was even personally invited to attend planning sessions for what became Allegany National Forest, a tract of more than a half million acres established in 1923. Thus, with rapidly declining timber resources on lands that became Allegany State Park, logging and chemical companies had very little to lose by selling their interest in southern Cattaraugus County and reestablishing their operations just below the New York State line.[47] To make this move more attractive, Fancher and DeHart Ames, a member of Fancher's political machine in Cattaraugus County, designed legislation guaranteeing that residual oil, gas, and timber rights would be retained by companies after their lands were sold off to New York State.[48]

On January 18, 1921, Ames, newly elected to the New York State Senate, introduced legislation that called for the creation of Allegany State Park, while Joseph McGinnies of Chautauqua County, another ally of Fancher's, introduced the bill in the state assembly.[49] By then Ames was a member of the Everett Commission, examining Indian policies. However, unlike Everett, Ames was hardly sympathetic to Indian land claims. During the state legislature's consideration of his Allegany State Park bill, Seneca residents of the Allegany Indian Reservation protested. The Seneca committee, which included John Jacobs, Joseph Watt, Windsor Pierce, DeForest Snow, Philo Nephew, and Henry John, stated that they were against passage of the bill for fear that it would interfere with Seneca property rights, lead to the appropriation of reservation lands, and "interfere with their enjoyment thereof." They maintained that any action threatening their rights guaranteed by law would also "infringe upon the jurisdiction and laws of the Government of the United States." John, who later was elected president of the Seneca Nation of Indians, and the other petitioners added: "We do not need to remind Your Excellency that while the people of said Reservations are restricted in their rights and powers as wards of the Government of the United States, they are at times all loyal to the State of New York, of which no better proof needs to be shown than that of the number of their sons who enlisted under the common flag in the recent World War." The Seneca petitioners concluded their letter by asking Governor Nathan Miller to veto the legislation.[50]

In several of the promotional writings for the park's creation before and during the state legislature's consideration of the bill, the park's potential impact on the Senecas was minimized or ignored altogether. On November 24, 1920, a press release pushing for the park's establishment maintained: "The tract lies south of the Allegheny River and between the Allegheny [sic] Indian Reservation . . . and the New York-Pennsylvania state line in Cattaraugus County. There are no villages or communities to be interfered with. The land is of little present value and is being denuded by chemical companies. Unless acquired now, this, the last opportunity now open to western New York, will be lost forever."[51] When the Senecas were mentioned during and after the bill was passed, they were presented as quaint vestiges of the past or as colorful entertainers for tourists.[52] As with the heavy-handed actions of National Park Service administrators in the same era, New York State officials had myopia toward reservation residents.[53]

Despite the Seneca protest, the Ames bill passed the Senate on April 15, 1921, and the assembly approved it three days later.[54] On May 2, Governor Miller signed the bill into law. The legislation was entitled "An Act to provide for the location, creation and management of the Allegany State Park in Cattaraugus County and for the purchase of lands: and making an appropriation thereof." Section 1 of the act defined the park's boundaries and stated that it "shall be forever reserved and maintained for the use of all the people, but the said Allegany State Park shall not constitute a part of the forest preserve." The law created the Board of Allegany State Park Commissioners, all appointed by the governor and approved by the state legislature. It gave them the power "to select, locate, and acquire lands" for the park, build roads and bridges, erect camps, reforest, and "provide for the protection and propagation of fish and game." Under the Allegany State Park Act, commissioners could appoint fish and game wardens, enforce fire regulations, lay out roads, and acquire lands, all done without the input of the Senecas. Importantly, section 9 of the act states: "The commission may exempt from the purchase of any lands or waters taken under this article, any oil, gas, lumber, or mineral rights thereon, with the right of access thereto, which exemption must be stated in the description filed in the office of the secretary of state and in the notice served on the owner, as provided by this section."[55] Soon after the bill's passage, Governor Miller appointed Fancher as chairman of the board of commissioners of Allegany State Park.[56]

The act was hailed by the regional newspapers of the day. In an editorial, "The Allegany State Park and What It Means," editors of the *Cattaraugus Republican* insisted that the act would usher in a new era of "almost limitless possibilities" for the city of Salamanca. The article referred to the city's new nom de plume—the Gateway to Allegany State Park—adding: "Salamanca people cannot too quickly recognize that almost overnight the great tract of wild lands to the south and west of this city, long regarded as almost worthless, has become one of our chief assets." Manifest Destiny reappeared in a new form. Just as the trans-Mississippi West, seen initially as "the Great American Desert," was conquered and transformed by Anglo-Saxon peoples and made into to the "garden of the world," southwestern non-Indian New Yorkers were now determined to transform their region into a tourist paradise. The editors predicted that urban dwellers from nearby cities would flock to the area for recreation. The article heaped most of the praise on Boss Fancher. The editorial referred to the act as "the crown jewel of Fancher's career in politics."[57]

On July 30, 1921, the park officially opened with a crowd estimated between five thousand and ten thousand people. It was an immediate success, with more than twenty thousand visitors in its first month. The newly appointed Allegany State Park Commission acquired its first lands six weeks before the opening of the park. The commission soon gobbled up seven thousand acres for the park at bargain-basement prices, with some lands obtained for as little as $4.50 an acre. The state park attracted hundreds of thousands of visitors to the area and expanded quickly. By the late 1940s, it had expanded to sixty-five thousand acres on lands adjacent to the Allegany Indian Reservation, becoming the largest of all New York state parks.[58]

Henry R. Francis, who was appointed the first executive secretary of the Allegany State Park Commission, was especially important in planning in the first years after the park's opening and worked closely with Robert Moses.[59] In his writings, he emphasized that the park was designed to provide wholesome and healthy camping facilities for urban dwellers, especially those coming from nearby Buffalo and Rochester. Francis described the commission's plans to acquire lands for cross-country skiing, picnicking, fishing, hiking, horseback riding, hunting, and swimming, as well as nature study. He recommended that canoeing be included as a future recreational activity, suggested that it could be developed along the Allegheny River between Salamanca and Onoville, and recommended that plots of land be provided for public use.[60] Hence, more than three decades before creation of the Allegheny Reservoir in the Kinzua Dam project, planners were looking to use waters in Seneca Country for recreational purposes. The commission also bred resentment when, in the mid-1920s, it assumed jurisdiction over the administration of Cuba Lake State Park, thus bringing it into direct conflict with Seneca land claims assertions.[61]

Right through the 1920s, the state's intrusion into Seneca existence remained unchecked. Albany policy makers continued to push for complete jurisdiction over Indian affairs. In October 1929, Secretary of the Interior Ray Wilbur wrote to the Senate Committee on Indian Affairs, recommending the expansion of state jurisdiction over Indian affairs in New York State. "In view of the fact that the State has heretofore always assumed the right to exercise sovereignty and jurisdiction over these people, I am strongly moved to recommend that the activities of the State in this respect be in no matter curtailed." He continued: "Rather, if any legislation by Congress along such lines is now to be had, that it be with a view of removing any doubts that may have heretofore existed with respect to the authority and jurisdiction of the State in the premises."[62] The same year, Edgar Meritt, the assistant commissioner of Indian affairs, testified before a Senate subcommittee that his federal agency "had practically nothing to do with the handling of the affairs of the New York Indians."[63]

The next year, in one of the more determined efforts to transfer full jurisdiction to Albany, Congressman Bertram Snell of Potsdam introduced legislation and held hearings on Capitol Hill.[64] After the state legislature passed a resolution in support of Snell's bill, five New York State commissioners—attorney general, education, health, social welfare, and mental hygiene—issued a separate report recommending the transfer of jurisdiction. The commissioners pointed out the wide disparities in annual financial costs between state and federal Indian policies, with Albany spending almost $500,000 to Washington's approximately $6,000.[65] Meanwhile, hundreds of Allegany and Cattaraugus Senecas signed a petition against transfer, filing it with the House Committee on Indian Affairs. They insisted that Congress not alter relations between the Seneca Nation and the U.S. and renege on "pledges to our people at the Treaty of Canandaigua, made so long ago and kept sacredly by us for so many years."[66]

The debate over the Snell bill occurred at a time when tensions between the Senecas and the state of New York had reached a boiling point. Just when the bill was being debated in Congress, two Cayuga women—Nancy Bowen and Lila Jimerson—who resided at the Cattaraugus Indian Reservation, were arrested for the murder of Clothilde Marchand, the wife of an internationally famous sculptor and museum exhibit designer. Henri Marchand had apparently had an affair with Jimerson, one of his models. On March 7, 1930, the deranged Bowen had clubbed Marchand's wife to death in Buffalo and both she and Jimerson had been arrested for the murder. Guy Moore, the local Erie County district attorney, stressed the sensationalist nature of the crime, labeling it an example of Indian witchcraft gone wild. He suggested that state criminal jurisdiction was needed, since the federal government's enforcement of law and order on the reservations in New York was insufficient. Within three weeks, in his rush to judgment, Moore had had the two women indicted, selected a jury, and put the women on trial for murder. News coverage, including a reprinting of a salacious diary allegedly written by Jimerson—one that proved to be a fake, demeaned the Hodinöhsö:ni´. Stories in New York State's newspapers spread nationwide, making outrageous claims about the immorality of Indian women and the so-called superstitious nature of Indian life as a whole.[67]

The Hodinöhsö:ni´ viewed the case as a clear example of two-sided white justice, since they saw Henri Marchand, who admitted seducing his models, as the calculating person behind the crime. Among those challenging racial stereotypes during the legal proceedings was a committee composed of Tuscarora chief Clinton Rickard, Seneca president Ray Jimerson, journalist/activist Alice Lee Jemison, and anthropologist Arthur C. Parker. Because of the anti-Indian hysteria surrounding the case, the Indians' defense committee beseeched famous attorney Clarence Darrow; Richard Templeton, the local U.S. attorney in Buffalo; and Vice President Charles Curtis, who was of Kaw Indian ancestry, to help the two women accused of murder. After much prodding and Vice President Curtis's interest in the case, the U.S. attorney intervened just four hours before the trial began, asserting federal jurisdiction in the case. After Jimerson fell ill with tuberculosis, the judge declared a mistrial of the two women. Instead of standing trial for a second time, Jimerson pleaded guilty to second-degree murder, but then recanted her confession. She and Bowen remained incarcerated for the year. In March 1931, Moore attempted to retry Jimerson for murder. She was acquitted in a second trial when Henri Marchand's philandering was fully revealed and suspicions about his own involvement in the murder were raised. Nancy Bowen subsequently pleaded guilty to second-degree manslaughter and was sentenced to time served.[68]

This murder case and other factors diverted attention from Congressman Snell's efforts to pass federal legislation to transfer criminal jurisdiction to Albany. The decade preceding the Marchand murder case had generated a new activism and renewed nationalism among the Hodinöhsö:ni´ as well as even more distrust of Albany officials. The state's burying of the Everett Commission report had fueled even more determined Hodinöhsö:ni´ efforts to seek compensation for land losses and resulted in a massive Iroquois Confederacy land claims suit involving six million acres, one that failed in federal court in 1927. Moreover, in the 1920s, the state had dismissed Seneca efforts to win back lands at Oil Spring.

By the late 1920s, the Cayuga land claim was also entangled in Seneca Nation efforts to seek justice. The Cayugas had been dispossessed by representatives of the state in "state treaties" in 1789, 1795, and 1807. The result was that some went to live with the Senecas.[69] Although the Senecas "spread their blanket" (a common Hodinöhsö:ni´ metaphor) and allowed the Cayugas to resettle in their territories, the newcomers had no land rights and had no way to secure title on these reservations. They were a minority often subject to the vicissitudes of Seneca politics.[70] Tensions between the two Indian nations had existed since Chief Peter Wilson's interference in Seneca politics during and after the Seneca Revolution. At the Everett Commission hearings, Cayugas voiced anger that a portion of their treaty annuities had been turned over to the Seneca Nation Council, allegedly to provide for the needs of individual Cayuga residents, especially those living at Cattaraugus.[71]

In 1906, hoping to retake land or secure financial compensation to buy land back in their homeland around Cayuga Lake, three Cayuga chiefs—Elon Eels, Ernest Spring, and David Warrior—had filed a memorial with the New York State commissioner of the land office, seeking compensation for the state's allowing white settlers to overrun Cayuga tribal lands and then making a substantial windfall by selling these lands, in violation of federal and state laws that limited profiting from them.[72] From that date onward to the time of the Marchand murder case, state officials either rejected the

Cayuga claim outright or pushed the questionable "solution" that Albany was willing to offer the Cayugas money to purchase Seneca Nation lands![73] In the first three decades of the twentieth century, the Cayugas were also divided, with two groups vying for power. Some local and state officials clearly attempted to further disharmony both within the Cayuga Nation and in its relations with the Seneca Nation. On November 15, 1931, Governor Franklin Roosevelt's office announced prematurely that it had reached a deal between the state, the Cayuga Nation, and the Seneca Nation. The "accord" claimed that the Cayugas would receive $247,609—a pittance for the sixty-four thousand acres lost in the Treaty of 1795—while the Senecas would be compensated with a one-time payment of $75,000 for allowing the Cayugas the right to reside within their nation.[74] Nowhere was there talk of resolving long-standing issues with the Senecas—fishing, hunting, and riparian rights, as well as their long-standing land claims.

The result was that both the Cayuga and Seneca leadership rejected the state's "solution." Hence, when Congressman Snell tried to continue his efforts to transfer jurisdiction to New York State, he was met with sizable Indian resistance to his plan and his bill went down to defeat.

The Onöndowa'ga:' and most other Hodinöhsö:ni' continued to see jurisdictional transfer as a direct threat to their sovereignty and continued to oppose similar efforts for the next two decades. Already suspicious of Albany's intentions, they were soon faced with the election of a New York governor to the presidency of the United States. While the hope was for federal intervention to promote economic relief and employment, much needed by both Indians and non-Indians facing the depths of the Great Depression, the Senecas were not overly impressed by a president's promises of a "new deal," since his track record as governor had not improved state relations with the Hodinöhsö:ni'.

Figure 18. Andrew John Jr., 1894. In the 1880s and early 1890s, John was elected president of the Seneca Nation of Indians four times. Although born on the Allegany Reservation, he had landholdings on Cattaraugus, some of which he donated to the expansion of the Thomas Asylum in the 1880s. He was a fervent opponent of the Dawes Act and the application of federal allotment policies to the Senecas. His political rivalry with William C. Hoag spanned nearly a quarter of a century. *Smithsonian Institution National Anthropological Archives, image NAA GN 00924A 06201200.*

Figure 19. William C. Hoag, February 27, 1904. Hoag, the most prominent Seneca politician of his era, was elected president of the Seneca Nation of Indians ten times from the early 1890s until his death in 1927. A controversial political leader who benefited from questionable leasing arrangements, he ran a well-oiled Seneca political machine for four decades. Hoag was also the most prosperous farmer among the Senecas and a promoter of agriculture among the Hodinöhsö:ni´. He was one of the founders of the Six Nations Agricultural Society, which founded the Indian Village at the New York State Fair a year after Hoag's death. *Smithsonian Institution National Anthropological Archives, image BAE GN 00944A 06203900.*

Figure 20. Marsh Pierce was spokesman for the Cornplanter heirs in the second half of the nineteenth century. Through his efforts, a schoolhouse was opened at the Cornplanter Grant in the late 1850s. In 1871 the Cornplanter Grant's lands were allotted. Seneca Cornplanter membership was soon incorporated into the political system of the Seneca Nation of Indians. *Reprinted from Thomas Donaldson, comp.,* The Six Nations of New York *(Washington, DC: U.S. Census Printing Office, 1892).*

FIGURE 21. Walter "Boots" Kennedy. A self-styled lawyer, Kennedy, who served on the Seneca Nation Council several times, was an important ally of Seneca president William C. Hoag. An ardent defender of Seneca treaty rights, he dominated the Everett Commission hearings on the Seneca reservations in 1920. *Courtesy Mathers Museum of World Cultures, Indiana University, Bloomington.*

Figure 22. Harriet Maxwell Converse. Converse, a poet, journalist, philanthropist, collector, museologist, and writer on the culture of the Six Nations, was the most prominent non-Indian advocate for the Hodinöhsö:ni´ in the last two decades of the nineteenth and the first three years of the twentieth century. She was adopted by the Snipe Clan of the Senecas and made a clan matron of the Iroquois Confederacy. *Courtesy Rare Books and Special Collections, Rush Rhees Library, University of Rochester.*

FIGURE 23. Edward Vreeland. The president of the leading bank in Salamanca, Vreeland was elected to Congress in 1899. From that date until he left Congress, he repeatedly introduced bills calling for the allotment of the Allegany Reservation. His efforts were largely supported by numerous non-Indian lessees on this reservation and were resisted by most Senecas. *Library of Congress, George Bain Collection, LC-DIG-ggbain-01214 (digital file from original negative).*

FIGURE 24. Albert T. Fancher, 1906. Fancher, a highly successful oil man, furniture magnate, and dairy farmer, was a New York State legislator and the Republican boss of Cattaraugus County for three decades until his death in 1930. He and his cohorts, including Edward Vreeland and James Whipple, promoted the allotment of Seneca lands with the aim of securing land titles for their non-Indian constituents. Fancher is most famous for being the "father" of Allegany State Park, sixty-five thousand acres that border the Allegany Indian Reservation and that have had a major impact on the Seneca Nation. *Reprinted from William J. Doty et al., eds.,* The Historic Annals of Southwestern New York. *Vol. 3. (New York: Lewis Historical Publishing Company, 1940).*

FIGURE 25. Alice Lee Jemison, circa early 1930s. This Seneca journalist-activist and niece of Seneca president Cornelius Seneca was a defender of Hodinöhsö:ni´ treaty rights. Working with Chief Clinton Rickard, she took an active role in challenging stereotypes in the media during the Marchand murder case in 1930–31. She worked with President Ray Jimerson in defending Seneca rights to fish and hunt on their federal treaty lands without state licenses. As one of the founders of the American Indian Federation in the mid-1930s, she was a major critic of the Indian New Deal; her activities placed her under surveillance by the Roosevelt administration. *Laurence M. Hauptman personal collection.*

•◄ 10 ►•

DÉJÀ VU

The intrusion into Seneca affairs continued into the 1930s, but this time the meddling was more from Washington than from Albany. Federal officials in the Department of the Interior aimed to transform federal Indian policies through what they outwardly referred to as self-rule. This federal effort was largely focused on promoting new constitutions and structures of elected government for Native American communities nationwide. However, the Senecas already had a constitution and an elected government that they had modified and lived under for more than eight decades.

The already-suspicious Senecas in New York, who had fought previously against congressional allotment legislation and more recently had strongly opposed the Snell bill, were not convinced that the new president, Franklin Roosevelt, was offering them anything really new. After all, he had been a two-term governor of New York, a state that had opposed Hodinöhsö:ni´ interests since its creation after the American Revolution.

After Roosevelt's election to the presidency in November 1932, progressive reformer Harold Ickes was appointed secretary of the interior and John Collier was named commissioner of Indian affairs. Along with Collier and Ickes, two attorneys—Felix Cohen and Nathan Margold—would make significant contributions to what became the "Indian New Deal." Importantly, Washington policy makers provided a significant amount of work relief, especially in WPA, PWA, and CCC projects, to Native Americans nationwide. They promoted Hodinöhsö:ni´ arts and cultural traditions, especially through the Seneca Arts Project, which ran from 1935 to 1941.[1] To their credit, from 1939 to 1942, attorneys in the Justice Department dealt with Seneca concerns about the severely undervalued and delinquent non-Indian leases on the Allegany Indian Reservation and brought a suit to that effect. It led to the cancellation of delinquent leases, which was confirmed in the federal court case *United States v. Forness* in 1942.[2]

With full presidential and Interior Department backing, Collier submitted the Wheeler-Howard bill to Congress in 1934. Congress radically altered the bill, eliminating some of Collier's progressive proposals, including establishment of a court of Indian affairs. On June 18, President Roosevelt signed the revised bill, known as the Indian Reorganization Act (IRA).[3] It was the centerpiece of the Indian New Deal.

The legislation included an end to the land allotment policies set forth in the Dawes Act. It authorized the return of unallotted surplus lands to tribal governments. Conservation efforts were encouraged by the establishment of Indian forestry units and by herd reduction on arid lands, although the arbitrary manner in which the latter program was applied led to Navajo resistance. The act established a revolving loan fund to assist organized tribes in community development. It also created an educational loan fund for Indians seeking avocational, high school, or college education. By waiving civil service requirements, it offered preference to Indians who sought employment in the Bureau of Indian Affairs (BIA). It helped some tribes increase their tribal land bases (especially when contrasted with the allotment period).[4] However, as the American Indian Policy Review Commission later documented, in the forty years after the act's passage, only 595,157 total acres were added to the Indians' land base. In the same period of time, 1,811,010 acres of Indians lands were condemned, mostly for dams, flood control, or hydroelectric projects.[5] Significantly, the IRA increased the personnel and supervisory responsibilities of the Interior Department and the BIA, adding a new layer of permanent administration to the BIA staff on top of an existing structure established by allotment policies.[6]

Despite what appeared to be some revolutionary features of the act— Indian preference in hiring, a revolving credit loan program for economic development, and the encouragement of scholarship assistance for Indian higher education—the Senecas and most Hodinöhsö:ni´ were suspicious of the motives behind the IRA. One Seneca wrote to Commissioner Collier in his faltering English: "We have been fooled time after time that most of the Indians have lost faith in the Saxon race we certainly have had some raw deal in back history we have never had a square deal."[7] In testimony before a congressional committee, President Ray Jimerson blasted the bill as being "too long and complicated, is full of new rules and regulations and is subject to Bureau interpretation."[8] The most vocal Seneca critic of the IRA was Alice Lee Jemison, a Cattaraugus Seneca who had worked for Jimerson in the tribal office. She was also the niece of Cornelius Seneca, three-time president of the Seneca Nation and one of its most respected leaders of the twentieth century.[9]

Members of the Seneca Nation had already spent more than eight decades under an elected government. Although the Senecas had heavily criticized their own governmental structure and many nostalgically looked back to the rule of a chiefs' council, they had largely accepted their government, however inefficient and at times corrupt. In the years that followed the revolution, they had formed a federation-style government composed of two very distinct residential reservation communities. They had brokered political compromises that managed to hold things together, In 1934 they asked themselves why Washington officials were now promoting the creation of a new elected government. They questioned why the U.S. government, which so often turned its back on its responsibilities under treaties, was finally committed to helping the Senecas? Why should President Roosevelt, a former governor of a state that had always been in opposition to Hodinöhsö:ni´ sovereignty, now promote an "Indian New Deal"?

Fearing new outside intrusion that would limit their sovereignty, the Senecas were most concerned with sections 16 and 17, which called for referenda to accept or reject the IRA, the establishment of a new form of elected tribal government, a new tribal constitution, and increased supervisory powers by the secretary of the interior. Article 16 read:

> Any Indian tribe, or tribes, residing on the same reservation, shall have the right to organize for its common welfare, and may adopt an appropriate constitution and by-laws . . . at a special election *authorized by the Secretary of the Interior.* . . . Amendments to the constitution and by-laws may be ratified and approved by the Secretary in the same manner as the original constitution and by-laws. . . . In addition to all the powers vested in any tribe or tribal council by existing law, the

constitution adopted by said tribe shall also vest in such tribe or its tribal council, the following rights and powers: To, employ legal counsel, the choice of counsel and fixing of fees to be *subject to the approval of the Secretary of the Interior*; to prevent the sale, disposition lease, or encumbrance of tribal lands, interests in lands, or other tribal assets without the consent of the tribe; and to negotiate with the Federal, State, and local Governments. The Secretary of the Interior shall advise such tribe or its tribal council of all appropriation estimates or Federal projects for the benefit of the tribe prior to the submission of such estimates to the Bureau of the Budget and the Congress.[10] (emphasis added)

Section 17 allowed the secretary of the interior to issue a charter of incorporation upon request and to establish the electoral machinery for voting on it. Section 17 also established a revolving loan fund to assist organized tribes in community development.

By the New Deal period, the Senecas did not want to turn back the clock and fight the battles of the 1840s, 1850s, and 1860s all over again. They had established order out of chaos and feared that the IRA would bring not only outside control but also increased political instability into their world. It is no wonder that unlike many Indian nations, they voted the IRA down—and not by a small margin. At Allegany, the vote was 298 against to 37 in favor, with 213 eligible voters not going to the polls, a traditional way of expressing opposition to a white referendum. At Cattaraugus, the vote was 475 against to 101 in favor, with 288 staying away from the polling booths. Although the allotted Cornplanter Grant had been formally incorporated into the Seneca Nation political structure in the late 1870s, a separate IRA referendum was held there on June 15, 1935. It should be noted that a significant percentage of the Indians there were Onondaga and Cayuga heirs of Chief Cornplanter. In the referendum, twenty-three Indians supported and seventeen opposed the act. Seneca leadership later vociferously and successfully questioned the right of non-Senecas to vote in the referendum, since seventeen votes were cast by Onondaga residents.[11]

Seneca dissatisfaction with the Roosevelt administration continued unabated. In 1935 Congress passed a bill sponsored by Representative Alfred Beiter and Senator James Mead that called for the repeal of the 1927 Seneca Conservation Act, including the concurrent jurisdiction over Seneca hunting and fishing on their own territories that had been set forth in the act. President Roosevelt vetoed the bill.[12] At the same time, with the immediate need to deal with the crisis of the Great Depression, the Roosevelt administration pushed hydroelectric projects and massive dam construction to create jobs and stimulate the economy.

In 1936 a major flood inundated downtown Pittsburgh. A flood control project for the Upper Allegheny River region, one whose origin dated back at least to 1908, was then revived.[13] In response, Congress passed the Copeland Omnibus Flood Control Act, which called for the Army Corps of Engineers to develop a comprehensive flood control plan.[14] That same year, the Seneca Nation Council sent representatives to Harrisburg in an attempt to slow the push for a dam that would impinge on their lands.[15] In 1938, in another act, Congress authorized the Army Corps of Engineers to develop a plan for thirty-nine reservoirs, nine of them above Pittsburgh along the Allegheny River, including the future Kinzua Dam in the vicinity of Warren, Pennsylvania. The act also placed the Corps of Engineers in charge of the design and implementation of future flood control projects, made provisions for the future development of hydropower at the dam, and gave the Federal Power Commission an equal voice in determining future projects.[16] In the same year, the Army Corps of Engineers hired Robert Moses, now head of the New York State Power Authority, and his staff as consultants to draw up plans for an Upper Allegheny River project.[17] In 1939 the Army Corps of Engineers issued a report to Congress recommending development of a hydroelectric dam on the Upper Allegheny River—a project that would require the removal of Senecas from the Cornplanter Grant and parts of the Allegany Indian Reservation.[18]

Although there was opposition to this dam by BIA personnel, it was war clouds on the horizon and the need to spend money for military preparedness that put off dam construction. Federal–Seneca relations remained tense after Congress passed the Selective Service Act of 1940. Once again, traditional, sovereignty-minded Hodinöhsö:ni´, including members of the Seneca Nation, became draft resisters, although hundreds did volunteer, serving with distinction in the Pacific, European, and North African fronts of the war.[19] To counter the negative publicity generated by draft resistance, several chiefs, not the Iroquois Confederacy's Grand Council, declared war on the Axis powers on the U.S. Capitol steps in 1942.[20] As early as May 1943, eighty-two Seneca men and women were in military service.[21]

During the Indian New Deal, Commissioner Collier had promised Congress that his agenda was the first stage of a larger aim, one to guide the Indians to self-rule and elevate them from reservation impoverishment. He presented it as a way to "emancipate" them from the federal bureaucracy that had regulated, controlled, and stifled their initiative for so long. Indeed, during the war, before a cost-cutting Congress, Collier indicated that the BIA was already making plans to that effect.[22] In 1945–46, the establishment of the Indian Claims Commission promoted by the New Dealers was pushed as a way for the federal government to buy out its past failures in administering Indian affairs and reduce its future treaty obligations.[23] In the postwar world, former Collier assistants such as William Zimmerman Jr. developed lists of Indian nations that could be "set free."[24] In 1948 Congress transferred criminal jurisdiction over the Hodinöhsö:ni´ to New York State, despite significant opposition from the Six Nations, both from elected Seneca leaders and from traditional Six Nations chiefs. This act and one passed in 1950 involving civil jurisdiction were the models for Public Law 280, passed by Congress in 1954, which transferred federal jurisdiction to five separate states.[25]

In 1956 the dam project for the Upper Allegany was revived when Congress appropriated $1 million to prepare a new study. For the next decade, the Seneca Nation and its supporters, who once again included the Quakers, resisted authorization for the building of the dam, but without success. By 1966, the dam was completed, taking nearly 10,000 acres of Seneca lands. In the years that followed this disaster, the Senecas rebuilt their nation, drawing inspiration from the realization that they had seen everything before and had survived many previous crises.[26]

———

In the years after 1848, the Senecas had been hardened in their resolve to survive. They repeatedly had to deal with years of internal political tensions as well as conflict with both state and federal officials. The Seneca Nation of Indians had faced constant and harsh criticisms from members of other Hodinöhsö:ni´ communities in New York because of the overthrow of their chiefs' council in 1848. Although they were culturally Hodinöhsö:ni´ and maintained two longhouses, they were set apart from the politics of the Grand Council at Onondaga. Instead, as late as the mid-1930s, they relentlessly defended their elected government by overwhelmingly voting down the provisions of the Indian Reorganization Act.

The years from the revolution of 1848 to World War II were years of preparation, when the leadership of the Seneca Nation learned valuable lessons to
meet future challenges. The Senecas won favorable decisions in court rulings,
such as the Pattison case over Oil Spring. With great staying power for four
decades, they won recognition and compensation in the courts and in congress
in the Kansas claims case. As early as 1866, they won a U.S. Supreme Court
case against New York State on the issue of taxation. From 1887 to 1914, the
Senecas successfully resisted allotment pushed by the "Salamanca Ring." They
adopted Harriet Maxwell Converse, who served as their chief publicist and
won over powerful supporters in Congress as well as influential clergymen
such as Bishop William Walker. In the process, two powerful Seneca political
figures—William C. Hoag and Andrew John Jr.—temporarily put away their
bitter intratribal rivalry and directed their energies to fighting the Vreeland
bills. The Senecas were also quite savvy in hiring two of the best attorneys of
the age—John Van Voorhis and George Decker—to defend their lands and
to secure justice before Congress and in the courts. While the Senecas didn't
succeed in stopping the transfer of federal criminal and civil jurisdiction to
New York State, which occurred in 1948 and 1950, their actions had delayed
congressional passage of this transfer for six decades.

Over the years the Senecas sought ways to protect their children from
the myriad of problems facing their community. At times they saw their
only alternative was to keep their children close to home, to insulate them
as best they could against the outside world. Although they were dissatisfied
with the quality of education and the assimilationist focus provided in the
state's district schools, they recognized the need to expose their children to
non-Indian ways. Thus they made compromises. They contributed moneys
and labor to repair schoolhouses and provided firewood to heat the buildings.
A few Senecas even served as teachers. However, on at least two occasions,
they instituted boycotts of the schools until administrators were replaced.
At other times, some parents, especially those who resided in Longhouse
districts at Allegany and Cattaraugus, encouraged nonattendance as a way
to protest. In another example of resistance, some parents sent their children
to the nearby boarding school at Tunesassa to be educated by the Quakers,
who had had long familiarity with and a bit more cultural sensitivity to the
Senecas. Moreover, some of the most prominent Allegany Seneca political
leaders—from William C. Hoag in the early 1870s to Calvin "Kelly" John
in the 1930s—were products of this educational institution.

Still other parents sent their children to far-off boarding schools. At Carlisle and other government-run or privately run boarding schools, the children interacted with large numbers of Native American children, including other pupils from Six Nations communities. While this was a harsh way to "save" their children, since their sons and daughters faced policies that attempted to change them, deny their Native language and customs, and transform their values, Hodinöhsö:ni´ parents were well aware that at schools such as Hampton, their children would receive three meals a day, somewhat better health care, and possibly a trade to help them survive in the rapidly changing world of industrial America. Some, such as Cleo Hewitt, a graduate of Hampton, returned to Seneca Country to teach. Nurse Nancy Seneca (Phillips), a graduate of Carlisle, was to save the day at the Thomas Asylum/School during a pandemic. Ray Jimerson, who attended Hampton, would be elected several times to the presidency of the Seneca Nation and fight for the recognition of Indian fishing rights.

During the Kinzua crisis, the Seneca Nation established the Seneca Educational Foundation with moneys provided in congressional legislation as "compensation." For the next twenty years, this small amount of money was used to provide higher education to a significant number of students, and many of those who benefited from program went on to work for the Seneca government. Onöndawa´ga:´ leaders also lobbied to get the New York State Board of Regents to issue a 1975 policy statement recognizing that Native Americans have the right to be taught about their own history. In 1989 Seneca was finally allowed to be used as the language requirement for high school graduation.

Survival took other forms. While scholars and many Hodinöhsö:ni´ rightly view the Thomas Asylum/School as a cold, depressing institution for children, its administration varied in compassion and ability from one decade to another. The asylum was originally founded at Cattaraugus by missionary Asher Wright with the support of the Seneca Nation as part of a reform movement—namely, as a refuge for orphans and children from all reservations within New York State who could not be provided for by their families. Compared with other Indian boarding schools from the end of the Civil War into the 1920s, it offered better health care. But after the death of the school's remarkable physician Albert D. Lake and the appointment of John Brennan, a rigid, much-hated disciplinarian, as the new superintendent, both the quality of the medical services provided and the overall administration of the Thomas School declined rapidly well into the 1940s. The Seneca push for health care, so manifested in the period 1880 to the early 1920s, was revived in the 1970s when the Health Action Group, mostly composed of determined Seneca women, pushed to obtain federal Indian Health Service coverage.

In the 1970s, attorneys for the Senecas successfully argued that they could hunt and fish without state licenses on their own reservations. In addition, from 1985 onward, Seneca attorneys brought a series of land claims suits against New York State. They used the very same argument employed by the Strong brothers in the *Christy* case in the 1880s and 1890s—that is, Albany's violations of the federal Trade and Intercourse Acts. In 1990, in congressional legislation, the Senecas secured more equitable leasing arrangements on the Allegany Indian Reservation, and in 2005, they won back fifty-one acres of the Oil Spring Indian Reservation. Moreover, as it had done as early as the 1860s, the Seneca Nation from the 1990s onward objected to and brought suit against state efforts to tax Indians and their enterprises on their reservations.

Since the creation of its elected government in 1848, the Seneca Nation had learned valuable lessons to meet the many challenges it faced during construction of the Kinzua Dam and after its completion in 1966. The Senecas fought the good fight for three decades in their attempts to stop it. Although they failed, along with their Quaker allies they skillfully brought national attention to the disgraceful treatment of American Indians in the United States. They generated more than a cause about one single dam; they helped create a movement that aimed to end Indian land loss nationally and recruited numerous political allies, both Indian and non-Indian.[27] For the next half century, they would successfully rebuild their community, much as they did after the disastrous Buffalo Creek Treaty of 1838.

•◄ ►•

ABBREVIATIONS USED IN THE NOTES

ACP	Arthur C. Parker
AD	Assembly documents
APS	American Philosophical Society
ARCIA	*Annual Report of the Commissioner of Indian Affairs*
BHML	Buffalo History Museum Library
BIA	Bureau of Indian Affairs
BN	*Buffalo (Evening) News*
COL	Columbia University
Coll.	collection
CR	*Cattaraugus Republican*
CU	Cornell University
CCF	central classified files
DHI	Jennings, *Iroquois Indians*
ER	*Everett Report*
FDR	Franklin Delano Roosevelt
FRC	Federal Record Center
HC	Haverford College
HISF	Hampton Institute student files
HUA	Hampton University Archives
ICC	Indian Claims Commission
IHS	Indian Health Service
IRA	Indian Reorganization Act
JKI	Joseph Keppler Jr.—Iroquois
KCNYIR	Kansas claims New York Indian records
LC	Library of Congress
M	microcopy
MP	Maris Pierce
MR	microfilm reel

MSS	manuscript collection
NA	National Archives, Washington, D.C.
NA II	National Archives, College Park, Md.
NYAR	New York Agency records
NYPL	New York Public Library
NYSA	New York State Archives
NYSDOHR	New York State Department of Health records
NYSDPW	New York State Department of Public Works
NYSED	New York State Education Department
NYSEDAR	New York State Education Department annual reports
NYSL	New York State Library, Manuscript Division
NYSSPIAR	New York State superintendent of public instruction annual reports
NYT	*New York Times*
NYYMF	New York Yearly Meeting of Friends
OF	official file
OIA	Office of Indian Affairs
OSI	Office of the Secretary of the Interior
PYMF	Philadelphia Yearly Meeting of friends
RG	record group
SC	special case file
SD	Senate document
SED	Education Department (New York State)
SNAR	Six Nations Agency records
SNI	Seneca Nation of Indians
SP	*Salamanca (Republican) Press*
Stat.	United States Statutes at Large
SW	Swarthmore College
TIS	Thomas Indian School (Thomas Asylum for Orphan and Destitute Indian Children)
TISAR	Thomas Indian School annual reports
UR	University of Rochester
USGPO	United States Government Printing Office
WMB	William M. Beauchamp
WHS	Wisconsin Historical Society
WR	*Whipple Report*

•◄ ►•

NOTES

Preface

1. Hauptman, *In the Shadow of Kinzua*; Hauptman, *Conspiracy of Interests*; Hauptman, *The Iroquois and the New Deal.*
2. Hauptman, "Indian Reorganization Act"; Hauptman, "American Indian Federation"; Hauptman, "Alice Lee Jemison"; Hauptman, "Raw Deal."
3. Hauptman, "Beyond Forensic History."
4. Hauptman, *In the Shadow of Kinzua.*
5. By far the best study on the revolution is Thomas S. Abler's "Factional Dispute and Party Conflict in the Political System of the Seneca Nation (1854–1895)." See also Society of Friends, *Documents and Official Reports*; Wilkins, *Documents of Native American Political Development*, 72–80, 265–67.
6. Donaldson, *Six Nations of New York*, 27–31. For the Kinzua Dam project, see Hauptman, *In the Shadow of Kinzua.*
7. There were also thirty-two Onondagas and five Oneidas living at Cattaraugus and eighty-seven Onondagas living at Allegany. Marcus Johnson [federal Indian subagent] to George Manypenny [commissioner of Indian affairs], September 30, 1854, *ARCIA* 1854, 26–27. My estimates of the percentage of Cayugas at Cattaraugus are based on the following: In 1845 there were 114 Cayugas on the Cattaraugus Indian Reservation; 44 left for Indian Territory the next year. By 1847, twenty-five had returned to Cattaraugus. Henry Schoolcraft, "Cattaraugus Indian Reservation," New York State Indian Census, 1845, NYSA. In 1890, 153 Cayugas and 1,355 Senecas were living at Cattaraugus. Donaldson, *Six Nations of New York*, 6. The late Pauline Seneca, a distinguished Cayuga elder, was married to Seneca nation president Cornelius Seneca. Her father, Sylvester C. Lay Jr., had been on the Seneca Nation Council, and her uncle Chester C. Lay had been president of the Seneca Nation. Author interview with Pauline Seneca, July 15–17, 1982.
8. Daniel Sherman [federal Indian agent] to Commissioner of Indian Affairs, October 9, 1877, *ARCIA* 1877, 165; Sherman to Commissioner of Indian Affairs, October 16, 1880, *ARCIA* 1880, 136. See also Abler and Elisabeth Tooker, "Seneca," 509; Abler, *Cornplanter*, 83–84, 187–88.

9. George-Shongo, *Ono'dowa'ga' Gano'kyëdoh Nogeh''oweh*, 17, 62; Abrams, *Seneca People*, 70–83.

10. See, for example, the revealing testimony of an aged Seneca military veteran named Huff about why the Senecas "put up" with their government, *ER*, 25.

11. William N. Fenton to Walter Taylor, January 28, 1965, Walter Taylor MSS, MR14, WHS; Wallace, *Death and Rebirth of the Seneca*; Wilson, *Apologies to the Iroquois*, 172.

12. 7 Stat., 9 (January 15, 1838). The corruption is well documented in pamphlets from 1840, 1841, and 1872 in Society of Friends, *Case of the Seneca Indians in the State of New York*. See also Manley, "Buying Buffalo from the Indians," 313–29. I deal with the treaty, its origins, and its impact in *Conspiracy of Interests*, 175–220, and *The Tonawanda Senecas' Heroic Battle against Removal*, 31–125. For the Treaty of 1842, see 7 Stat., 586 (May 20, 1842).

13. See note 12.

14. In a tribal referendum on May 23, 1964, women won the right to vote in Seneca tribal elections. Two years later, in another referendum, they received the right to hold office. "Seneca Women Given Right to Hold Office," *SR*, April 7, 1966.

15. Daniel Sherman [federal Indian agent] report to Commissioner of Indian Affairs, October 21, 1874, *ARCIA* 1874, 183; Cong. Rec., 57th Cong., 2d sess. (December 15, 1902), 36, 1:337.

16. Author interview with George Heron, September 29, 1984. Heron was president of the Seneca Nation of Indians during the Kinzua crisis.

Chapter 1

1. I further develop this point in Hauptman, "The Meddlesome Friend." In my fieldwork for more than forty-five years, many Allegany and Cattaraugus Senecas have expressed to me that "outsiders" were responsible for the revolution and that the election system was imposed on the Senecas. Some are nostalgic about the old system of chiefs and their council rule.

2. Quaker publications related to the events leading up to the revolution include pamphlets from 1840, 1841, and 1872 in Society of Friends, *Case of the Seneca Indians in the State of New York*; Society of Friends; *Documents and Official Reports* (1857); and several others through 1872.

3. For background on Seneca land losses from 1797 to 1842, see Hauptman, *Conspiracy of Interests*, 1–23, 121–220.

4. New York State Census, 1865; French, *Gazetteer of the State of New York*, 150–51; Whitford, *History of the Canal System*, 1:914–19.

5. The Stryker frauds are documented in U.S. Congress, H.R. Rep. 92. For more on Stryker, see Hauptman, *Conspiracy of Interests*, 178–81, 186–88, 255n19.

6. For McLane, see Lyman C. Draper MSS, MR4, 133, WHS, reprinted in John, *Notes of Border History*. Solomon W. McLane to William Medill [commissioner of Indian affairs], February 16, 1849; Solomon W. McLane and Zachariah

Jimeson to Thomas Ewing [secretary of the interior], November 7, 1849, OIA, NYAR, M234, MR587, RG75, NA; Maris Pierce to Joseph Elkinton, April 17, 1851, NYYMF MSS, SW (copy in SNI Archives). List of members of the Seneca Mission Church in Severance, *Buffalo Historical Society Publications*, 379–80. David George-Shongo, director of the Seneca-Iroquois National Museum, claims that the first president's name was inaccurately recorded and that it was actually Solomon Williams Lane. *Seneca Nation of Indians Official Newsletter*, December 23, 2016, and January 13, 27, 2017; George-Shongo, *Ono'dowa'ga' Gano'kyëdoh Nogeh''oweh*, 3–4.

7. Abler, "Factional Dispute and Party Conflict," 155.

8. Ibid., 157.

9. Ibid., 110 passim.

10. For the early problems caused by leasing, see *ARCIA* 1851, 265.

11. The corruption is well documented in Society of Friends, *Case of the Seneca Indians in the State of New York*, 1–53. See also Manley, "Buying Buffalo from the Indians," 313–29.

12. Society of Friends, *Documents and Official Reports*, 15–20. For John Seneca's genealogy and church affiliation, see Howland, "Seneca Mission at Buffalo Creek," 156–57. For the register of members, see Severance, *Buffalo Historical Society Publications*, 379–80.

13. Society of Friends, *Documents and Official Reports*, 16–18.

14. Ibid., 19–20.

15. Ibid.

16. Ibid., 20.

17. New York State Legislature, *Laws of New York*, chap. 150 (May 8, 1845), 146.

18. Ibid.

19. Ibid. For the divisive impact of these state laws, see Fenton, "The Seneca Indians by Asher Wright," 315–16. The legislature continued its attempts to incorporate the Senecas under state law well after 1845. See, for example, New York State Legislature, *Laws of New York*, chap. 365 (November 15, 1847).

20. Jemison quoted in "Council of the Seneca Nation," *Commercial Advertiser*, August 27, 1845, OIA, NYAR, M234, MR586, RG75, NA.

21. John Mitten quoted in ibid.

22. Maris Pierce to George T. Trimble, March 16, 1846, PYMF MSS, HC (copy on file in SNI Archives).

23. Electoral results of Seneca election, 1846, OIA, NYAR, M234, MR 586, RG75, NA.

24. "The Memorial of the Undersigned Chiefs of the Assembled in Public Council, on the Cattaraugus Reservation: on 3d Day of December 1845," pamphlet, NYSL.

25. Society of Friends, *Report of the Proceedings at an Indian Council Held at Cattaraugus in the State of New York, June, 1846*, 35–36.

26. Ibid., 28–30.

27. See note 1. Thomas's remarkable entrepreneurial abilities are documented Dilts, *Great Road*, 10–12, 32–50, 56, 62; Stover, *History of the Baltimore and Ohio Railroad*, 20–25, 30–33, 37.

28. Members of the Seneca Nation of Indians refer to the United States–Seneca Treaty of 1842, an accord that returned the Allegany and Cattaraugus Reservations but not the Buffalo Creek and Tonawanda Reservations, as the "Compromise Treaty." Members of the Tonawanda Band of Senecas refer to the same accord as the "Compromised Treaty," since none of their lands were returned in 1842. They were "allowed" to repurchase seventy-five hundred acres after another federal treaty in 1857. See 7 Stat., 586 (May 20, 1842). For Thomas's and the Hicksites' roles at this treaty, see Hauptman, "Statesmen, Salvation Seekers, and the Senecas," 51–83.

29. For the Senecas' adoption of Philip Thomas, see "Council of the Seneca Nation at Cattaraugus," *Commercial Advertiser*, August 18, 1845; Society of Friends, *Report of the Proceedings of an Indian Council Held at Cattaraugus in the State of New York, 7th Month, 1845*, 33–34; Society of Friends, *Documents and Official Reports*, 4. See also Philip Thomas to George Manypenny [commissioner of Indian affairs], June 7, 1853, OIA, M 234, NYAR, MR588, RG75, NA.

30. Fenton, "Toward the Gradual Civilization of the Indian Natives," 567–81.

31. Philip Thomas to William Medill, August 28, 1846, OIA, NYAR, M234, MR586, RG75, NA. See also Philip Thomas to William Medill, May 15, 1846, September 25, 1846; Philip Thomas to T. Hartley Crawford, July 31, 1845, OIA, NYAR, M234, MR586, RG 75, NA; Philip Thomas to William Medill, March 10, August 30, September 9, and November 25, 1848, OIA, NYAR, M234, MR 587, RG75, NA. After the revolution, Thomas broke with Wilson after the Cayuga chief was accused of corruption. The Baltimore business magnate blamed Wilson's fall from grace on the chief's frequent presence as a delegate to the political cesspool of Albany. Philip Thomas to President Millard Fillmore, February 24, 1851, OIA, NYAR, M234, MR587, RG75, NA.

32. Peter Wilson to Asher Wright, March 4, 1844, William Clement Bryant MSS, Letterbook II, BHML. For a description of his studies in medical school, see Peter Wilson to Asher Wright, December 8, 1842, William Clement Bryant MSS, Letterbook II, BHML.

33. For criticisms of Wilson, see Chiefs' Petition to Remove Peter Wilson as the Seneca Interpreter, October 27, 1848, OIA, NYAR, M234, MR586, RG75, NA. He was accused of being a drunk, an adulterer, and a brawler. William Jemerson [Seneca Nation clerk] to Commissioner of Indian Affairs, February 10, 1851; Philip Thomas to President Millard Fillmore, February 24, 1851, with attached women's petition [from Margaret Two Guns, Nancy Jimerson, Lucy King, Julia Silverheels, Rachel Bigdeer, Widow George, and Mrs. Allen

Jimeson], February 10, 1851, OIA, NYAR, M234, MR587, RG75, NA. Wilson survived these criticisms and later represented the Six Nations Council as the Cayuga representative in pursuit of the Kansas claims.

34. By mid-century, more than two hundred Onondagas and Cayugas were living in Seneca territory, mostly at Cattaraugus, *ARCIA* 1852, 27. Peter Wilson to William Medill, July 1, 1847, OIA, NYAR, M234, MR586, RG75, NA. For Seneca support of Wilson, see Henry Two Guns to Philip Thomas, September 14, 1846, OIA, NYAR, M234, MR586, RG75, NA. As late as 1853, prominent Senecas were defending Wilson. See John Luke and Zachariah L. Jimeson to Philip Thomas, May 14, 1853; Ely S. Parker to President of the United States, March 21, 1853, OIA, NYAR, M234, MR588, RG75, NA. For the 1847 epidemic, see Fenton, "Seneca Indians by Asher Wright," 320.

35. Peter Wilson to Philip Thomas, December 23, 1847, OIA, NYAR M234, MR586, RG75, NA; Peter Wilson to Philip Thomas, July 18, 1848, OIA, NYAR M234, MR587, RG75, NA.

36. Philip Thomas to William Medill, March 10, 1848.

37. Philip Thomas to William Medill, September 9, 1848. For the accusations against Thomas and Wilson, see Maris Pierce to Joseph Elkinton, February 21, 1849; Maris Pierce to Mary Jane Pierce, February 13, 1849, MP MSS; Maris Pierce to President Zachary Taylor, March 13, 1849, BHML; Maris Pierce to Joseph Elkinton, June 10, 1850, NYYMF, SW (copy on file in SNI Archives). Later Thomas defended himself from these accusations: Philip Thomas to William Medill, December 15, 1848, OIA, NYAR, M234, MR587, RG75, NA. Maris Pierce to Joseph Elkinton, April 17, 1851, MP MSS, BHML.

38. Abler, "Factional Dispute and Party Conflict," 125.

39. Maris Pierce to George Lindsey, January 25, 1847; W. P. Angel [federal Indian subagent] to William Medill, March 17, 1847, OIA, NYAR, M234, MR586, RG75, NA; Israel Jemison to William Marcy [secretary of war], March 18, 1848; Israel Jemison, Seneca White, and Chiefs Council to Philip Thomas, April 19, 1848; Petition of Allegany Seneca Chiefs to Congress [includes Governor Blacksnake] to President of the United States, March 29, 1848; Chiefs' petition to the President of the United States, January 25, 1849 OIA, NYAR, M234, MR587, RG75, NA.

40. Warriors' petition to William Marcy, March 23, 1848; John Bennett, John Green Blanket, et al. to William Marcy, October 11, 1848; Petition of Headmen and Warriors to Secretary of War, January 26, 1848, OIA, NYAR, M234, MR587, RG75, NA.

41. Seneca women's petition, October 13, 1848, OIA, NYAR, M234, MR587, RG75, NA.

42. Subagent Shankland report to Commissioner of Indian Affairs, December 30, 1848, with attached census, October 30, 1848, *ARCIA*, 1848–49, 571.

43. Ibid.

44. Resolutions adopted by the constitutional convention of the Seneca Nation of Indians, December 4, 1848, OIA, NYAR, M234, MR587, RG, NA. The adopted constitution has been conveniently reprinted in Wilkins, *Documents of Native American Political Development,* 75–82.

45. Seneca Nation Council minutes, June 1854, SNI Archives.

46. Abler, "Factional Dispute and Party Conflict," vii, 115, 118–20, 123–25, 152–58. Abler's conclusions here appear quite accurate. I compared the names of delegates who approved the Seneca constitution of 1848 with names found on the membership lists of the Reverend Thompson Harris's Seneca Mission Church at Buffalo Creek and the Reverend Asher Wright's United Mission Church at Cattaraugus. See "List of members of the Seneca Mission at Buffalo Creek" in Severance, *Buffalo Historical Society Publications,* 379–80.

47. I compared the names of delegates who approved the 1848 Seneca constitution with the names of chiefs who signed the 1838 and 1842 treaties.

48. Wilkins, *Documents of Native American Political Development,* 75–82.

49. Seneca Chiefs to President James K. Polk, December 7, 1848, OIA, NYAR, M234, MR587, RG75, NA.

50. Chiefs' petition to President of the United States, January 25, 1849, OIA, NYAR, M234, MR 587, RG75, NA.

51. Fifty-one Seneca Warriors [opposed to the new government] to President of the United States, January 29, 1849, OIA, NYAR, M234, MR587, RG75, NA.

52. William L. Marcy to Maris Pierce, February 14, 1849, MP MSS, BHML; Philip Thomas to William Medill, February 2, 1849, in "Society of Friends, Joint Committee on Indian Affairs of the 4 Yearly Meetings of Baltimore, Philadelphia, New York, and Genesee, 1849," pamphlet in NYSL.

53. Maris Pierce to Joseph Elkinton, February 21, 1849, April 9, 1849; Maris Pierce to Mary Jane Pierce, February 13, 1849, March 12, 1849; Maris Pierce to Thomas Ewing [secretary of the newly created Interior Department], March 8, 1849; Maris Pierce to President Zachary Taylor, March 13, 1849, MP MSS, BHML.

54. Solomon W. McLane to William Medill, February 16, 1849, OIA, NYAR, M234, MR587, RG75, NA.

55. Gua-na-ea to President Zachary Taylor, April 24, 1849, in Society of Friends, *Documents and Official Reports,* 23–24.

56. Philip Thomas to William Medill, March 23, May 9, 1849; Philip Thomas to Thomas Ewing, April 8, 1849, OIA, NYAR, M234, MR587, RG75, NA.

57. Maris Pierce to President Zachary Taylor, March 13, 1849, OIA, NYAR, M234, MR587, RG75, NA.

58. New York State AD 189, chap. 378 (March 27, April 11, 1849), 530, 721; New York State Legislature, *Laws of New York,* chap. 420 (April 11, 1849), 576.

59. Peacemakers' and clerk's affidavit regarding first election, May 1, 1849, OIA, NYAR, M234, MR 587, RG75, NA; George-Shongo, *Ono'dowa'ga' Gano'kyëdoh Nogeh''oweh*, 6.

60. Zachary Taylor "to his children and friends in the Seneca Nation," May 2, 1849, OIA, NYAR, M234, MR 587, RG75, NA.

Chapter 2

1. See Abler, "Factional Dispute and Party Conflict," vi–viii.

2. Stephen Osborne [federal Indian subagent] to Luke Lea [commissioner of Indian affairs], September 30, 1852, *ARCIA* 1852, 25.

3. Solomon W. McLane and Zachariah Jimeson to Thomas Ewing, November 7, 1849, OIA, NYAR, M234, MR587, RG75, NA.

4. Maris Pierce to Joseph Elkinton, November 29, 1849, MP MSS, BHML.

5. Maris Pierce to Joseph Elkinton, February 21, 1849, February 10, 1850, MP MSS, BHML; Abrams, *Seneca People*, 70.

6. George-Shongo, *Ono'dowa'ga' Gano'kyëdoh Nogeh''oweh*, 70.

7. Maris Pierce to Joseph Elkinton, June 10, 1850, HC (copy in SNI Archives). By 1853 Pierce had finally concluded that the chiefs' efforts to convince Washington officials about the need to return to a council of chiefs–style government was futile. Maris Pierce to Philip Thomas, January 27, 1853, MP MSS, BHML.

8. Maris Pierce to Joseph Elkinton, May 7, 1851, HC (copy in SNI Archives).

9. Memorial to the President of the United States, March 12, 1852; Memorial to New York State Legislature, March 22, 1852, OIA, NYAR, M234, MR588, RG75, NA.

10. Seneca chiefs to President Millard Fillmore, July 8, 1852, OIA, NYAR, M234, MR588, RG75, NA.

11. Millard Fillmore to Luke Lea, July 16, 1852, OIA, NYAR, M234, MR588, RG75, NA.

12. Seneca chiefs to President of the United States, July 8, 1852, OIA, NYAR, M234, MR588, RG75, NA; Abrams, *Seneca People*, 70–71.

13. John Luke, John Hudson, and Peter Snow to Fillmore, September 29, 1852, OIA, NYAR, M234, MR588, RG75, NA.

14. John Luke, John Hudson, Joshua Turkey to Commissioner George Manypenny, February 19, 1855, OIA, NYAR, M234, MR588, RG75, NA. Nevertheless, the ex-chiefs continued to lobby to turn back the clock.

15. Ibid.

16. As early as January 27, 1853, Maris Pierce concluded that these efforts to convince Washington officials were hopeless. Maris Pierce to Philip Thomas, January 27, 1853, MP MSS, BHML. Nevertheless, the ex-chiefs continued appealing to Washington officials. See Henry Two Guns [elected president in May 1854], Israel Jemison, et al., ex-chiefs' petition to George Manypenny, December 15, 1853, OIA, NYAR, M234, MR588, RG75, NA.

17. C. P. Washburne to Commissioner of Indian Affairs, October 20, 1851, *ARCIA* 1851, 265; Abrams, *Seneca People*, 70–72; Hogan, "City in a Quandary," 84; Hungerford, *Men of Erie*, 189–95; Thomas Wistar, "Report of the Committee on the Civilization and Improvement of the New York Indians," *The Friend*, June 10, 1865, 325. Hogan incorrectly states that railroad leases were legal since they were confirmed by the New York State Legislature,

18. Hoag benefited by questionable leasing. Seneca Nation Council minutes, 1880s–1920s. See also Hogan, "City in a Quandary," 85–88.

19. Mason, "Geography of Allegany State Park," 35–38; Hogan, "City in a Quandary," 79–101.

20. Seneca [ex-]chiefs to President Millard Fillmore, July 8, 1852, OIA, NYAR, M234, MR588, RG75, NA.

21. Seneca Nation Council minutes, 1861.

22. Nathaniel Strong to Commissioner of Indian Affairs, January 20, 1857, OIA, NYAR, M234, MR588, RG75, NA.

23. Marcus Johnson [federal Indian subagent] to Commissioner of Indian Affairs J. W. Denver, September 30, 1857, *ARCIA* 1857, 20.

24. Society of Friends, *A Brief Sketch*, 20, 53.

25. Herrick, *Empire Oil*, 22, 35–61, 424–25, 437; Abler, "Factional Dispute and Party Conflict," viii, 169–73; Hogan, "City in a Quandary," 79–101; Brewer, "Oil and Gas Geology," 6–8; Mason, "Geography of Allegany State Park," 34–40; B. B. Weber to Commissioner of Indian Affairs, November 30, 1903. *ARCIA* 1903, 225.

26. According to George Abrams, the impeachment apparently was related to President Job King's granting of the Manley-Nash leases to all the oil and mineral reserves on the Allegany Reservation. Abrams, *Seneca People*, 80, 82. Although initially approved by the Department of the Interior, they were later canceled.

27. See note 25; Rowan, "New York State Produces Oil for the World," 2:991–1010.

28. *Seneca Nation v. Philonus Pattison*. A transcript of court proceedings and testimony at the Cattaraugus County Court in 1857–58 can be found at the Cattaraugus County Courthouse, Little Valley, New York. Copies of Blacksnake's map and papers are also filed there. *Seneca Nation v. Philonus Pattison*, New York Court of Appeals, Vol. 87, Case 1 (1860–61), NYSA. See also Congdon, *Allegany Oxbow*, 197–202. For greater detail, see Hauptman, *Conspiracy of Interests*, 162–74.

29. For the Genesee Valley Canal, see Whitford, *History of the Canal System*, 1:708–13, 1:1010–14; 2:1030–36.

30. The Senecas won a hard-fought land claims settlement in 2005 over fifty-one acres at Oil Spring. See "Settlement of Cuba Lake Claim," *SNI Official Newsletter*, February 11, 2005; "U.S. Court Approval Clears Way for Restoration of Seneca Nation Sovereign Land," *SNI Official Newsletter*, July 29, 2005.

31. New York State Legislature, *Laws of New York,* 63rd sess., chap. 254 (May 9, 1840), 26–27. New York State Legislature, *Laws of New York,* 64th sess., chap. 166 (May 4, 1841), 134–36.
32. Notice of Tax Sales, October 11, 13, 1856, OIA, NYAR, M234, MR588, RG75, NA; L. Burrows [New York State comptroller] to DeWitt Littlejohn [New York State Assembly speaker], with attachments concerning tax sales of Seneca lands, January 9, 1857, Society of Friends, *Documents and Official Reports,* 80–81; Abrams, *Seneca People,* 72–73.
33. Philip Thomas to George W. Manypenny, June 6, 1855, with attached notice of a land sale and unpaid tax payments; Philip Thomas to George W. Manypenny, [no month or day] 1857, OIA, M234, NYAR, MR 588, RG75, NA. Philip Thomas to George T. Trimble, Amos Willetts, and William C. White, November 26, 1856, papers and letters relating to the work of the joint Indian committee of four yearly meetings, 1835–1863, File 21: 1856–57, NYYMF (transferred from Haviland Record Room, Friends School, Manhattan, to Swarthmore College; copy on file in SNI Archives).
34. Memorial of the President John Luke and the Seneca Nation and Councilors to the New York Assembly and Senate, January 1, 1857, in Society of Friends, *Documents and Official Reports,* 82–84.
35. Ibid.
36. Philip Thomas to Commissioner George Manypenny, [no month or day] 1857, OIA, NYAR, M234, MR588, RG75, NA; New York State Legislature, Senate Doc. 85; George Manypenny to [New York State] Governor Myron Clark, December 22, 1856; Myron Clark to E. Merriam, December 26, 1856; [New York State] Governor John King to DeWitt Littlejohn, January 17, 1857, all in Society of Friends, *Documents and Official Reports,* 77–91. Philip Thomas to J. B. Pierce, MP MSS, February 24, 1852, BHML.
37. For the Quaker School, see chapter 6. For the Thomas Asylum/School, see chapter 5.
38. Philip Thomas to James W. Denver, July 27, 1857, OIA, M234, NYAR, MR 588, RG75, NA. See also Hauptman, *Tonawanda Senecas' Heroic Battle against Removal,* 110.
39. George Manypenny to [New York State] Governor Myron Clark, December 22, 1856, in Society of Friends, *Documents and Official Reports,* 49–51.
40. New York State Legislature, Senate Doc. 85.
41. "Act to Relieve the Seneca Nation of Indians from Certain Taxes on the Allegany and Cattaraugus Reservations," *Laws of New York* (January 22, 1857), reprinted in Society of Friends, *Documents and Official Reports,* 90–91.
42. *Joseph Fellows, Survivor of Robert Kendle, Plaintiff in Error v. Susan Blacksmith and Ely S. Parker, Administrator of John Blacksmith, Deceased,* 66 U.S. 366 (March 5, 1857).
43. *The New York Indians,* 72 U.S. 761 (May 16, 1867). For *Fellows v. Blacksmith,* see 60 U.S. 366 (March 5, 1857).

44. "The Taxes on the Indian Reservation," *CR*, May 18, 1871.

45. See Hauptman, *In the Shadow of Kinzua*, chapter 1.

46. Nathaniel T. Strong wrote that the Indian regiments formed in New York State had not been accepted there "upon the grounds of being Indian." Nathaniel Strong to Commissioner William Dole, November 21, 1861, OIA, NYAR, M234, MR589, RG75, NA.

47. Wooster King to "My dear friend," December 11, 1861; Cornelius Plummer to Nathaniel Plummer, December 11, 1862; Cornelius Plummer to Jesse Plummer, February 20, 1862, April 1, 1862; Levi Williams to Father, June 1, 1862, Willet Pierce to Father, June 5, 1862, Civil War Coll., Seneca-Iroquois National Museum; Asher Wright to D. E. Sill [federal Indian agent], February 6, 1864, OIA, NYAR, M234, MR590, RG75, NA; Company K, Fifty-Seventh Pennsylvania Volunteer Infantry, regimental books, records of the adjutant general's office, RG 94, NA; Bates, *History of the Pennsylvania Volunteers*, 2:246–84.

48. D. C. Leach [federal Indian agent] to Commissioner William Dole, September 22, 1862, *ARCIA* 1862, 345.

49. For more on the heroic exploits of the Iroquois, mostly Senecas, in D Company, see Laurence M. Hauptman, *The Iroquois in the Civil War*, 25–45.

50. James C. Fitzpatrick, "The Ninth Corps," *New York Herald*, June 30, 1864; "Chief Silverheels," *Warren (Pa.) Mail*, August 23, 1887.

51. Seneca petition [about illegal enlistments of Seneca boys], General Canby to War Department, January 14, 1864; General E. D. Townsend to Secretary of War, December 3, 1863, March 24, 1864; General E. D. Townsend to Secretary of War [Edwin Stanton], April 12, 1864; authorization for Chief Samuel George (Onondaga) to act as spokesman to get Six Nations underage soldiers discharged, January 4, 1864, OIA, NYAR, M234, MR590, RG75, NA. See also Hauptman, *The Iroquois in the Civil War*, 108–9.

52. The federal Indian agent reported 150 cases. D. E. Sill to William E. Dole, September 22, 1862, *ARCIA* 1862, 346; Asher Wright's report to John Manley, September 30, 1864, *ARCIA* 1864, 455.

53. Resolution of the Seneca Nation Tribal Council, Cattaraugus Reservation [A. Sim Logan, clerk], November 7, 1864, OIA, NYAR, M234, MR590, RG75, NA; Commissioner William Dole's report, [no month or day] 1864, *ARCIA* 1864, 44.

54. This political upheaval was related to whether the Seneca Nation should pursue the Kansas claims under the fraudulent Treaty of 1838. *ARCIA* 456–64; *ARCIA* 1865, 454–56. See chapter 3.

55. President Henry Silverheels to Commissioner William Dole, December 13, 1864, OIA, NYAR, M234, MR590, RG75, NA.

56. "Indians Ask Rule by Chiefs: Cattaraugus Delegation Will Request Washington to Permit Change," *NYT*, May 14, 1926.

Chapter 3

1. For the two treaties, see *WR*, 23–24; 7 Stat., 550 (January 15, 1838).
2. For the ICC and modern Seneca land claims actions, see Hauptman, *In the Shadow of Kinzua*, 187–205.
3. According to attorney George Shattuck, "I used the argument of the state's violation of the Federal Trade and Intercourse Acts in the Oneida land claims case before the United States Supreme Court." Author interview with George Shattuck, August 25, 1983. *Oneida Nation of New York v. County of Oneida, et al.*, 414 U.S. 661. See also Shattuck, *Oneida Land Claims*, 7, 38, 50, 62, 95. From 1985 to 2006, Arlinda Locklear and Jeanne Whiteing, attorneys for the Seneca Nation of Indians, used the very same arguments. I worked for both these attorneys.
4. 7 Stat., 550 (January 15, 1838).
5. According to the federal Indian subagent, about two hundred Iroquois from New York left for Kansas, then Indian Territory, in 1846. Of these, seventy-four died of disease and other causes, eighty-nine returned to New York, and twenty-five remained in the West. W. H. Angel's list of Indians, June 25, 1848, OIA, NYAR, M234, MR587, RG75, NA. All other sources indicate that thirty-two of these Indians remained in the West. Smith, *Indian Tribal Cases*, 2.
6. 11 Stat., 735; 12 Stat., 991 (November 5, 1857). For more on this federal treaty, see Hauptman, *Tonawanda Senecas Heroic Struggle against Removal*, 101–13.
7. See Miner and Unrau, *End of Indian Kansas*.
8. *ARCIA* 1857, 8.
9. Seneca Nation Council resolution, June 2, 1858, OIA, NYAR, M234, MR589, RG75, NA. George Abrams incorrectly puts the date as 1857. Abrams, *Seneca People*, 73.
10. Letter of Edward Purse [Pierce] to Philip Thomas, September 10, 1858, in Thomas, *Address to Edward Pierce*.
11. Abrams, *Seneca People*, 73. Throughout the late 1850s and the 1860s, Strong and Wilson continued to push for Seneca Nation action on its Kansas claims. Wilson appears to have remained persona non grata to some of his own Cayugas. One petition in 1860 indicated that Wilson had been deposed as chief and had "no legal right to transmit any kind of business with the [U.S.] Government in their name." See petition by Cayuga Indians to Commissioner A. B. Greenwood, February 29, 1860, OIA, NYAR, M234, MR 590, RG75, NA. For favorable portraits of the two men, see their obituaries in *CR*: January 18, 1872 (Strong); April 11, 1872 (Wilson). Both Strong and Wilson had "nine lives," emerging from condemnation and political defeat on several occasions.
12. Civil Appropriations Act, 11 Stat., 425 (March 3, 1859); 1859 report by H. S. Stevens, "Census and Testimony Relative to New York Indians in Kansas, 1859," BIA, SC29: KCNYIR, Box 7, RG75, NA.

13. E. A. Hayt [commissioner of Indian affairs] to Carl Schurz [secretary of the interior], March 29, 1878, in U.S. Congress, House of Representatives, Committee on Indian Affairs, H.R. Doc. 673. See also Hiram Price [commissioner of Indian affairs] to Secretary of the Interior [Henry Teller], February 9, 1883, in U.S. Congress, H.R. Doc. 2001; *New York Indians v. United States*, 170 U.S. 1 (April 11, 1898).

14. During the Civil War, federal Indian agent E. L. Terry complained to the commissioner of Indian Affairs that no one was coming to the aid of the destitute "New York Indians" in Kansas, who were "now outcasts," victims of "lawless violence," and facing "extinction." Terry to Commissioner of Indian Affairs William Dole, August 18, 1862, OIA, NYAR, M234, MR 590, RG75, NA.

15. *ARCIA* 1862, 43.

16. Maris Pierce to Mary Jane Pierce, February 2, 1864, Maris Pierce MSS, BHML.

17. Daniel Two Guns, Joshua Turkey, and Nathaniel Strong, February 19, 1864; Nathaniel T. Strong to Commissioner William Dole, April 1, 1864, OIA, NYAR, M234, MR590, RG75, NA.

18. Peter Wilson, Israel Jemison, et al. to Commissioner of Indian Affairs, April 29, 1864, OIA, NYAR, M234, MR590, RG75, NA.

19. Maris Pierce to Mary Jane Pierce, April 24, 1864, MP MSS, BHML.

20. Resolution of the Seneca Nation Tribal Council, Cattaraugus Reservation [A. Sim Logan, clerk], November 7, 1864, OIA, NYAR, M234, MR590, RG75, NA; Commissioner William Dole's report, [no month or day] 1864, *ARCIA* 1864, 44.

21. John Manley [federal Indian agent] to Commissioner of Indian Affairs, September 30, 1864, *ARCIA* 1864, 453–54; Remarks of John Manley, undated, *ARCIA* 1864, 456–64.

22. Remarks of John Manley, *ARCIA* 1864, 464.

23. President Henry Silverheels to Commissioner William Dole, December 13, 1864, OIA, NYAR, M234, MR590, RG75, NA.

24. C. B. Rich [federal Indian agent to commissioner of Indian affairs], September 30, 1865, *ARCIA* 1865, 454–56.

25. Maris Pierce to Benjamin Hallowell, January 7, 1867, SC (copy on file in SNI Archives).

26. Joseph Scattergood to Asher Wright, March 2, 10, 1869, William Clement Bryant MSS, Letterbook II, BHML; S. Rep. 145, 41st Cong., 2d sess., May 3, 1870, in DHI, MR49.

27. Prucha, *American Indian Treaties*, 334–58.

28. Joseph Scattergood to Asher Wright, March 2, 10, 1869. See, for example, S. 640, 43rd Cong., 1st sess. (March 30, 1874), in DHI, MR 49.

29. U.S. Congress, H.R. Doc. 2001; U.S. Congress, H.R. Doc. 2002; U.S. Congress, H.R. Doc. 673; U.S. Congress, H.R. Doc. 1858.

30. "Salamanca Brevities," *CR*, January 26, 1883; "Salamanca Brevities," *CR*, February 2, 1883; "The Seneca Indians—Prospects of the Indians Establishing a School," *CR*, February 16, 1883.

31. For John's final defeat, which led him to a new "career" in Washington, see "The Election Controversy," *CR*, December 4, 1891; Viola, *Diplomats in Buckskin*, 184–85.

32. This was referred to as the Bowman Act; 27 Stat., 426 (January 28, 1893).

33. *New York Indians v. United States*, 30 Ct. Cl.413 (1895), dismissed. Appealed to the United States Supreme Court: 170 U.S.1, 614 (1898). Judgment for "New York Indians." Reversed and remanded to U.S. Court of Claims; 33 Ct. Cl.510, 521. Judgment for "New York Indians." Appealed to U.S. Supreme Court: 170 U.S. 464 (1899). Dismissed. Judgment for "New York Indians." For a chronology of congressional action and court decisions, see Smith, *Indian Tribal Cases*, 1–4.

34. 31 Stat., 27 (February 9, 1900).

35. E. A. Hitchcock to Commissioner of Indian Affairs, March 17, 1904, with undated report by Special Agent Guion Miller, BIA, SC29: KCNYIR, Box 3: Seneca, RG75, NA.

36. Census rolls of New York Indians, compiled by A. W. Ferrin, federal Indian agent, BIA, SC29: KCNYIR, Box 4, RG75, NA; B. B. Weber to Commissioner of Indian Affairs, November 27, 1902, *ARCIA* 1902, 258–60.

37. See note 35. For the special agent's list of accepted applications, see the report of Special Agent Guion Miller, 1903–5: Lists of Names of Applicants for Shares of the New York Indian Money Awarded by the Court of Claims, BIA SC29: KCNYIR, Box 3, RG75, NA.

38. New York Indians Seneca [applications] Rejected Records Relating to Kansas Claims of New York Indians, BIA, SC29, KCNYIR, Box 3, RG75, NA.

39. Case of Hattie R. Calhoun; Answer [legal brief] of Seneca Nation, Petition of Senecas Who Have Not Been Enrolled by the Secretary of the Interior, March 28, 1905, *New York Indians v. United States*, No. 17,861, BIA, SC29: KCNYIR, Box 6, RG75, NA.

40. See note 38.

41. B. B. Weber [federal Indian agent] to Commissioner of Indian Affairs, August 26, 1906, *ARCIA* 1906, 286–91.

42. *New York Indians v. United States*, 40 Ct. Cl.448 (May 15, 1905). For the brief by those denied, see note 39.

43. B. B. Weber to Commissioner of Indian Affairs, August 26, 1906; report of Special Agent Guion Miller, 1903–1905: Lists of Names of Applicants for Shares of the New York Indian Money Awarded by the Court of Claims, BIA SC29: KCNYIR, Box 3, RG75, NA.

44. *WR*, 23–24. For a fuller discussion of this treaty, see Hauptman, *Conspiracy of Interests*, 144–61; cf. Prucha, *American Indian Treaties*, 144–45.

45. *Seneca Nation v. Harrison B. Christy [Christie]* 2 N.Y.S. 546 (Sup. Ct. 1888), affirmed 27 N.E. 275 (N.Y. 1891); appeal dismissed 162 U.S. 283 (1896).

46. *WR*, 23–24.

47. *American State Papers*, 2:868.

48. U.S. Senate, *Journal of the Executive Proceedings*, 3:601 (February 29, 1828).

49. Ibid., 3:603 (April 4, 1828).

50. Richard Montgomery Livingston report to Secretary of War Peter B. Porter, December 25, 1828, OIA, records of the Seneca Agency in New York, M234, MR 808, RG75, NA.

51. Ibid.

52. *WR*, 23–24.

53. Manley, "Red Jacket's Last Campaign," 149–62.

54. Abrams, *Seneca People*, 80–82.

55. Hiram Price [commissioner of Indian affairs] to Secretary of the Interior, April 15, 1881 (filed copy in Seneca-Iroquois National Museum).

56. Benjamin G. Casler [federal Indian agent] to Commissioner of Indian Affairs, October 14, 1881, *ARCIA* 1881, 142.

57. Ibid.; "An Important Decision," *CR*, October 26, 1888; T. W. Jackson [federal Indian agent] to Commissioner of Indian Affairs, August 1889; *ARCIA* 1889, 266; New York State Legislature, *Laws of New York*, chap. 150 (May 8, 1845). For a more detailed analysis of this case, see Hauptman "*Seneca Nation v. Christy*," 947–79.

58. See note 52.

59. W. Peacock [federal Indian agent] to Commissioner of Indian Affairs, September 22, 1884, *ARCIA* 1884, 139–40; W. Peacock to Commissioner of Indian Affairs, August 25, 1885, *ARCIA* 1885, 160–61; W. Peacock to Commissioner of Indian Affairs, August 30, 1886, *ARCIA* 1886, 207; Strong, *Autobiography*; Strong, *Wah-ke-nah and Her People*.

60. 2 NYS 546 (Sup. Ct. 1888); "An Important Decision," *CR*, October 26, 1888.

61. 27 N.E. 275 (N.Y.1891). For the Trade and Intercourse Act cited in the decision, see 2 Stat., 139–46 (March 30, 1802).

62. For Andrews, see Bergan, *History of the New York Court of Appeals*, 114; and New York Court of Appeals, *There Shall Be a Court of Appeals*, 96–97.

63. For Chancellor Sims's views on the Onondagas, see *WR*, 41–45.

64. Hagan, "Reformers' Images of the American Indian," 145–54.

65. 27 N.E. 275 (N.Y. 1891).

66. Ibid.

67. "The Treaty Upheld," *NYT*, April 24, 1891.

68. "Against the Senecas," *CR*, May 8, 1891.

69. 162 U.S. 283 (1896).

70. *Oneida Nation of New York v. County of Oneida, et al.*, 414 U.S., 661. See note 3.

71. *City of Sherrill v. Oneida Indian Nation*, 125 S. Ct. 1478 (2006).

Chapter 4

1. Donaldson, *Six Nations of New York*, 6–9, 11.

2. Ibid., 9.

3. For the origins of the Gaiwi:yo:h, see Wallace, *Death and Rebirth of the Seneca*, 236–85; Wallace, "Origins of the Longhouse Religion," 442–48; Deardorff, "Religion of Handsome Lake," 77–107; Tooker, "On the Development of the Handsome Lake Religion," 35–50.

4. "Three-quarters of the people are professed Christians"; Arthur C. Parker, *Analytical History of the Seneca Indians*, 154.

5. Wallace, "Origins of the Longhouse Religion," 447.

6. Elisabeth Tooker, *Iroquois Ceremonial of Midwinter*, 21.

7. Deardorff claims that a direct line existed from Owen Blacksnake at Allegany right through Edward Cornplanter. Tooker concluded that "there is no legitimate inheritance of all the Good Message [of Handsome Lake]. There are many." Tooker, "On the Development of the Handsome Lake Religion," 48.

8. Parker quoted in Tooker, "On the Development of the Handsome Lake Religion," 46. Parker allegedly learned this from Edward Cornplanter, a fact disputed by Merle Deardorff.

9. For example, a Cattaraugus Seneca opened the Green Corn ceremony in 1894; "Pagan Gospel Ended Adjourned," *Syracuse Herald*, August 22, 1894.

10. For Edward Cornplanter, see Parker, *Parker on the Iroquois*, 14, 21 32–33, 35; Fenton, "Aboriginally Yours," 177–95; Fenton, *The Great Law and the Longhouse*, 106.

11. Fenton, "Aboriginally Yours," 181.

12. "Indians at Pow-wow [actually at Thanksgiving ritual] Observe Old Rites; Representatives of the Six Nations Meet on Onondaga Reservation near Syracuse; Ancient Faith Is Taught; Chief [Edward] Cornplanter Expounds Religion of Handsome Lake and Braves Dance and Tell Their Sins," *NYT*, November 25, 1909. Cornplanter was a Longhouse preacher and teacher, not a chief.

13. Bilharz, "First among Equals?" 101–12; Caswell, *Our Life among the Iroquois Indians,* vii–xxv; Bowen, "Women of the Seneca Nation." For critiques of women's "declension" studies among the Iroquois, see Shoemaker, "The Rise and Fall of Iroquois Women"; Shoemaker, "From Longhouse to Log House."

14. George-Shongo, *Ono'dowa'ga' Gano'kyëdoh Nogeh''oweh*, 34–35; Abrams, *Seneca People,* 100; "Seneca Women Given Right to Hold Office," *SP*, April 7, 1966.

15. Kossuth Bishop et al. to George Scattergood, December 11, 1878, with attached memorial signed by Alexander John, Martin Jimerson, George Titus, Dr. James Shongo, thirty-three women, and others, February 1, 1879, OIA, NYAR, M234, MR596, RG75, NA.

16. See chapter 10.

17. The most widely cited versions of the Gayaneshä'go:wa:h—the Hodinöhsö:ni' Great Law—are in Gibson, *Concerning the League*, xxviii–xxxi, 418, 486–99, and (the Seth Newhouse version) Parker, *Parker on the Iroquois*, sections 40, 44–54, 95.

18. For a good, brief summary of women's traditional roles, see Tooker, "Women in Iroquois Society," 109–24.

19. Jordan, *Seneca Restoration*, 224–77; Brown, "Reservation Log Houses," 29–31.

20. Wallace, *Death and Rebirth of the Seneca*, 312.

21. Abler, *Cornplanter*, 110–11; Fenton, *Great Law and the Longhouse*, 653–59, 674; Wallace, *Death and Rebirth of the Seneca*, 179–83.

22. Wilkins, *Documents of Native American Political Development*, 78.

23. Rothenberg "Mothers of the Nation," 81.

24. Author interview with Rovena Abrams, February 23, 2011. In interviews in the 1980s, Senecas and Cayugas (with Seneca fathers) in their seventies, eighties, and nineties reflected about their grandmothers and mothers who were herbalists. See Austin, *Ne′ Ho Niyo′* Dë:Nö′, 2:26 (Hazel Black), 2:249 (Rhoda Titus), 2:261 (Katie Waterman), 2:271 (Mattie Young).

25. Donaldson, *Six Nations of New York*, 59–60.

26. Ibid., 49–51. Seneca women continue to run crafts booths at the Erie County Fair. Author interview with Jean Lorette, September 25, 2011. They also do so at the Indian Village at the New York State Fair, which the author last attended on Indian Day, September 4, 2015.

27. Wallace, *Death and Rebirth of the Seneca*, 278.

28. For the impact on Seneca family and community life, "Seneca Civilization: The Result of Deadly Firewater; Tommy Halftown, and Indian Brave Yanked to the Happy Hunting Ground by a Locomotive Engine," *CR*, December 13, 1889; "Reservation Tragedy: Jesse Jimerson Killed in a Shooting Affray," *CR*, August 16, 1902; "Carouse May Have a Fatal Result," *CR*, January 30, 1903.

29. Donaldson, *Six Nations of New York*, 60.

30. Harriet S. Caswell, *Our Life among the Iroquois Indians*, 101.

31. See note 25.

32. President Andrew John Jr. and Seneca Nation Council protest letter to the secretary of the interior, reprinted in *CR*, February 17, 1888. For the failure to successfully prosecute whiskey cases, see "The Indian Whiskey Cases," *CR*, January 25, 1895. As early as 1709, New York Colony passed a law attempting to regulate the distribution of alcohol to Indians. See Mancall, *Deadly Medicine*, 106. While the federal government attempted, with limited success, to regulate the trade in alcohol from 1802 onward, the New York State Legislature passed a law regulating the sale of alcohol to Indians in 1855. Unrau, *White Man's Wicked Water*, 92.

33. "New York Indians," *New York Herald*, February 2, 1890.

34. For the role of band music at federal Indian boarding schools, see Hauptman, "From Carlisle to Carnegie Hall."

35. Parker, *Analytical History of the Seneca Indians*, 152–53. Author interview with Pauline Seneca, July 15–17, 1982. Seneca was the daughter of Sylvester C. Lay Jr. and the niece of Chester C. Lay.

36. Daniel Sherman to Commissioner of Indian Affairs, October 15, 1878, *ARCIA* 1878, 111–12.

37. Daniel Sherman to Commissioner of Indian Affairs, October 9, 1877, *ARCIA* 1877, 164.

38. Hoag employed fifty Indians on his farm and paid them two to four dollars per day. He annually raised a substantial amount of berries (one thousand bushels). Donaldson, *Six Nations of New York*, 50.

39. Thomas Lappas, "For God and Home and Native Land"; William M. Beauchamp, "Iroquois Temperance Work," *Syracuse Post-Standard*, October 20, 1902.

40. I am a non-Indian member of this organization and have been honored twice by the organization for my writings about the Iroquois. Over the past forty years, I have attended at least half of the annual Peter Doctor Memorial Foundation awards dinners.

41. Rebecca Bowen, "Women of the Seneca Nation," paper delivered at Seneca Nation Women's Conference, Allegany Indian Reservation, August 5, 2011.

42. See chapter 7.

43. Seneca suffrage petition of November 1, 1920, SNI Archives. (The original is in the Joseph Keppler Jr. Iroquois MSS, Division of Rare and Manuscript Collections, CU.) The other fifteen names on the petition were those of non-enrolled Senecas and non-Indians.

44. See note 14.

45. United States Bureau of the Census, *12th Census of the United States*, 1900; Siener, "Buffalo," 233–37; Goldman, *High Hopes*, 131–48; author interview with Jeanne Marie Jemison, September 13, 1986. Jemison's father worked in the Lackawanna steel plants after World War I. In other interviews in the 1980s, Senecas and Cayugas (with Seneca fathers) reflected about fathers and grandfathers who worked in different occupations outside of farming. See Austin, *Ne' Ho Niyo' Dë:Nö'*, 1:170–73, 2:91, 2:105, 2:129, 2:105, 2:253. Edward Cornplanter joined traveling shows as an acrobat and minstrel, and others were musicians in theatrical orchestras and bands. Donaldson, *Six Nations of New York*, 49–51.

46. "New York Indians Till 23,472 Acres but Many Only Hunt or Work on Highways," *NYT*, August 16, 1925.

47. "Indians Elect a Captain [Isaac Seneca]," *NYT*, December 8, 1899; "Seneca to Direct the Indians," *Philadelphia Inquirer*, December 7, 1899; Jenkins, *Real All-Americans*, 59–62, 72, 81, 136.

48. Morgan, *League of the Ho-de-no-sau-neé*, 109–10.

49. For George, see Hauptman, "Samuel George," 5–22.

50. Author interviews with Lee Lyons and Oren Lyons, September 8, 1984. Lee Lyons was a runner for the Grand Council at Onondaga, and I was privileged to meet him. I was on the Cattaraugus Indian Reservation in July 1984 when designated Hodinöhsö:ni' runners came through, carrying a message of peace,

symbolized by wampum strings, from the Grand Council to the Olympic Games in Los Angeles.

51. John Cummings, *Runners and Walkers*, 51.

52. There is no adequate scholarly biography of Deerfoot. All writings on him focus on the history of running; offer too little on the Senecas, their history, and their culture; and contain errors. Cummings, *Runners and Walker*, 51–62; Lovesey, *Five Kings of Distance*, 15–40; Hadgraft, *Deerfoot*; E. S. Sears, *Running through the Ages*, 132–38. For a brief summary, see Tanner, "Deerfoot," 5:194. Tanner and several other authors cited above incorrectly list Deerfoot's year of death as 1897. He died in 1896. Deerfoot's impressive lacrosse stick is in the collections of the Rochester Museum and Science Center.

53. Harriet Maxwell Converse, "Deerfoot, the Seneca Runner," *Buffalo Express*, July 22, 1894.

54. Lucas, "Deerfoot in Britain," 13; Cummings, *Runners and Walkers*, 51–54.

55. Foreman. *Indians Abroad*, 120–25.

56. *Times* (London), October 3, 1861; Lucas, "Deerfoot in Britain," 14–19; Cummings, *Runners and Walkers*, 54–55.

57. Descriptions of Deerfoot and his early successes in Great Britain are in the *Times* (London), September 24, October 3, October 15, and December 5, 17, 1861. See also "Deerfoot the Indian Runner," *Commercial Advertiser* (New York), October 10, 1861.

58. Lucas, "Deerfoot in Britain," 15.

59. "Deerfoot the Indian Runner," *New York Evening Post*, December 31, 1861; Lucas, "Deerfoot in Britain," 13–19.

60. *Bell's Life*, April 1862.

61. Lucas, "Deerfoot in Britain," 15. Accusations of fixed races occurred several more times during Deerfoot's stay in England. See, for example, *New York Clipper*, January 18, 1862.

62. Lucas, "Deerfoot in Britain," 16; Lovesey, *Five Kings of Distance*, 31–36.

63. Lucas, "Deerfoot in Britain," 16; Lovesey, *Five Kings of Distance*, 37–38; Lupton and Lupton, *Pedestrian's Record*, 188.

64. *Chicago Tribune* reporter quoted in "Extraordinary Racing—Indians versus Horses," *New York Evening Post*, August 2, 1865.

65. Harriet Maxwell Converse, "Deerfoot, the Seneca Runner," *Buffalo Express*, July 22, 1894; "Deerfoot Is No More: Noted Indian Runner Dies on the Cattaraugus Reservation," *NYT*, January 20, 1896. Cummings and others inaccurately put his date of death as 1897.

66. "Deerfoot's Grave," *Buffalo Express*, April 1, 1900.

67. Lucas, *Olympic Games, 1904*, 48, 54 (photo of Pierce with other runners), 64. See also Matthews, *America's First Olympics*.

68. Hewitt, "Iroquois Game of Lacrosse," 189–91; Beauchamp, "Iroquois Games," 269–77; Morgan, *League of the Ho-de-no-sau-nee*, 291–98; Wulff, "Lacrosse among the Seneca," 16–22. See also Fisher, *Lacrosse*, and especially Vennum, *American Indian Lacrosse*.

69. Wallace, *Death and Rebirth of the Seneca*, 319.

70. Fenton, *Great Law and the Longhouse*, 27.

71. Ibid., 130

72. Vennum, *American Indian Lacrosse*, 53–69, 113, 317; Morgan, *League of the Ho-de-no-sau-neé*, 293.

73. Morgan, *League of the Ho-de-no-sau-neé*, 294–99; Vennum, *American Indian Lacrosse*, 69–70, 80–81, 177, 183.

74. Beers, *Lacrosse*; Vennum, *American Indian Lacrosse*, 253–64.

75. Fisher, *Lacrosse*, 102–8.

76. "Lacrosse at Buffalo," *NYT*, July 2, 1901.

77. "Indians at Bay Ridge [Brooklyn]: Seneca Indians Beaten Easily by the Crescent Athletic Club," *NYT*, May 24, 1903; "Indians Win at Lacrosse: Seneca Beat Stevens Institute on Hoboken Grounds," *NYT*, May 23, 1903; "Cornell and Indians Tie in Lacrosse," *NYT*, May 26, 1903; "Cornell Beats Indians at Lacrosse," *NYT*, April 20, 1907.

78. "Indians Win at Lacrosse: Seneca Beat Stevens Institute on Hoboken Grounds," *NYT*, May 23, 1903.

79. Quoted in Fisher, *Lacrosse*, 105–6.

80. Ibid., 107–8.

81. Austin, *Ne' Ho Niyo' Dë:Nö'*, 2:253.

82. Author interviews with Francis Kettle, July 27, 1977, and June 8, 1978; author interview with Arleigh Hill, July 25, 1978; "Rochester to Lone Ranger: Tonto Was a Lacrosse Star Here in the 1930s," *Rochester Times-Union*, February 15, 1955.

83. Laurence M. Hauptman, Seneca field notes, 1972–2017.

84. Seneca infant mortality in 1890: 23 deaths of 104 births. Donaldson, *Six Nations of New York*, 7.

Chapter 5

1. Fenton, "Toward the Gradual Civilization of the Indians Natives," 567–81. For the Wrights' mission, see Abler, "Protestant Missionaries and Native Cultures," 25–37; Fenton, "Seneca Indians by Asher Wright," 302–21; Caswell, *Our Life among the Iroquois Indians*. There is no adequate history of the Thomas Asylum. For a recent attempt, see Burdich, *Thomas Indian School*. Burdich earlier wrote "'No Place to Go': The Thomas Indian School and the 'Forgotten' Children of New York."

2. New York State Legislature, *Laws of New York,* chap. 233 (1855). Tribal affiliations and/or reservation residence of students at the Thomas Asylum/School are listed in many of its annual reports. My approximate estimate of tribal affiliations is based on my readings of all the institution's annual reports.

3. Holt, *Indian Orphanages*, 57–60, 65–66.

4. Fenton, "Toward the Gradual Civilization of the Indians Natives," 567–81. For Hoag and Kennedy, see TISAR, 1915, 8. I personally knew three Hodinöhsö:ni

who taught at the school: Caroline Hewitt (Seneca), Pauline Seneca (Cayuga), and Virginia Snow (Cayuga).

5. New York State Legislature, *Laws of New York,* chap. 162 (1875).

6. Daniel Sherman to Commissioner of Indian Affairs, October 14, 1876, *ARCIA* 1876, 114.

7. "The Indian Children: What the State Is Doing for Them: The Thomas Asylum: Where They Are Educated and Taught Various Useful Skills," *CR,* August 20, 1897.

8. New York State Legislature, *Laws of New York,* chap. 585 (1927); New York State Legislature, *Laws of New York,* chap. 654 (1929).

9. United States Department of the Interior, National Park Service, *Historic American Building Survey,* 1–6. The limited number of days (two) that the infirmary/clinic/hospital was open did not change from 1887 through the early 1970s. *ARCIA* 1887, 182; author interview with Wini Kettle, April 15, 1971; author interview with Marilyn Anderson, September 26, 2011. Anderson is the former director of the Seneca Nation of Indians Department of Health.

10. Author interview with Marlene Johnson, July 17, 1992. Over the years, I have greatly benefited from discussions with Johnson, a former residential student at the Thomas Indian School. Johnson served as chair of the National Advisory Commission on Indian Education.

11. TISAR, 1890, 6.

12. TISAR, 1910, 32.

13. Despite one-sided interpretations of the Thomas Indian School, Hodinöhsö:ni´ elders (not just Seneca) have had diverse opinions about the school. See interviews in Austin, *Ne´ Ho Niyo´* Dë:Nö´: 1:192–98 (Virginia Snow), 1:139–40 (Mary Pembleton), 1:250 (Florence White), 1:88–90 (Calvin Kettle), 2:155–56 (Arthur Nephew), 2:74 (Lambert Griffin), 2:104–6 (Alta Jimerson), 2:181–83 (Norma Patterson), 2:95 (Rubena Jacobs), 2:250 (Rhoda Titusm), 2:90 (Andrew Herne).

14. Asher Wright report to John Manley, September 30, 1864, OIA, NYAR, M234, MR590, RG 75, NA.

15. *WR,* 67.

16. New York State Legislature, *Report on Indian Affairs,* 1930, 5–7 (pamphlet in NYSL).

17. T. W. Jackson [federal Indian agent] to Commissioner of Indian Affairs, August 31, 1888, *ARCIA* 1888, 201. Although Jackson pointed out the poor health conditions, he blamed much of the problem on Seneca hereditary factors as well as on unsanitary conditions at Allegany and Cattaraugus. See also note 7.

18. By the 1920s, "the status of Indian health was at least two generations behind the national average." DeJong, *"If You Knew the Conditions,"* 19. See also DeJong's excellent article "'They Are Kept Alive.'"

19. Daniel Sherman to Edward P. Smith [commissioner of Indian affairs], July 28, 1873, OIA, NYAR, M234, MR 591, RG 75, NA. There is no previous study focusing on Wright's medical career.

20. Asher Wright to Daniel Sherman, July 19, 1873, OIA, NYAR, M234, MR 591, RG 75, NA.

21. Frederick Parker quoted in Caswell, *Our Life among the Iroquois Indians*, 307.

22. Fenton, "Seneca Indians by Asher Wright," 302–21.

23. See note 20.

24. As early as 1873, Wright proposed that the Office of Indian Affairs provide him with medical supplies. Daniel Sherman to Commissioner Edward P. Smith, July 28, 1873, OIA, NYAR, M234, MR591, RG75, NA.

25. Daniel Sherman to Commissioner Edward P. Smith, October 15, 1875, *ARCIA* 1875, 336. Smith had visited the New York Agency in October 1874. *ARCIA* 1876, 114; Caswell, *Our Life among the Iroquois Indians*, 205–6.

26. Arthur Wright report, September 19, 1863, *ARCIA* 1863, 381; Asher Wright report to John Manley, September 30, 1864, OIA, NYAR, M234, MR590, RG75, NA.

27. See note 20. At least two Hodinöhsö:ni´ were trained in and practiced Western medicine as physicians from the 1820s to the late nineteenth century. They were Jacob Jemison, Mary Jemison's grandson; a naval surgeon who was killed by Barbary pirates; and Peter Wilson, a Cayuga chief.

28. Daniel Sherman report to Commissioner of Indian Affairs, June 5, 1875, with attached report from Dr. E. A. Meader to Sherman, May 31, 1875, OIA, NYAR, M234, MR592, RG75, NA; *ARCIA* 1875, 88.

29. See note 20.

30. Dr. Albert. D. Lake's physician's report, TISAR 1888, in *Medical Register* 49 (August 4, 1888): 97–99.

31. Joseph F. Murphy, "Health Problems of the Indians," 347–53.

32. See note 20.

33. Daniel Sherman to Commissioner of Indian Affairs, June 5, June 30, 1875, OIA, NYAR, M234, MR592, RG75, NA.

34. Daniel Sherman to Commissioner of Indian Affairs, March 11, May 28, 1876, OIA, NYAR, M234, MR593, RG75, NA; July 27, August 16, September 22, 1876, OIA, NYAR, M234, MR593, RG75, NA; November 26, 1877, OIA, NYAR, M234, MR594, RG75, NA; April 9, April 28, August 17, 1878, OIA, NYAR, M234, MR595, RG75, NA. Seneca protest to the Seneca Nation Council, November 12, 1877, OIA, NYAR, M234, MR594, RG75, NA.

35. Daniel Sherman to Commissioner of Indian Affairs, March 11, 1876. There is no explanation for the disparity in salaries, with the assistant receiving more than the licensed physician.

36. Dr. W. H. Curtis to Daniel Sherman, January 8, 1875, OIA, NYAR, M234, MR592, RG75, NA.

37. Daniel Sherman to Commissioner of Indian Affairs, August 18, 1877, OIA, NYAR, M234, MR 594, RG 75, NA.

38. Caswell, *Our Life among the Iroquois Indians*, 182–90.

39. D. M. Pettit and B. F. Hall to Daniel Sherman, [no day or month] 1876, OIA, NYAR, M234, MR593, RG75, NA. Sherman to Commissioner of Indian

Affairs, November 26, 1877. Dr. Lake's salary was held up by the annuity issue. A. D. Lake to Commissioner of Indian Affairs, May 15, 1878, OIA, NYAR, M234, MR 595, RG75, NA.

40. Caswell, *Our Life among the Iroquois Indians,* 303.

41. Albert Lake [protest about not being paid] to employees at New York Agency, 1877, OIA, NYAR, M234, MR594, RG75, NA. Statement of proposed changes in employees of New York Agency, August 2, 1880, OIA, NYAR, M234, MR596, RG75, NA.

42. TIS treasurers' reports, October 1918–March 1919, Box 2; July 1922, Box 3, TIS records, NYSA.

43. See note 7.

44. For example, one of its superintendents (Valkenburg) was confined to an asylum, allegedly for mental illness, after his administration was accused of irregularities. "Thomas Indian Orphan Asylum Investigation Discontinued," *CR,* March 17, 1893.

45. My conclusions here are based on readings of the history of individual Indian boarding schools as well as Adams, *Education for Extinction,* 125–35; Cahill, *Federal Fathers and Mothers,* 222; and DeJong's "'They Are Kept Alive.'"

46. TISAR, 1923, 7.

47. When I was interviewing Rick Jemison, then a Seneca Nation judge, I noticed Dr. Lake's portrait on the wall of the Seneca courthouse that had been the Thomas Indian School hospital, constructed in 1930. Author interview with Rick Jemison, March 21, 2012.

48. Albert D. Lake, "Anasthetics," medical degree thesis, 1867, Cleveland Medical College, Dittrick Medical History Center, Case Western Reserve Medical School; "Leading Physician Dies," *BN,* March 15, 1923; "Dr. Albert D. Lake," *Jamestown Evening Journal,* March 15, 1923; Hafner, *Directory of Deceased American Physicians,* 1:889; Ellis, *History of Cattaraugus County,* 239–48.

49. Dr. Lake constantly complained about overcrowding. See TISAR, 1908, 18–19; TISAR, 1911, 34–37; TISAR, 1912, 39–41; TISAR, 1916, 32–33; TISAR, 1917, 32–33; TISAR, 1918, 34–35. As late as 1920, he was still advocating for the building of new dormitories, arguing that the closing of the Carlisle Indian School had put a strain on Thomas and left "our institution the only place accessible for resident pupils of all the reservations of the state." TISAR, 1920, 30–32.

50. TISAR, 1890, 7, 18; TISAR, 1895, 22; TISAR, 1896, 21–23.

51. TISAR, 1908, 34. He was also critical of the children's diet at the school, recommending more vegetables, insisting that the amount allocated was insufficient. TISAR, 1896, 21–23.

52. TISAR, 1910, 27.

53. TISAR, 1912, 41; TISAR, 1921, 13.

54. TISAR, 1915, 44.

55. TISAR, 1911, 36. As early as 1896, Lake had observed, "Indeed there can be no question that the death rate on the several Indian reservations is much greater than in any other portion of the state." TISAR, 1896, 21–23.

56. TISAR, 1911, 36.

57. Ibid., 35.

58. TISAR, 1916.

59. Annual report of the Lake Mohonk Conference, 1912, 34–35.

60. TISAR, 1881, 13–14.

61. See note 45. For more comparisons, see, for example, Adams, *Education for Extinction*, 130–31 (tuberculosis and trachoma); Putney, "Fighting the Scourge," 78–109 (tuberculosis), 141–69 (trachoma); DeJong, "'They Are Kept Alive'"; Child, "Homesickness, Illnesses, and Death."

62. Dr. Lake was aided by Dr. J. C. Davis of Versailles in combatting the smallpox epidemic. "Indians to Be Vaccinated " *NYT*, October 9, 1888; O'Brien, "History of Public Health." In a telegram, President Andrew John Jr. recommended a quarantine. John to Commissioner of Indian Affairs, September 24, 1888, BIA, CCF 24098-1888, Box 483, RG75, NA. There were two smallpox scares after that, leading to vaccinations on several reservations in New York; *ARCIA* 1902, 259. There was one case of smallpox at the school in 1922. Thomas Indian School superintendent diaries, Box 2, TIS, NYSA.

63. I examined every Thomas Indian School report from 1912 to 1922 and found no cases of polio. For statistics on the 1916 epidemic, see Persico, *History of Public Health*, 84.

64. TISAR, 1917, 34. See the chart on trachoma cases in DeJong, *"If You Knew the Conditions,"* 27. Only 0.2 percent of Native New Yorkers contracted the disease—the second-lowest percentage nationwide.

65. *Report on State Department of Health, 1905–1911*, 22, NYSDOHR (transcript in NYSL).

66. See note 17.

67. TISAR, 1902, 20–21; TISAR, 1921, 13.

68. TISAR, 1907, 18; TISAR, 1911, 34; TISAR, 1914, 53; TISAR, 1915, 43; TISAR, 1918, 34.

69. TISAR, 1911, 34–37; TISAR, 1917, 33. By 1921, the funding was nearly twice as much as in 1917–18.

70. TISAR, 1918, 34–35. The literature on this epidemic is immense. See Bristow, *American Pandemic*; Barry, *Great Influenza*; Kolata, *Flu*; Crosby, *America's Forgotten Pandemic*.

71. By the first weeks of October 1918, Buffalo, then the nation's tenth-largest city, was overwhelmed by the epidemic. It had a shortage of doctors and nurses because many medical professionals were still in Europe, since World War I had not ended. *BN*, October 7, 1918; Bucki, "A History of Buffalo's Medical Response."

72. *Public Health Report* (U.S. Public Health Service), May 19, 1919, 1008–9. For
    a discussion of the disease's impact on other Native American communities,
    see Crosby, *America's Forgotten Pandemic*, 256–57. According to Crosby, the
    high rate of mortality from influenza among Alaska Natives led one physician to
    conclude in racist fashion that it was due to their "genetic weakness" (228). For
    the disease's impact on one federal Indian boarding school (five hundred cases
    at the Chemawa Indian Industrial School), see Bristow, *American Pandemic*,
    40–43.
73. TISAR, 1919, 8–9, 32–34. TIS superintendent's daily diaries, October 23,
    25, 27, 31, 1918, February 3, 1919, Box 2, TIS, NYSA.
74. Rubena Jacobs interview in Austin, *Ne′ Ho Niyo′* Dë:Nö′, 2:95–99.
75. TIS superintendent's daily diaries, October 23, 25, 27, 31, 1918, February 3,
    1919, Box 2, TIS, NYSA.
76. TISAR, 1919, 8–9, 32–34. Nancy Philips graduated from Carlisle in 1897. See
    "Indian Trained Nurses," *New York Herald Tribune*, May 27, 1888; "Indians as
    Nurses," *Philadelphia Inquirer*, May 22, 1898. See also the following Carlisle
    publications: *Indian Helper*, June 4, November 12, 1897, December 15, 1899;
    The Red Man, May–June 1897, June 1910, October 1911; and *The Red Man
    and Helper*, July 19, 1901. Nancy Seneca and Isaac Seneca files, Cumberland
    County Historical Society, Carlisle, Pennsylvania.
77. TISAR, 1919, 8–9.
78. Ibid., 32–34.
79. TIS treasurers' reports, March 1919, Box 2, TIS, NYSA.
80. TISAR, 1919, 32–34.
81. TISAR, 1920, 30–32.
82. TISAR, 1921, 13.
83. TISAR, 1922, 15.
84. "Leading Physician Dies," *BN*, March 15, 1923; "Dr. Albert D. Lake," *James-
    town Evening Journal*, March 15, 1923. More than sixty years later, one Seneca
    tribal elder, Gertrude Nimham, a student at the school in the World War I
    era, called Lake a "good doctor." She also claimed that the physician had a
    drinking problem and sometimes showed up "half-drunk." Gertrude Ninham
    interview in Austin, *Ne′ Ho Niyo′* Dë:Nö′, 2:160–62. We have no way to judge
    the accuracy of Nimham's comments. However, Lake's advocacy on behalf of
    improved health care for the Hodinöhsö:ni' and his solid statewide reputation
    in the medical profession suggest that Nimham was mistaken.
85. United States Department of the Interior, *Historic American Building Survey*,
    1–6.
86. New York State Legislature, *Report on Indian Affairs*, 5–7; "History of TIS
    Clinic," *Si Wong Geh*, May 28, 1975.
87. TISAR, 1931, 11; TISAR, 1936–38, "Financial Statement." For the hype,
    see TISAR, 1932. See also TISAR, 1931, photograph of hospital; TISAR,
    1933–34.

88. "History of TIS Clinic," *Si Wong Geh,* May 28, 1975. Author interview with Wini Kettle, April 15, 1971; author interview with Marilyn Anderson, September 26, 2011; author interview with Rick Jemison, March 21, 2012. All three were directly involved in Seneca Nation health care improvements in the 1970s and after.

89. Alice Lee Jemison to President Franklin D. Roosevelt, June 20, 1935, OF 296, FDR Presidential Library, Hyde Park, New York.

90. New York State Governor's Committee on the Utilization of the Thomas Indian School, meeting minutes, October 29, 1956, and January 31, 1957, records of the New York State Museum, Box 19, Folder 18, NYSA. William N. Fenton report, December 12, 1957, records of the New York State Museum, Box 10, Folder 19, NYSA.

91. In my many interviews with Senecas over the past forty-five years, Brennan appears to have been the most despised of the Thomas Indian School superintendents. He came under heavy criticism in the mid-1940s from Willard W. Beatty, the federal director of Indian education at the BIA. Beatty, a leading progressive educator, saw the Thomas Indian School under Brennan's leadership as a hostile environment for children. Beatty, "An Informal Report on the Thomas Indian School, 1946," BIA CCF 1940–52 (N.Y.), 5874-1943-210, RG75, NA.

92. Karen Kalaijian and Anthony Golda, "Indian Health Services in Western New York State: Past, Present, and Future," July 1975, report to the New York State commissioner of health, NYSDOHR, subject files of the executive deputy commissioner, Box 16, "Indian Health Services" folder, NYSA; "Profile Summary of Allegany and Cattaraugus," New York State Legislature, Standing Committee on Governmental Operations, Subcommittee on Indian Affairs, report, 1971, 41, subject and hearing files, 1968–72, Box 3, NYSA; "History of TIS Clinic," *Si Wong Geh,* May 28, 1975.

93. For the remarkable work of Seneca women and Lionel John in turning around Seneca health care in the 1970s, see Hauptman, *In the Shadow of Kinzua,* 143–62.

Chapter 6

1. Author interviews of Anna Lewis, May 4, 1978, and June 10, 1983. I also interviewed Louis R. Bruce Jr., Lincoln White, Laura Chodos, Leo Soucy, Marlene Johnson, and Lloyd Elm about historic problems related to educating Native Americans in New York State.

2. Board of Regents, *Native American Education.*

3. New York State Legislature, *Laws of New York,* 1848, chap. 114 (April 30, 1846); Birdseye, *Indian Education in New York State.* This informational handout was updated on several occasions and distributed by the Native American Indian Unit in the New York State Department of Education.

4. Bowen, *Education at Ohi:yo.*

5. See Hauptman, *In the Shadow of Kinzua*, 89.
6. New York State Legislature, *Laws of New York*, 1856, chap. 71 (April 1, 1856).
7. NYSSPIAR, 1858, 25–28.
8. Joseph E. Hazard [superintendent of schools at Allegany and Cattaraugus] to Andrew Draper [New York State superintendent of public instruction], September 15, 1888, NYSSPIAR, 1889, 849–50.
9. NYSSPIAR, 1873, 100.
10. E. M. Petit to Victor Rice [New York State superintendent of public instruction], September 30, 1866, NYSSPIAR, 1867, 93–95. An added month of instruction was provided by moneys from a donation made by the Philadelphia Yearly Meeting of Friends.
11. Ibid.
12. See note 8.
13. Joseph E. Hazard to Andrew S. Draper, October 13, 1891, NYSSPIAR, 1892, 551–52; NYSSPIAR, 1892, 652.
14. The author would like to thank Jaré Cardinal, former director of the Seneca-Iroquois National Museum, for pointing this out to me.
15. See note 10.
16. E. M. Petit to Abram B. Weaver [New York State superintendent of public instruction], September 30, 1868, NYSSPIAR, 1869, 87–89.
17. *WR*, 60 passim. According to Joseph E. Hazard, superintendent of district schools at Allegany and Cattaraugus, "Experience has taught me that male teachers are not as successful in these schools as lady teachers, hence during the past year ladies only have been employed." Joseph E. Hazard to Andrew S. Draper, August 31, 1889, NYSSPIAR, 1890, 654.
18. Annual report of the NYSED, 1923, 89–98.
19. C. E. Benton [superintendent of schools at Allegany and Cattaraugus] to Abram B. Weaver, December 13, 1871, NYSSPIAR, 1872, 102–4.
20. Annual report of the NYSED, 1923, 89–98.
21. John Archer [superintendent of schools at Allegany and Cattaraugus] to Neil Gilmour [New York State superintendent of public instruction], November 15, 1874, NYSSPIAR, 1875, 117; John Archer to Neil Gilmour, November 30, 1876, NYSSPIAR, 1877, 116.
22. John E. Leach [superintendent of schools at Allegany and Cattaraugus] to William B. Ruggles [New York State superintendent of public instruction], December 26, 1884, NYSSPIR, 1885, 157.
23. See chapter 5.
24. John Archer to Neil Gilmour, November 30, 1876, NYSSPIAR, 1877, 2:116.
25. John Archer to Neil Gilmour, December 10, 1879, NYSSPIAR, 1880, 85.
26. I based this conclusion on a survey of all the annual reports of the superintendent of public instruction from 1854 to 1900, most of which contain statistics of attendance. For the push for a compulsory attendance law, see W. K. Harrison report, July 31, 1899, NYSSPIAR, 1899, 536.

27. W. H. Campbell to Neil Gilmour, November 10, 1882, NYSSPIAR, 1883, 123–25.
28. *WR*, 60.
29. Ibid., 30.
30. Ibid., 79.
31. Joseph E. Hazard to Andrew S. Draper, October 13, 1891, NYSSPIAR, 1892, 552.
32. G. W. Boyce to S. F. Crooker, November 13, 1893, NYSSPIAR, 1893, 652–54.
33. W. K. Harrison report, 1896, NYSSPIAR, 1897, 581–82.
34. See note 26.
35. AD 12, March 16, 1914.
36. Andrew S. Draper, "The Indian Problem, in the State of New York," September 10, 1889, NYSSPIAR, 1890, 662–92.
37. Ibid.
38. Annual reports of the Lake Mohonk Conference, 1877, 110; 1888, 25, 84, 87–88, 93, 98, 102–3; 1889; 1891, 57, 78, 95, 108.
39. Johnson, "Schooling the 'Savage,'" 74–82.
40. See note 36.
41. Ibid.
42. See chapter 7.
43. Compare NYSSPIAR, 1882, 91–93, with NYSSPIAR, 1903, 691.
44. "Compulsory Indian Education: Assembly Bill Applies to Allegany and Cattaraugus Counties," *NYT*, January 1900.
45. Annual report of the NYSED, 1923, 89–98. The explosive *Everett Report* was never published, apparently censored.
46. Ibid., 91, 98.
47. Ibid., 91.
48. Ibid., 97.
49. New York State Legislature, *Report on Indian Affairs* (transcript on file at New York State Library).
50. Annual report of the NYSED, 1933, 153–56; annual report of the NYSED, 1934, 138–39.
51. Author interview with Pauline Seneca, July 15–17, 1982. Seneca, a Cayuga elder married to Seneca president Cornelius Seneca, attended district school on the Cattaraugus Indian Reservation as well as the Quaker School and taught for many years in the district schools and at Thomas Indian School.
52. Annual report of the NYSED, 1953, 1:25–26.
53. Annual report of the NYSED, 1955, 258 (statistical table).
54. Interviews in Austin, *Ne' Ho Niyo' Dë:Nö'*: 1:50–51 (Caroline Hewitt), 2:52 (Bernice Crouse), 1:132 (Florence Parker), 1:212 (Esther Sundown), 2:113 (Elsie Johnson), 1:256 (Rachel White).
55. Esther Sundown interview in Austin, *Ne' Ho Niyo' Dë:Nö'*, 1:212.
56. Interviews in Austin, *Ne' Ho Niyo' Dë:Nö'*: 2:24–27 (Hazel Pierce Black), 1:69 (Johnson Jimerson).

57. Interviews in Austin, *Ne' Ho Niyo'* Dë:Nö': 1:69 (Ruth Kenjockety), 1:237 (Milton Wheeler).

58. Elsie Jimerson interview in Austin, *Ne' Ho Niyo'* Dë:Nö', 2:111–14.

59. Rachel White interview in Austin, *Ne' Ho Niyo'* Dë:Nö', 1:256.

60. Bowen, *Education at Ohi;yo'*. For Quaker schools among the Senecas, see Kinney, "Letters, Pen, and Tilling the Field"; Barton, *Quaker Promise Kept*, 29–80, 99–104.

61. Jackson, *Sketch of the Manners, Customs, Religion and Government*; Jackson, "Halliday Jackson's Journal," 117–47, 325–49.

62. Wallace, *Death and Rebirth of the Seneca*, 221–321.

63. Kinney, "Letters, Pen, and Tilling the Field," 4.

64. Ibid., 54–55.

65. Ibid., 70.

66. Ibid., 4–5.

67. Nicholas, "A Little School," 1–21.

68. For Senecas at Dartmouth, see Calloway, *Indian History of an American Institution*, 89–94, 103.

69. Kinney, "Letters, Pen, and Tilling the Field," 211–14.

70. For the schism between the Orthodox and Hicksite sects, see Barbour et al., *Quaker Crosscurrents*, 121–30.

71. Kinney, "Letters, Pen, and Tilling the Field," 240–43; Barton, *Quaker Promise Kept*, 29.

72. Bowen, *Education at Ohi;yo'*, 5.

73. *ARCIA* 1877, 164.

74. C. E. Benton [superintendent of Allegany and Cattaraugus schools] to Abram B. Weaver [New York State superintendent of public instruction], December 13, 1871, NYSPIAR, 1872, 102–4.

75. See chapters 8 and 9 for more on Willie Hoag. He entered the school in 1872. Barton, *Quaker Promise Kept*, 62.

76. Congdon, *Allegany Oxbow*, 89, 121–26.

77. Bowen, *Education at Ohi;yo*, 5–6; Barton, *Quaker Promise Kept*, 38–40, 58.

78. *WR*, 1087–92.

79. Ibid., 1091.

80. Perry Jemison interview in Austin, *Ne' Ho Niyo'* Dë:Nö', 1:63.

81. Nettie Watt interview in Austin, *Ne' Ho Niyo'* Dë:Nö', 1:234.

82. Dema Stoffer interview Austin, *Ne' Ho Niyo'* Dë:Nö', 1:201.

83. *WR*, 60.

84. Florence Lay interview in Austin, *Ne' Ho Niyo'* Dë:Nö', 1:95.

85. Bernice Crouse interview in Austin, *Ne' Ho Niyo'* Dë:Nö', 2:52.

86. Iva Calendine interview in Austin, *Ne' Ho Niyo'* Dë:Nö', 2:48.

87. Hazel Pierce Black interview in Austin, *Ne' Ho Niyo'* Dë:Nö', 2:24–27.

88. Barton, *Quaker Promise Kept*, 68–72.

89. Ibid. A major measles epidemic hit the school population hard in the late 1880s.

90. For a partial listing of Hodinöhsö:ni´ students who attended, see Barton, *Quaker Promise Kept*, 99–104. For the incredible work of former Quaker School students in opposing the Kinzua Dam and helping rebuild the Seneca Nation after the dam was opened, see Hauptman, *In the Shadow of Kinzua*.

Chapter 7

1. Author interview with John Mohawk, March 20–21, 2001. Mohawk was an enrolled member of the Seneca Nation, a professor at SUNY Buffalo, a journalist, a philosopher, and a former editor of *Akwesasne Notes*.

2. The best treatment of the Carlisle Indian Industrial School is Bell, "Telling Stories out of School." See also Witmer, *Indian Industrial School*, which lists tribal affiliations for students, some of which are inaccurate. For the educational philosophy of the school's founder, see Pratt, *Battlefield and Classroom*.

3. See note 2.

4. The best account of Native Americans at Hampton is Brudvig, "'Bridging the Cultural Divide.'" Brudvig's dissertation is a more nuanced and thorough study than Donal F. Lindsey's *Indians at Hampton, 1879–1923*. Other helpful accounts include Engs, *Educating the Disenfranchised and Disinherited*; Adams, "Education in Hues"; and Ahern "'Returned Indians.'"

5. Owl, "Hampton Indians at Cattaraugus Indian Reservation"; author interview with W. David Owl, July 28, 1977.

6. Author interviews with Caroline Hewitt and Pauline Seneca, June 4, 1978; Caroline Hewitt interview in Austin, *Ne´ Ho Niyo´ Dë:Nö´*, 1:50–51; author interview with W. David Owl, July 28, 1977.

7. Brudvig, "'Bridging the Cultural Divide,'" 346–47.

8. Quoted in Adams, *Education for Extinction*, 45.

9. Pratt, *Battlefield and Classroom*, 37–40; Brudvig, "'Bridging the Cultural Divide,'" 62–70.

10. See tables 2 and 3.

11. Seneca Applications for Admission to Hampton, HISF, HUA; Brudvig, "'Bridging the Cultural Divide,'" 348–99; Owl, "Hampton Indians at Cattaraugus Indian Reservation"; Brudvig, "First Person Accounts."

12. Brudvig, "'Bridging the Cultural Divide,'" 85–87. See Waldron, "The Indian Health Care Question."

13. Eric Foner, "Liberated and Unfree," review of Douglas R. Edgerton, *The Wars of Reconstruction*, *NYT*, February 2, 2014.

14. Adams, "Education in Hues," 164–71.

15. Annual report of the Lake Mohonk Conference, *1892*, 39–42.

16. Adams, *Education for Extinction*, 326–28; *ARCIA* 1912.

17. Hollis Burke Frissell report to Commissioner of Indian Affairs, August 23, 1894, *ARCIA* 1894, 415–17.

18. Ibid
19. Ibid.
20. Brudvig, "'Bridging the Cultural Divide,'" 123–25, 189–90.
21. Adams, *Education for Extinction*, 175.
22. Ibid. See also note 17.
23. See table 3.
24. Walter David Owl file, HISF, HUA.
25. See note 20.
26. Adams, *Education for Extinction*, 191–206; Cross, "Making Citizens of Savages," 33–48.
27. See, for example, "Program for Indian Citizenship Day, February 8th, 1910," Caroline Hewitt file, HISF, HUA.
28. Brudvig, "'Bridging the Cultural Divide,'" 136–54.
29. Each entry form listed the student's religion. Most Senecas listed themselves as church members. Although Evelyn Twoguns did not list herself as belonging to a church, she was made a member of St. John's Church on the campus. Evelyn Twoguns files, HISF, HUA.
30. For recruitment efforts, see Clara M. Snow, "A Visit to the New York Reservations," *SW* 21 (November 1892): 170–71; and her "Glimpses of New York Reservations Life," *SW* 26 (August 1897): 155.
31. Clara M. Snow and Caroline Andrus employment records, HISF, HUA.
32. See note 30.
33. Ibid.
34. Ibid.; Snow, "Glimpses of New York Reservations Life," 155.
35. Brudvig, "'Bridging the Cultural Divide,'" 282.
36. This was true for almost all the application files I read. Two students had attended a largely African American school before. Both Elnora and Bernedena Seneca had attended Lincoln Institute. Elnora Seneca files, Bernedena Seneca files, HISF, HUA.
37. Evelyn Twoguns files, HISF, HUA. Noah Twoguns went off to war in the fall of 1861. Noah Twoguns to Asher Wright, September 21, 1861, William Clement Bryant MSS, Letterbook II, BHML.
38. For more on Doxon and the Hodinöhsö:ni' club at Hampton, see Brudvig, "'Bridging the Cultural Divide,'" 119. See also Lucinda George, "Indian Day, 1900," and Charles Doxon, "Industrial Education," in Brudvig, "First Person Accounts." For the Oneidas at Hampton, see Hauptman, *Oneida in Foreign Waters*, 23–37.
39. Frances Halftown (poor eyesight); Alice "Edita" Jemison (government funding ran out); Marian Pierce (family request); Lucinda Doxtator, Elsie Scanandore, and Lettie Scott (finished schooling elsewhere); anonymous (unsatisfactory conduct), HISF, HUA.

40. For the outing system, see Trennert, "From Carlisle to Phoenix," 267–91; Richard Henry Pratt, "The True Origin of the Indian Outing System at Hampton (Va.) Institute," *Red Man* (September–October 1885): 2; Pratt, *Battlefield and Classroom*, 194.

41. Author interview with W. David Owl, July 28, 1977; Owl to Miss Andrews, June 2, August 9, and August 20, 1914, September 24, 1916, Owl files, HISF, HUA. Owl's outing had a long-term impact. The late Keith Smiley, whose family owns Mohonk Mountain House, looked up to Owl as a mentor and they remained friends for more than fifty years. Author interview with Keith Smiley, May 3, 1984.

42. Anonymous Seneca (to protect privacy), HISF, HUA.

43. Elnora Seneca file, HISF, HUA.

44. W. J. Easton's evaluation reports for Evelyn Twoguns's outing, Evelyn Twoguns file, HISF, HUA.

45. Mrs. Hyde's evaluation report of Caroline Hewitt's outing, 1908; Miss Clarey's and Mrs. I. G. Scoville's evaluation of Caroline Hewitt's outing of 1909, Carolyn Hewitt file, HISF, HUA.

46. Mrs. H. H. Lawton's evaluation of Caroline Hewitt's outing, 1910, Caroline Hewitt file, HISF, HUA.

47. Application of Caroline Hewitt to Hampton Institute, May 30, 1905, Martha Jamerson to H. B. Frissell, May 20, 1905, Caroline Hewitt questionnaire, 1908, Caroline Hewitt's student record, Hewitt to "Dear Friend," February 8, 1906, Hewitt to Miss Townsend, January 24, 1917, Caroline Hewitt file, HISF, HUA; Hewitt interview in Austin, *Ne´ Ho Niyo´* Dë:Nö´, 1:50–51; author interviews with Caroline Hewitt and Pauline Seneca, June 4, 1978.

48. See note 47.

49. Caroline Hewitt alumna reports, 1912, 1921, 1926; *SW*, November 1919, July 1922; (Carlisle) *Arrow*, October 13, 1913, March 27, 1914; (Carlisle) *Redman*, October 1913, Caroline Hewitt file, HISF, HUA.

50. Caroline Hewitt academic transcript, 1905–11, Edith Dobie recommendation for Caroline Hewitt, undated, Caroline Hewitt file, HISF, HUA.

51. See table 2. For personal reminiscences by male Cattaraugus Seneca students (Francis Kennedy and Samuel George) who attended Hampton, see Brudvig, "First Person Accounts."

52. See table 3.

53. Victor Gordon file, HISF, HUA.

54. Archie Tallchief and Solon Scott files, HISF, HUA.

55. Asher Wright Parker file, HISF, HUA.

56. These five students require anonymity, HISF, HUA.

57. Raymond Jimerson, Leroy Jimerson, Laverne Leonard Seneca, Wilbur Seneca, and Cephas Watt files, HISF, HUA.

58. Raymond Jimerson file, HISF, HUA.

59. U.S. Congress, *Hearings on S. 5302*, 16–17.

60. Brudvig, "'Bridging the Cultural Divide,'" 298–31. Adams, *Education for Extinction*, 252, 322, 327–28; Adams, "Education in Hues," 164–71.

61. W. David Owl to Sydney Frissell, August 1, 1960, W. David Owl files, HISF, HA.

62. Brudvig, "'Bridging the Cultural Divide,'" 322.

63. Lindsey, *Indians at Hampton*, 170. Cf. Brudvig, "'Bridging the Cultural Divide,'" 319–29.

64. Adams, *Education for Extinction*, 327–28; Lindsey, *Indians at Hampton*, 32, 95–97.

65. Author interview with W. David Owl, July 28, 1977.

66. Ellen Crouse, Caroline Hewitt, Rogene Pierce, Elsie Scanandore, Joel Scanandore, Lydia Scanandore, Jacob Seneca, and Evelyn Twoguns files, HUA; Evelyn Twoguns to Miss Hilts, May 21, 1931, Evelyn Twoguns files, HISF, HUA.

67. Evelyn Twoguns to H. B. Frissell, January 9, 1916; Evelyn Twoguns to "My Fellow Endeavorers," January 17, 1923; Evelyn Twoguns to Miss Hilts, May 27, 1937, Evelyn Twoguns files, HISF, HUA. Twoguns kept Hampton staff abreast of her career in the Indian Service as well as events and conditions at Cattaraugus. She corresponded more frequently than any other Seneca. On June 30, 1927, she wrote: "Rev. Owl is now a full-fledged minister as he finished at the Rochester Theological Seminary in May. He has the Baptist Church on this [Cattaraugus] reserve. I saw him preach for the first time at the prayer meeting last night. He does quite well." Twoguns to Caroline Andrus, June 30, 1927, Evelyn Twoguns file, HISF, HUA.

68. See table 3.

69. Caroline Hewitt to Miss Townsend, January 24, 1917; Hewitt to Caroline Andrus, October 12, 1918, Caroline Hewitt file, HISF, HUA. 68.

70. See note 68.

71. Brudvig, "'Bridging the Cultural Divide,'" 333–37.

72. Adams, *Education for Extinction*, 327.

73. See note 71.

74. Elsie Scanandore and Lucinda Doxtator files, HISF, HUA.

75. Brudvig, "'Bridging the Cultural Divide,'" 344–46.

76. Ibid., 347.

Chapter 8

1. 25 USC 1041a.

2. [Dawes] General Allotment Act, 24 Stat., 388–91 (February 8, 1887). Burke Act, 24 Stat., 182–83 (May 8, 1906). For the devastating impact of federal allotment policies on one Iroquoian community, see Hauptman and McLester, *Oneidas in the Age of Allotment*.

3. The best scholarly history of the Ogden Land Company is Conable, "A Steady Enemy."

4. For the Seneca position on the Ogden Land Company claim, see U.S. Congress, S. Doc. 154, 1.

5. In September 1990, I provided oral and written testimony before the House of Representatives Committee on Interior and Insular Affairs and the Senate Committee on Indian Affairs on the history of these leases and their impact on the Senecas. U.S. Congress, *Hearings on H.R. 5367*; U.S. Congress, *Hearings on S. 2895*. For more detail, see Hauptman, *Iroquois Struggle for Survival*, 15–43; Hauptman, *The Iroquois in the Civil War*; Hauptman, "Historical Background to the Present Day Seneca Nation-Salamanca Lease Controversy; Hauptman, "Compensatory Justice"; Hauptman, "Senecas and Subdividers."

6. New York State Legislature, *Laws of New York*, chap. 133 (March 16, 1865); New York State Legislature, *Laws of New York*, chap. 211 (March 25, 1865).

7. New York State Legislature, Senate, Senate Doc. 24.

8. Seneca Nation Council minutes, February 10, 1868.

9. The *Jamestown Journal* later noted: "The decision [in the New York Supreme Court by Judge Baker] left the [non-Indian] people of Salamanca absolutely without any rights on the [Allegany] reservation." "Indian Leases at Salamanca," February 19, 1875; President William Krouse and the Seneca Nation Tribal Council Resolution, December 6, 1871, OIA, NYAR, M234, MR591, RG75, NA.

10. C. W. Armstrong, Clerk, New York State Legislature, Joint Resolution, January 18, 1871, in Governor John Hoffman, Letter of Transmittal of Joint Resolution of the New York State Legislature, January 18, 1871, OIA, NYAR, M234, MR591, RG75, NA.

11. Hudson Ansley [town supervisor of Salamanca] to Commissioner of Indian Affairs, February 6, 1871, with resolution of Cattaraugus County Board of Supervisors, November 30, 1870, OIA, NYAR, M234, MR592, RG75, NA. "These improvements were made on what were supposed to be leases legally granted by the New York State Legislature; but the courts have decided that neither the Indians nor the state have power to make such lease." Federal Indian agent Daniel Sherman to Commissioner of Indian Affairs, November 1, 1874, *ARCIA* 1874, 23.

12. Abrams, *Seneca People*, 77–78.

13. John W. Street [attorney and claims agent for Atlantic and Great Western Railroad] to Commissioner of Indian Affairs, August 29, 1874, OIA, NYAR, M234, MR592, RG75, NA. A year before, the Seneca Nation had questioned the legality of these railroad leases. James G. Johnson [attorney for Seneca Nation] to Commissioner of Indian Affairs, July 17, 1873, OIA, M234, MR591, RG75, NA.

14. Hudson Ansley to Secretary of the Interior, July 10, 1873, OIA, NYAR, M234, MR 591, RG75, NA.

15. President Peter Snow and Seneca Nation Council protest of congressional bill H.R. 2264, January 23, 1873; James G. Johnson to Commissioner of Indian Affairs, July 17, 1873, OIA, NYAR, M234, MR591, RG75, NA.

16. H. S. Cunningham to Commissioner of Indian Affairs, September 15, 1868, *ARCIA* 1868, 24.

17. Daniel Sherman to Commissioner of Indian Affairs, October 24, 1874, *ARCIA* 1874, 24. Sherman recommended that the federal government extinguish the Ogden Land Company preemption claim. He also described the Senecas as being "quasi independent sovereignties in the heart of the State of New York" for too long and said they should be made citizens since they were "completely adapted to civilized life" (22). He continued to push this agenda until 1880, when he was replaced as agent. For Sherman's support for the first leasing bill of 1875, see Cong. Rec. 913–14, 43rd Cong., 2d sess., February 2, 1875. Sherman later claimed that he helped draft the 1880 lease extension bill. Daniel Sherman to Commissioner of Indian Affairs, October 16, 1880, *ARCIA* 1880, 136.

18. H.R. 1053, January 12, 1874, 43d. Cong. 1st sess., OIA, NYAR, M234, MR592, RG75, NA; "The Indian Lands," *Jamestown Journal*, January 23, 1874.

19. President Peter Snow and Seneca Tribal Council protest, January 31, 1874, OIA, NYAR, M234, MR 592, RG75, NA.

20. U.S. Congress, S. Doc. 122.

21. *ARCIA* 1874, 22.

22. For Bogy, see Unrau, "Lewis Vital Bogy."

23. 18 Stat., 330 (February 19, 1875); "Washington: Approved," *Albany Argus*, February 22, 1875.

24. Seneca Nation of Indians protest, Seneca Nation Council minutes, February 20, 1875, SNI Archives.

25. C. Delano statement about the act of February 19, 1875, and appointment of three commissioners to survey Allegany Indian Reservation, March 30, 1875, OIA, NYAR, M234, MR593, RG75, NA. Abler, "Factional Dispute and Party Conflict," 200.

26. Approval of two Eugene Nash mineral lease agreements by the secretary of the interior, Carl Schurz to Commissioner of Indian Affairs, March 1, 1878, OIA, NYAR, M234, MR595, RG75, NA. On September 21, 1878, the Interior Department revised its earlier decision and refused to approve the Manley-Nash leases. A. Bell [acting secretary of the interior] to Commissioner of Indian Affairs, September 21, 1878, OIA, NYAR, M234, MR595, RG75, NA.

27. Abrams, *Seneca People*, 79.

28. *ARCIA* 1875, 88.

29. Ibid., 335–36; *ARCIA* 1873, 173–74; *ARCIA* 1876, 113–14; *ARCIA* 1880, 135–37. Even a prominent Quaker do-gooder pointed to the recent allotment of Cornplanter as a model for Allegany. Joseph Scattergood to Arthur Wright, July 31, 1872, William Clement Bryant MSS, Letterbook II, BHML.

30. Notice of Special Election, August 29, 1876 [in lieu of disputed election of May 1876], OIA, NYAR, M234, MR593, RG75, NA; Abrams, *Seneca People*, 80.

31. Laura Wright to William Clement Bryant, November 11, 1878, William Clement Bryant MSS, Letterbook II, BHML.
32. Certified Copy of All the Evidence and Proceedings of the Seneca Nation Impeachment of Job King, January 8–11, 1879, OIA, NYAR, M2324, MR596, RG75, NA; Harrison Halftown report about election of May 7, 1878, OIA, NYAR, M234, MR 595, RG75, NA. John Manley denied the charge, as did federal Indian agent Daniel Sherman, who defended King. Transcript of Trial of Impeachment, Seneca Nation Council minutes, 1879; Abler, "Factional Dispute and Party Conflict," 201–2, 214–23.
33. John Kennedy to James Miller; W. D. Waddington to Daniel Sherman, November 8, 1879, OIA, NYAR, M234, MR 596, RG75, NA. The complaint read: "The people have lost confidence in their councilors to guard their interests in a proper manner, and respectfully ask the friends to help us." Kossuth Bishop et al. to George Scattergood, December 11, 1878, with attached memorial signed by Alexander John, Martin Jimerson, George Titus, Dr. James Shongo, thirty-three women, and others, February 1, 1879, OIA, NYAR, M234, MR596, RG75, NA.
34. *ARCIA* 1884, 139–40; *ARCIA* 1885, 159–60; *ARCIA* 1886, 207.
35. Seneca Nation Council minutes, March 11, 1891. However, annual salaries for the chief operating officers of the Seneca Nation had substantially increased by 1901: the president received $250 and expenses; the treasurer $300; and the clerk $200. This was not the case for other elected officials. When tribal councilors were in attendance at council meetings, they were merely receiving three dollars per day and expenses. Seneca Nation Council minutes, June 31, 1901.
36. A. W. Ferrin [federal Indian agent] to Commissioner of Indian Affairs, July 25, 1899, *ARCIA* 1899, 256–57.
37. Seneca Nation Council minutes, 1854, SNI Archives.
38. Donaldson, *Six Nations of New York*, 38.
39. The Senecas had various motives to push for allotment. The most prominent Senecas to advocate land in severalty were Harrison Halftown, longtime clerk of the Seneca Nation; Lester Bishop, former tribal councilor from Cattaraugus and Sunday school teacher at the Thomas Indian School; and Myron Silverheels, former Seneca tribal councilor from Allegany and candidate for presidency of the Seneca Nation in 1876. Others who pushed for allotment included Henry Silverheels, a minister; John Kennedy, a longtime political gadfly and critic of the elected council; Lowell Strong, the nonenrolled son of Chief Nathaniel T. Strong and Hoag's brother-in-law; and Nathaniel Patterson, the brother of Seneca president Franklin Patterson, Hoag's major political ally.
40. For more than twenty years, John lobbied on Capitol Hill against the allotment of Seneca lands, starting in 1882: "Washington from Our Special Correspondent," *New York Herald*, January 14, 1882; Letter from Washington," *Troy Times*, March 3, 1882.

41. "Rejoiced Together: Senecas, Squatters and Latter-Day Salamancans," *CR*, April 15, 1892; "The Seneca Oil Leases," *CR*, May 17, 1897.

42. On October 22, 1890, the Seneca Tribal Council accused John and his delegation of going to Washington to advocate for the ninety-nine-year lease. On January 17, 1900, the council adopted a resolution that was sent to the commissioner of Indian affairs, the chairman of the Senate Committee on Indian Affairs, and Congressman Edward Vreeland, indicating that they should not listen to John or meet him, since he was not an official delegate of the Seneca Nation. Seneca Nation Council minutes, SNI Archives.

43. Viola, *Diplomats in Buckskin*, 184–85.

44. On Hoag's death, the *New York Times* observed: "Representative of the best type of Indian," who had "a keen interest in the customs of his ancestors and had a thorough knowledge of their lore." He "owned one of best collections of Indian relics in Southwestern New York." "Hoag, Indian Chief, Dies," *NYT*, August 1, 1927. Equally positive was Thomas Donaldson's assessment. He also inaccurately claimed that Hoag worked his large farm and did not rent his lands out. Donaldson, *Six Nations of New York*, 49. See also *New York Herald*, February 2, 1890. For a less flattering portrait of Hoag and Seneca politics during his era, see New York State Legislature, *Report of the Special Committee Appointed by the Assembly of 1905 to Investigate the Conditions Existing upon the Several Indian Reservations of the State*, 101–45, 183–284.

45. Congdon, *Allegany Oxbow*, 163–93. "These galoots [Hoag's political party] have their Tom Platt and their Tammany. They know a thing or two. . . . They have two tracts . . . and they elect their treasurer from the Cattaraugus reservation and their president from the Allegany reservation. Next year, the President will be treasurer and the treasurer will be president. Isn't that a game? Just swap, that's all." *Brooklyn Daily Eagle*, November 22, 1905.

46. See note 44.

47. Andrew John Jr. quoted in "Legislation Asked for the Senecas: A More Equitable Distribution of Their Money Desired," *New York Tribune*, December 31, 1897.

48. "Ryan Act in Court, *CR*, May 31, 1901.

49. For the General Allotment Act, see 24 Stat., 388–91 (February 2, 1887). For the Burke Act, see 34 Stat., 182–83 (May 8, 1906).

50. *WR*, 1074–88, 1092–1122. The report also indicated that John Kennedy, Henry and Myron Silverheels, and John Jimeson also favored allotment by 1889 (71).

51. Ibid., 1039–43.

52. Ibid., 71, 1067–71, 1186–90.

53. Ibid., 71, 1123–29.

54. Ibid., 59–79. See also "The Indian Question: Investigating the Cattaraugus Reservation," *CR*, August 10, 1888.

55. *WR*, 78–79.

56. Petition of Andrew John Jr., Clerk William Patterson, and sixteen tribal councilors, January 26, 1888, attached to T. W. Jackson report, February 14, 1888, BIA records, CCF, 4375-1888, NY, Box 447, RG75, NA.

57. T. W. Jackson report, February 14, 1888.

58. 26 Stat., 558 (September 30, 1890). "For Ninety-nine Years: Let Salamancans Rejoice," *CR*, October 3, 1890. See also U.S. Congress, S. Doc. 45. After the ninety-nine-year lease was signed and formally went into effect, a major celebration by Hoag's Seneca supporters and white Salamancans occurred. "Rejoiced Together: Senecas, Squatters and Latter-Day Salamancans," *CR*, April 15, 1892.

59. *ARCIA* 1902, 218–20.

60. *ARCIA* 1888, LXXV.

61. For a sampling of Whipple's efforts at passing legislation in Albany, see "The News This Morning: Defeat of Whipple Bill Leads to Celebration by Senecas," *New York Tribune*, June 17, 1890; A. W. Ferrin to Commissioner of Indian Affairs, September 14, 1891, *ARCIA* 1891, 316; A. W. Ferrin to Commissioner of Indian Affairs, August 31, 1894, *ARCIA* 1894, 215. The Senecas continued to object throughout the decade. Seneca Nation Council minutes, December 28, 1899, SNI Archives.

62. President John and the Seneca Nation protest, July 15, 1890, BIA, CCF 21726-1890, RG75, NA.

63. Seneca Nation Council minutes, March 11, 1891; *ARCIA* 1891, 316.

64. For the best brief summaries of Converse's extraordinary life, see Parker, "Harriet Maxwell Converse"; Fenton, "Converse, Harriet Maxwell." Her obituary can be found in "White Woman Chief Dies," *New York Herald*, November 20, 1903; "Chiefs Mourn GA-IE-WA-NOH," *New York Sun*, November 20, 1903. For the combined Episcopal and Longhouse rites at her funeral, see "Indians Mourn at Mrs. Converse's Bier," *NYT*, November 23, 1903.

65. Harriet Maxwell Converse, "Hon. Thomas Maxwell 'Reminiscences of the Southern Tier,'" MSS in Maxwell family file in Chemung County Historical Society, Elmira, New York; "Hon William Maxwell," *Elmira Telegram*, undated in Maxwell family file in Chemung County Historical Society, Elmira, New York. See also "Death of Thomas Maxwell," *Elmira Advertiser*, November 5, 1864.

66. Parker, *Life of General Ely S. Parker*, 48, 134, 162–64, 223. Arthur C. Parker, the general's grandnephew, became the executor of her estate and, after her death, edited her major work on the Hodinöhsö:ni´: *Myths and Legends of the New York Iroquois*. See also Porter, *To Be an Indian*, 45–46, 70–71.

67. "The Six Nations: Defense of the Indian Character and Morals: Views of Mrs. Converse," *Buffalo Courier*, June 9, 1894; "The Seneca Indians: Letter in Their Defense from Mrs. Converse," *Elmira Telegram*, October 20, 1895; Harriet Maxwell Converse, "A Plea for the Rights of Empire State Indians," *Washington Times*, March 21, 1902; "New York Indian Lands," *New York Tribune Weekly*

Review, March 29, 1902; "Senecas to Fight in Court: A Woman [Converse] Unites Them in a Stand for Their Lands," *New York Sun*, November 30, 1902.

68. Converse's residence was described as "a most interesting museum. The walls are covered with Indian relics and the cases are filled with all kinds of curios." "Chief of Six Nations: Harriet Maxwell Converse Possesses Honors of a Rare Character," *New York Recorder*, December 1, 1892. See also *Commercial Advertiser* (New York City), December 23, 1892. According to Arthur C. Parker, the residence was a gathering place for Hodinöhsö:ni´ as well as other Native peoples from all over the Americas, whether they were in need or not. Converse, *Myths and Legends*, 20–21.

69. Melvil Dewey, who headed the New York State Library at the time, credited her with building the collections of the New York State Museum. Dewey to Converse, July 30, 1898, Harriet Maxwell Converse scrapbook, WMB MSS, MR27, NYSL. George Hamell, a well-respected former curator at the New York State Museum, while recognizing her philanthropy, pointed out the many flaws in Converse's knowledge of Iroquoian arts and folklore. George Hamell to author, personal communication, January 8, 2018. Jesse Cornplanter, a noted Seneca raconteur and artist, regretted that his father, Edward, and Converse "had stripped the community of its oldest ceremonial gear to fill up the empty cases of new museums in New York and later in Albany. Jesse would afterward protest at the finest ethnological art being locked in museums under glass and irretrievable once it got into public hands." Fenton, "'Aboriginally Yours,'" 182. I heard similar criticisms among the Hodinöhsö:ni´ in the 1970s.

70. Edward Cornplanter saw her as an art patron, benefactor, and trusted adviser. Edward Cornplanter to Harriet Maxwell Converse, January 17, March 23, April 23, May 31, August 21, September 6, October 8, November 30, December 26, 1900; May 22, July 19, 1901; August 9, October 16, 1901; January 21, May 28, September 29, October 6, 1902; April 18, April 23, May 4, 1903; undated 1903, JKI MSS, MR1, CU.

71. See, for example, "Friend to the Indians: Harriet Maxwell Converse Has Returned from the Great Council," *Buffalo Express*, February 14, 1902; "Senecas to Fight in Court: A Woman [Converse] Unites Them in a Stand for Their Lands," *New York Sun*, November 30, 1902. Working with the chiefs, she also helped raise money and arrange ceremonies to honor famous Hodinöhsö:ni´ and to remind New Yorkers of their Indian past: "Monuments to the Indian: The Memory of the American Indian to Be Perpetuated in Bronze," *New York World*, June 19, 1892; "[Ely S. Parker Re-]Buried in the Land of His People," *New York Tribune*, January 21, 1897; "Deerfoot's Funeral," *Buffalo Express*, April 2, 1900.

72. "Rites of Adoption by the Seneca Indians on the Cattaraugus Reservation, June 15, 1885," pamphlet in NYSL. "Harriet Maxwell Converse, "How I Became a Seneca Indian," ACP MSS, Box 2, Folder 8, UR.

73. Harriet Maxwell Converse Adopted by the Senecas," *New York World*, April 8, 1891.

74. Chiefs Daniel La Fort, Abraham Hill, Thomas Webster, Thomas Williams, and Baptist Thomas certify "that Harriet Maxwell Converse has been duly elected and installed to the Chieftain ship [*sic*] of the Six Nations of the New York Indians on the 18th day of September in the year 1892 at the condolence held at the Tonawanda Indian Reservation," ACP MSS, Box 2, Folder 8, UR; "Queen of the Indians: How Harriet Maxwell Converse Became Chief of the Six Tribes," *Commercial Advertiser* (New York), December 23, 1892.

75. Fenton, *Great Law and the Longhouse*, 6–8, 27, 99, 130, 209, 618. For the importance of the Condolence Council ritual in Iroquoian diplomacy, see Fenton, "Structure, Continuity and Change."

76. Fenton, *Great Law and Longhouse*, 6.

77. There are several different versions of the Gayaneshä'go:wa:h, the Great Law of Peace. The two most cited are told by John Arthur Gibson and Seth Newhouse. See Gibson, *Concerning the League*, and (for the Seth Newhouse version) Parker, *Parker on the Iroquois*, 3:7–64.

78. See notes 67 and 71.

79. George-Shongo, *Ono'dowa'ga' Gano'kyëdoh Nogeh''oweh*, 112n113, 51.

80. Andrew, John Jr. quoted in "Legislation Asked for the Senecas: A More Equitable Distribution of Their Money Desired," *New York Tribune*, December 31, 1897.

81. See note 42. See also Seneca Nation Council minutes; "Ryan Act in Court," *CR*, May 31, 1901.

82. For Congressman Vreeland, see Doty, Congdon, and Thornton, *Historic Annals of Southwestern New York*, 3:140–42.

83. Ibid., 3:10–17; editorial, *SP*, March 21, 1930; "Ex-Senator Fancher Dies on a Train: Former New York State Legislator Amassed a Fortune in Oil Industry," *NYT*, March 21, 1930; Herrick, *Empire Oil*, 424–25, 437. For more on Fancher, see Hauptman, "Park Boss."

84. Hauptman, "Governor Theodore Roosevelt," 1–7. In addition to the Indian Rights Association, the Lake Mohonk Conference of Friends of the Indian and the U.S. Board of Indian Commissioners annually called for the allotment of tribal lands in New York. For a study of these reformers, see Hagan, *Indian Rights Association*.

85. Chauncey H. Abrams to Harriet Maxwell Converse, November 26, 1901, ACP MSS, Box 2, Folder 8, UR. Abrams and Edward Cornplanter later honored the work of Converse on behalf of the Hodinöhsö:ni' at her funeral. "Chiefs Mourn Ga-e-wa-noh," *New York Sun*, November 23, 1903.

86. Edward B. Vreeland to Merrill E. Gates, January 10, 1902, records of the U.S. Board of Indian Commissioners, 1899–1918. For Commissioner of Indian Affairs William Jones's endorsement of Vreeland's efforts, see *ARCIA* 1904, 199–20.

87. Annual report of the Lake Mohonk Conference, 1902, 92–95.

88. Iroquois Confederacy protest against Vreeland bill (H.R. 10079), February 12, 1902, JKI MSS, MR1, CU. The bill was one of several introduced by Vreeland in 1902 and 1903.

89. Converse also attempted to foster unity, but severe divisions continued: Andrew John Jr. to Harriet Maxwell Converse, February 4, February 8, March 5, 1902; Harriet Maxwell Converse to Andrew John Jr., April 9, 1902; C. C. Lay to Harriet Maxwell Converse, April 9, 1902; William C. Hoag to Harriet Maxwell Converse, April 9, 1902, ACP MSS, UR. Harriet Maxwell Converse to Joseph Keppler, March 15, 1902, JKI MSS, MR1, CU.

90. Harriet Maxwell Converse to Joseph Keppler Jr., September 18, 1902, JKI MSS, MR1, CU; Harriet Maxwell Converse to Joseph Keppler Jr., December 18, 1902, JKI MSS, MR1, CU.

91. For Judge Andrews's role, see Harriet Maxwell Converse to Joseph Keppler Jr., December 18, 1902, JKI MSS, MR1, CU; Charles Andrews, "The Ogden Land Company," *New York Sun*, March 15, 1902.

92. Andrew John Jr. to Harriet Maxwell Converse, February 4, 1902. Arthur C. Parker, executor of her estate, indicated that at the time of her death, on November 18, 1903, "her fortunes had dwindled almost to nothing." Parker, "Harriet Maxwell Converse," 30.

93. U.S. Congress, *Hearings on H.R. 12270*, 70–71.

94. Ibid., 71.

95. Ibid., 72.

96. Converse, "A Plea for the Rights of Empire State Indians," *Washington Times*, March 21, 1902.

97. Annual report of the Lake Mohonk Conference, 1902, 64–69; William Walker to Daniel Smiley, October 18, 1902, Smiley family MSS, HC; William Walker to Merrill E. Gates, March 11, 1902, records of the U.S. Board of Indian Commissioners, 1899–1918, RG75, NA. Walker is also quoted in opposition to the Vreeland bills in "Misrepresenting the Indians," *Rochester Post Express*, January 6, 1903, and "Sharks Cheat Indians," *New York Tribune*, September 25, 1903. The Senecas adopted Walker around 1900. Parker, *Life of General Ely S. Parker*, 331.

98. Van Voorhis's opinions can be found in U.S. Congress, *Hearings: Allotment of Lands in Severalty to the Indians of New York*, 18–41; U.S. Congress, *Hearings on H.R. 7262*, 6–16, 39–57. See also John Van Voorhis to Charles J. Bonaparte [secretary of the interior], February 11, 1904, records of the U.S. Board of Indian Commissioners, 1899–1918, RG75, NA. As early as 1900, Standard Oil was seen as being behind efforts to get at Seneca lands. "The Oil Trust Balked in Indian Grab," *New York World*, February 4, 1900.

99. For Quay, see Kehl, *Boss Rule in the Gilded Age*. Comparisons with the Oklahoma experience were frequently made. See "Sharks Cheat Indians," *New York Tribune*, September 25, 1903.

100. For Sulzer's attacks against the bills, see 38 Cong. Rec. 4253–55 (1904). Vreeland attacked Sulzer for criticizing the bills and for making judgments four hundred miles from his New York City base: 38 Cong. Rec. 5200–5206 (1904). The reformer Sulzer was later impeached as mayor of New York City for breaking with the Tammany machine, which controlled city politics. See Lifflander, *Impeachment of Governor Sulzer.*

101. 36 Cong. Rec. 337 (1902).

102. For example, Vreeland's H.R. 7262, introduced on December 11, 1903.

103. Memorial of 629 Adult Members of the Seneca Nation Protesting against the Passage of House Bill No. 12270 Providing for the Allotment of the Lands of the Nation in Severalty, January 15, 1903, JKI MSS MR6, CU.

104. Annual report of the Lake Mohonk Conference, 1902, 96. John had great ability to get publicity. He even won support in the ethnic press of the day. See "An Indian's [John's] Protest against Land Piracy," *Irish World*, February 2, 1902. The Senecas received favorable support from major New York City newspapers: the *New York Sun*, the *New York Tribune*, and the *Brooklyn Daily Eagle.*

105. U.S. Congress, Senate, *Hearings: Allotment of Lands in Severalty to the Indians of New York*, 81–89, 102.

106. Testimony of William Hoag in Warren K. Moorhead, [undated] Preliminary Report on the New York Indians, records of the U.S. Board of Indian Commissioners, 1899–1918, RG75, NA. See also U.S. Congress, Senate, *Hearings: Allotment of Lands in Severalty to the Indians of New York*, 19–20.

107. William C. Hoag report on meeting with Van Voorhis's law firm, Seneca Nation Council minutes, January 28, 1904, SNI Archives. For Converse's obituary, see "White Woman Chief Dies," *New York Herald*, November 20, 1903; "The Indians' Friend Dead," *New York Sun*, November 20, 1903. For her funeral according to both Episcopal and Longhouse rites, see "Indians Mourn at Mrs. Converse's Bier: Pay Loving Tribute to the 'Great White Mother.'" *NYT*, November 23, 1903.

108. Francis Leupp to Darwin R. James, March 27, 1906, records of the U.S. Board of Indian Commissioners, 1899–1918, RG75, NA.

Chapter 9

1. "New York Indians," *New York Herald*, February 2, 1890.

2. F. A. Gaylord, "Report on State Land in the Vicinity of Cuba Lake," 1913; F. A. Gaylord to A. B. Strough, July 13, 1914; Albert E. Hoyt to Delbert Snyder, records of the Seneca Nation of Indians, Department of Law (Justice), Allegany Indian Reservation.

3. For more on the Oil Spring (Cuba Lake) case, see chapter 2. For more on the Oil Spring and Grand Island claims, see Hauptman, *In the Shadow of Kinzua*, 186–99.

4. New York State Legislature, AD 40, 1906.

5. Document 28, "Minority Report from the Committee on Conservation of Natural Resources, and Reasons Therefor," in New York State Constitutional Convention, *Documents of the Constitutional Convention*, 14–17.

6. Document 1, "Members on the Committee on Relations with the Indians," in New York State Constitutional Convention, *Documents of the Constitutional Convention*, 3; Document 2, "Names and Post Office Addresses of Delegates to Constitutional Convention," in New York State Constitutional Convention, *Documents of the Constitutional Convention*, 1–8.

7. Document 26, "Report of the Committee on Relations to the Indians, Relative to Proposed Amendment No. 769 (Int. 707)," in New York State Constitutional Convention, *Documents of the Constitutional Convention*, 1.

8. Ibid., 2–3.

9. Ibid., 4–5. "Lawmakers Seek Justice for the Indians: Constitutional Convention Urged to Wipe Out the Tribal Courts in the State," *NYT*, August 8, 1915.

10. Ibid., 1–10.

11. Ibid.

12. An Act to Prevent Taking Fish by Net in the Waters of Cattaraugus Creek and Its Mouth, New York State Legislature, *Laws of New York,* chap. 590 (1886); Act for the Protection of Game in the Counties of Chautauqua and Cattaraugus, New York State Legislature, *Laws of New York,* chap. 430 (1886). In Kent, *Fish and Game Laws,* 36, 46.

13. " Indians Must Have Licenses," *SP*, December 8, 1908.

14. See George P. Decker, "New York Iroquois and State Game Laws," 1908, typescript, NYSL. For attorney George Decker's extraordinary career, see Hauptman, *Seven Generations of Iroquois Leadership,* 124–42.

15. *United States v. Winans*, 198 U.S. 371 (1905).

16. 215 N.Y. 42; 165 App. Div. 881 (1915).

17. *People of the State of New York on the Relation of Kennedy v. Becker, as Sheriff of Erie County*, 241 U.S. 556 (1916).

18. *ER*, 244–95.

19. Ibid., 197.

20. Ibid., 190–91.

21. Ibid., 261–62.

22. Ibid.

23. Ibid., 288–93.

24. See, for example, Hauptman, *Seven Generations of Iroquois Leadership,* 117–63.

25. For Senecas in World War I, see Krouse, *North American Indians in the Great War,* 39, 53, 120–21, 139, 152, 160.

26. Jesse J. Cornplanter questionnaire, Wanamaker-Dixon MSS, Mather Museum of World Cultures, Indiana University; Jesse J. Cornplanter to Carleton Perry, April 1, 1938, Indian Arts Project MSS, RMSC. See also Fenton, "Aboriginally Yours," 176–95.

27. Zissu, "Conscription, Sovereignty, and Land," 537–66.

28. Walter Kennedy to Arthur C. Parker, July 25, 1918, Society of American Indian MSS, WHS.
29. Zissu, "Conscription, Sovereignty, and Land," 548.
30. *United States v. Boylan, et al.*, 256 F. 468 (1919); 265 F.186 (1920).
31. See note 24.
32. Indian Citizenship Act, 43 Stat., 253 (June 2, 1924). Protest of Indian Citizenship Act, Seneca Nation Council minutes, 1924, SNI Archives. Immediately after the war. Congress began to consider this move and the Hodinöhsö:ni' reacted: "Chiefs of Six Nations to Reject Citizenship," *Syracuse Post Standard*, May 9, 1920.
33. 44 Stat., 932 (1927).
34. U.S. Congress, *Hearings on S. 5302*. For the Seneca protest against the bill, see pages 19–21; for Ray Jimerson's testimony see pages 16–17; for Warren Kennedy's testimony, see pages 14–16; for Alice Lee Jemison's testimony, see pages 6–10; for Cephas Watt's testimony, see pages 10–14.
35. Ray Jimerson to Senator Burton Wheeler, February 6, 1934, Senator Robert Wagner Sr. MSS, legislative files, Box 224, Indians file, Georgetown University; Robert Galloway [Seneca tribal attorney] to Governor Herbert Lehman, January 28, 1933, Governor Herbert Lehman MSS, MR86, Seneca Nation of Indians file, Columbia University.
36. Jimerson tried to get a federal appointment for Alice Lee Jemison in an effort to further Seneca Nation objectives. Ray Jimerson to Congressman James Mead, January 28, 1933, with attached resolution of Seneca Nation Tribal Council and résumé of Alice Lee Jemison; Alice Lee Jemison to John Collier, with attached resolutions of Seneca Nation Tribal Council, January 28, 1933, and December 30, 1933, BIA CCF, 1907–39, 19086-1934-162, New York, RG75, NA.
37. Veto message of President of Franklin D. Roosevelt, in U.S. Congress, S. Doc. 70. For the Seneca response, see Alice Lee Jemison to President Franklin D. Roosevelt, June 20, 1935, records of President Franklin D, Roosevelt, OF 296, FDR Presidential Library.
38. *People v. Redeye*, 358 N.Y.S.2d 632 (1974).
39. Fish and Wildlife Laws of New York State, article II, title 7, section 11-0707, paragraph 8, *McKinney's Consolidated Laws of New York Annotated*, 252; Seneca Nation of Indians fishing laws for Allegany, Cattaraugus, and Oil Spring territories.
40. New York State Legislature, *Laws of New York*, 1921, chap. 468 (1921).
41. New York State Office of Parks, Recreation, and Historic Preservation (OPRHP), *Allegany State Park. Master Plan/Draft Environmental Statement, April 14, 2010* (Albany: OPRHP, 2010), 27, 42–43.
42. Robert Moses pushed the building of the Kinzua Dam, which he argued would benefit the park. Charles E. Congdon interview conducted by William N. Fenton, December 4, 1964, William N. Fenton MSS, Kinzua Dam folder,

American Philosophical Society, Philadelphia. For Moses, see, for example, "State Council of Parks Backs Federal Plan to Buy Reservation and Remove Indians," *SRP*, January 21, 1946.

43. Mason, "Geography of Allegany State Park," 35–38.

44. Rowan, "New York State Produces Oil for the World," 1010.

45. New York State Association, *A Park Plan for New York State*, 26–35.

46. See 36 Stat., 961 (March 1, 1911). This was known as the Weeks Act.

47. After the establishment of Allegany State Park, the forest supervisor of the U.S. Department of Agriculture indicated that there was not the necessary supply of wood within the bounds of the state park for the operation of chemical companies—even those that still occupied thirteen thousand acres of land. L. L. Bishop to Chauncey J. Hamlin, August 3, August 5, 1922, Chauncey J. Hamlin MSS, Box 3, Folder 10; Correspondence Re: Allegany State Park, 1922–24, BHML.

48. In the New York State Archives, an index of deeds for lands acquired by the Allegany State Park Commission and approved by the New York State Attorney General's Office lists numerous chemical and lumber companies that sold lands but retained mineral and timber rights.

49. For a brief summary of Ames's career, see "DeHart Henry Ames," in Doty, Congdon, and Thornton, *Historic Annals of Southwestern New York*, 3:92–93.

50. Seneca petition, 1921, legislative bill jacket, New York State Assembly, *Laws of New York, 1921,* chap. 468. Henry John was elected Seneca president in 1934 and died in office on December 3, 1935. George-Shongo, *Ono'dowa'ga' Gano'kyëdoh Nogeh''oweh,* 129, 129n116.

51. Alleghany [*sic*] State Park Association press release, November 24, 1920, Charles C. Adams MSS, Box 11, Folder 1, NYSL.

52. Edward Brown [park consultant], "Allegheny [*sic*] State Park," *Hobbies* 1 (March 1921): 3–13. Brown later expanded his report. See Henry R. Francis, "The Recreation Resources of the Allegany State Park," *Hobbies* 2 (February 1922): 1–24, reprinted as a separate pamphlet, located in NYSL. For the full report by Francis, see Commissioners of the Allegany State Park, *First Annual Report,* appendix C. Francis also published a promotional pamphlet, "The Allegany State Park," for the Buffalo, Rochester, and Pittsburgh Railway, which was reprinted several times from 1922 onward.

53. Robert H. Keller and Michael F. Turek, *American Indians and National Parks* (Tucson: University of Arizona Press, 1998), xiii–xiv; Mark D. Spence, *Dispossessing the Wilderness* (New York: Oxford University Press, 1999), 4. Stephen Mather, the head of the national park, gave his formal endorsement to the creation of Allegany State Park. Edward F. Brown, "Allegheny [*sic*] State Park," *Hobbies* 1 (March 1921): 13; Mather to Chauncey J. Hamlin, March 7, 1921, legislative bill jacket, Series 12590, New York State Assembly, *Laws of New York*, chap. 468 (1921).

54. *Journal of the Senate of the State of New York, 1921*, 1464; *Journal of the Assembly of the State of New York, 1921*, 2699.
55. New York State Assembly, *Laws of New York*, chap. 468 (May 2, 1921).
56. Commissioners of the Allegany State Park, *First Annual Report*.
57. "The Allegany State Park and What It Means," *CR*, May 5, 1921, editorial.
58. Minutes of the 119th Meeting of the Commissioners of the Allegany State Park Commission, April 12, 1952, Chauncey J. Hamlin MSS, Box 3, Folder 11, BHML; Ames, "Allegany State Park," 765–74; Ward, "The Allegheny [*sic*] Park," 286–87; Congdon, *Allegany Oxbow*, 5–10.
59. Francis was in frequent contact with Robert Moses. Henry Francis to Robert Moses, September 18, September 25, October 31, 1923; Robert Moses to Henry Francis, November 2, November 23, 1923, RM MSS, Box 2, Allegany State Park folder, NYPL. Compare Francis's "The Recreation Resources of the Allegany State Park," *Hobbies* 2 (February 1922): 1–24, and his other writings cited in note 52 with the Moses-backed New York State Association, *Park Plan for New York*, 26–35, with a proposal for the new park bond issue.
60. Henry R. Francis, "The Recreation Resources of the Allegany State Park," *Hobbies* 2 (February 1922): 1–24; Henry Francis, "The Recreation Resources of The Allegany State Park," in Commissioners of the Allegany State Park, *First Annual Report*; Francis, "Allegany State Park" (promotional pamphlet).
61. For more detail, see Hauptman, *In the Shadow of Kinzua*, 53–58, 195–97.
62. Quoted in New York State Legislature, *Report on Indian Affairs, 1930*, 1–2, transcript in NYSL.
63. U.S. Congress, *Hearings on S. Res. 79*, 12:4865.
64. U.S. Congress, *Hearings on H.R. 9720*, 1. For more on Hodinöhsö:ni' opposition to the Snell bill, see Rickard, *Fighting Tuscarora*, 95–96.
65. See note 62.
66. U.S. Congress, *Hearings on H.R. 9720*, 19–20.
67. Harring, "Red Lilac of the Cayugas," 64–94.
68. Ibid.
69. I was the expert witness for the Cayuga Nation of New York in their land claim; *Cayuga Nation of New York and Seneca-Cayuga Tribe of Oklahoma and the United States as Plaintiff-Intervenor*, 165 F. Supp. 266 (N.D.N.Y., 2001). Based on a finding of fact, the Cayugas were awarded $247.8 million in this federal district court action. The case was appealed and the decision was overturned by the federal court of appeals in a finding of law in 2005: *Cayuga Indian Nation v. Pataki*, 413 F.3d 266 (2d Cir. 2005).
70. See, for example, the case of Cayuga Harold K. Bishop of the Fourth Infantry, Third Division, who lost his life estate at Cattaraugus while serving in the American Expeditionary Force during World War I. Krouse, *American Indians in the Great War*, 138–39.
71. *ER*, 210–47.

72. Cayuga chiefs memorial to New York State commissioners of the Land Office, February 14, 1906, Papers Relating to Claim of Cayuga Indian Nations against State of New York, 1780–1910, compiled by Edward H. Leggett, MSS 11597M, NYSL.

73. *Proceedings of the [New York State] Commissioners of the Land Office, 1910,* 27–32, 107–53, 306, 334–35, 364; *Proceedings of the [New York State] Commissioners of the Land Office, 1911,* 128–31; *Proceedings of the [New York State] Commissioners of the Land Office, 1924,* 54–60; "To Pay Indian Claim of 1795," *NYT,* March 5, 1913; Governor Al Smith, Executive Chamber News Release, January 31, 1924, Governor Al Smith MSS, MR12, NYSA.

74. "1795 Cayuga Claim on State Settled," *NYT,* November 15, 1931; New York State governor's news release: "In the Matter of the Application of the Cayuga Nation of Indians within the State of New York; Approval of the Settlement of Their Claim by the Governor," December 17, 1931, Governor FDR MSS, MR27, NYSA; "Senecas Oppose State Agreement," *NYT,* November 18, 1931.

Chapter 10

1. For a fuller analysis, see Hauptman, *Iroquois and the New Deal,* 136–76.

2. *U.S. v. Forness, et al.* (Salamanca Trust Co., et al., defendant-intervenors), 37 F. Supp. 337 (February 14, 1941); 125 *Fed. Rep.,* 2d Ser., 28 (January 20, 1942); "Our Indian Landlords Finally Get a Break," *NYT,* January 21, 1942.

3. 48 Stat., 984 (June 18, 1934); Hauptman, "Indian Reorganization Act," 131–48; Hauptman, "Raw Deal," 15–24.

4. See note 3.

5. American Indian Policy Review Commission, *Final Report,* 1:309–10.

6. Barsh, "BIA Reorganization Follies of 1978," 12.

7. George F. Newton to John Collier, October 28, 1934, 4894-1934-066, Part 12A, Records Concerning the Wheeler-Howard Act, Box 9, RG75, NA.

8. Ray Jimerson testimony in U.S. Congress, *Hearings on H.R. 7902,* 9:389.

9. For more on Jemison, see Hauptman, "Alice Lee Jemison," 175–86.

10. See note 3.

11. Haas, *Ten Years of Tribal Government under IRA,* 18. Federal Indian agent W. K. Harrison and his BIA community worker, anthropologist William N. Fenton, helped conduct the referendum, although Fenton privately expressed his concerns to the Senecas, since he was clearly opposed to the IRA. Author interviews with William N. Fenton, June 28, 1978, and May 18, 1983. For the Seneca protest over the referendum at Cornplanter, see Merrill Bowen to John Collier, June 18, 1935; Mitchell S. Pierce to Harold Ickes, June 17, 1935; John Collier to W. K. Harrison, July 30, November 18, 1935; Shipe and Faris Report, October 14, 1936, 9562-1936-066, New York, General Records Concerning Indian Organization, 1934–1956, RG75, NA.

12. See chapter 9.

13. Rosier, "Dam Building and Treaty-Breaking," 347.

14. Smith, "The Politics of Pittsburgh Flood Control, 1908–1936," 5–24; Smith, "The Politics of Pittsburgh Flood Control, 1936–1960," 3–24.

15. Author interviews with Merrill Bowen, August 26, 1983, and September 28, 1984. Bowen, the Cornplanter Seneca spokesman during the Kinzua crisis and editor of the *Kinzua Planning Newsletter*, went with several Seneca delegates to Harrisburg to protest in 1936. For the Interior Department's initial opposition to the Kinzua Dam during the New Deal, see John D. Reeves and A. D. Wathen to Commissioner of Indian Affairs, December 30, 1936; Oscar L. Chapman [assistant secretary of the interior) to Louis Johnson [assistant secretary of war], June 6, 1940, BIA CCF, 1907–39, 2691-29-052, New York, RG75, NA; Oscar L. Chapman to Secretary of War, August 28, November 23, December 31, 1940; E. K. Burlew [acting secretary of the interior] to Secretary of War, May 2, 1940, NYAR, Box 4, Cornplanter Dam folder, FRC, NA, NYC.

16. 52 Stat., 1215 (June 28, 1938). See also 55 Stat., 638 (August 18, 1941).

17. William N. Fenton interview of Charles E. Congdon, December 4, 1964, WNF MSS, Kinzua Dam folder, APS.

18. The Covell report is reprinted in U.S. Congress, H.R. Doc. 300, 22–87.

19. *Ex Parte Green* 123 F2d 862 (1941). The draft resistance case can be followed in *NYT*: October 10, October 12, 1940; February 27, May 15, August 15, 1941; October 21, 1941; *New York Herald Tribune*: October 21, 1941; *Niagara Falls Gazette*: December 27, 1941.

20. Resolution of Iroquois Declaration of War, June 12, 1942, William Zimmerman Jr. to Jesse Lyons, June 22, 1942; Department of the Interior press release, June 12, 1942, BIA CCF, 1940–52, ACC 53A-367, Box 1056, File 26556-1942-054, New York, RG75, NA; William Zimmerman Jr. to Jesse Lyons, June 22, 1942, BIA CCF, 1940–52, ACC 53A-367, Box 1056, File 26556-1942-061, New York, RG75, NA; Department of the Interior press release, June 12, 1942, BIA CCF, 1940–52, ACC 53A-367, Box 1056, File 26556-1942-061, New York, RG75, NA; author interview with Louis R. Bruce Jr., June 30, 1982.

21. "Indians Erect Roll of Honor for 82 in U.S. Armed Services," *SP*, May 10, 1943.

22. John Collier testimony in U.S. Congress, *Hearings on H.R. 166*.

23. Fixico, *Termination and Relocation*, 21–41.

24. William Zimmerman Jr. testimony in U.S. Congress, *Hearings on S. Res. 41*, part 3, 547.

25. 62 Stat., 1224 (July 2, 1948); 64 Stat., 845 (September 13, 1950).

26. See Hauptman, *In the Shadow of Kinzua*.

27. The Kinzua Dam and its impact on the Seneca Nation had national reverberations. See American Indian Chicago Conference, *Declaration of Indian Purpose*, 37.

•◄ ►•

BIBLIOGRAPHY

Archival Records and Manuscript Collections

American Philosophical Society
    Fenton, William N., MSS
    Speck, Frank, MSS
    Tooker, Elisabeth, MSS
    Wallace, Anthony F. C., MSS
Buffalo History Museum Library
    Bryant, William Clement, letterbooks
    Gansworth, Howard, MSS
    Hamlin, Chauncey J., MSS
    Holland Land Company MSS
    Indian Collection MSS (photographs)
    Parker, Arthur C., MSS
    Parker, Ely S., MSS
    Parker, Isaac Newton, MSS
    Pierce, Maris B., MSS
Case Western Reserve Medical School, Dittrick Medical History Center
    Lake, Albert D., thesis: "Anasthetics"
Cattaraugus County Courthouse (Little Valley, New York)
    Map book (Indian reservations)
    Chief Blacksnake testimony in *Seneca Nation v. Philonus Pattison*
Chemung Historical Society, Elmira, New York
    Converse, Harriet Maxwell, vertical file
    Maxwell family vertical file
Columbia University
    Lehman, Herbert, MSS
Cornell University
    Bates, Erl, MSS
    Cornell Cooperative Extension MSS
    Fellows, Joseph, MSS
    Keppler Jr., Joseph, Iroquois MSS
    Reed, Daniel, MSS

Columbia University
     Lehman, Herbert, MSS
Cumberland County Historical Society
     Files of Seneca students at Carlisle
     Photographic records
Federal Records Center, National Archives, New York City
     RG75, records of the New York Agency, 1938–49
Georgetown University
     Wagner Sr., Robert F., MSS
Hampton University Archives
     Employee files
     Seneca student files
Haverford College, Haverford, Pennsylvania
     Indian Committee of the Society of Friends, records of the Philadelphia
          Yearly Meeting
     Smiley family (Lake Mohonk Friends of the Indian) MSS
     Tunesassa Friends School MSS
Historical Society of Pennsylvania, Philadelphia
     Indian Rights Association MSS
Library of Congress
     Roosevelt, Theodore, MSS
     Schoolcraft, Henry Rowe, MSS
Mather Museum of World Cultures, Indiana University, Bloomington
     Wanamaker Collection, including Joseph Dixon interviews and questionnaires
          of American Indians who served in World War I
National Archives, Washington, D.C.
     BIA central classified files, 1881–37
     Carlisle Indian School files
     Census rolls, 1885–40, New York Agency
     Correspondence of the Office of Indian Affairs, M234, RG75
     Records of the New York Agency, 1824–81, microfilm reels 583–96
     Records of the New York Emigration Agency, 1829–51, microfilm reel 597
     General records concerning Indian organization, 1934–56
     Ratified Indian treaties, 1722–69, M668, microfilm reels 2, 3, 9, 12
     Records concerning Indian organization, 1934–56
     Records concerning the Wheeler-Howard Act
     Records relating to the negotiation of ratified and unratified treaties, 1801–69,
          T494, microfilm reels 1, 2, 4, 6, 8
     Records of the United States Board of Indian Commissioners
     Special Case File 29: Records relating to the New York Indians, the Treaty
          of 1838, and the Kansas claims
National Archives II, College Park, Maryland
     Cartographic records

Records of the Indian Claims Commission, RG279
Records of the secretary of the interior, RG48
Newberry Library
    Jennings, Francis, William N. Fenton, and Mary A. Druke, eds. *Iroquois Indians: A Documentary History of the Six Nations and Their League* (microfilm reels 48–50)
New York Public Library, Manuscript Division
    Moses, Robert, MSS
New York State Archives, Albany
    Indian annuity records
    Indian census rolls (including Schoolcraft census, 1845)
    New York State Board of Charities, Department of Social Welfare
        Thomas Indian School superintendents' daily diaries
        Thomas Indian School treasurers' monthly reports
        Thomas Indian School unrestricted correspondence files (unrelated to individual student files)
    New York State Council of Parks minutes
    New York State Department of Education, Native American Indian Education Unit
    New York State Museum records
    New York State Department of Law, Litigation Bureau
        Landmark case files
    New York State governors' records
        Hughes, Charles Evans
        Miller, Nathan
        Morgan, Edmund
        Roosevelt, Franklin D.
        Seymour, Horatio
        Smith, Alfred E.
    New York State Department of Health records
    New York State Legislature
        Committee on Governmental Operations, Subcommittee on Indian Affairs, subject and hearings files, 1968–72
New York State Library, Manuscript Division, Albany
    Adams, Charles C., MSS
    Bliss, Asher, MSS
    Everett Commission. *Assembly Report of the Indian Commission to Investigate the Status of the American Indian Residing in the State of New York,* March 17, 1922
    Leggett, Edward H., comp. *Papers Relating to Claim of Cayuga Indian Nations against State of New York, 1780–1910*
    Parker, Arthur C., MSS
    Society of American Indians MSS (microfilm)
    Stillman, Lulu, MSS

New York State Museum
    Beauchamp, William, MSS (includes Harriet Maxwell Converse scrapbooks)
    Harriet Maxwell Converse Collection
Pennsylvania State Archives, Harrisburg
    Deardorff, Merle H., MSS
Roosevelt Presidential Library, Hyde Park, New York
    Franklin D. Roosevelt official files series
St. John Fisher College, Lavery Library
    Decker, George, MSS
Seneca Nation of Indians Archives
    Seneca Council minutes, 1854–50
Seneca Nation Department of Law (Justice)
    Records relating to Oil Spring land claims, 1985–2005
Seneca–Iroquois National Museum
    Pamphlet series on Seneca culture
    Photographic Collection
Smithsonian Institution, National Anthropological Archives
    Bureau of American Ethnology Collection
    Hewitt, J. N. B., MSS
State University of New York, College at Buffalo
    Reilly, Paul G., Indian Claims Commission MSS
State University of New York, College of Environmental Sciences and Forestry
    Moon, F. Frederick, MSS
Swarthmore College
    Baltimore Yearly Meeting of Friends MSS
    New York Yearly Meeting of Friends (Haviland Record Room Collection)
University at Albany, SUNY
    Manley, Henry S., MSS
University at Buffalo, SUNY, Charles B. Sears Law Library
    Howard Berman Collection
    Indian Claims Collection (Peter Sullivan, New York State assistant attorney
        general)
University of Rochester
    Dewey, Thomas E., MSS
    Morgan, Lewis Henry, MSS
    Parker, Arthur C., MSS
    Parker, Ely S., MSS
Wisconsin Historical Society
    Montezuma, Carlos, MSS
    Taylor, Walter, MSS
Yale University, Beinecke Library
    Pratt, Richard Henry, MSS
Yale University, Sterling Library
    Collier, John, MSS

Court Cases

Cherokee Nation v. Georgia, 30 U.S. 1 (1831).

Cherokee Tobacco, 78 U.S. 616 (1871).

City of Sherrill v. Oneida Indian Nation, 125 S. Ct. 1478 (2006).

County of Oneida, et al. v. Oneida Indian Nation of New York, 414 U.S. 226 (1985).

Deere, et al. v. St. Lawrence River Power Co., et al., 22 F.2d 851 (1927).

Ex Parte Green, 123 F.2d 862 (1941).

In Re New York Indians, 72 U.S. 761 (1866).

Kennedy v. Becker, 241 U.S. 566 (1916).

Lonewolf v. Hitchcock, 187 U.S. 553 (1903).

New York Indians v. United States, 40 Ct. Cl. 448 (1905).

[New York State] Department of Taxation and Finance v. Milhelm Attea & Bros., Inc., et al., 512 U.S. 61 (1994).

Oneida Indian Nation of New York v. County of Oneida, et al., 94 S. Ct. 772 (1974).

People v. Redeye, 358 N.Y. 2d 289 (1974).

Seneca Nation v. Harrison B. Christy, 2 N.Y.S. 546 (Sup. Ct., 1888), affirmed 27 N.E. 275 (N.Y., 1891), appeal dismissed, 162 U.S. 208 (1896).

Seneca Nation of Indians v. Philonus Parrison, 87 Casel (N.Y., 1860–61).

United States v. Boylan, et al., 256 F.468 (1919); 265 F.186 (1920).

United States v. Cattaraugus County, 67 F. Supp. 294 (W.D.N.Y., 1946); 71 F. Supp. 413 (W.D.N.Y.).

United States v. Elm, 25 Fed. Cas. 1006 (1877).

United States v. Forness, et al. (Salamanca Trust Co., et al., defendant-intervenor), 37 F. Supp. 337 (1941); 125 *Red. Rep.*, 2d Series, 928 (1942).

United States ex. rel. John D. Lynn v. Frederick W. Hamilton, et al. 233 F.685 (W.D.N.Y, 1915).

United States v. Winans, 198 U.S. 371 (1905).

Winter v. United States, 207 U.S. 564 (1908).

Woodin v. Seeley, 25 N.Y.S. 818 (1931).

Interviews Conducted by the Author

Cornelius Abrams Jr., September 29, 1984, and March 21, 1986, Allegany Indian Reservation

Rovena Abrams, February 23, 2011, Allegany Indian Reservation

Marilyn Anderson, May 4–5, 1977, New Paltz, New York; September 26, 2011, Cattaraugus Indian Reservation

Duwayne "Duce" Bowen, March 21, 1986, Allegany Indian Reservation

Merrill Bowen, August 26, 1983, and September 28, 1984, Allegany Indian Reservation

Ethel Bray, August 15, 2001, Allegany Indian Reservation

Louis R. Bruce Jr. (former commissioner of Indian affairs), December 10, 1980, and June 30, 1982, Washington, D.C.

Ramona Charles, July 21, 1982, May 14, 1986, and September 18, 2007, Tonawanda Indian Reservation

Laura Chodos (New York State Board of Regents), February 24, 1986, Albany

Lloyd Elm (former director of Indian education for the Buffalo, New York, and Saint Paul, Minnesota, school systems), July 31, 2005, Canton, New York

William M. Fenton, June 28, 1978, and May 18, 1983, Slingerlands, New York

George Heron (former president of the Seneca Nation of Indians), September 28, 1984, Allegany Indian Reservation

Tyler Heron, August 10, 2012, Allegany Indian Reservation

Caroline Hewitt, June 4, 1978, Cattaraugus Indian Reservation

Arleigh Hill, July 25, 1978, Rochester, New York

Jeanne Marie Jemison, August 26, 1977, Herndon, Virginia; August 23, 1978, Tysons Corner, Virginia; July 14, 1982, New Paltz, New York; September 6, 1984, March 21, 1986, and September 13, 1986, Cattaraugus Indian Reservation

Rick Jemison, March 21, 2012, Cattaraugus Indian Reservation

Calvin John (former president of the Seneca Nation of Indians), May 2, 1987, and May 4, 1997, Allegany Indian Reservation

Hazel Dean John, July 16, 1984, April 18, 1986, and January 30, 1987, Albany

Maurice John Sr. (former president of the Seneca Nation of Indians), May 30, 2012 (telephone interview)

Randy John, January 31, 2012, Allegany Indian Reservation

Marlene Johnson (former chair of the Presidential Commission on Indian Education), July 9, 1992, Olean, New York; August 15, 2001, Allegany Indian Reservation

Fred Kennedy, September 25, 2011, Dunkirk, New York

Francis Kettle (former president of the Seneca Nation of Indians), July 27, 1977, and June 8, 1978, Cattaraugus Indian Reservation

Wini Kettle, April 15, 1971, New Paltz, New York; July 28, 1978, Cattaraugus Indian Reservation

Anna Lewis (New York State Education Department, Native American Unit), May 4, 1978, New Paltz, New York; June 10, 1983, Albany

Jean Loret, September 25, 2011, Dunkirk, New York

Lee Lyons, September 8, 1984, Syracuse

Oren Lyons, September 8, 1984, Syracuse

John Mohawk, March 20–21, 2001, Buffalo

Carole Moses, July 18, 2001, Allegany Indian Reservation

W. David Owl, July 28, 1977, Cattaraugus Indian Reservation

Genevieve Plummer, July 28, 1972, Allegany Indian Reservation

Jack Preston, May 4, 1975, New Paltz, New York

Cyrus M. Schindler Sr. (former president of the Seneca Nation of Indians), May 31, 2012 (telephone interview)

Martin Seneca Jr., June 11, 2011, Cattaraugus Indian Reservation

George Shattuck, August 25, 1983, Syracuse

Pauline Seneca, June 4, 1978, and July 15–17, 1982, Cattaraugus Indian Reservation

Keith Smiley, May 3, 1984, New Paltz, New York

Leo Soucy (New York assistant commissioner of education), March 4, 1986

Corbett Sundown, May 22, 1980, Tonawanda Indian Reservation
Lincoln White (assistant commissioner for Indian affairs educational policies, BIA), July 1, 1982, Washington, D.C.

Federal, State, and Seneca Nation Government Publications

American Indian Policy Review Commission. *Final Report.* 2 vols. Washington, D.C.: USGPO, 1977.

American State Papers: Documents, Legislative and Executive of the Congress of the United States, Class 2; Indian Affairs. 2 vols. Washington, D.C.: Gales and Seaton, 1832–34.

Austin, Alberta, comp. *Ne´ Ho Niyo´ Dë:Nö´—That's What It Was Like.* 2 vols. Lackawanna, N.Y.: Rebco Enterprises for the Seneca Education Department, 1986–89.

Bardeau, Phyllis E. W. *Definitive Seneca: It's in the Word.* Edited by Jaré Cardinal. Salamanca, N.Y.: Seneca–Iroquois National Museum, 2011.

Birdseye, Ruth. *Indian Education in New York State, 1846–1953/1954.* Albany: New York State Education Department, 1954.

Board of Regents of the University of the State of New York. *Native American Education.* Position Paper 22. Albany: New York State Education Department, 1975.

Bowen, Rebecca. *Along the Ohi:yo.* Parts 1 and 2. Salamanca, N.Y.: Seneca Nation Archives, n.d.

———. *Education at Ohi:yo´: A Brief History.* Salamanca, N.Y.: Seneca Nation Archives, n.d.

Cohen, Felix S. *Handbook of Federal Indian Law.* Washington, D.C.: U.S. Department of the Interior, 1942; reprint, Albuquerque: University of New Mexico Press, 1971.

Commissioners of the Allegany State Park. *First Annual Report.* Salamanca, NY: Commissioners of the Allegany State Park, 1922.

Cowen, Philip A. *Survey of Indian Schools.* Albany: New York State Department of Education, 1940.

Donaldson, Thomas, comp. *The Six Nations of New York.* Washington, D.C.: U.S. Census Printing Office, 1892.

George-Shongo, David. *Ono´dowa'ga´ Gano´kyëdoh Nogeh''oweh (Seneca Nation of Indians): The 160 Years of Republican Government.* Salamanca, N.Y.: Seneca Nation of Indians, Archives Department, 2009.

Haas, Theodore H. *Ten Years of Tribal Government under IRA.* Washington, D.C.: United States Department of the Interior, 1947.

Kappler, Charles J., comp. *Indian Affairs: Laws and Treaties.* 5 vols. Washington, D.C.: USGPO, 1904–41. Volume 2 reprinted as *Indian Treaties, 1778–1883.* New York: Interland, 1972.

New York State Board of Charities. Annual reports of the Thomas Asylum/School, 1875–1929.

New York State Board of Land Commissioners. Proceedings of the commissioners, 1906–24.

New York State Commissioner of Education. Annual reports, 1901–40.

New York State Commissioners of Allegany State Park. Annual reports, 1921–50.

New York State Constitutional Convention. *Documents of the Constitutional Convention of the State of New York, 1915.* Albany: J. B. Lyon, 1915.

New York State Court of Appeals. *There Shall Be a Court of Appeals: 150th Anniversary of the State Court of Appeals.* Albany: New York State Court of Appeals, 1997.

New York State Department of Social Welfare. Annual reports of the Thomas Indian School, 1930–56.

New York State Legislature. *Laws of New York.*

New York State Legislature, Assembly. *Assembly Journal.*

———. *Report of the Indian Commission to Investigate the Status of the American Indian Residing in the State of New York (Everett Report).* Albany: New York State Assembly, 1922.

———. *Report of the Special Committee Appointed by the Assembly of 1905 to Investigate the Conditions Existing upon the Several Indian Reservations of the State.* Albany: New York State Assembly, 1906.

———. *Report of the Special Committee to Investigate the Indian Problem of the State of New York (Whipple Report).* 2 vols. Albany: Troy Press, 1889.

———. *Report on Indian Affairs,* Albany: New York State Assembly, 1930.

———. Standing Committee on Governmental Operations, Subcommittee on Indian Affairs. Hearings, October 14–15, 1970.

New York State Legislature, Joint Legislative Committee on Indian Affairs. Reports, 1944–59.

New York State Legislature, Senate. *Senate Journal.*

———. Senate Doc. 24. *Remonstrance of Seneca Indians of the Cattaraugus Reservation against the Passage of Any Law Authorizing an Allotment or Lease of Their Lands to White People,* February 7, 1868.

———. Senate Doc. 85. *Report of the Judiciary Committee on the Memorial of the President and Councilors of the Seneca Nation of Indians for Relief from Taxes,* January 22, 1857.

———. Subcommittee on Indian Affairs of the Subcommittee on Governmental Operations. Public hearings, 1970–71.

New York State Office of Parks, Recreation, and Historic Preservation. *Allegany State Park. Master Plan/Draft Environmental Statement.* 3 vols. Albany: New York State Office of Parks, Recreation, and Historic Preservation, 2010.

New York State Superintendent of Public Instruction. Annual reports, 1854–1900.

Persico, Joseph. *History of Public Health in New York State.* Albany: New York State Department of Health, 1968.

Seneca Nation of Indians. Annual reports, 2006, 2008, and 2014.

United States Bureau of the Census. First through fifteenth censuses, 1790–1930.

United States Congress. *Congressional Record.*

United States Congress, House of Representatives. H.R. Doc. 300. *Hearings: Allegheny River, N.Y. and Pennsylvania, Allegheny Reservoir.* 76th Cong., 1st sess. Washington, D.C.: USGPO, 1939.

———. H.R. Rep. 92. 31st Cong., 1st sess., September 9, 1850.

United States Congress, House of Representatives, Committee on Indian Affairs. *Hearings on H.R. 106: Investigation of Indian Affairs.* Parts 1 and 2. 76th Cong. 1st and 2d sess. Washington, D.C.: USGPO, 1943–44.

———. *Hearings on H.R. 166: Investigate Indian Affairs.* 78th Cong., 1st sess., March 23, 1943; 2d sess., February 2, February 16, 1944.

———. *Hearings on H.R. 7902.* Washington, D.C.: USGPO, 1934.

———. *Hearings on H.R. 7262: Allotment of Lands in Severalty to the Indians in New York.* 58th Cong, 2d sess. Washington, D.C.: USGPO, 1904.

———. *Hearings on H.R. 9720: Indians of New York.* 71st Cong., 2d sess. Washington, D.C.: USGPO, 1930.

———. *Hearings on H.R. 12270 for the Allotment of Lands in Severalty among the Seneca Nation of New York Indians.* 57th Cong., 1st sess. Washington, D.C.: USGPO, 1902.

———. H.R. Doc. 673. *New York Indian Lands in Kansas.* 48th Cong., 1st sess., March 5, 1883. *Congressional Serial Set*, Vol. 2255, 48–1.

———. H.R. Doc. 1858. *Indian Beneficiaries under Treaty Concluded at Buffalo Creek, January 15, 1838.* 52nd Cong., 1st sess., July 13, 1892. *Congressional Serial Set*, Vol. 3048.

———. H.R. Doc. 2001. *Indian Treaty of Buffalo Creek, New York.* 47th Cong., 2d sess., March 2, 1883, 1–4. *Congressional Serial Set*, Vol. 2160, 47–2.

———. H.R. Doc. 2002. *Allowance of Claims in the Office of the Quartermaster-General, Commissary General, and Third Auditor.* 47th Cong., 2d sess., March 3, 1883.

United States Congress, House of Representatives, Committee on Interior and Insular Affairs. *Hearings on H.R. 5367: To Provide for the Renegotiation of Certain Leases of the Seneca Nation.* September 13, 1990. 101st Cong., 2d sess. Washington, D.C.: USGPO, 1990.

United States Congress, House of Representatives, Subcommittee on Indian Affairs of the Committee on Interior and Insular Affairs. *Hearings on H.R. 1794, H.R. 3343, and H.R. 7354: Kinzua Dam (Seneca Indian Relocation),* May 18–December 10, 1963. 88th Cong., 1st sess. Washington, D.C.: USGPO, 1964.

United States Congress, Senate. S. Doc. 45. 55th Cong., 2d sess., 1892.

———. S. Doc. 70: *The Taking of Fish and Game within Certain Indian Reservations in the State of New York.* 74th Cong., 1st sess., June 17, 1935.

———. S. Doc. 122: *Protest of the President, Councilors and People of the Seneca Nation of Indians Made in Their National Council against the Passage of the Bill H.R. No. 3080 to Authorize the Seneca Nation to Lease Their Lands within the Cattaraugus and Allegany Reservations, and to Confirm Existing Leases.* 43d Cong., 1st sess., 1874.

———. S. Doc. 154: *The Ogden Land Company*. 54th Cong., 2d sess., 1897.

———. S. Doc. 1038: *Contagious and Infectious Diseases among the Indians*, 62–63. *Congressional Serial Set* 6365, 1912.

United States Congress, Senate, Committee on Indian Affairs. *Hearings: Allotment of Lands in Severalty to the Indians of New York*. 58th Cong, 2d sess. Washington, D.C.: USGPO, 1903.

———. *Hearings on S. 5302: An Act to Amend the Act Entitled "An Act to Grant the State of New York and the Seneca Nation of Indians Jurisdiction Over the Taking of Fish and Game within the Allegany, Cattaraugus, and Oil Spring Indian Reservations, Approved January 5, 1927."* 72nd Cong., 2d sess. Washington, D.C.: USGPO, 1933.

United States Congress, Senate, Committee on the Post Office and Civil Service. *Hearings on S. Res. 41: Officers and Employees of the Federal Government*. 80th Cong., 1st sess. Washington, D.C.: USGPO, 1947.

United States Congress, Senate, Select Committee on Indian Affairs. *Hearings on S. 2895: To Provide for the Renegotiation of Certain Leases of the Seneca Nation*, September 18, 1990. 101st Cong., 2d sess. Washington, D.C.: USGPO, 1990.

United States Congress, Senate, Subcommittee of the Committee on Indian Affairs. *Hearings on S. Res. 79*, 1920.

United States Congress, Senate, Subcommittee on Indian Affairs of the Committee on Interior and Insular Affairs. *Hearings on S. 1836 and H.R. 1794: Kinzua Dam (Seneca Indian Relocation)*, March 2, 1964. 88th Cong., 2d sess. Washington, D.C.: USGPO, 1964.

United States Congress, Senate, Subcommittee on Interior and Insular Affairs. *Hearings on S. 1683, S. 1686, S. 1687: New York Indians*. Washington, D.C.: USGPO, 1948.

United States Department of the Interior, National Park Service. *Historic American Building Survey: Thomas Asylum for Orphan and Destitute Indian Children (Thomas Indian School)*. Washington, D.C.: U.S. Department of the Interior, 1974.

United States Department of the Interior, Secretary of the Interior. Annual reports.

United States Department of the Interior, Commissioner of Indian Affairs. Annual reports.

Whitford, Noble E. *History of the Canal System of the State of New York*. 2 vols. Supplement to the annual report of the engineer and surveyor of the State of New York. Albany: Brandon Printing, 1906.

Periodicals

Albany Argus
Albany Times Union
Bell's Life (London)
Brooklyn Eagle
Buffalo Courier
Buffalo Courier Express
Buffalo Express

Buffalo News
Carlisle Arrow
Cattaraugus Republican
Chicago Tribune
Commercial Advertiser (Buffalo)
Commercial Advertiser (New York City)
Elmira Advertiser
Elmira Telegram
The Friend
Hobbies (Buffalo Society of Natural Sciences)
Indian Helper (Carlisle Institute)
Indian Truth (Indian Rights Association)
Jamestown (NY) Post-Journal
Nation
New York Clipper
New York Evening Post
New York Herald
New York Herald Tribune
New York Recorder
New York Sun
New York Times
New York Tribune
New York World
Niagara Fall Gazette
Oh He Yoh Noh (Allegany Indian Reservation)
Olean Times-Herald
Public Health Report (U.S. Public Health Service)
Redman (Carlisle Institute)
Rochester Democrat and Chronicle
Rochester Post Express
Rochester Times Union
Salamanca Press (formerly *Salamanca Republican-Press*)
Schenectady Gazette
Seneca Nation of Indian's Official Newsletter
Si Wong Geh (Cattaraugus Indian Reservation)
Southern Workman
Syracuse Herald-American
Syracuse Post-Standard
Talks and Thoughts of the Hampton Students
The Times (London)
Troy Times
Warren (Pa.) Mail
Washington Post
Washington Times

Books, Booklets, Pamphlets

Abler, Thomas S. *Cornplanter: Chief Warrior of the Allegany Senecas.* Syracuse: Syracuse University Press, 2007.

————, ed. *Chainbreakers: The Revolutionary War Memoirs of Governor Blacksnake as Told to Benjamin Williams.* Lincoln: University of Nebraska Press, 1989.

Abrams, George H. J. *The Seneca People.* Phoenix: Indian Tribal Series, 1976.

Adams, David Wallace. *Education for Extinction: American Indians and the Boarding School Experience 1875–1928.* Lawrence: University Press of Kansas, 1995.

Adams, William. *Historical Gazetteer and Biographical Memorial of Cattaraugus County. N.Y.* 2 vols. Syracuse: Lyman, Horton, 1893.

American Indian Chicago Conference. *Declaration of Indian Purpose.* Chicago: American Indian Chicago Conference, 1961.

Barbour, Hugh, Christopher Densmore, and Elizabeth Moger, eds. *Quaker Crosscurrents: Three Hundred Years of Friends in the New York Yearly Meetings.* Syracuse: Syracuse University Press, 1995.

Barry, John N. *The Great Influenza: The Epic Story of the Deadliest Plague in History.* New York: Viking Books, 2004.

Barsh, Russel L., and James Youngblood Henderson. *The Road: Indian Tribes and Political Liberty.* Berkeley: University of California Press, 1980.

Barton, Lois. *A Quaker Promise Kept: Philadelphia Friends' Work with the Allegany Seneca, 1795–1960.* Eugene, OR: Spencer Butte Press, 1990.

Bates, Samuel P., comp. *History of the Pennsylvania Volunteers.* Vol. 2. Harrisburg: Singerly, 1869.

Beers, William George. *Lacrosse: The National Game of Canada.* Montreal: Dawson Brothers, 1869.

Bergan, Francis. *The History of the New York Court of Appeals, 1847–1932.* New York: Columbia University Press, 1985.

Bilharz, Joy. *The Allegany Senecas and Kinzua Dam: Forced Relocation through Two Generations.* Lincoln: University of Nebraska Press, 1998.

Bristow, Nancy K. *American Pandemic: The Lost Worlds of the 1918 Influenza Epidemic.* New York: Oxford University Press, 2012.

Burich, Keith. *The Thomas Indian School and the Irredeemable Children of New York.* Syracuse: Syracuse University Press, 2016.

Cadwalader, Sandra L., and Vine Deloria Jr., eds. *The Aggressions of Civilization.* Philadelphia: Temple University Press, 1984.

Cahill, Cathleen D. *Federal Fathers and Mothers: A Social History of the United States Indian Service.* Chapel Hill: University of North Carolina Press, 2011.

Calloway, Colin G. *The Indian History of an American Institution: Native Americans at Dartmouth.* Hanover, N.H.: Dartmouth College, 2010.

Campisi, Jack, Michael Foster, and Marianne Mithun, eds. *Extending the Rafters: Interdisciplinary Approaches to Iroquoian Studies.* Albany: State University of New York Press, 1984.

Caro, Robert. *Power Broker: Robert Moses and the Fall of New York.* New York: Random House, 1974.

Caswell, Harriet S. *Our Life among the Iroquois Indians.* 1892. Paperback reprint, Lincoln: University of Nebraska Press, 2007.

Cohen, Felix S. *The Legal Conscience: Selected Papers of Felix Cohen.* Edited by Lucy Kramer Cohen. New Haven, Conn.: Yale University Press, 1960.

——— *On the Drafting of Tribal Constitutions.* Edited by David Wilkins. Norman: University of Oklahoma Press, 2007.

Congdon, Charles E. *Allegany Oxbow: A History of Allegany State Park and the Allegany Reserve of the Seneca Nation.* Little Valley, N.Y.: Straight, 1967.

Converse, Harriet Maxwell. *Myths and Legends of the New York State Iroquois.* Edited by Arthur C. Parker. New York State Museum Bulletin 125. Albany: New York State Museum, 1908.

Cornplanter, Jesse. *Legends of the Longhouse.* New York: Lippincott, 1938.

Crosby, Alfred W. *America's Forgotten Pandemic: The Influenza of 1918.* New York: Cambridge University Press, 1989. Originally published in 1976 as *Epidemic and Peace, 1918.*

Cummings, John. *Runners and Walkers: A Nineteenth Century Sports Chronicle.* Chicago: Regnery Gateway, 1981

Curtin, Jeremiah. *Seneca Indian Myths.* 1922. Paperback reprint, New York: Dover, 2001.

DeJong, David H. *"If You Knew the Conditions": A Chronicle of the Indian Medical Service and American Indian Health Care, 1908–1955.* New York: Lexington Books, 2008.

Deloria Jr., Vine, and Raymond J. DeMallie, comps. *Documents of American Indian Diplomacy: Treaties, Agreements, and Conventions, 1775–1949.* 2 vols. Norman: University of Oklahoma Press, 1999.

Densmore, Christopher. *Red Jacket: Iroquois Diplomat and Orator.* Syracuse: Syracuse University Press, 1999.

Dilts, James D. *The Great Road: The Building of the Baltimore and Ohio: The Nation's First Railroad, 1828–1953.* Palo Alto, Calif.: Stanford University Press, 1993.

Doty, William J., Charles E. Congdon, and Lewis H. Thornton, eds. *The Historic Annals of Southwestern New York.* 3 vols. New York: Lewis Historical Publishing Company, 1940.

Ellis, Franklin, ed. *History of Cattaraugus County, New York.* Philadelphia: L. H. Evarts, 1879.

Engelbrecht, William. *Iroquoia: The Development of a Native World.* Syracuse: Syracuse University Press, 2004.

Engs, Robert F. *Educating the Disenfranchised and Disinherited: Samuel Chapman Armstrong and Hampton Institute, 1839–1893.* Knoxville: University of Tennessee Press, 1999.

Fear-Segal, Jacqueline, and Susan D. Rose, eds. *The Carlisle Indian Industrial School: Indigenous Histories, Memories, and Reclamations.* Lincoln: University of Nebraska Press, 2016.

Fenton, William N. *The Great Law and the Longhouse: A Political History of the Iroquois Confederacy.* Norman: University of Oklahoma Press, 1998.

———. *The Iroquois Eagle Dance: An Offshoot of the Calumet Dance*. 1953. Paperback reprint, Syracuse: Syracuse University Press, 1991.

———. *The Little Water Society of the Senecas*. Norman: University of Oklahoma Press, 2002.

———, ed. *Symposium on Local Diversity*. Bulletin 149. Washington, D.C.: Bureau of American Ethnology, 1951.

Fenton, William N., and John Gullick, eds. *Symposium on Cherokee and Iroquois Culture*. Bulletin 180. Washington, D.C.: Bureau of American Ethnology, 1961.

Fisher, Donald M. *Lacrosse: A History of the Game*. Baltimore: Johns Hopkins University Press, 2002.

Fixico, Donald L. *American Indians in a Modern World*. Lanham, Md.: Alta Mira Press, 2008.

———. *The Invasion of Indian Country in the Twentieth Century: American Capitalism and Tribal Natural Resources*. Niwot: University Press of Colorado, 1998.

———. *Rethinking American Indian History*. Albuquerque: University of New Mexico Press, 1997.

———. *Termination and Relocation: Federal Indian Policy, 1945–1960*. Albuquerque: University of New Mexico Press, 1986.

Foreman, Carolyn. *Indians Abroad, 1492–1938*. Norman: University of Oklahoma Press, 1942.

Francis, Henry R. *The Allegany State Park*. Salamanca, N.Y.: Buffalo, Rochester, and Pittsburgh Railway, 1922.

French, J. H. *Gazetteer of the State of New York*. Syracuse: R. Pearsall Smith, 1860.

Gibson, John Arthur. *Concerning the League: The Iroquois Tradition as Dictated in Onondaga*. Edited and translated by Hanni Woodbury, in collaboration with Reg Henry and Harry Webster, based on Alexander A. Goldenweiser's manuscript. Memoir 9. Winnipeg: Algonquian and Iroquoian Linguistics, 1992.

Goldman, Mark. *High Hopes: The Rise and Decline of Buffalo*. Albany: SUNY Press, 1983.

Graymont, Barbara. *The Iroquois in the American Revolution*. Syracuse: Syracuse University Press, 1972.

Hadgraft, Rob. *Deerfoot: Athletics' Noble Savage: From Indian Reservation to Champion of the World*. Southend-on-Sea, UK: Desert Island Books, 2007.

Hafner, Arthur W., comp. *Directory of Deceased American Physicians, 1804–1929*. 2 vols. Chicago: American Medical Association, 1993.

Hagan, William T. *The Indian Rights Association: The Herbert Welsh Years*. Tucson: University of Arizona Press, 1985.

Hale, Horatio E. *The Iroquois Book of Rites*. 2 vols. Philadelphia: D. G. Brinton, 1883.

Hauptman, Laurence M. *Between Two Fires: American Indians in the Civil War*. New York: Free Press/Simon and Schuster, 1995.

———. *Conspiracy of Interests: Iroquois Dispossession and the Rise of New York*. Syracuse: Syracuse University Press, 1999.

———. *Formulating American Indian Policy in New York State, 1970–1986*. Albany: SUNY Press, 1988.

———. *In the Shadow of Kinzua: The Seneca Nation of Indians Since World War II.* Syracuse: Syracuse University Press, 2014.

———. *The Iroquois and the New Deal.* Syracuse: Syracuse University Press, 1981.

———. *The Iroquois in the Civil War: From Battlefield to Reservation.* Syracuse: Syracuse University Press, 1993.

———. *The Iroquois Struggle for Survival: World War II to Red Power.* Syracuse: Syracuse University Press, 1986.

———. *An Oneida Indian in Foreign Waters: The Life of Chief Chapman Scanandoah.* Syracuse: Syracuse University Press, 2016.

———. *Seven Generations of Iroquois Leadership: The Six Nations since 1800.* Syracuse: Syracuse University Press, 2008.

———. *The Tonawanda Senecas' Heroic Battle against Removal: Conservative Activist Indians.* Albany: SUNY Press, 2011.

Hauptman, Laurence M., and L. Gordon McLester III, eds. *The Oneidas in the Age of Allotment, 1860–1920.* Norman: University of Oklahoma Press, 2006.

Herrick, John. *Empire Oil: The Story of Oil in the Empire State.* New York: Dodd Mead, 1949.

Hewitt, J. N. B. *Iroquois Cosmology.* Part I. Washington, D.C.: Bureau of American Ethnology, 1899–1900.

———. *Iroquoian Cosmology.* Part II. Washington, D.C.: Bureau of American Ethnology, 1928.

Holt, Marilyn I. *Indian Orphanages.* Lawrence: University Press of Kansas, 2004.

Hungerford, Edward. *Men of Erie: A Story of Human Effort.* New York: Random House, 1946.

Jackson, Halliday. *Sketch of the Manners, Customs, Religion and Government of the Seneca Indians in 1800.* Philadelphia: T. C. Gould, 1830.

Jenkins, Sally. *The Real All-Americans.* New York: Random House, 2008.

Jennings, Francis, William N. Fenton, Mary Druke, and David R. Miller eds. *The History and Culture of Iroquois Diplomacy: An Interdisciplinary Guide to the Treaties of the Six Nations and Their League.* Syracuse: Syracuse University Press, 1985.

John, Randy. *The Social Integration of a Native American Population.* New York: Garland, 1995.

———, comp. *Seneca People: Places and Names.* Edited by Jaré Cardinal. Salamanca, N.Y.: RAJ Publications, 2017.

———, ed. *Notes of Border History: Taken on a Trip to the western part of Penna. & the adjoining parts of the New York & Ohio, from Jan. 30th to March 9th. 1850.* Transcribed by Jaré R. Cardinal. Salamanca, N.Y.: RAJ Publications, 2017.

Jordan, Kurt. *The Seneca Restoration: A Local Political Economy.* Gainesville: University of Florida Press, 2008.

Kehl, James. *Boss Rule in the Gilded Age: Matt Quay of Pennsylvania.* Pittsburgh: University of Pittsburgh Press, 1981.

Kent, George E., comp. *The Fish and Game Laws of the State of New York.* Troy, N.Y.: Troy Press, 1888.

Kolata, Gina. *Flu: The Story of the Great Influenza Pandemic of 1918 and the Search for the Virus That Caused It*. New York: Farrar, Straus, Giroux, 1999.

Krouse, Susan Applegate. *North American Indians in the Great War*. Lincoln: University of Nebraska Press, 2007.

Lafitau, Joseph François. *Customs of the American Indians*. 2 vols. Edited by William N. Fenton. Translated by Elizabeth Moore. Toronto: Champlain Society, 1974.

Lake Mohonk Conference of Friends of the Indian. Annual reports, 1883–1916.

Lifflander, Matthew L. *The Impeachment of Governor Sulzer*. Albany: SUNY Press, 2012.

Lindsey, Donal F. *Indians at Hampton, 1879–1923*. Urbana: University of Illinois Press, 1994.

Lucas, Charles J. P. *The Olympic Games, 1904*. Saint Louis: Woodward and Tiernan, 1905.

Lupton, James M. K., and James L. Lupton. *The Pedestrian's Record*. London: W. H. Allen, 1890.

Lovesey, Peter. *Five Kings of Distance*. New York: St. Martin's Press, 1981.

Mancall, Peter C. *Deadly Medicine: Indians and Alcohol in Early America*. Ithaca, N.Y.: Cornell University Press, 1995.

Matthews, George R. *America's First Olympics: The St. Louis Games of 1904*. Columbia: University of Missouri Press, 2005.

Metcalf, R. Warren. *Termination's Legacy: The Discarded Indians of Utah*. Lincoln: University of Nebraska Press, 2002.

Miner, H. Craig, and William Unrau. *The End of Indian Kansas: A Study of Cultural Revolution, 1854–1871*. Lawrence: Regents Press of Kansas, 1978.

Morgan, Lewis Henry. *League of the Ho-de-no-sau-nee, or Iroquois*. Rochester: Sage and Brothers, 1851. Paperback reprint with introduction by William N. Fenton, New York: Corinth Books, 1962.

New York State Association. *A Park Plan for New York State with a Proposal for the New Park Bond Issue*. New York: Committee on State Park Plan of the New York State Association, 1922, 1924.

Parker, Arthur C. *An Analytical History of the Seneca Indians*. Rochester: Lewis Henry Morgan Chapter of the New York State Archaeological Association, 1926.

———. *The Life of General Ely S. Parker: Last Grand Sachem of the Iroquois and General Grant's Military Secretary*. Buffalo Historical Publications 23. Buffalo: Buffalo Historical Society, 1919.

———. *Parker on the Iroquois*. Edited by William N. Fenton. Syracuse: Syracuse University Press, 1968.

———. *Seneca Myths and Folk Tales*. 1923. Paperback reprint with introduction by William N. Fenton, Lincoln: University of Nebraska Press, 1989.

Peabody, Francis Greenwood. *Education for Life: The Story of Hampton Institute, Told in Connection with the Fiftieth Anniversary of the Foundation of the School*. Garden City, N.Y.: Doubleday, Page, 1918.

Pevar, Stephen L. *The Rights of Indians and Tribes*. 4th ed. New York: New York University Press, 2012.

Philp, Kenneth R. *Termination Revisited: American Indians in the Trail to Self-Determination, 1933–1953.* Lincoln: University of Nebraska Press, 1999.

Porter, Joy. *To Be an Indian: The Life of Iroquois-Seneca Arthur Caswell Parker.* Norman: University of Oklahoma Press, 2001.

Porter, Robert Odawi, ed. *Sovereignty, Colonialism and the Indigenous Nations.* Durham, N.C.: Carolina Academic, 2005.

Pratt, Richard Henry. *Battlefield and Classroom: Four Decades with the American Indians, 1867–1904.* Edited by Robert M. Utley. New Haven, Conn.: Yale University Press, 1964.

Prucha, Francis Paul. *American Indian Policy in the Formative Years: The Indian Trade and Intercourse Acts, 1790–1834.* Cambridge, Mass.: Harvard University Press, 1962.

———. *American Indian Treaties: A History of an Anomaly.* Berkeley: University of California Press, 1994.

———. *The Great Father: The United States Government and the American Indians.* 2 vols. Lincoln: University of Nebraska Press, 1984.

———, ed. *"Americanizing" the American Indians: Writings of Friends of the Indians.* Cambridge, Mass.: Harvard University Press, 1973.

Richter, Daniel K. *The Ordeal of the Longhouse: The Peoples of the Iroquois League in the Era of Colonization.* Chapel Hill: University of North Carolina Press, 1992.

Rickard, Clinton. *Fighting Tuscarora: The Autobiography of Chief Clinton Rickard.* Edited by Barbara Graymont. Syracuse: Syracuse University Press, 1973.

Rites of Adoption by the Seneca Indians on the Cattaraugus Reservation. No place or publisher listed, June 15, 1885.

Sears, E. S. *Running through the Ages.* Jefferson, N.C.: McFarlane, 2001.

Severance, Frank H., ed. *Buffalo Historical Society Publications.* Vol. 6. Buffalo: Buffalo Historical Society, 1903.

Shattuck, George C. *The Oneida Land Claims: A Legal History.* Syracuse: Syracuse University Press, 1991.

Smith, E. B., comp. and ed. *Indian Tribal Claims Decided in the Courts of the United States, Briefed and Compiled to June 30, 1947.* Westport, Conn.: Praeger, 1976.

Society of Friends. *A Brief Sketch of the Efforts of the Philadelphia Yearly Meeting of the Religious Society of Friends to Promote the Civilization and Improvement of the Indians; also of the Present Condition of the Tribes in the State of New York.* Philadelphia: Indian Committee of the Philadelphia Yearly Meeting of Friends, 1866.

———. *The Case of the Seneca Indians in the State of New York, 1840.* Reprint, Stanfordville, N.Y.: Earl Coleman Publisher, 1979.

———. *Documents and Official Reports Illustrating the Causes Which Led to the Revolution of the Seneca Indians in the Year 1848, and to the Recognition of Their Representative Republican Constitution by the Authorities of the United States and of the State of New York.* Baltimore: William Wooddy and Son, 1857.

———. *Further Proceedings of the Joint Committee Appointed by the Friends Constituting the Yearly Meetings of Genesee, New York, Philadelphia, and Baltimore for*

Promoting the Civilization and Improving the Condition of the Seneca Nation of Indians From the Year 1847 to the Year 1850. Baltimore: William Wooddy and Son, 1850.

———. *Memorial of the Seneca Indians to the President of the United States Also an Address From the Committee of Friends Who Have Extended Care to These Indians and an Extract from the Report of the Commissioner of Indian Affairs*. Baltimore: William Wooddy and Son, 1850.

———. *Report of the Proceedings of an Indian Council Held at Cattaraugus in the State of New York, 7th Month, 1845*. Baltimore: William Wooddy, 1845.

———. *Report of the Proceedings at an Indian Council Held at Cattaraugus in the State of New York, June, 1846*. Baltimore: William Wooddy, 1846.

Stave, Bruce M. *The New Deal and the Last Hurrah: Pittsburgh Machine Politics*. Pittsburgh: University of Pittsburgh Press, 1970.

Stover, John T. *History of the Baltimore and Ohio Railroad*. West Lafayette, Ind.: Purdue University Press, 1987.

Strong, James Clark. *The Autobiography of James Clark Strong*. Los Gatos, Calif.: privately printed, 1910.

———. *Wah-ke-nah and Her People: The Curious Customs, Traditions, and Legends of North American*. New York: G. P. Putnam, 1893.

Talbot, Edith Armstrong. *Samuel Chapman Armstrong: A Biographical Study*. New York: Doubleday, Page, 1904

Tome, Philip. *Pioneer Life or Thirty Years a Hunter*. 1854. Reprint, Mechanicsburg, Pa.: Stackpole Books, 2006.

Thomas, Philip Evan. *An Address to Edward Purse [Pierce], President of the Seneca Nation, November 1, 1858*. Pamphlet in New York State Library.

Tooker, Elisabeth. *The Iroquois Ceremonial of Midwinter*. Syracuse: Syracuse University Press, 1970.

Trigger, Bruce G., ed. *Handbook of North American Indians*. Vol. 15: *The Northeast*. Washington, D.C.: Smithsonian Institution, 1978.

Troutman, John W. *Indian Blues: American Indians and the Politics of Music, 1879–1934*. Norman: University of Oklahoma Press, 2009.

Unrau, William E. *White Man's Wicked Water: The Alcohol Trade and Prohibition in Indian Country, 1802–1892*. Lawrence: University Press of Kansas, 1996.

Upton, Helen M. *The Everett Report in Historical Perspective: The Indians of New York*. Albany: New York State American Revolution Bicentennial Commission, 1980.

Vecsey, Christopher, and William A. Starna, eds. *Iroquois Land Claims*. Syracuse: Syracuse University Press, 1988.

Vennum, Thomas. *American Indian Lacrosse: The Little Brother of War*. Baltimore: Johns Hopkins University Press, 1994.

Viola, Herman J. *Diplomats in Buckskin: History of Indian Delegations in Washington City*. Washington, D.C.: Smithsonian Institution Press, 1981.

Wallace, Anthony F. C. *The Death and Rebirth of the Seneca*. New York: Alfred A. Knopf, 1969.

Whalen, Kevin. *Native Students at Work: American Indian Labor and Sherman Institute's Outing Program, 1900–1945*. Seattle: University of Washington Press, 2016.

Wilkins, David E. *American Indian Politics and the American Political System*. 3rd ed. Lanham, Md.: Rowman and Littlefield, 2010.

———. *American Indian Sovereignty and the United States Supreme Court: The Masking of Justice*. Austin: University of Texas Press, 1997.

———, ed. *Documents of Native American Political Development, 1500s to 1933*. New York: Oxford University Press, 2009.

Wilkins, David E., and K. Tsianina Lomawaima. *Uneven Ground: American Indian Sovereignty and Federal Law*. Norman: University of Oklahoma Press, 2001.

Wilson, Edmund. *Apologies to the Iroquois*. 1959. Paperback reprint edition with introduction and correspondence by William N. Fenton, Syracuse: Syracuse University Press, 1991.

Winegard, Timothy C. *For King and Kanata: Canadian Indians and the First World War*. Winnipeg: University of Manitoba Press, 2012.

Witmer, Linda F. *The Indian Industrial School, Carlisle, Pennsylvania, 1878–1918*. 3rd ed. Carlisle, Pa.: Cumberland County Historical Society, 2002.

Articles and Chapters in Edited Volumes

Abler, Thomas S. "Friends, Factions and the Seneca Nation Revolution of 1848." *Niagara Frontier* 21 (Winter 1974): 74–79.

———. "Protestant Missionaries and Native Cultures: Parallel Careers of Asher Wright and Silas T. Rand." *American Indian Quarterly* 26 (Winter 1992): 25–37.

———. "Seneca Moieties and Hereditary Chieftainships: The Early Nineteenth Century Political Organization of an Iroquois Nation." *Ethnohistory* 51 (Summer 2004): 459–88.

Abler, Thomas S., and Elisabeth Tooker. "Seneca." In *North American Indians*, Vol. 15: *The Northeast*, edited by Bruce G. Trigger, 505–17. Washington, D.C.: Smithsonian Institution, 1978.

Adams, David Wallace. "Beyond Bleakness: The Brighter Side of Indian Boarding Schools." In *Boarding School Blues: Indian Educational Experiences*, edited by Clifford Trafzer, Jean A. Keller, and Lorene Sisquoc, 35–64. Lincoln: University of Nebraska Press, 2006.

———. "Education in Hues: Red and Black at Hampton Institute, 1878–1893." *South Atlantic Quarterly* 76 (Spring 1977): 159–76.

Ahern, Wilbert H. "The 'Returned Indians': Hampton Institute and Its Indian Alumni, 1879–1893." *Journal of Ethnic Studies* 10 (Winter 1983): 263–304.

Ames, DeHart H. "Allegany State Park." In *The Historic Annals of Southwestern New York*, edited by William Doty, Charles E. Congdon, and Lewis H. Thornton, 2:765–74. Chicago: Clarke, 1940.

Barsh, Russel L. "American Indians and the Great War." *Ethnohistory* 38, no. 3 (1991): 276–303.

————. "The BIA Reorganization Follies of 1978: A Lesson in Bureaucratic Self-Defense." *American Indian Law Review* 7 (1979): 1–50.

Beauchamp, William M. "Iroquois Games." *Journal of American Folklore* 9 (1896): 269–77.

Berkhofer Jr., Robert F. "Faith and Factionalism among the Senecas: Theory and Ethnohistory." *Ethnohistory* 12 (1965): 99–112.

Burdich, Keith. "'No Place to Go': The Thomas Indian School and the 'Forgotten' Children of New York," *Wicaza Sa Review* 2 (2007): 93–110.

Bilharz, Joy A. "First among Equals? The Changing Status of Seneca Women." In *Women and Power in Native North America*, edited by Laura Klein and Lillian Ackerman, 101–12. Norman: University of Oklahoma Press, 1995.

Brewer Jr., Charles. "Oil and Gas Geology of the Allegany State Park." *New York State Museum Circular* 10 (May 1931): 1–22.

Bucki, Deborah B. "A History of Buffalo's Medical Response to the Great Influenza Pandemic." In *Medical History in Buffalo: Collected Essays*, edited by Lilli Sentz, 209–30. Buffalo: School of Medical and Biomedical Sciences, State University of New York, 1996.

Child, Brenda. "Homesickness, Illnesses, and Death: Native American Girls in Government Boarding Schools." In *Wings of Gauze: Women of Color and the Experience of Health and Illness*, edited by Barbara Blair and Susan E. Cayleff, 169–79. Detroit: Wayne State University Press, 1993.

Coffey, Louis. "Mediated Settlement of a Native American Land Claim." *CPA Journal* (June 2006): 1–6.

Cohn, Benjamin. "History and Anthropology: The State of Play." *Comparative Studies in Society and History* 22 (April 1980): 198–221.

Congdon, Charles E. "The Park Region and Its History." In *The Book of the Museum*, edited by Frank H. Severance, 293–98. Publications of the Buffalo Historical Society 25. Buffalo: Buffalo Historical Society, 1921.

Cross, Lezlie. "Making Citizens of Savages: Columbia's Roll Call at the Hampton Institute." *Journal of American Drama and Theatre* 24 (Spring 2012): 33–48.

Deardorff, Merle H. "The Cornplanter Grant in Warren County." *Western Pennsylvania Historical Magazine* 24 (March 1941): 1–22.

————. "The Religion of Handsome Lake: Its Origins and Development." *Bureau of American Ethnology Bulletin* 149 (1951): 77–107.

David H. DeJong. "'They Are Kept Alive': Federal Indian Schools and Student Health, 1878–1918." *American Indian Quarterly* 31 (Spring, 2007): 256–82.

Fenton, William N. "Aboriginally Yours: Jesse J. Cornplanter, *Hah-Yonh-Wonh-Ish*, the Snipe, Seneca, *1889–1957*." In *American Indian Intellectuals*, edited by Margot Liberty, 176–95. Saint Paul, Minn.: American Ethnological Society, 1978.

————. "Converse, Harriet Maxwell." In *Notable American Women, 1607–1950*, edited by Edward T. James, Janet Wilson James, and Paul S. Boyer, 1:375–77. Cambridge, Mass.: Harvard University Press, 1971.

————. "Fishing Drives among the Cornplanter Seneca." *Pennsylvania Archaeologist* 12 (1942): 48–52.

———. "Locality as a Basic Factor in the Development of Iroquois Social Structure." *Bureau of American Ethnology Bulletin* 149 (1951): 35–54.

———. "Pennsylvania's Remaining Indian Settlement." *Pennsylvania Park News* 44 (1945): 1–2.

———. "Place Names and Related Activities of the Cornplanter Seneca." *Pennsylvania Archaeologist* 15, nos. 2–4 (1945).

———. "Place Names and Related Activities of the Cornplanter Seneca." *Pennsylvania Archaeologist* 16, no. 2 (1946).

———. "Structure, Continuity and Change in the Process of Treaty Making." In *The History and Culture of Iroquois Diplomacy: An Interdisciplinary Guide to the Treaties of the Six Nations and Their League*, edited by Francis Jennings, William N. Fenton, Mary A. Druke, and David R. Miller, 3–36. Syracuse; Syracuse University Press, 1985.

———. "Toward the Gradual Civilization of the Indian Natives: The Missionary and Linguistic Work of Asher Wright (1803–1875) among the Senecas of Western New York." *Proceedings of the American Philosophical Society* 100 (1956): 567–81.

———, ed. "Seneca Indians by Asher Wright (1859)." *Ethnohistory* 4 (1957): 302–21.

Graymont, Barbara. "New York State Indian Policy after the Revolution." *New York History* 58 (October 1976): 438–74.

Gunther, Gerald. "Governmental Power and New York Indian Lands: A Reassessment of a Persistent Problem of Federal–State Relations." *Buffalo Law Review* 7 (Fall 1958): 1–14.

Hagan, William T. "Reformers' Image of the American Indian." In *'They Made Us Many Promises': The American Indian Experience, 1524 to the Present*, edited by Philip Weeks, 145–54. Wheeling, Ill.: Harlan Davidson, 2002.

Harmon, Alexandra, Colleen O'Neill, and Paul C. Rosier. "Interwoven Economic Histories: American Indians in a Capitalist America." *Journal of American History* 98 (December 2011): 698–722.

Harring, Sydney. "Red Lilac of the Cayugas: Traditional Indian Law and Culture Conflict in a Witchcraft Trail in Buffalo, New York, 1930." *New York History* 73 (January 1992): 64–94.

Hauptman, Laurence M. "Alice Lee Jemison: A Modern 'Mother of the Nation.'" In *Sifters: Native American Women's Lives*, edited by Thelma Perdue, 175–86. New York: Oxford University Press, 2001.

———. "The American Indian Federation and the Indian New Deal: A Reinterpretation." *Pacific Historical Review* 52 (November 1983): 378–402.

———. "Beyond Forensic History: Observations Based on a Forty-Year Journey through Iroquois Country." *Journal of the West* 49 (Fall 2010): 10–19.

———. "Compensatory Justice: The Seneca Nation Settlement Act." *National Forum* 71 (Spring 1991): 31–33.

———. "Ditches, Defense, and Dispossession: The Iroquois and the Rise of the Empire State." *New York History* 79 (October 1998): 325–58.

———. "From Carlisle to Carnegie Hall: The Music Career of Denison Wheelock." In *The Oneidas in the Age of Allotment, 1860–1920*, edited by Laurence

M. Hauptman and L. Gordon McLester III, 112–38. Norman: University of Oklahoma Press, 2006.

———. "Governor Blacksnake and the Seneca Indian Struggle to Save the Oil Spring Reservation." *Mid-America* 81 (Winter 1999): 51–73.

———. "Governor Theodore Roosevelt and the Indians of New York State." *Proceedings of the American Philosophical Society* 119 (February 1975), 1–7.

———. "The Historical Background to the Present Day Seneca Nation–Salamanca Lease Controversy: The First Hundred Years." In *Iroquois Land Claims*, edited by Christopher Vecsey and William A. Starna, 101–22. Rockefeller Institute Working Paper 20. Albany: Rockefeller Institute of Government, 1985.

———. "The Indian Reorganization Act." In *The Aggressions of Civilization: Federal Indian Policy Since the 1880s*, edited by Vine Deloria Jr. and Sandra Cadwalader, 131–48. Philadelphia: Temple University Press, 1984.

———. "The Iroquois School of Art: Arthur C. Parker and the Seneca Arts Project, 1935–1941." *New York History* 60 (July 1979), 282–312.

———. "The Meddlesome Friend: Philip Evan Thomas among the Onöndowa'ga:´, 1838–1861." In *Proceedings of the Conference on Quakers and American Indians, November 2016*, edited by Ignacio Gallup-Diaz and Geoffrey Plank, 136–57. Leiden, Netherlands: Brill, 2019.

———. "Park Boss: Albert T. Fancher and Allegany State Park." *New York Archives* 17 (Winter 2018), 26–30.

———. "Raw Deal: The Iroquois View the Indian Reorganization Act of 1934." In *Studies on Iroquoian Culture*, edited by Nancy Bonvillain, 15–24. Rindge, N.H.: Man in the Northeast, 1980.

———. "Samuel George (1795–1873): A Study of Onondaga Indian Conservatism." *New York History* 70 (January 1989): 4–22.

———. "*Seneca Nation v. Christy*: A Background Study." *Buffalo Law Review* 46 (Fall 1998): 947–79.

———. "Senecas and Subdividers: Resistance to Allotment of Indian Lands in New York, 1875–1906." *Prologue: The Journal of the National Archives* 9 (Summer 1977): 105–17.

———. "Statesmen, Salvation Seekers and the Senecas: The Supplemental Treaty of Buffalo Creek, 1842." *New York History* 78 (January 1997): 51–82.

———. "Who Owns Grand Island (Erie County, New York)?" *Oklahoma City University Law Review* 23 (Spring–Summer 1998): 151–74.

Hogan, Thomas E. "City in a Quandary: Salamanca and the Allegany Leases." *New York History* 55 (January 1974): 79–101.

Hewitt, J. N. B. "Iroquois Game of Lacrosse." *American Anthropologist* 5 (1892): 189–91.

Howland, Henry R. "The Seneca Mission at Buffalo Creek." In *Buffalo Historical Publications*, vol. 6, edited by Frank H. Severance, 125–61. Buffalo: Buffalo Historical Society, 1903.

Jackson, Halliday. "Halliday Jackson's Journal to the Seneca Indians, 1798–1800." Edited by Anthony F. C. Wallace. *Pennsylvania History* 19 (April–July 1952): 117–47, 325–49.

Johnson, Ronald M. "Schooling the 'Savage': Andrew S. Draper and Indian Education." *Phylon* 35 (1974): 74–82.

Lappas, Thomas. "For God and Home and Native Land: The Haudenosaunee and the Women's Christian Temperance Union, 1884–1921." *Journal of Women's History* 29 (Summer 2017): 62–85.

Lucas. John. "Deerfoot in Britain: An Amazing American Long Distance Runner, 1861–1863." *Journal of American Culture* 69 (Fall 1983): 13–19.

Manley, Henry S. "Buying Buffalo from the Indians." *New York History* 27 (July 1947): 313–29.

———. "Indian Reservation Ownership in New York." *New York State Bar Bulletin* 32 (April 1960): 134–38.

———. "Red Jacket's Last Campaign." *New York History* 31 (April 1950): 149–68.

Mason, Carol. "The Geography of Allegany State Park." *New York State Museum Circular* 16 (August 1936): 1–68.

Murphy, Joseph, F. "Health Problems of the Indians." *Annals of the American Academy of Political and Social Science* 37 (1911): 347–53.

Nicholas, Mark. "A Little School, a Reservation Divided: Quaker Education and Allegany Seneca Leadership in the Early Republic." *American Indian Quarterly* 30 (2006): 1–21.

O'Brien, H. R. "History of Public Health in Chautauqua, Cattaraugus, and Allegany Counties." *New York State Journal of Medicine* 44 (1944): 21–33.

Owl, W. David. "Hampton Indians at the Cattaraugus Indian Reservation." *Southern Workman* 65 (April 1, 1936): 105–9.

Parker, Arthur C. "Harriet Maxwell Converse." In *Myths and Legends of the New York Iroquois*, by Harriet Maxwell Converse, 1908. Reprint, *New York State Museum Bulletin* 125 (1981): 14–30.

Philp, Kenneth R. "Termination: A Legacy of the Indian New Deal." *Western Historical Quarterly* 14 (April 1983): 165–80.

Porter, Robert Odawi. "Decolonizing Indigenous Governance: Observations on Restoring Greater Faith and Legitimacy in the Government of the Seneca Nation." *Kansas Journal of Law and Public Policy* 8 (Winter 1999): 97–141.

Pound, Cuthbert W. "Nationals without a Nation: The New York State Tribal Indians." *Columbia Law Review* 22 (February 1922): 97–102.

Rosier, Paul C. "Dam Building and Treaty Breaking: The Kinzua Dam Controversy, 1936–1958." *Pennsylvania Magazine of History and Biography* 119 (October 1995): 345–468.

Rothenberg, Diane. "The Mothers of the Nation." In *Women and Colonization: Anthropological Perspectives*, edited by Mona Etienne and Eleanor Leacock, 63–87. New York: Praeger, 1980.

Rowan, Rae L. "New York State Produces Oil for the World." In *The Historic Annals of Southwestern New York*, edited by William Doty, Charles E. Congdon, and Lewis H. Thornton, 2:991–1010. Chicago: Clarke, 1940.

Shoemaker, Nancy. "From Longhouse to Log House: Household Structures among the Seneca in 1900." *American Indian Quarterly* 15 (1991): 329–38.

———. "The Rise and Fall of Iroquois Women." In *Native Women's History in Eastern North America before 1900: A Guide to Research and Writing*, edited by Nancy Shoemaker, 303–29. Lincoln: University of Nebraska Press, 2007.

Siener, William H. "Buffalo." In *The Encyclopedia of New York State*, edited by Peter Eisenstadt and Laura-Eve Moss, 233–37. Syracuse: Syracuse University Press, 2005.

Smith, Roland. "The Politics of Pittsburgh Flood Control, 1908–1936." *Pennsylvania History* 42 (January 1975): 5–24.

———. "The Politics of Pittsburgh Flood Control, 1936–1960." *Pennsylvania History* 44 (January 1977): 3–24.

Tanner, Edwin P. "Deerfoot (1828–January 1897)." In *Dictionary of American Biography*, edited by Allen Johnson and Dumas Malone. New York: Charles Scribner's Sons, 1930.

Tooker, Elisabeth. "The League of the Iroquois: Its History, Politics, and Ritual." In *Handbook of North American Indians*. Vol. 15: *The Northeast*, edited by Bruce G. Trigger, 107–34. Washington, D.C.: Smithsonian Institution, 1978.

———. "On the Development of the Handsome Lake Religion," *Proceedings of the American Philosophical Society* 133 (1989): 35–50.

———. "On the New Religion of Handsome Lake." *Anthropological Quarterly* 41 (1968): 187–200.

———. "Women in Iroquois Society." In *Extending the Rafters: Interdisciplinary Approaches to Iroquois History*, edited by Jack Campisi, Michael Foster, and Marianne Mithun, 109–24. Albany: SUNY Press, 1984.

Trennert, Robert. "From Carlisle to Phoenix: The Rise and Fall of the Outing System, 1878–1930." *Pacific Historical Review* 52 (August 1983): 267–91.

Unrau, William E. "Lewis Vital Bogy." In *The Commissioners of Indian Affairs, 1824–1977*, edited by Robert Kvasnicka Herman Viola, 109–14. Lincoln: University of Nebraska Press, 1979.

Waldron, Martha. "The Indian Health Care Question." *In Twenty-Two Years of the Hampton Normal and Agricultural Institute at Hampton, Virginia: Record of Negro and Indian Graduates*, edited by Helen Ludlow, 193–202. Hampton, Va.: Hampton Normal and Agricultural Institute, 1893.

Wallace, Anthony F. C. "Origins of the Longhouse Religion." In *Handbook of North American Indians*. Vol. 15: *The Northeast*, edited by Bruce G. Trigger, 442–48. Washington, D.C.: Smithsonian Institution, 1978.

Ward Jr., Hamilton. "The Allegheny Park: The Story of Its Establishment." In *The Book of the Museum*, edited by Frank H. Severance, 286–92. Publications of the Buffalo Historical Society 25. Buffalo: Buffalo Historical Society, 1921.

Wulff, Roger. "Lacrosse among the Seneca." *Indian Historian* 10 (1977): 16–22.
Zissu, Erik M. "Conscription, Sovereignty, and Land: American Indian Resistance during World War I." *Pacific Historical Review* 64 (November 1995): 537–66.

Theses and Dissertations

Abler, Thomas S. "Factional Dispute and Party Conflict in the Political System of the Seneca Nation (1845–1895): An Ethnohistorical Analysis." PhD dissertation, University of Toronto, 1969.
Bell, Genevieve: "Telling Stories out of School: Remembering the Carlisle Indian Industrial School." PhD dissertation, Stanford University, Palo Alto, Calif., 1998.
Borgia, Melissa E. "An Overview of Language Preservation at *Ohi:yo*, the Seneca Allegany Territory." PhD dissertation, Indiana University of Pennsylvania, Indiana, Pa., 2010.
Brown, Dorcas. "The Reservation Log Houses." Master's thesis, SUNY Oneonta, 2000.
Brudvig, Jon L. "'Bridging the Cultural Divide': Hampton Institute's Experiment in American Indian Education, 1876–1923." PhD dissertation, College of William and Mary, Williamsburg, Va., 1996.
Conable, Mary. "A Steady Enemy: The Ogden Land Company and the Seneca Indians." PhD dissertation, University of Rochester, 1995.
Kinney, Jill. "Letters, Pen, and Tilling the Field: Quaker Schools among the Seneca Indians on the Allegany River, 1798–1852." PhD dissertation, University of Rochester, 2009.
Putney, T. Diane. "Fighting the Scourge: American Indian Morbidity and Federal Policy, 1897–1928." PhD dissertation, Marquette University, Milwaukee, 1980.
Rothenberg, Diane B. "Friends Like These: An Ethnohistorical Analysis of the Interaction between Allegany Senecas and Quakers, 1798–1823." PhD dissertation, City University of New York, 1976.

Documentaries

Douglas, Ron, dir. *Unseen Tears: The Impact of Native American Residential Boarding Schools in Western New York*. Buffalo: Native American Community Services of Erie and Niagara Counties, 2009.
Forbes, Allan, and George Heron, dir. *Land of Our Ancestors*. Rochester: Seneca Nation of Indians, 1994.
Gazit, Chana, and David Stewart, dir. *Honorable Nations*. Arlington, Va.: PBS, 1991.
Marzuki, Marcy, writer. *Indian Warriors: The Untold Story of the Civil War*. New York: History Channel, 2006.

Website

Brudvig, Jon L., comp. "Hampton Normal & Agricultural Institute: American Indian Students (1878–1923)," Twofrog, 1999–2012, www.twofrog.com /hampton.html (accessed December 23, 2013).

•◄ ►•

INDEX

White, Edward, 173
White, James, 123, 129
White, Rachel, 105
White, Willis, Jr., 172
White Chief, 9
White Seneca, 8, 9
White Woman's Reservation, 8, 45
Widow George, 208–9n33
Wilbur, Ray, 182
Wild West shows, 61
Willard, Frances, 60
Williams, Frank, 118
Williams, Lewis, 118
Wilson, Charles, 60
Wilson, John, 18
Wilson, Peter, 14–16, 23–25, 38–41,
    184, 208n31, 209n33, 215n11,
    225n27. See also Cayuga Indians;
    Seneca Revolution of 1848;
    Thomas, Philip Evan
Wilson, Woodrow, 135
women, Seneca, 13, 20, 66, 82, 102,
    153, 183–84; attempt to prevent
    Seneca Nation political schism,
    56; awarded voting rights and
    office holding, 57–58; changing
    political role, 56–57, 177, 183;
    education of, 108, 111–12, 118–20,
    125–28, 132–33; Great Law and,
    54–58, 161–62; and health care
    improvements, 91–93, 201; and
    horticulture, 54–58; influence
    at Big Tree Treaty (1797), 57;
    influence at Canandaigua Treaty
    (1794), 57; "keepers of the
    kettle," 10; matrilineage, 54–55;
    Nineteenth Amendment (U.S.

Constitution) and, 61; role in
    fomenting Seneca Revolution of
    1848, 9–11, 16–17; selling crafts,
    58, 220n26; Seneca Women's
    Female Benevolent Society,
    61; as teachers, 97, 105, 111,
    118–20, 131, 230n17; temperance
    movement and, 58–61; women's
    suffrage, Seneca, 56–61, 206n14
wood chemical industry, 28, 178–79,
    248n47. See also Allegany Indian
    Reservation, Allegany State Park
Woolman, Abner, 108
World Court, 176
World's Fairs, 67–68. See also names of
    individual expositions
World War I, 79, 88, 89, 105, 170,
    175, 180, 249n70
World War II, 198
Wright, Arthur, 81
Wright, Asher, 6–7, 14–16, 18, 19, 55,
    59, 64, 76, 77, 79, 80–83, 92, 107,
    201. See also Presbyterians; Seneca
    Revolution of 1848; Thomas
    Indian School; United Mission
    Church (Seneca Mission/Asher
    Wright Memorial Presbyterian
    Church); Wright, Laura
Wright, Laura, 59, 76, 80, 81, 83–84,
    92, 153

Young Chief, 12
Young Joe, 18
Young King, 6, 67

Zátopek, Emil, 63
Zimmerman, William, Jr., 199

CPSIA information can be obtained
at www.ICGtesting.com
Printed in the USA
LVHW030002210519
618494LV00006B/160/P